RHODES

RHODES

Antony Thomas

BBC BOOKS

To President Mandela,
who has given South Africa a second chance

Acknowledgements

There's not space enough to thank all those who made the series and this book possible. My personal list must begin with the memory of my grandparents, Edward and Elsa Thomas, as well as the late Bigvai Masekela, who accepted me as a son and opened my eyes to South Africa. I would like to thank Kenneth Griffith for planting the seed, and Charles Denton, Margaret Matheson and Scott Meek for giving me the means as well as their continual creative support. I owe a great debt to Jonathan Altaras, Will Boyd, Nadine Gordimer, Roger James, Phyllis Johnson, David Martin, Sheila Nevins, and Lynton and Pippa Stephenson for their encouragement and support at crucial times; Francis Dobbs and Doe Mayer for their meticulous research; Michael Wearing for keeping the flame alive at the BBC; and Alan Yentob for making the *Rhodes* series possible. Thank you Vivian Bickford-Smith, Richard Dawkins, Miranda Hearn, Heather Holden-Brown, Kate Lock, Tom Lodge and Khadija Manjlai for your invaluable help and advice. Thank you David Drury, Maurice Cain, Charles Salmon and the entire cast and crew of the *Rhodes* series for a magnificent achievement. Finally, my special thanks to Nigel Stafford-Clark for your enormous creative contribution to the book and the series, and Nigel Crewe for supporting this obsession from the very beginning to the very end.

Frontispiece: Cecil Rhodes

This book is published to accompany the BBC television dramatisation *Rhodes*, which was first broadcast in 1996. The series was produced by the BBC Drama department.
Executive Producers: Michael Wearing and Antony Thomas
Producers: Charles Salmon and Scott Meek. Director: David Drury

Published by BBC Books, an imprint of BBC Worldwide Publishing,
BBC Worldwide Limited, Woodlands, 80 Wood Lane, London W12 0TT.

Designed by Andrew Shoolbred and BBC Books
Picture research: Anne-Marie Ehrlich

First published 1996
© Antony Thomas 1996
The moral right of the author has been asserted.

ISBN 0 563 38742 4

Set in Janson
Printed and bound in Great Britain by Butler & Tanner, Frome and London
Jacket printed by Lawrence Allen Ltd, Weston-super-Mare

CONTENTS

The idea gleaming and dancing before one's eyes like a will-of-the-wisp at last frames itself into a plan. Why should we not form a secret society with but one object, the furtherance of the British Empire and the bringing of the whole uncivilised world under British rule, for the recovery of the United States, for the making the Anglo-Saxon race but one Empire?

What a dream, but yet it is probable, it is possible.

CECIL RHODES (AGED 23) IN HIS *CONFESSION OF FAITH*

The conquest of the earth, which mostly means the taking it away from those who have a different complexion or slightly flatter noses than ourselves, is not a pretty thing when you look into it too much. What redeems it is the idea only. An idea at the back of it; not a sentimental pretence but an idea; and an unselfish belief in the idea – something you can set up, and bow down before, and offer a sacrifice to...

JOSEPH CONRAD, *HEART OF DARKNESS*

INTRODUCTION

A belief in Rhodes became a substitute for religion.

SIDNEY LOW, EDITOR OF THE *ST JAMES GAZETTE*

(1888–1897)

As protection against unfair influence, we oblige our politicians to declare their 'special interests'. It seems only fair that biographers should be asked to do the same.

My 'special relationship' with Cecil Rhodes dates back to the late 1940s, when, as a small child growing up in Cape Town, I would be taken by my grandparents to the botanical gardens in the city centre to spend a few reverential moments before the statue of Cecil Rhodes.

Rhodes is caught in mid-stride at the junction of the main walkways. In his right hand, he grips one of those broad-brimmed Boer hats that were to become his trademark in later life. His left hand is raised, the extended fingers permanently reaching for the north, reaching for Africa. The stone plinth beneath his feet bears the simple legend 'Your Hinterland is There'.

I have often thought that a devout Catholic child, standing before a statue of the Virgin or, at the very least, some important saint, must experience similar emotions to those I felt in Rhodes's 'presence' all those years ago. And I don't use religious imagery lightly. To my grandparents, Rhodes was much more than a dead hero. He was an ideal. He represented everything they aspired to and defined who they were. He gave meaning to the word 'English'. 'Common sense, determination, boundless energy, good humour, sincerity, plainness in living and in speech, clear perception of essential facts – these qualities which are distinctively English were distinctively present in Cecil Rhodes's character.'[1]

Such were the sentiments of the editor of the *Cape Argus*, writing on the day after Rhodes's death. They were certainly my grandparents' sentiments and, when in their care, my nightly devotions always included the simple prayer (which somehow skirted around the problem of our Celtic origins) – 'Dear God, thank you for making me English!'

It was a prayer that made perfect sense to disciples of a man who claimed 'the highest standards of human perfection ... Justice, Liberty and Peace' for his race and described the English as '[God's] chosen instrument in carrying out the divine idea over the whole planet'[2] ... I contend that we are the finest race in the world and that the more of the world we inhabit the better it is for the human race...'[3]

By these pronouncements, Rhodes was offering us something more than a definition of ourselves. He was justifying our presence in this part of Africa. Through him, expropriation had been transformed into a duty, a sacred duty 'for the betterment of humanity'.[3]

At this distance it's not difficult to understand Rhodes's appeal to my grandparents' class and generation (harder, though, to imagine how any shred of this creed could continue to influence long after their deaths). They *needed* Rhodes's encouragement and endorsement. Their England was in sudden, painful decline. A Labour administration was in power 'at home', India was 'lost' for ever to the Empire and our 'dear General Smuts' had been defeated by alien Afrikaners.

It is not within the scope of this introduction to describe my own political journey; sufficient to say that by my mid-20s I was committed to the struggle for a non-racial South Africa. Rhodes belonged to a childhood I believed I had left behind for ever.

This was certainly my attitude in 1970, when I was approached by the actor/writer Kenneth Griffith to direct a documentary on the life of Cecil Rhodes. Kenneth had developed a highly idiosyncratic style of storytelling. For 90 minutes he would stand before the camera and deliver a fiery monologue on the life of an important historical figure. As far as possible, his aim was to describe every incident in the authentic setting, 'so that ghosts could rise'.

Kenneth's account of Rhodes's life was a revelation. In prose crackling with Celtic indignation, he revealed a man who had elbowed his way to a fortune in the no-holds-barred mêlée of the Kimberley diamond rush and then used that fortune to fund mercenary armies, to murder, steal, bribe, cheat and corrupt in a headlong rush to secure as much of Africa's land and mineral wealth as he could lay his hands on. It was strong stuff, graciously described by the reviewer in the *Daily Telegraph* as 'a brilliant speech for the prosecution'.[4]

For me, it was also painful stuff. Rhodes had been such an important part of my childhood identity that I could not avoid feelings of self-disgust. My heritage had been laid bare and it was seen to be rotten, rotten to the core.

What started as a professional need to verify the accuracy of Kenneth's account (and accurate it was, down to the last detail) soon developed into a voracious appetite for any biography, letter or paper that could throw further light on the life and career of Cecil Rhodes. In some respects the information I uncovered was more damning than anything Kenneth had presented. There was, for instance, a compelling account of an assassination contract drawn up between Rhodes and a young adventurer,[5] but even more serious was damning evidence of Rhodes's contribution to the political evolution of South Africa in his dual role as the Cape's prime minister and minister of native affairs; evidence, it should be said, that no-one had sought to conceal.

My grandparents, like many English-speaking South Africans, believed in the essential humanity of the English tradition – the Rhodes tradition – in South African politics. Rhodes, they used to tell me, was a father to the natives. They loved to describe how he rode unarmed into the centre of the Matabele 'rebellion' (against *his* administration) and how the chiefs and elders had sat at his feet like so many penitent children, laid down their arms and entreated for peace.

It was this fatherly concern, this sense of justice and decency, that set us apart from the brutal Afrikaners who were turning our country into an international pariah. At least, that was the message I received as a child.

Not so. If anyone can be accused of laying the foundations of apartheid, it was 'that most English of Englishmen'[6] Cecil John Rhodes. In 1887 – 61 years before the Nationalists came to power in South Africa – he had stood before a packed House of Assembly in Cape Town and declared:

> These are my politics on native affairs, and these are the politics of South Africa ... The native is to be treated as a child and denied the franchise ... We must adopt a system of despotism, such as works so well in India, in our relations with the barbarians of South Africa.[7]

Seven years later Rhodes drew up his blueprint for a new South Africa. Far from being 'the economically illogical legacy of the frontier, the creation of Afrikaner nationalism',[8] this was an English plan, devised by English capitalists who had made – and were continuing to make – their fortunes from South Africa's diamonds and South Africa's gold. It promised to solve the country's labour problems at a stroke. Stripped to its essentials, the plan sought to end black self-sufficiency by confining rural Africans to tribal reserves and imposing a tax on every hut. To survive, Africans would have to enter the cash economy and sell their labour to whites.

Rhodes assured his parliamentary colleagues that if his bill became law, they would no longer regard Africans as a problem but as an asset, adding with characteristic 'wit': 'When I see the labour troubles that are occurring in the United States, and ... are going to occur with the English people in their own country ... I feel rather glad the labour question here is connected with the native question ...'[9]

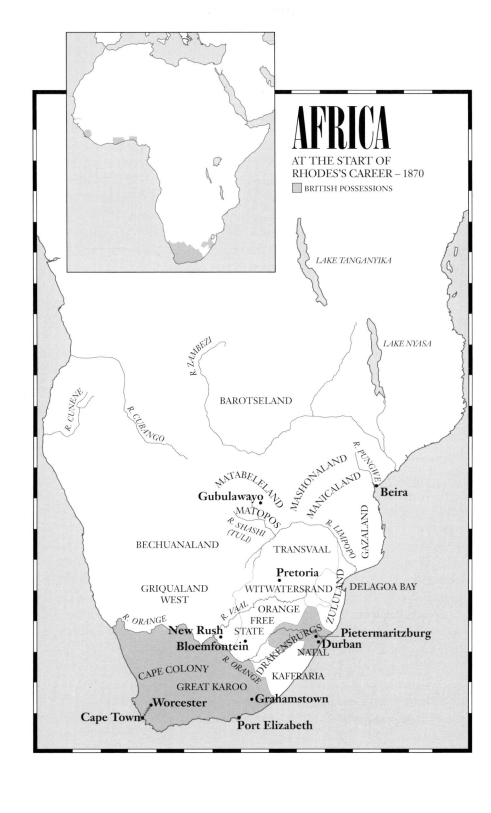

AFRICA

AT THE START OF
RHODES'S CAREER – 1870

▨ BRITISH POSSESSIONS

LAKE TANGANYIKA

LAKE NYASA

R. ZAMBEZI

R. CUNENE

R. CUBANGO

BAROTSELAND

MATABELELAND

MASHONALAND

MANICALAND

R. PUNGWE

Gubulawayo

Beira

MATOPOS

R. SHASHI (TULI)

GAZALAND

BECHUANALAND

TRANSVAAL

R. LIMPOPO

Pretoria

GRIQUALAND
WEST

WITWATERSRAND

DELAGOA BAY

ZULULAND

R. ORANGE

R. VAAL

ORANGE
FREE
STATE

New Rush

Bloemfontein

DRAKENSBURGS

Pietermaritzburg

Durban

NATAL

R. ORANGE

KAFERARIA

CAPE COLONY

GREAT KAROO

Worcester

•**Grahamstown**

Cape Town

Port Elizabeth

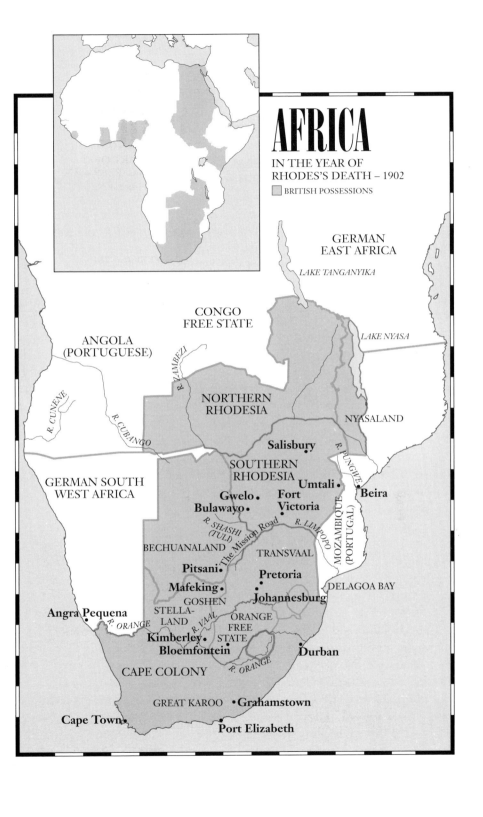

AFRICA

IN THE YEAR OF
RHODES'S DEATH – 1902

BRITISH POSSESSIONS

GERMAN
EAST AFRICA

LAKE TANGANYIKA

CONGO
FREE STATE

ANGOLA
(PORTUGUESE)

LAKE NYASA

R. ZAMBEZI

NORTHERN
RHODESIA

NYASALAND

R. CUNENE

R. CUBANGO

Salisbury

SOUTHERN
RHODESIA

R. PUNGWE

GERMAN SOUTH
WEST AFRICA

Umtali

Beira

Gwelo

Fort
Victoria

Bulawayo

*R. SHASHI
(TULI)*

The Mission Road

R. LIMPOPO

MOZAMBIQUE
(PORTUGAL)

BECHUANALAND

TRANSVAAL

Pitsani

Pretoria

Mafeking

Johannesburg

DELAGOA BAY

Angra Pequena

GOSHEN

STELLA-
LAND

R. ORANGE

R. VAAL

ORANGE
FREE
STATE

Kimberley

Bloemfontein

Durban

CAPE COLONY

R. ORANGE

GREAT KAROO

Grahamstown

Cape Town

Port Elizabeth

In tandem with these territorial changes, Rhodes and his ministers imposed apartheid in the towns. Those non-whites who had long been an integral part of urban life now experienced segregation in schools, sports, prisons, hospitals, theatres and on public transport. They were disqualified from jury duty (a privilege enjoyed since the early years of British administration in the Cape) and removed, in their thousands, from the electoral rolls.[10]

So much for the 'father of the native peoples', and so much for that English tradition of justice, liberty and peace in South African politics.

Of course there is a counter-argument, and I've heard it time and time again from latter-day apologists. The man must be judged in the context of his time. Every major European power and a few also-rans had joined the unseemly scramble for land in Africa. What we might now describe as murder, coercion and theft were the common currency of empire-building. As for segregation, Rhodes was simply responding to popular (white) will. Understand the times. The defence rests.

There is an arrogance implicit in this argument. It assumes a moral development over the past 100 years that we have no right to claim. It ignores the tensions and ideological crosscurrents in Rhodes's day is deaf to those clear contemporary voices that were raised in protest against him and his methods.[11] Above all, a view of Rhodes that makes him the 'dupe' of a flawed ideology does injustice to a man of his undoubted genius, a man blessed with extraordinary powers of foresight and perception.

The more one learnt about Rhodes through his letters, his speeches and the recollections of his contemporaries, the clearer it became that this was not someone who could be set aside in another time and another *Zeitgeist*. In a real sense he remains with us, here and now.

I am aware that the greatest sin a biographer can commit is to view the past from the narrow perspective of his own time, to ignore the historical context and make assumptions about character and motive that are based on contemporary fads and theories – and there have certainly been some ludicrous attempts to reach Rhodes by these routes.[12]

That said, the closer one gets to Rhodes, the more one recognizes a contemporary mind and contemporary methods. With astonishing prescience, his friend and biographer W.T. Stead described Rhodes as 'the first of the new Dynasty of Money Kings which has been evolved in these later days as the real rulers of the Modern World'.[13]

Rhodes achieved a near-monopoly of the world's diamonds by manipulating the money markets, by audacious takeovers and the secret purchase of shares. He had a perfect understanding of public relations and the power of the press, acquiring newspapers, both openly and secretly, in the belief that 'the press rules the minds of men'.[3] He probed the soft underbelly of the English Establishment and discovered corruption, self-deception and greed, and used his discoveries to his own advantage. As the Americans would say, he worked the system. He learnt that nobody, not even Queen Victoria herself, could resist him, and that famous journalists and distinguished politicians – politicians who remain popular heroes to this day – could be bought with flattery and a few thousand pounds.[14]

And Rhodes's motives? Simply stated by one biographer, 'Rhodes's foible was size'. Today, we have come to recognize a species of 'Money King' who must acquire for acquisition's sake. We no longer expect ideological or even economic justification for the absorption of another motor-manufacturing plant or television network, but in the nineteenth century the public was more particular. Moral rectitude was required, and Rhodes was always careful to provide it.

When his mercenaries had destroyed the Matabele nation, thereby adding another 70,000 square miles (181,400 square kilometres) to 'his' Rhodesia (today's Zimbabwe), Rhodes announced to his exultant British shareholders that the value of their investment had increased by 2000 per cent. At the same time, he assured them that profiteering was a patriotic duty:

> Whenever the man in the street sneers [at you] remind him that it was an undertaking which he had not the courage to take part in himself as one of the British people. The Imperial Government would not touch it. The Cape Government was too poor to do so ... It has been done [by you] ... It has been done also – which the English people like – without expense to their exchequer.[15]

It would be dangerous to pursue the analysis too far and conclude that Rhodes's Imperial 'ideal' and his intoxicating rallying call to an English 'master race' were no more than public relations ploys. As I hope to show, the relationship between motive and presentation is subtle. One thing, though, is certain. Rhodes only embraced his Imperial ideal when it served his purpose. If there was ever a conflict of interest, he could be as anti-imperialist as any Fenian or Boer. Faced with an attempt to stop the distribution of confiscated Matabele cattle and land among his young mercenaries, Rhodes threatened to declare independence, warning British administrators that if they dared to restrain him, they would find themselves facing 'a new Republic, which would cause more blood ... than the whole Matabeleland nation is worth'.[16]

I have no way of describing the weeks and months spent studying Rhodes's letters and speeches, as well as the many articles, diaries and biographies that touch his life, except to invoke Joseph Conrad and Marlow's journey into the 'Heart of Darkness'. My descent into evil was, in some unnerving way, a journey of self-discovery. Everything about the man, down to the rhythms of his speech, was so recognizable, so familiar. As the evidence of his betrayals and shifting allegiances accumulated, as his disastrous legacy in Britain and southern Africa became clearer, so Rhodes the man took a stronger and stronger hold. I found myself marvelling at his persuasive powers, his extraordinary ability 'to get inside the other man's head' and achieve virtually anything he wanted. I was stunned by the brilliance of his stratagems and the extent to which he was prepared to take risks. I began to experience the pain of his personal life. I even developed a taste for his peculiar brand of black humour. Childhood identification was beginning all over again.

Nothing contributed more to my sense of the man than a collection of letters the 17-year-old Rhodes had written to various members of his family from the cotton farm in Natal, which he eventually abandoned for the diamond fields.

Here was a boy, bursting with charm and energy, who, at this very young age, had an intuitive feeling for Africa and her people. Indeed, his descriptions of the Natal landscape compare favourably with anything the great Anthony Trollope could offer when he toured the colony seven years later. The young Rhodes seized every opportunity to experience the country. Riding for days at a time and sometimes alone, he enjoyed an easygoing relationship with the local Africans, regularly sharing their food and hospitality. Above all, he began to appreciate their values, particularly the value they placed in a man's trust. When work started on his cotton fields he introduced the revolutionary scheme of paying his workers in advance in order to 'earn a good name' among them. And there's certainly no evidence to suggest they ever let him down.[17]

In one letter to his mother he considered the possibility of acquiring a piece of 'good, flat land' that had already been cleared and cultivated by a local chief. The problem (for the chief) was that this land lay within an area already set aside for the colonists, 'so he can be turned off and the fruit of his labours turned to a white man's advantage'.[17] Rhodes considered his options carefully. It might be legal to take the man's land, but was it right...? Evidently not. The chief stayed where he was.

Was this really the same boy who grew into the Cecil Rhodes who seized close to a million square miles (2.6 million square kilometres) of Africa,[18] brushing his critics aside with that dreadful riposte 'I prefer land to niggers!'?

The more I discovered about him, the clearer it became that Rhodes's progress from cotton farmer and young diamond digger to 'African Colossus' had the shape and scale of classical tragedy – the massive tragedy of a young man's corruption in pursuit of power.

Driven by an early sense of his own mortality (at the age of 19 he suffered his first heart attack), forever cutting corners and taking risks in a race against time, expending so much of his energy persuading others (and himself) that *his* was the only course, Rhodes remained a compelling tragic 'hero' to the very end.

It seems that no-one, before or since, has elicited so many contradictory judgements from biographers and commentators. One obituary described him as 'massive, plain and honest'. To other writers he was 'immoral'. He was 'amoral'. He was 'almost immeasurably great'. He was a 'genius' below whose 'fascinating surface, the worms of falsehood and corruption [crept]'. He was a 'cynic'. He was 'incapable of cynicism'. But it was Basil Williams, one of the earlier biographers, who came as close as anyone to a Rhodes I can recognize with this observation:

> The worst of a man of such dominating personality is that his evil example is as potent as the good. He was no cynic ... but his Kimberley training led him deliberately to adopt a pose of cynicism, which had effects as baleful as if he had himself been a cynic to the core.[19]

It is the 'pose' and its 'baleful effects' that are the key. Whether dealing with emperors, queens or paramount chiefs, white bigots or rebellious blacks, rich or poor, men of God or the profanest diggers, Rhodes had the imagination and the skill to enter their world and play the role best calculated to seduce them to his cause. I don't believe, though, that he once lost sight of himself during those performances or entirely forgot the boy who could worry over a piece of ground that was his by law, but not by right. Self-knowledge there always was and, if one reads the texts carefully enough, self-disgust as well.

Today, the traveller along the path of Rhodes's spirit finds only neglect and decay. The seaside cottage where he died is now squeezed ignominiously against the mountain by a road and a railway line running parallel to the beach. The place is open to the public eight hours a day, but I must confess I have never come across another visitor during my many pilgrimages.

Bishop's Stortford, the English town of his birth, barely acknowledges him. His only monument is a simple brass plate in St Margaret's Church, which reads: 'In memory of Cecil John Rhodes, Premier of Cape Colony and Founder of Rhodesia, Fifth Son of the Vicar'.

Netteswell House, his birthplace, survives on bar takings and stage bookings, thanks to a brutally ugly leisure centre tacked on to the back. The

15

house itself is lucky to receive 15 visitors a week (6000 can be expected at Anne Hathaway's cottage on a summer weekend). The local grammar school that Rhodes attended between the ages of eight and 16 is now a unisex hair salon. Stylists and clients know nothing of Cecil Rhodes.

Much the same can be said of the other milestones in his life – the original De Beers boardroom, his Inyanga estates, his tomb in the Matopos hills. Sometimes there's an occasional visitor; invariably there are faded photographs and untended displays, watched over by an elderly curator who seems surprised that anyone should be taking an interest. The only spark of passion I have ever encountered was during a visit to the Matopos in 1970. Joshua Nkomo's guerillas had made an unsuccessful attempt to blast Rhodes's body out of its granite tomb, and their detonators were still scattered about the site when we arrived.

The statue of Rhodes in the Cape Town gardens that I remember so vividly from childhood is now discoloured and corroded. Streaks of white birdlime on either side of the face give his eyes, nose and mouth the appearance of a mask, detached from the rest of the head. Over the years rainwater, flowing from a crease in the brim of his farmer's hat, has eaten a large, rusty hole in his right leg. People stroll past uninterested, unseeing – in the very heart of the city that once honoured him with the most extravagant state funeral in its history.

Groote Schuur, his estate at the foot of Table Mountain, *is* maintained, but visitors are not encouraged. The great house was willed to the nation and became the official residence of the South African head of state, until Nelson Mandela broke with tradition.

The Rhodes scholarships are his only lasting memorial, but these have been awarded to students he would not have endorsed and for purposes quite different from those he intended.[20] In all other respects we have disengaged from him and moved on. But do we have the right to disengage so easily? Is it wise?

On a visit to one of the many neglected sites I remember complaining about public ignorance and indifference towards Rhodes. People, I told the curator, *should* visit this place.

'In penitence or in celebration?' came the unexpected question.

'Neither. Simply in recognition', I answered.

Defeat and occupation have forced other nations to examine their past, to acknowledge mistakes and delusions and to try to rebuild on what is best. We in Britain have not had this experience. Perhaps we are the weaker for it.

Rhodes had a huge and lasting impact on the course of British and South African history. He was alive and very influential in the early years of this century, and his business methods are still chillingly familiar as the century draws to a close. He was also a brilliant, charismatic man whose life story is an extraordinary mixture of high adventure, deception and betrayal – and on an unimaginable scale.

For all these reasons I became obsessed by a single thought as I learnt more and more about Cecil Rhodes. Might it not be possible to bring this important story to a mass audience through the medium of television drama?

In 1983 I approached Charles Denton and Margaret Matheson of Zenith Productions with the idea of writing a drama series on the life of Cecil Rhodes. It was (to borrow Rhodes's own words) 'a mad thought, the thought of a lunatic'. Firstly, there was the scale of his life. It was not possible to compress his story into the four to six hours that now seem to be the obligatory maximum for the so-called television mini-series. Huge sets were essential, beginning with the re-creation of early Kimberley and the diamond mines. Extras would be needed by the thousand, and all in costume. Whole cavalries and regiments of warriors would be required, along with ox-waggons, stage-coaches and at least two nineteenth-century trains. Above all, the series needed Africa – its people, its scenery and its wildlife.

The short answer is that the Rhodes series took 13 years from conception to fulfilment.

————— ONE —————

1902

The man was great, almost immeasurably great …
Cecil Rhodes stands on a pedestal of his own.

W.T. STEAD, *THE LAST WILL AND TESTAMENT OF CECIL JOHN RHODES*

And on the pedestal these words appear:
'My name is Ozymandias, king of kings:
Look on my works, ye Mighty, and despair!'
Nothing beside remains. Round the decay
Of that colossal wreck, boundless and bare
The lone and level sands stretch far away.

SHELLEY, *OZYMANDIAS*

March was insufferable the most exceptional spell of oppressive weather anyone could remember. It was already early autumn in the colony, a time when a cooling breeze could be expected off the Atlantic. But for once the wind failed. There was neither cloud nor breath of air to relieve the pitiless heat beating down on Cape Town out of a cloudless sky and thrown back from mountain and sea.[1]

This heat was killing him, suffocating him. His face was purple, bloated, wet with sweat beneath his tousled grey hair. His breath came in short, fitful gasps. He wandered from room to room, his clothes thrown open, trying to breathe. He flung himself on to the couch in the darkened drawing room. He started up and then dropped into a chair, but still he could not breathe. He laboured upstairs to his bedroom and paced about, every now and then stopping at the window[2]. From here he had 'a wondrous view' across his lake of magnificent blue hydrangeas, his great masses of bougainvilleas and plumbago, his regiments of rhododendrons, fuchsias, roses and Ceylon lilies, his plantations of gigantic pines, all marching in disciplined lines towards the mountain – *his* mountain, where he liked to sit 'and think in continents'.[3]

Nothing 'petty or finikin' was permitted in his domain.[4] Every project,

18

every enterprise, had to be on a large scale. His pets were lions; they too were big – big like his ideas. When asked by his staff how many yards he wished to plant with rhododendrons, he replied, 'Five miles!'[5]

He had bought this Groote Schuur estate 10 years earlier. The grounds had to be fashioned out of raw wilderness, the main house gutted and massively enlarged. His vision, as he described it to his architect, was 'Big and simple, barbaric if you like.'[6]

He was 38 years old at the time, but already Cecil Rhodes was prime minister of Cape Colony, chairman of Consolidated Gold Fields and managing director of the De Beers Mining Company, which held (and still holds) a virtual monopoly of the world's diamond production and distribution. The previous year his young mercenaries had seized 80,000 square miles (207,200 square kilometres) of Africa in his name, but that was only a beginning.[7] Hadn't the British prime minister himself turned to Rhodes and said, 'Take all you can and ask me afterwards'?[8]

In those heady days Groote Schuur had matched the scale of his ambition, but now the place was killing him. Not a breath of air stirred the hangings at the open bedroom window or rustled the leaves of the oaks that surrounded the house. The white walls, white colonnades and white gables were a pain to his eyes.[9]

Groote Schuur.

Late in the afternoon of 4 March he left Groote Schuur for the last time. He was driven to his small seaside cottage at Muizenberg in the first car he had ever owned, a 12–14 hp Wolseley, which he had been as delighted with 'as a child with a new toy'.[10] But the time for such pleasures was over. Now his sufferings were 'almost indescribably painful'.[11]

His sickroom in the cottage was small, square and whitewashed with an iron bedstead in the centre of the bare floor. A hole had been smashed in one wall to create a cross-draught; openings had been cut into the ceiling and trays of ice were laid out beneath the tin roof. A punka rigged up over his head was kept going night and day by servants who squatted outside on the verandah. An oxygen cylinder was kept at his bedside 'but afforded him only temporary relief'.[11]

Rhodes was suffering from an aneurysm of the aorta – the blockage and consequent swelling of the large vessel distributing blood from the heart to the body. As his condition worsened the enlarged aorta began to fill the right lung cavity, causing severe pain and loss of breath. He could not lie down as this tightened his chest, making it extremely difficult for him to breathe. To relieve these symptoms, a broad band had been stretched lengthways along the bed so that Rhodes could rest against it and maintain a permanent sitting position. Silver tubes drained the fluid from his swollen legs.

For nearly three weeks after his arrival at the cottage daily medical bulletins appeared on the editorial pages of the *Cape Argus* and the *Cape Times*. To spare the patient's feelings, a special issue was struck off for him 'in which the bulletin merely stated that "Mr. Rhodes had passed a somewhat restless night" and added a few commonplaces.'[10] Special prayers were said on his behalf in churches, and telegrams poured in from all parts of the world. The *Argus* reported that 'The Message sent by Her Majesty the Queen [Alexandra] was pathetic: "I am greatly touched at your sad illness, and pray God that your life may be spared." The cable was read to Mr. Rhodes, who was moved to tears.'[12]

Crowds gathered outside the cottage. Some even forced their way into the grounds, giving the servants 'the greatest trouble in keeping the outlook from the windows free.'[13]

No female nurse was permitted to attend Rhodes, but his closest friend and confidant, Dr Leander Starr Jameson, was 'nurse and sister, as well as brother to [him], and Mr. Rhodes could scarcely endure [Jameson] out of his sight'.[9] Colonel Elmhirst Rhodes, DSO, a serving officer in the Boer War, was given compassionate leave to be at his brother's side, and Rhodes's favourite young men were summoned from far and wide. Jack Grimmer, the former De Beers clerk who now managed Rhodes's vast Inyanga estates, made the 1200-mile (1930-kilometre) journey in 'rapid' time. As the *Argus* was delighted to report, the sight of young Jack brought immediate relief to the dying man: '... and that young gentleman was a tower of strength in the sick room, especially at times when the patient was in great pain and, in degree, less tractable'.[12]

The sensitive 'Flippie' Jourdan was brought to Rhodes's bedside from Worcester in the Cape, and found it 'most heart-rending to see him sit on the edge of the bed, at one moment gasping for breath, and at another with his head sunk so low that his chin almost touched his chest.'[13]

According to Gordon Le Sueur, another young favourite:

[On] about March 23 [Rhodes] seemed to be sinking, but suddenly developed a craving to go home to England. All species of animals, when they feel the end approaching, wish to go home to die, and so it was with Rhodes ... And then it was for Jameson to go and tell him that he would be dead before he reached Cape Town docks. For all that, he clung to the idea, and cabins were reserved on the mail steamer 'the Saxon', sailing on March 26. His cabin was fitted with electric fans, oxygen tubes, and refrigerating pipes in readiness for him. Strangely enough, on the morning of Wednesday March 26, he rallied considerably ...[10]

Rhodes's condition had so improved that Le Sueur and Jourdan felt confident enough to leave the cottage for Cape Town. They even speculated that Rhodes might be able to sail on the *Saxon*.

But it was not to be.

Shortly before 6.00 p.m. on Wednesday 26 March 1902, 'to the accompaniment of the thunder of the surf breaking on the beach in front of his little bedroom, the greatest of modern Englishmen ... passed away'.[11] He was 48 years old.

The end had been 'perfectly quiet and peaceful. Those who were privileged to see the remains tell us that ... a half-smile remained after his death.'[12]

Dr Jameson made the announcement to the waiting crowd. When asked for the great man's last words, he replied: 'So little done. So much to do.'

A final stroke of public relations. When asked later by a trusted friend whether the report was true, Jameson was said to have answered, 'Nonsense! ... Do you think Rhodes was a poet?'[14]

It was Rhodes's banker, Sir Lewis Michell, who had claimed that those words were 'murmured' in his presence,[11] but Sir Lewis was not a witness to the death. Those who were described a parting more simply human. After reaching out to Jameson and muttering 'Good bye. God bless you!'[12] Cecil

The cottage at Muizenberg where Rhodes died.

Rhodes looked up at young Grimmer and said 'Turn me over, Jack!' ... and then expired.[15]

No matter. Jameson's announcement was more appropriate to the man and the moment, and it was this version that newspaper editors, speech writers and archbishops seized upon in their glowing testimonials to 'one of the greatest men of modern times'.[12]

The news was broadcast to Cape Town that evening 'in a fortuitous and singular Manner'. Someone had the good sense to contact Mr O'Callaghan, the manager of the International Hotel in the city centre, where the weekly promenade concert was in progress. 'Mr. O'Callaghan at once stopped the performance and requested the bandmaster to play the Dead March [from] "Saul". The night was beautifully clear and still ... and the strains of the familiarly plaintive air penetrated the entire ... district.'[12]

Young Jourdan hurried back from Cape Town to Muizenberg. He leaves us this description of his dead idol:

> The light fell fully on his Caesar-like face, and showed off his strong fea-tures and massive head to great advantage … I thought I had never seen him look more beautiful … He reminded me so much of the pictures I had seen of Napoleon Bonaparte … Even in death he looked determined, dignified and masterful.
>
> As I stood there in the lonely simple room, and realized for the first time that I should never see his genial smile or his beautiful clear blue eyes light up, or hear his kind and friendly voice again, I could no longer restrain myself, and I felt the warm drops trickle down my cheeks.[13]

But this was not the time for tender reverie. Grim duties had to be per-formed. After taking a plaster cast of the face, Jameson and two other doc-tors performed a full autopsy.

> The major finding … confirmed the clinical diagnosis of a dilation of the ascending aorta the "size of a man's wrist" with a "saccular dilation from the transverse portion as large as a child's head" … The lungs were filled with fluid, congested with blood and compressed …[16]

In the early hours of 27 March the body was placed in a temporary coffin and transported by special train to Rondebosch, the nearest station to Groote Schuur. Jameson, Colonel Rhodes and Jack Grimmer were among the six mourners who accompanied the body. At Rondebosch station, a horse-drawn hearse was waiting.

It was a still, clear, moonlit night. Le Sueur and the entire Groote Schuur staff were awake and awaiting the homecoming. At 4.00 a.m. they heard the sound of the distant train. Le Sueur walked out on to the veran-dah. Half an hour later he heard the sound of wheels and horses' hooves, and saw lights appearing round the bend of the front drive.

> The effect was weird in the extreme – the semi-darkened house with the little group of servants standing with bared heads waiting for the procession which slowly made its way between the great oaks which line the gravelled drive – waiting for the master who was coming home for the last time.
>
> There was a brilliant full moon that Thursday morning before Good Friday, and its rays shining through the oak leaves cast a pattern of patches of gold and black darkness upon the drive.
>
> Slowly the hearse approached, no sound being heard but the scrunching of the gravel beneath the horses' hoofs [sic] and the measured tread of the little band of mourners, who had now been joined by Mrs. Stuart and Mr.

Theo Schreiner. Then it stopped before the door … The coffin was borne in by the undertaker's men … Not a word was spoken by any of us, as in silence the Chief entered his home for the last time.

The cover, not yet screwed down, was moved so as to expose the face … We stood round as if dazed, until the dreary silence was broken by a woman's sob, and Mrs. Stuart came forward and placed a spray of white flowers upon [the coffin]. So Cecil Rhodes entered his house for the last time.[17]

The following day 'the whole British Empire was in mourning'.[13] Telegrams and cables of condolence were received from all parts of the world. Flags were flown at half-mast, and the principal business places in Cape Town closed for the day. The government announced that a state funeral would be held.

In columns heavily bordered in black, the Cape newspapers described the world's reaction to the passing of 'a great Empire-builder such as has not been seen since the days of ancient Rome'.[12] The German Kaiser sent 'a message of sympathy to His Majesty [King Edward VII] on the loss of so distinguished a subject as Mr. Rhodes'.[18] The American papers published 'longer obituaries than any since the death of Queen Victoria, except on the death of President McKinley'.[19] In the emotion of the moment Britain's colonial rivals seemed willing to suspend their criticisms of Rhodes. According to the Cape papers, the press comments in the European capitals were unexpectedly sympathetic. 'They recognized his colossal work for the British Empire and his colonising genius.'[19]

Unsurprisingly, the English press 'dwelled upon the noble ends for which he worked, the grandeur of his ideas, his courage and pertinacity, the intensity of his patriotism, and the clear conception of the Imperial destinies of the British race'.[12] Her Majesty, Queen Alexandra, sent another 'touching' telegram, and ordered a Cape Town florist to prepare a wreath bearing the simple message 'From the Queen'. It would remain permanently on Rhodes's coffin 'during the whole of the obsequies and [be] buried with the great statesman's remains'. Two other wreaths shared this honour. They were 'From his brothers and sisters' and 'From Dr. L.S. Jameson, Friendship'.[20]

From London it was announced that a memorial service would be held at St Paul's Cathedral, to be attended by the lord mayor and the Corporation of the City of London. Proposals were put forward for a permanent memorial at Rhodes's birthplace, Bishop's Stortford, and a bust in Westminster Abbey.[18]

But it was in Rhodes's own territory, his putative United States of South Africa, that the greatest demonstrations of public sorrow and public adulation were seen – demonstrations unequalled before or since. Cities and towns literally closed down. Everywhere flags flew at half-mast. From Salisbury, the capital of the country that bore his name, the *Herald* reported that 'Rhodesia, like a widow, sits numbed in her bereavement'.[21]

Over the Easter weekend 30,000 people filed through the oak-panelled hall of Groote Schuur into the mortuary chamber, 'passing the catafalque with heads bared in deep silence...'. The *Cape Times* described 'A ceaseless procession of men, women and children, some in deep mourning, some in their working clothes, all however wearing some touch of black crêpe in their garments.'[5]

The writer went on to assure his readers that 'Very many coloured people were present to pay their modest tribute of respect, for Mr. Rhodes was always a friend to the coloured man, and there were not a few aboriginal natives among those who came to mourn.'[5]

Le Sueur records wreaths and floral tributes arriving 'by the ton'.[10] According to a *Cape Argus* report, the funeral chamber and the adjoining rooms were soon filled to capacity, forcing the paper to publish an appeal to 'persons desiring of showing their respect for the deceased' to send any further tributes to the Cape Parliament, where the body would be lying in state between the hours of 9.00 a.m. and 12 noon on Thursday 4 April, the day of the funeral service.[18]

In those three hours 15,000 people passed through the Parliament building to pay their respects. Thousands more had been pouring into Cape Town from all parts of the country since the previous day. It was 'a throng, the like of which has never been seen in the thoroughfares of the city before'. Entire buildings were draped in purple and black. 'Men, women and children in deep mourning stood on footpaths, filled the balconies, peopled the windows, and occupied every elevated position which could afford them a view...'.[22]

All traffic had been cleared from the streets by the time a contingent of mounted police appeared at the head of Adderley Street, Cape Town's main thoroughfare. Behind them, members of the Cape Parliament, the Bar, the civil service, the Church, the armed services, the business community, the teaching professions, the press, and any other institution deemed important to the life of the colony, slow-marched to the strains of Beethoven.[23] The coffin of Matabele teak was borne on a gun carriage draped with a Union Jack, the flag of Rhodes's Chartered Company and a white silk ensign from the Loyal Women's Guild bearing the inscription, 'Farewell, Great Heart'.[22]

His Grace the Archbishop of Cape Town delivered the funeral address, taking his text from 2 Samuel: 'Know ye not that there is a prince and a great man fallen this day in Israel'. After alluding very briefly, as archbishops must, to certain features of Rhodes's character 'which *some* might wish had been other than they were' (my italics), His Grace made it clear that he was not to be included in that disagreeable minority. He exhorted the congregation to learn from Rhodes's 'large, unselfish, patriotic views, and not to rest until they be realized'. Following his great example, they should dedicate their lives 'to the expansion and consolidation of the British Empire, to the provision of new markets for British merchandise, and to a new country for British colonists'.[24]

In a highly significant passage, His Grace posed a rhetorical question or two: 'But men will ask, what about his religion? Why did he pay no attention to its outward observances?'[24] Rhodes was famously agnostic and often a fierce critic of Christian missionary activity in Africa.[25] No matter. Between God and Mammon, the prince of the Established Church knew where a man's patriotic duties lay, and Rhodes's life was held up before that congregation as an example of Christian dedication to a cause that his Grace described (using Rhodes's own words) as 'the betterment of humanity and … the increase of the sum of human happiness'.[24]

The funeral procession passing down Adderly Street, Cape Town.

As the choir sang 'Father in Thy gracious keeping/leave we now thy servant sleeping', the coffin returned to the streets for another memorable procession – this time to the railway station, where a massive banner proclaimed 'To live in hearts we leave behind is not to die'.[26] The funeral train, engines attached, stood in readiness. The De Beers saloon, in which he had so often travelled, had been prepared as a funeral car. Everything, but everything, was draped in purple and black – the station entrances, the platforms, the locomotives and the carriages, inside and out.

> The troops lining the platform, [stood] with reversed arms as the coffin was borne to the de Beers saloon, where with lighted candles burning at the head, the bier had been prepared for its reception … To the minute at five o'clock the train steamed out of the station.[22]

The 1000-mile (1600-kilometre) journey to Rhodes's chosen burial ground in the Matopos was one of the most extraordinary pageants ever documented. Heavy with ritual and symbolism, it has been beautifully described by his biographer, Sarah Gertrude Millin:

> The body of Rhodes passed along the path of his spirit: from Cape Town where he had ruled, through the Western Province of his vineyards, to Kimberley that had begotten his dreams, along his own railway in Bechuanaland, through the country of his name, to the hills where he had made his peace with the sons of Moselikatze [Mzilikazi].[27]

Through stations draped in the purple and black, where guards of honour lined the platforms and military bands played funeral marches; past towns where churches tolled the minute bell and all places of business were closed; alongside British military encampments 'where sentries, perched on the roofs of the little block-houses, [stood] like statues with arms reversed'[26] the funeral train bore Rhodes's body to his African Valhalla. 'For a thousand miles, men, women and children swarmed from their homesteads for a last glimpse of what remained of their beloved friend.'[23]

In the larger towns the train would stop, and 'Farmers and their wives from the back veldt, old and young colonists, many of them with streaming eyes, brought their wreaths and laid them reverently on his coffin'.[23] Some bore simple messages of grief or gratitude others showed a more positive spirit: 'Generations will Rise Up and Call him Blessed.'[22]

At one town, 'as the train entered the station, children strewed flowers before the engine, while the platform was crowded by a large gathering, principally diggers and Mr. Rhodes's old constituents'.[22] In Kimberley, Rhodes's diamond capital, 'two thousand workmen from De Beers marched through the town, four abreast, headed by their own brass band, playing the tunes of well-known hymns'.[22] Le Sueur wrote: 'One can almost say that every man, woman and child turned up to take part in the stream of people who passed the coffin between the hours of 6 a.m. and 10 a.m.'[26]

From Kimberley to Mafeking an armoured train preceded the first locomotive and searchlights swept the night veld. The Boer War was not yet over.[28]

The railhead was at Bulawayo, former capital of the vanquished Matabele. From here a great funeral trek, consisting of a stream of mailcoaches, 'innumerable Cape carts' and men on horseback, cycle and foot set off in one great procession, five miles long,[29] for the Matopos – that primeval landscape of massive granite boulders, chaotically heaped one upon the other. This was the sacred ground of the Matabele, the final resting place of Mzilikazi, founder of their nation, whose corpse, 'sitting upright in a stone chair'[30] at the mouth of a high cave, still surveyed the lands he had conquered; lands that his successors had lost to Rhodes.

When he had first been taken to this place Rhodes had stared at the eyeless skull under its headdress of blue jay feathers and whispered, 'What a poet that man was!' It was an experience that had touched his imagination.

> I admire the grandeur and loneliness of the Matoppos ... [he wrote in his final will], and therefore I desire to be buried in the Matoppos on the hill which I used to visit and which I called the View of the World in a square to be cut in the rock on the top of the hill covered with a plain brass plate with these words thereon – 'Here lie the remains of Cecil John Rhodes'.

To his chosen site close to the tomb of Mzilikazi his coffin was taken, drawn on a gun carriage by a team of twelve black oxen. 'The hill was swarming with the Matabele he had won and betrayed and won again' and, as the coffin was hauled up the granite slope, 'They gave him, alone of white men before or since, the royal salute ... "Bayete!"'[29]

Even in death, Rhodes had demonstrated his supreme power over men's imaginations, be they white or black, rich or poor, humble or mighty.

As the coffin was lowered by chains into the granite tomb the white mourners sang 'Now the labourer's task is o'er', and the Bishop of Mashonaland read the poem 'C.J.R.' 'from the heart and pen of prophet–poet Rudyard Kipling':[29]

> So huge the all-mastering thought that drove,
> So brief the term allowed –
> Nations, not words, he linked to prove
> His faith before the crowd ...

The ceremony at Rhodes's grave in the Matopos.

Another poet (anonymous) even imagined Rhodes's ascent into paradise 'as angels chant the Welcome Song':

> Called home while still in manhood's prime;
> Transferred to spheres of grander work;
> The Master needs thee – oh, reward sublime!
> The Master beckons! Go receive thy crown.[31]

Others portrayed Rhodes as a Messiah, who would return to this earth in a glorious Second Coming 'when all his dreams are realised and his schemes completed as the "over-lord" of a new Africa, bearing in its ripened civilisation the impress of his genius'.[32]

It is not difficult to understand what had inspired the adulation and hyperbole. His had, indeed, been a spectacular life. In his brief, 30-year career Rhodes had not only monopolized the world's diamonds and a fair share of the world's gold, he had carved a personal empire out of the heart of Africa. His railways and telegraph lines straddled the continent. He had given his name to two vast countries, Southern Rhodesia (today's Zimbabwe) and Northern Rhodesia (Zambia), and British protection to Bechuanaland (Botswana) and Nyasaland (Malawi). His Chartered Company claimed exclusive mineral rights over 'a territory of nearly one million square miles'[33] (2.6 million square kilometres), comparable to all of Hitler's conquests in Europe and Africa when the Third Reich was at its zenith and German panzers stood at the gates of Moscow.

But the Rhodes myth was sustained by something even greater than diamonds, gold and unimaginable tracts of land. It rested on something he liked to call 'My Idea'. Through his speeches, his writings and his brilliant propaganda, Rhodes was able excite the English imagination to an extent that has seldom been equalled before or since and at his death the excitement peaked. Everywhere the call went out – 'Raise his banner!', 'Carry on the great work!', 'Follow his example!'[12]

Hadn't Rhodes dreamt of a single African nation, stretching from the Cape to the Sudan, 'a country fit for White Men, fit for Englishmen; richer, more populous than the United States of America'?[34] Hadn't he called for 'the bringing of the whole uncivilised world under British rule, for the recovery of the United States, for the making of the Anglo-Saxon race but one Empire'?[35]

No wonder men fantasized about his glorious Second Coming. The best was yet to come. 'However high is the regard in which we hold him now, it will be left to future generations to gain the full measure of his greatness.'[23] Rhodes shared this opinion. Once, when he sat talking late into the night with his friend, Dr Jameson, he was asked how long he expected to be remembered. After a second or two Rhodes replied, 'I give myself four thousand years!'[36]

Such things were not to be. Other writers, with a clearer vision, could penetrate the fog of propaganda, could separate fact from fiction and distinguish the 'pirate flag' of a 'speculator and gamester' from the banner of 'truth and justice which knows no race or colour'.[37]

That distinction was made by the great South African writer Olive Schreiner a full seven years before Rhodes's death. Once Britain had made peace with the Boers and emotions had cooled, others began to take stock. The contradiction between Rhodes's imperial ambitions and the methods he used to achieve them – the very point that Miss Schreiner had made – began to worry the British. English-speaking South Africans, like my grandparents, might continue to worship him, but in Britain he would not remain a hero, not even an imperial hero. As early as 1921 an eminent English biographer would write disapprovingly: '[Rhodes] lowered the standard of public life at the Cape and even at home in England.'[38] G.K. Chesterton judged him even more harshly: 'Rhodes had no principles whatever to give the world ... What he called his ideas were the dregs of Darwinism which had already grown not only stagnant, but poisonous.'[39]

The English Establishment had never liked him. He was altogether too cynical, too clear-sighted, too damned clever. They had been happy to collude with him when he served their purpose, but he was never one of them.

The rise of fascism would further tarnish Rhodes's reputation, making him guilty by association. Spengler, the German philosopher, once hailed Rhodes as 'the first man of a new age – the first precursor of a Western type of Caesar, whose day is yet to come'.[40] And when a new Caesar did appear in the shape of Adolf Hitler, he excited men's imaginations with the very words Rhodes had used to whip up English hysteria 40 years earlier: 'I believe that the German people are called by the divine destiny to be leaders of the world for the glory of the German being as well as for the benefit of the human race.'[39] Change one word and you have a Rhodes quotation. Hitler said himself that the only person who understood the historical conditions for maintaining British supremacy was Cecil Rhodes, who had been ignored by his own people.[40]

There was another connection that deserves special mention. From an early age Rhodes had acknowledged his debt to the Jesuits. So had Heinrich Himmler. In Rhodes's case, they were the inspiration for his plan to create 'a secret society ... placed at our universities and schools ... in every Colonial legislature ... [which would] crush all disloyalty and every movement for the severance of the British Empire'.[41] For Himmler, the Jesuits were the inspiration behind a plan to establish an élite corps, placed in universities, schools and every occupied town and village. Thanks to some deft manoeuvring by his trustees, Rhodes's secret society evolved into the community of Rhodes scholars (see pp. 332-333). Himmler's secret society came to be known as the SS.

Parallels like these were too awkward, too embarrassing for the English to accept. Backs would turn, eyes would be averted. There would be no bust of Rhodes in Westminster Abbey and no memorial to his greatness in Bishop's Stortford, the place of his birth. He reminds us of connections and responsibilities we prefer to forget.

The record of Rhodes's death and funeral is a testament to mass hysteria, racial delusion, mysticism, pageantry – and meticulous stage management. In dread and fascination we have watched other nations indulge in such things. But the English?

'Know thyself.' The year 1902 is too close for such complacency.

In Rhodesia young men were still laying down their lives for Rhodes's

'Idea' in the early 1980s. South Africa retained a political system firmly based on it well into this decade. (Ironically, though, his political heirs in that country came to hate him for committing one rash act he would regret for the rest of his life.)[42]

In Britain, our political system owes nothing to Cecil Rhodes, but the emotions he could excite and manipulate are still depressingly familiar.

For our own sake more than his, we should not turn our backs on Cecil Rhodes. There is a great deal that he can tell us.

TWO

'A DELICATE, GOLDEN-HAIRED LITTLE FELLOW'

'Why did I come to Africa?', he once replied to a friend.
'Well, they will tell you that I came out on account of my
health, or from a love of adventure – and to some extent that
may be true; but the real fact is that I could no longer stand
the eternal cold mutton'.[1]

Bishop's Stortford lies 30 miles (48 kilometres) to the north of London. The M11 motorway and a regular train service to London's Liverpool Street station have transformed the quiet Hertfordshire village of Rhodes's birth into a typical British dormitory town, unexceptional except for a weekly street market which suggests older links with agriculture and the land.

On South Road, two semi-detached Georgian houses have been united with a 1960s leisure centre and uniformly plastered in white stucco in an attempt to give coherence to the whole. The sign outside tells us that this complex is called the Rhodes Centre.

In earlier times, the two original houses, Thorleybourne and Netteswell House, had distinct and separate identities; Netteswell, the house on the right, being variously described as 'cramped' and 'an ugly, grey-stone, three-storeyed' home.[2] It was here that the Colossus of Africa entered this world at 7.30 p.m. on 5 July 1853.

Biographers have repeatedly raked through the known fragments of Rhodes's early life in their efforts to explain the man he became. A recent American biographer even went as far as to engage the services of a professor of psychiatry to assist him with a 'psychodynamic interpretation' of Rhodes's background and early life. Although it may be entertaining to hear that the birth of a younger brother gave Rhodes feelings of 'bitterness and resentment' against his father which would 'curdle his relations with powerful figures, usually older men, who stood in the way of his dreams'[3] this approach

Netteswell House, Bishop's Stortford – Rhodes's birthplace.

tells us more about the American writers than it does about Cecil Rhodes.

The man himself wasn't exactly helpful. He deflected the primary question, 'Why did you come to Africa?', with a joke about cold mutton.

'Mr. Rhodes never talked about himself', a contemporary informs us, 'except…' – and this is crucial – '…if it were to illustrate some important point which he was trying to drive home.'[4] That was the Rhodes technique, particularly in later life. If he wanted to make an important political point or simply enhance his image, he would construct a parable and pass it off as personal experience. 'When I was scolded by the Kaiser', or 'When Lord Grey told me that Groote Schuur had burnt down' or 'When I was walking with General Gordon'. Journalists and writers loved it. He was sharing a confidence, inviting them to eavesdrop on private conversations between great men. It was the raw material that legends are spun from.

Before he publicized these personal parables, Rhodes liked to test them on friends and courtiers to rehearse and hone them until he was sure of the effect.

Not all his personal stories were inventions. Some were factual and have been corroborated by contemporary witnesses, others were embellishments; but whether they were true, half-true or pure fiction, they all had one important thing in common: they served his purpose. Reminiscence without purpose was a waste of time, and Rhodes could not bear to waste time. For that reason his childhood was seldom visited. It served no purpose. It was too ordinary.

There was one childhood story, though, which he particularly liked. It tells of a visit he paid, when he was '10 or 12', to the home of an elderly admiral whom he found planting acorns:

> I said to him, very gently, that the planting of oak-trees by a man advanced in years seemed to me rather imaginative. He seized the point at once and said: 'I know I cannot expect more than to see them beyond a shrub; but with me rests the conception and the shade and the glory.[5]

This anecdote was included in a political speech made in 1895 when Rhodes was very conscious of his failing health. It tells us that in the last decade of his life he wanted his public to think of him as a great visionary who might not survive to see his dreams fulfilled, but it brings us no closer to Rhodes, the child.

From the evidence we have his childhood and background were indeed ordinary, and it is that ordinariness which makes the man so exceptional. Rhodes was born in an age when Britain was still an aristocratic country. Government, Church and army were led by men from landed and titled families, brought up in a tradition of service to the state. One day Rhodes would have to deal with this aristocratic elite, and it would give him one of his most audacious and exciting victories; but in that campaign he was the outsider, moving in. He had none of the advantages of aristocratic wealth and connection.[6]

Rhodes was the sixth surviving child of the Rev. Francis William and Louisa Rhodes. An older brother, Basil, had died in infancy, and a younger brother died the year after Rhodes was born. Three more brothers followed. All survived. This family of nine children and four adults (there were never less than two servants in the house) shared the 'cramped' quarters on South Road.

Rhodes's father was the first and last in a long line of Rhodeses to enter the Church. In later life, Rhodes would jokingly refer to his ancestors as 'keepers of cows'. This is misleading. The Rhodeses were, indeed, from yeoman stock, but in the early eighteenth century an ancestor, William Rhodes, moved his family from Cheshire and purchased a large farm in St Pancras – now part of central London but then in open country. Subsequent generations profited from rising land values and purchased several businesses, including a brick and tile factory. From such a background, Cecil Rhodes would never know the struggles of men who have risen from extreme poverty, but neither could he expect the position and wealth that were the entitlements of the English upper classes. In this highly stratified society, Rhodes was born into the very middle of the middle ground. In a sense, that was nowhere.

> The meaning of Rhodes' ancestry lies in its lack of meaning ... Rhodes him-
> self recognized this when he set no name beside his own on his tombstone;
> not of ancestor or of birthplace. He was that being, Cecil John Rhodes,
> belonging to nobody, belonging to everybody – self-contained.[7]

What do we really know of this child, born in a vicarage in Bishop's Stortford? A school companion, writing to Rhodes in later life, told him: 'You
were a delicate, golden-haired little fellow then.'[8] A former nanny remembered him as 'good-looking, with fair hair, and the nice agreeable way of
speaking which runs in the family'.[9] Another witness described 'a grubby
little boy with ruffled hair'.[9] Some spoke of him as delicate, others as 'deli-
cate-looking' but 'healthy enough'. Depending on the source, his hair can be
fair or dark; his eyes 'deep blue' or 'a thoughtful grey'. There are similar
variations in the early accounts of his behaviour and character. 'He was a shy
and solitary spirit, full of strange silences.' 'He was a bright, fairly clever lad,
with nothing dreamy about him.' The common denominator – as the early
photographs confirm – is a picture of an attractive, slender, thoughtful child.

There are plenty of anecdotes illustrating early grit and determination. A
retired schoolmaster, writing to *The Times* a year after Rhodes's death, still
remembered 'a pretty, delicate child in a plaid frock' standing with his nurse
among the spectators at a cricket match:

> The batsman hit a ball to leg, which without touching the ground, struck
> the little fellow full on the arm. I rushed up, fearing the bone was broken,
> but on testing it found it was not. I was struck by the Spartan way, almost
> indifference with which the child bore pain.[10]

In similar vein, we hear that Rhodes liked his bath cold. 'He took it very cold
... "one, two", and then came a splash.'[11] In a little confessional album on
display in the Rhodes Centre you can still see his motto, written in a childish
hand: 'Do or Die'. As these stories accumulate one can't help wondering
how many thousands – nay, hundreds of thousands – of middle-class Victorian boys had childhood thoughts and childhood experiences no different
from these.

In their efforts to rescue young Cecil Rhodes from the crowd, several
biographers have poked about in the darker recesses of Netteswell House
and discovered 'tensions', 'intense sibling rivalries' and 'murderous feelings'.
Rhodes's mother, we are told, was 'pitifully overworked – worn out by child
rearing and child bearing'. His father was cold, severe and remote.

Certainly, the Rev. Francis Rhodes was well into middle age when Cecil
Rhodes was a child. This was the vicar's second marriage. His first wife,

Elizabeth, had died in childbirth, and nine years would pass before he took Louisa Peacock as his bride. Francis Rhodes was 46 years old when Cecil was born and perhaps less capable of forming a close relationship with his son than a younger father might have been. But does this necessarily make him 'cold' and 'severe', or justify talk of 'a smouldering anger that fuels a son's rivalry with his father [and] shows up in the entrepreneur's dogged intensity to succeed'?[12] This was Victorian England, after all. Fathers seldom enjoyed demonstrative relationships with their sons, but these omissions did not create a generation of megalomaniacs.

In the following description of Francis Rhodes, a nanny gives us a clear picture of a typical Victorian paterfamilias:

> [He stood] a little apart from his family, interfering but seldom in the daily discipline save when his ire was roused by some particularly aggravating boyish escapade ... [He] was the final arbiter only in the worst mis-demeanours and on those occasions he favoured the cane.[13]

People liked and respected the Rev. Francis Rhodes. During his 15 years as curate in the parish of Brentwood, he was known as 'the good Mr. Rhodes'.[14] Never pompous or verbose – he was famous for his 10-minute sermons – Francis Rhodes was remarkably tolerant of people who held views that differed from his own. He disliked hypocrisy, and made 'downrightness of speech' the universal principle of his home. 'Subterfuge and insincerity were unknown.'[15]

Rhodes's father was also an active and energetic man, and here we might usefully speculate on the influences that shaped Cecil Rhodes. During his time as vicar of Bishop's Stortford, the Rev. Rhodes raised £20,000 to establish a training college for 'mistresses in elementary schools'.[14] He also dragooned the burghers of Bishop's Stortford into backing his scheme to expand the local grammar school and oversaw the completion of an entire new building – today's unisex hair salon.

Rhodes had this to say about his dealings with his father:

> My father frequently, and I am now sure wisely, demolished many of my dreams as fantastical, but when I had rebuilt them on more practical lines, he was ready to listen. He never failed to put his finger on the weak spots, and his criticisms soon taught me to consider a question from every possible point of view.[16]

Of course, this might have been another of his fables but, if it was, it certainly indicated fond memory, and there is evidence enough in the family correspondence of an easy, warm relationship between father and son.[17]

Rev. Francis Rhodes   **Louisa Rhodes**

In later years Rhodes's friends noted that he used to speak of his father 'with admiration'.[18]

As to the suggestion that Rhodes's mother was 'pitifully overworked', etc., one can only answer that the Rhodeses were a Victorian middle-class family, where large numbers of children were the norm and servants attended to the chores. (Baby Cecil didn't even feed at his mother's breast.) This is not to suggest that Louisa Rhodes led an easy life, but if the implication is that Cecil Rhodes was starved of normal maternal affection, there is plenty of evidence to the contrary in his loving letters to his mother and in this observation, made to a close friend: 'My mother got through an amazing amount of work; she must have had the gift of organisation, for she was never flustered and seemed always to have ample time for all our many, and to us, important affairs.'[16]

In Rhodes's relationships with his brothers and sisters there is certainly no suggestion of 'sibling rivalries', let alone 'murderous feelings'. On the contrary, Rhodes showed genuine affection and loyalty and a touching, almost paternal concern for their welfare when he was as young as 17.[19] Indeed, most of the clan 'buzzed about Cecil' until the end of his days, enjoying his support and patronage.

Herbert, the first-born, was eight years older than Rhodes. Cecil adored his elder brother and, in spite of the difference in their ages, the two of them spent days walking and riding together. An extrovert with a wild sense of humour, Herbert had, to borrow his mother's phrase, 'every sort of sense [but] common sense'.[20]

> It was Herbert who on pony-back chas'd the village children right into their school house; it was Herbert who ranged his younger brothers in a row, each armed with a stick, and led them in a soldier's charge through and through their father's rows of peas, and brooked no breach of his authority.[20]

A master remembered Herbert breaking out of a school walk to scale the scaffolding of an unfinished building and then running out 'on a horizontal pole, where, without apparent effort, he [stood] unsupported, haranguing his school fellows'. Herbert was 'passionate … amenable to no restraint'. He was also a born actor, 'with a face like India rubber and an extraordinary command of expression'. He could howl 'with big tears dropping onto the floor … when administered a sharp correction [in class]', but the moment the master's back was turned 'all signs of grief disappeared' and Herbert would entertain his fellow pupils with 'hideous grimaces', resuming his 'agonised countenance' immediately the master looked round to discover the cause of the disturbance.[21]

Two sisters – Louisa and Edith – were next in line. Described as 'small and dark, quiet, rather prim and old-maidish',[22] Louisa spent most of her adult years living 'quietly at Iver',[23] near the spot where Pinewood Film Studios now stand. Rhodes always found time for weekends in Iver whenever he was staying in London.

Edith was a very different character, a 'strapping, robust girl'[22] who was 'careless in attire … she displayed splendid disregard for conventionalities, and freely asserted her right to independent action'. Edith is described as being 'extremely like her brother … [with] a large share of his determined spirit'.[22]

There was one occasion, many years later, when Edith wrote to Rhodes suggesting she should stay with him at Groote Schuur. Rhodes instructed his secretary to write back and decline the pleasure, remarking, 'I am very fond of my sister, and it would be very pleasant to have her here, but I am afraid the house is not big enough for two of us!'[23]

A friend once said of Edith, 'Had she been a man she, too, would have made a new country, or if there were no more new countries, she would have built an island out in the ocean!' Apparently, she was 'immensely pleased when this remark was repeated to her.'[23]

After Edith, there were Basil (who lived for only 11 days) and Francis William. 'Frankie', as he was known, had charm and panache. In later life

Rhodes would describe him as 'a very gallant fellow on the battlefield and also in the ladies' boudoir'. He achieved minor distinction in the dragoons, serving in India, Uganda and the Sudan, where he was awarded a DSO. He eventually resigned with the rank of colonel to throw in his lot with his famous younger brother. Within a year he was condemned to death for participating in the plot to overthrow President Kruger. He survived, only to be besieged at Ladysmith in 1899, and died six years later in Groote Schuur.

Ernest, the next brother, also joined forces with Rhodes. He had resigned his army commission with the rank of captain to emigrate to Australia, but was persuaded to move to South Africa where he was rewarded with the position of manager of Rhodes's Consolidated Gold Fields company.

Cecil was next in line, followed by Frederick and Elmhirst, the brother who was given compassionate leave to be at Rhodes's bedside during those final days in the cottage at Muizenberg.

Arthur Montagu, the next youngest, would also enjoy his brother's patronage. After failing as an ostrich farmer, he was rewarded with a large estate in Matabeleland. When the 'rebellion' was quelled Arthur put in a substantial claim for damages to mealie crops that had never existed, as his brother knew only too well. 'Cecil Rhodes had most of these claims submitted to him, and across his brother's he wrote: "This is the most impudent claim that has yet been submitted".'[23] Unfortunately, there is no record to tell us whether compensation was paid.

The youngest brother, Bernard, would also start out in life as a soldier. Like Elmhirst, he served in the Boer War, but otherwise seems to have led a rather aimless existence: '[Rhodes] was very fond of him, but objected to … what he called [his] useless life.' When a visitor to Groote Schuur told Rhodes he knew Bernard, his host replied, 'Ah, yes! Bernard is a charming fellow; he rides, shoots and fishes; in fact, he is a loafer.'[23]

Rhodes adopted a similar tone when he once described his brothers' military capabilities: 'I have four brothers, each in a different branch of the British army, and not one of them could take a company through Hyde Park Gate.'[23]

This remark should be received in the spirit intended – as a joke – and not, as one biographer would have us believe, as a sign of deep-seated contempt. Until the end of his life Rhodes expressed his affection and loyalty in the trust he placed in his abler brothers and in his continual generosity towards the whole clan, including the most undeserving members. His contemporaries certainly interpreted his feelings correctly when they decided that the wreath from Rhodes's brothers and sisters should remain in the place of honour on the coffin, along with the offerings from Her Majesty the Queen and Dr L.S. Jameson.

Rhodes as a boy.

One question mark hangs over this picture of a loving, well-adjusted family. Of the nine brothers and sisters, only one, Ernest, would marry. Rhodes's contemporaries and the early biographers had no problems with that. In Victorian and Edwardian times, wanderlust and the spirit of adventure were considered plausible explanations for the desire to remain single. However, later biographers have worried and fretted over the issue. Some, as we have seen, applied fashionable psychoanalytical dogma to the 'problem' of the eight unmarried Rhodeses. No doubt fashions will change again. Future biographers may well turn to geneticists, or perhaps neuro-scientists, for an explanation of bachelorhood based on the pathology of the brain. As things stand there are no clear answers, but we do ourselves a disservice when we stretch the available evidence so far that demons rise in the Victorian vicarage on South Street.

Family life was not restricted to this one home. Sophy Peacock,

Mrs Rhodes's unmarried sister, lived in the manor house at Sleaford, a train ride away in Lincolnshire, and all the children would spend time with their favourite aunt. Frank, her godson, was her particular favourite, but 'dear Aunt Sophy' and the Lincolnshire countryside would feature strongly in Cecil Rhodes's own life. He made many friends in the area and learnt to ride there, despite the fact that 'he never had a good seat or hands'.[9] Another family retreat was Twyford House, a small late-Stuart manor on the river Stour and the home of William Arthur Rhodes, the vicar's brother. According to young Cecil, this was always his 'favourite place'.

With financial help from Aunt Sophy, the Rev. Francis Rhodes was able to provide the best education for his three oldest boys. Herbert was sent to Winchester; Frank and Ernest went to Eton. There is no clear explanation why Cecil Rhodes should have gone no further than the local Bishop's Stortford grammar school, the establishment that his father had done so much to improve. Some biographers have cited his poor health; others have suggested that 'the family had grown larger than their father's purse'.[24] Rhodes has given us no clue, but there was never a suggestion, from him or anyone else, that he had been unfairly treated by his father.

Rhodes was a conscientious but undistinguished pupil. History and geography were said to be his favourite subjects, and he made the school cricket eleven when he was 13. His two academic achievements were a classical scholarship and a silver medal for elocution.

Two interesting fragments survive from Rhodes's schooldays. The first is a letter, written to him years later by an old school companion, who remarks: 'Do you remember that the boys always called you Rhodes? We never used your Christian name.'[21] And so it would be for the rest of his life. To the world, he was Mr Rhodes. Among a certain set in London, he was 'The Emperor'. To his young men he was 'The Old Man' or 'The Chief'. To his intimate friends, he was 'Rhodes'. No one dreamt of calling him Cecil. Even his letters to his mother were signed 'Your affectionate son, C.J. Rhodes'.

The second 'fragment' is an interview with Robert Yerburgh, son of the rector of Sleaford and one of Rhodes's closest childhood friends. He recalled Rhodes's 'precocious power of observation', and provided an illustration that made another point altogether.

When the two boys used to ride together through the Lincolnshire countryside, 'instead of gazing at a pretty girl looking over a gate, [Rhodes] was all eyes for the country he passed through, and always remembered which farm was well cultivated and which slackly managed'.[20] His nanny, Mrs Newman, said much the same thing: 'He didn't look at women, even as a boy, always shy of them.'[11]

However, there was nothing shy or retiring about the letter that Rhodes wrote to his Aunt Sophy two weeks after his 15th birthday:

> I cannot deny, for it would only be hypocrisy to say otherwise, that I still, above everything, should like to be a barrister; but I agree with you it is a very precarious profession.
>
> Next to that, I think a clergyman's life is the nicest and therefore I shall try most earnestly to go to college, because I have fully determined to be one of those two, and a college education is necessary for both.[25]

In the 1860s and for many decades to come, entry to university without a public school education was only within reach of the exceptionally gifted. To make up for possible shortcomings, the Rev. Francis Rhodes removed his son from school when Cecil was 16 years old with the intention of tutoring him personally, butfate intervened.

> Soon after leaving the grammar school, Cecil fell ill. As soon as he was well enough to go out, he was sent to be overhauled by the family doctor, John Edward Morris, who afterwards recalled that the boy was so nervous and anxious when he came into the consulting room, that he had to be sent off to take a walk in the fields to calm himself down. When he returned, Dr. Morris examined him and realised, but did not openly tell him, that his lungs were affected. As there was a tendency to consumption in the family, the Vicar, with the doctor's approval, decided that a long sea voyage would be the best cure.[26]

Most biographers now believe this was a misdiagnosis. Certainly, there are no references to tubercular lesions in the records of the Muizenberg autopsy. A popular hypothesis since the mid-1960s is that Rhodes suffered from what doctors now call an atrial septal defect – in layman's language, a hole in the heart.[27] A recent biographer takes a third line and argues that Rhodes was not ill at all when he first went to Africa. His thesis is that Rhodes simply wanted an opportunity 'to postpone answers to his own questions about a profession and his ambiguity about whether he could gain entrance to one of the colleges of the Universities of Oxford or Cambridge'.[28] For some time to come, Rhodes would certainly debate the possibility of returning to England to qualify for the Church or the legal profession, but this does not dispose of the commonly held view that Rhodes was originally sent to Africa because of illness. His frequent assurances about his health in his letters home would seem strange from a teenager with no reason to expect anything else, and there can be no doubt that Rhodes was severely ill at the age of 19 and again the following year. Indeed, he would continue to be dogged by ill health for the rest of his life and clearly thought that *he* knew what the problem was. 'I always feel my lungs to be a sort of skeleton in the cupboard, ever ready to pounce down and take me off'[29] he wrote to his brother Frank shortly after his 22nd birthday. The obsession with death would continue throughout his 20s and beyond: 'I have that inner conviction that if I can live... The fear is shall I have the time and the opportunity?'[30]

Whatever it was, something persuaded Francis Rhodes that his son should terminate his studies and take a long sea voyage. The obvious destination was South Africa. Herbert was already in Natal, where he had received a grant of 200 acres (81 hectares) to farm cotton under an emigration scheme. Aunt Sophy agreed to provide the funds for Rhodes's passage and an additional lump sum of £2000.

There is no surviving record of Rhodes's departure from Bishop's Stortford, or indeed from the docks at Gravesend, except one rather sad aside in a letter he wrote to his mother which has been seized upon by biographers of the 'dysfunctional family' school: 'I was so sorry I did not see my father to say goodbye to – and shake hands with, but I daresay we shall some day meet again.'[31]

There is, however, a very touching record of Rhodes's last night in London, which was provided, years later, by a Mrs Bennett. She and her husband had been attending a concert at the Albert Hall. Mrs Bennett could not recall the programme, but she remembered that the music had been very moving because the young man sitting next to her suddenly burst into tears. His sobs soon became so loud that he started to attract attention, so she leaned across and tried to calm him. After the concert the young man apologized for his behaviour and explained that the next day he was sailing for Africa, the doctors having told him that a sea voyage was his only chance of life. His heart was heavy at leaving England and the music had been too much for him. The Bennetts invited him back to their hotel and asked his name. It was Cecil Rhodes.[32]

On the following day Cecil Rhodes sailed out of Gravesend on a 322-ton wooden barque, the *Eudora*. His destination was South Africa. At this stage of his life, the only thing that can be said with any certainty is that fate had provided him with an opportunity to be in the right place at exactly the right time.

THREE

'AN UNPROFITABLE AND TURBULENT BACKWATER'

Our possessions in Southern Africa are not merely worthless but pernicious – the source not of increased strength, but of weakness – enlarging the range of our responsibilities, while yielding no additional resources for properly sustaining them.

LORD GREY, GOVERNOR OF CAPE COLONY (1854–1861)

For the first 70 years of the nineteenth century men despaired of South Africa. The land was poor. Vast tracts of the interior consisted of scrub and semi-desert and there seemed little prospect of the mineral wealth that had attracted immigrants to the United States and Australia. There were no navigable rivers, and travellers overland had to negotiate formidable mountain barriers. Worst of all, there was conflict: white against black, white against white, black against black.

Three main groups of people inhabited this land when the first Europeans settled in the year 1652. The original South Africans – San hunter-gatherers (or Bushmen) and the related Khoi-Khoi herders – predominated in the south and west. The north and east were inhabited by Bantu-speaking Africans* with more advanced skills who had been migrating slowly southwards for centuries (just how slowly can be judged from archaeological evidence of their presence in the area of present-day Johannesburg dating back to the seventh century).[1]

It is sad to report that some historians have felt it necessary to rewrite this early chapter of South Africa's history for propaganda purposes. The

---

*Because racial classification and segregation have played such an important part in the political history of South Africa, we are forced to use racial labels to make any sense of events. Throughout the rest of the text, 'white' will apply to people of European descent. The word 'Coloured' will be used to denote people of mixed descent. As Vivian Bickford-Smith points out in his excellent study (p. 201), from the 1890s onwards the term 'Coloured' was generally used as a self-descriptive ethnic label in the Cape by people who were not accepted as white and did not think of themselves as natives or Africans.

'African' will apply to Bantu-speaking Africans only, although the Khoi-San, their descendants and many whites would properly regard themselves as African. 'Black' will be used as a collective term for all non-whites.

45

claim has frequently been made that Europeans and Africans entered the territory of present-day South Africa simultaneously and that the latter waged a blitzkreig against the indigenous people, annihilating the Khoi-San in their drive to the south. The inferences they would have us draw are only too clear: neither European nor African has prior claim to this land and the rights of the present-day black majority should be judged in the context of their history – that is, as foreign invaders who exterminated the original South Africans.

On the first point the propagandists are in error by at least a thousand years. On the second point, there is enough evidence (physical and linguistic) to suggest that the Khoi-San lived harmoniously in the midst of Bantu-speaking Africans and that the two groups intermingled. The typical Khoi-San features – the flatter face, the finer nose and the high cheek bones – are particularly evident in areas like the southern Transkei, where President Mandela was born.

A Khoi-Khoi beauty.

The earliest Europeans to reach the Cape were the Portuguese, but it was their later seaborne rivals, the Dutch, who first established a permanent settlement there. In 1652, Jan van Riebeck landed in Table Bay with a small force of soldiers and civilians (126 men in all). The home authority was not the government of Holland but the board of the Dutch East India Company – the so-called 'Council of Seventeen' – in Amsterdam. Because of the wretched diet on board their ships, fatality rates were high on the long sea voyages to and from the company's rich eastern empire, based in Java. As a halfway house between Europe and the East, the Cape seemed an ideal depot for resupplying ships with fresh provisions, but there was no intention of founding a colony. As far as the directors in Amsterdam were concerned, the place had no value except as a company farm.

Van Riebeck was ordered to plant vegetable gardens and to establish a store-

Khoi-Khoi herders below Table Mountain.

house, a granary and a hospital. He was also expected to buy what meat he could from the local herders, whom the Portuguese had called Hottentots and the Dutch called Caepmans, but who called themselves Khoi-Khoi – 'Men of Men'.

In spite of the original intention of the Council of Seventeen, the settlement inevitably expanded. The Dutch were joined by German settlers and, later, by French Huguenots fleeing persecution during the reign of Louis XIV. As the growing settler population moved away from Table Bay and established farms in the valleys and hills of the Cape peninsula, the need for labour became paramount. The Khoi-San were not co-operative, and slaves were imported from the Guinea coast, Angola and Madagascar and from the Dutch possessions in the Far East – principally Java, but also Sri Lanka and the Malay peninsula. These slaves worked in homes, in artisan workshops and in the fields.

In the Cape, as in all colonial societies well into the nineteenth century, there were no taboos against sexual relations between the races. (Marriage, of course, was another matter.) Liaisons between the white masters and their African and Asian slaves produced the ancestors of today's Cape Coloureds. Ironically in view of later political developments, sexual relations between the races were so prevalent that very few members of the older South African families of Dutch descent can claim that pernicious label 'pure white'.

Under the iron rule of the East India Company there was no freedom 'either as to private life, political life or religious life'.[2] Dutch was imposed as the official language in schools, in commerce, in churches and in the conduct of public affairs. The only form of Christian worship and doctrine tolerated in the settlement was the 'sombre and stern Calvinism of the seventeenth century, hostile to all new light, thoroughly imbued with the spirit of the Hebrew records of the Old Testament, and with but little of the Christian spirit of kindness and mercy taught in the New'.[3]

From the late 1700s all further immigration ceased, 'and so a small, homogeneous, inbred community developed at the far end of Africa ... There was no commerce to speak of. Slaves were kept in their place by brutal punishment ... Society was sterile and immobile'.[4]

This isolated group at the southern tip of Africa would eventually be known as the 'Afrikaners'. Their language, a basic form of Dutch with a rich infusion of English, Javanese and African words, would come to be known as 'Afrikaans'. 'Boer' (literally 'farmer' in this language) would sometimes be used as a synonym for Afrikaner, and sometimes to denote those independent-minded (and frequently economically backward) Afrikaners who trekked into the interior to escape the Dutch East India Company and, later, British rule. These people survived as migrant stock farmers, driving their cattle over vast distances and living out of their waggons. When and if they settled, the poor grazing land in so much of the South African interior necessitated huge farms of up to 6000 acres (2400 hectares).

These migrations out of the colony began in the early years of the eighteenth century when Boers met Africans, whom they called 'Kaffirs'.* A state of intermittent hostility between the two peoples continued well into the next century, when the encounters would be 'dignified with the name Kaffir Wars, but to begin with, they were little more than reciprocal cattle raids'.[4]

In 1794 Holland was overrun by troops of the French Republic. Britain captured the colony the following year, with the intention of denying the French a strategically important base. In 1802 the Cape was briefly restored to the Dutch, but was recaptured when hostilities resumed four years later. When the British took permanent control in 1806 there were 26,000 Afrikaners in the Cape and almost equal numbers of Africans and Khoi-San,

---

*Kaffir is an Arabic word meaning infidel or non-believer. It has become a term of vicious abuse in South Africa in this century, with connotations similar to the American use of the word 'nigger'. However, during the eighteenth and most of the nineteenth century the word was not considered abusive.

Boer family on Trek.

making a grand total of 75,000 people in the entire colony.[5] This was equivalent to the population of just one American city, New York, which had also been established as a Dutch settlement in the seventeenth century.

From the very beginnings of British rule there was friction between Englishman and Afrikaner. The early administrators believed in the potential equality of the races and enraged the Boers with their attempts at even-handed treatment. In 1813, a commission was appointed to investigate the violent treatment of Coloured slaves and servants by their Boer masters. The subsequent use of Coloured troops in an attempt to arrest and even shoot a white farmer provoked the frontier rebellion of Slagter's Nek in 1815. The six Boer ringleaders were sentenced to be hanged in front of their families, but the gallows broke under the combined weight of the condemned men. Appeals for clemency were then brushed aside by the British officer in charge of the proceedings. Half dead, the six unfortunate Boers were forced to wait 'many hours' until a second gallows was constructed and the grisly process could be concluded. Slagter's Nek would not be forgotten.[6]

Events came to a head in 1834, when slavery was abolished 'in all lands subject to the British crown'. A value of £3 million was placed on the slaves of the colony, but little more than a third of this amount was offered in

Trekking through the Transvaal.

compensation. 'Even this was paid in such a manner that much of it fell into the hands of fraudulent agents before it reached the Boers.'[7]

The more prosperous Afrikaners, who had made their wealth in trade and settled agriculture, tended to remain in the Cape, but between 1835 and 1837, 10,000 of the more irreconcilable Boers moved out in a series of migrations that would eventually be known as the Great Trek. In one of these parties was a boy who had just turned 10 in the year 1835. His name was Johannes Paulus Kruger.

Roaming with their families and cattle, flushing out or enslaving the indigenous people, the trek Boers drove on across the plain between the Orange and the Vaal rivers and settled in territories that would soon be known as the Boer republics of the Orange Free State and the Transvaal. Here, by force of arms, the trekkers compelled Africans to work for them and expropriated African land.

> The simple language of the Old Testament had a meaning for [the Boers], much of it applying to a people leading a similar life to their own, wandering in the wilderness, depending on flocks and herds, fighting heathen tribes for existence. The Boers looked upon Kaffirs as the descendants of Cain, considering any attempt to Christianise them as trying to nullify God's curse.[8]

One group of trekkers moved eastwards across the Drakensberg mountains into an area of violent conflict between black and black. A series of bloody wars and forced migrations had made the Zulus under Shaka and his half-brother Dingaan the dominant power in this region, and it was here, along the shores of the Indian Ocean, that the trekkers established their independent republic of Natalia.

The British viewed these developments with alarm. It had never been their intention to waste resources on an unprofitable backwater at the far end of Africa. The principle had been clearly stated from the very beginning. In 1809 Lord Caledon, the then governor, wrote: 'The true value of this colony is it's [sic] being considered an outpost subservient to the protecting of our East India Possessions.'[9] But now the British were being forced to spread their responsibilities over a wider and wider area, thanks to those intransigent Boers.

Clearly, a Boer presence along the coast could not be tolerated, and in 1845 the British expelled the intruders by force, claiming the colony of Natal for the Crown. In addition to the obvious strategic motive, the British claimed a second consideration, namely 'to protect the natives and raise them on the scale of humanity'.[10] Evidently, the treatment of 'natives' was not an issue in the weak Boer republics inland and would not become an issue as long as these territories remained weak and inland. Here, under Boer rule, Africans and people of mixed race were compelled to carry passes and to reside outside the towns unless granted special dispensation. (They were even forbidden to walk on the pavements in towns.) They had virtually no protection under the law, and individual whites were free to inflict their own savage punishments without fear of prosecution.[11] These injustices were enshrined in the laws of the Boer republics. The opening preamble to the Transvaal constitution read: 'The people will permit no equality between white and Coloured inhabitants, either in Church or State.'

These considerations did not prevent Britain granting formal recognition to the Transvaal in 1852 and to the Orange Free State two years later.

With the annexation of Natal, the British were now responsible for two South African colonies separated by 300 miles (483 kilometres) of African territory, which they called Kaffraria. There were 1800 miles (2900 kilometres) of border to defend and an area twice the size of the British Isles to administer – responsibilities out of all proportion to the single limited objective of securing the Cape route. 'Our possessions in Southern Africa are not merely worthless, but pernicious,' grumbled Lord Grey, the Governor of the Cape in the 1850s, '[they are the] source not of increased strength, but of weakness – enlarging the range of our responsibilities, while yielding no additional resources for properly sustaining them.'[12]

With attitudes like these, it is hardly surprising that only the bare minimum was spent on the development of the two colonies. As late as 1877 Cape Town, the most important centre in British South Africa, was dismissed by Anthony Trollope as a 'ragged' and 'unprepossessing town … in a very grand setting'.[13] The poverty and backwardness in the rest of the colony defied description.

The Cape's principal export and source of revenue was wool. There was a brief boom in 1862, when the American Civil War disrupted supplies, but peace in the United States brought slump to South Africa. To make matters worse, the colony was gripped by a severe and prolonged drought throughout the mid-1860s. Ripples from the farmers' plight soon spread outwards, and insolvencies occurred on a daily basis. Banks collapsed. Farms were abandoned. Artisans left their rented houses in the towns and migrated to other countries.

As if drought and slump were not enough, the Suez Canal, now under construction, brought the promise of a shorter sea route from Europe to the Far East. The Cape's only tangible asset seemed under threat.

Hare-brained schemes were devised in a desperate bid to raise additional revenue. These included an attempt to establish a silkworm industry in the Cape and to promote cotton-growing in Natal – a proposition that attracted the attention of an irrepressible adventurer 'with every sort of sense but common sense'[14] called Herbert Rhodes.

But salvation, when it came, was from an entirely different quarter.

Along the banks of the Orange river, which marked the northern border of Cape Colony, was a farm called 'de Kerk', jointly owned by a Mr Schalk van Niekerk and his stepfather. One day, van Niekerk was visiting a cottage on his land occupied by a Boer family named Jacobs. As he glanced at the Jacobs children playing 'klip-klip' or 'five stones', a particularly bright stone caught his eye. He was told that it had been found on the river bank. As van Niekerk had a reputation in the district as a collector of unusual stones, Mrs Jacobs made him a present of 'die mooi klip' – the pretty pebble.

Van Niekerk may have suspected there was something unusual about his find, but he did nothing about it until John O'Reilley, a big-game hunter and pedlar, passed through the district on his way to Colesberg, the nearest large settlement. Van Niekerk showed the stone to O'Reilley and, encouraged by his interest, asked him to take it to Colesberg in the hope that someone there might be able to identify it. There is no record of any business transaction between farmer and trader, but legend has it that Mr Lorenzo Boyes, the resident magistrate in Colesberg, tested the stone for hardness by scratching the letters D & P on the window of Draper & Plewman's, the grocers. Boyes immediately forwarded the stone to Dr William Atherstone, a resident of Grahamstown, who had earned a formidable reputation in the colony as both surgeon and geologist.

The stone duly arrived in an unregistered envelope addressed to 'The Country's Leading Mineralogist, Thursford House, Grahamstown'. According to Dr Atherstone's account, on fine days he received his post sitting under a large pear tree in his garden. When he opened Boyes's envelope something dropped out. It was only after reading the magistrate's letter that Atherstone realized what he had let fall. He scrambled about in the grass without success, and then called his daughter.

> Together in the greatest excitement, we searched among the grass of the lawn until we found the pebble. I had never seen a rough diamond before, but upon taking its specific gravity and hardness, examining it by polarized light and so on, I at once decided that it was a genuine diamond of considerable value. I took it to my next-door neighbour and old friend, Bishop Rickards, bidding him to test it, which he did, cutting his initials and the date on one of the panes of glass in the window of the Bishop's sitting room. This pane of glass was afterwards taken out and carefully framed, and is still, I believe, preserved by the Roman Catholic priests in charge of Grahamstown.[15]

Atherstone decided to make a dramatic announcement at a dinner given that evening by the lieutenant-governor. He also wrote to Lorenzo Boyes, confirming that the stone was a real diamond weighing $21\frac{1}{2}$ carats, prophetically adding 'where that came from there must be lots more'.

The stone was sent to London, where it was valued at £500 and came to be known as the 'Eureka' diamond. But there was no immediate rush to the Cape. A Professor James R. Gregory of London University dampened expectations with a report that first appeared in the *Journal of the Society of Arts* in November 1868 and was subsequently reprinted in the Cape newspapers. The professor had been sent to South Africa by a Hatton Garden diamond dealer and, in his report, he claimed to have 'made a very lengthy examination of the districts where diamonds are said to have been found'. His conclusion was unequivocal: '[I] saw no indication that would suggest the finding of diamonds or diamond bearing deposits in any of these localities.'

In spite of this prognosis, diamonds continued to be discovered. Gregory defended his corner by suggesting that these new finds had either been planted deliberately to lure immigrants to the most unpromising corner of an unpromising country or had been carried there by ostriches (where the ostriches were supposed to have found diamonds was not stated).

Atherstone was incensed at being cast as either a dupe or an impostor, and an angry exchange of letters and articles was published in London and the Cape. At the height of this controversy, Schalk van Niekerk returned centre stage and announced a discovery that would settle the issue for once and for all (and incidentally enrich South African slang with a new word, 'gregory', meaning an 'outrageous blunder').[16]

The Eureka had boosted van Niekerk's reputation locally, and when a 'native shepherd' discovered a very unusual stone near the banks of the Orange river he was advised to take it to the 'expert'. By now, van Niekerk had no difficulty recognizing a diamond. He offered the shepherd 500 sheep, 10 oxen and a horse in exchange for a magnificent stone of 83 carats, which would subsequently be known as the 'Star of Africa'. Van Niekerk sold it to a trading company for £11,200. It was then taken to Cape Town, where the colonial secretary held it up before the members of the House of Assembly and declared, 'Gentlemen, this is the rock upon which the future success of South Africa will be built'.

The first to work the river diggings were the blacks and the Boers. They were close at hand, they knew the land and they had the equipment. Very soon, the original discoveries on the Orange river would be augmented by richer finds along the banks of the Vaal, which joins the Orange a few miles west of the farm de Kerk. A sleepy, forgotten land was about to awake.[17]

After the local people came the colonists from the Cape and Natal; after them, the foreigners: seasoned diggers from the Australian gold fields; forty-niners from California; ships' deserters; fallen aristocrats; veterans of the American Civil War; young men fresh from England's prestigious public schools; and whole families escaping the slums and ghettos of Central Europe.

The diamond rush was on, but Cecil Rhodes had come to grow cotton.

---FOUR---

COTTON

'Ah, yes!' Rhodes used to say in later years, whenever
he was told that something was impossible,
'They told me I couldn't grow cotton.'[1]

After a voyage of 75 days, the wooden sailing barque *Eudora* dropped anchor off Durban bay in the British crown colony of Natal. At low tide a ridge of sand barred entry to the port, and the passengers had to be taken ashore in rowing boats. Sometime in the early afternoon of 1 September 1870 Cecil Rhodes set foot on African soil for the first time.[2]

Speculation and invention are now no longer necessary. At last, Cecil Rhodes has a voice, thanks to a remarkable collection of letters, written mostly to his mother but intended for the whole family. Indeed, in his first letter home Rhodes made it clear that he expected the entire correspondence to be copied out and distributed to his aunts and uncle.[2]

Through these letters we discover a young man, bursting with charm and enthusiasm, who enjoyed an uncomplicated and loving relationship with every member of his family. There is certainly no suggestion of an intimidating or remote father. 'Give my best love to papa',[3] ... 'Please thank father for his letter, but if I ever am a clergyman, I will come home and go to college first',[4] ... 'Please thank father for his kindness ...'[4] and so on.

The letters reveal a special closeness between mother and son, but Rhodes loved his brothers and sisters as well, relishing every scrap of news from them, especially news of their triumphs and achievements. They were given affectionate nicknames – Ernest was 'the Professor'[4] and Frank was 'the Duke'. Rhodes fantasized that his dashing older brother would soon be joining him in South Africa: 'Fancy the Duke at full gallop after a velde-beeste on the boundless prairies of the Transvaal!'[5]

In the letters to his family Rhodes tried hard to minimize his hardships and disappointments and to stress what was positive and exciting. He wanted them to share his sense of wonder, to savour every new sight, sound and smell.

Rhodes, aged 14.

In 1870, the port where Rhodes had landed was a miserable jumble of tin-roofed buildings covered in blown sand,[6] so Durban did not get a mention in the letters. Instead, Rhodes asked the family to lift their eyes, as he had done, and experience the grandeur of the setting; to imagine hills, covered in thick bush, 'rising one above the other, right down to the shore'. Bands of 'kaffirs'[7] roamed these shores – 'fine looking men, [holding] themselves very erect', with their hair dressed with porcupine quills and carrying snuff boxes 'in a hole bored through their ears'. These fine specimens would 'rather shock your modesty', he told them at the vicarage, describing how they paraded stark naked with 'nothing on, except a band round the middle'.[2]

Rhodes was expecting Herbert when he arrived at Durban, but instead of a brother, two letters were waiting for him at the port. One informed him that Herbert had left for the diamond fields, 500 miles (800 kilometres) in the interior.[2] Twenty pounds was enclosed. The second letter was from Dr

Durban bay, 1870.

Sutherland, surveyor-general of Natal, asking Rhodes to call on him. It was Dr Sutherland's duty to show new settlers to their lands. He lived near Pietermaritzburg, not far from the Umkomaas valley, where Herbert had received his grant of 200 acres.

There was no complaint in Rhodes's account of his reception at the port; no hint of the disappointment he must have felt after a 6000-mile (9650-kilometre) journey and almost 11 weeks at sea.

To Pietermaritzburg, then, a 57-mile (92-kilometre) journey by coach and four:

> To look at the horses, you would think they could not go four miles. Have you ever seen the horses in a gypsy's travelling house? Well, these here look very like those. Yet ... they rattle down the steepest hills at an awful rate; and you every minute expect to be over, but they never stumble and we performed the journey in nine hours, and changed the horses five times.[2]

The country, with its steep hills and deep valleys, enchanted Rhodes: 'Take the downs at Brighton and there is Natal.'[2]

He slept overnight in Pietermaritzburg, and on the following morning rode to the surveyor-general's office, where he could expect directions to his new home. Instead, he was invited to stay with Dr Sutherland and his family until Herbert's return. (It was said that Mrs Sutherland was particularly keen to welcome the young immigrant into her home.) Rhodes offered no explanation for this unexpected generosity, but one doesn't have to carry speculation too far. There's evidence enough in the letters of immense charm at work, as well as a remarkable ability to empathize with others regardless of their race or status. Rhodes, of course, was not one to boast of these gifts; at least, not at this stage of his life. His only concern, it seems, was to ensure that his brother would not be lowered in the family's estimation because of his failure to appear at the port. So it was Herbert who was portrayed as the darling of the Sutherland household: 'They all speak well of Herbert. He seems to have made so many friends and to bear such a high character for honest dealing and hard work. In fact, they all seem to like and respect him so much.'[2]

Rhodes was not one to sit around in the surveyor-general's house. Whether he felt genuinely better or wanted to spare his family the worry, he lost no opportunity to reassure them that he was fit and ready for an active life: 'I have been very well ever since I left England, and never felt better in my life'[2] and 'I can assure you that as yet I have never regretted coming out here. I feel so much stronger and better in every way.'[3]

Within a day or two of his arrival he rode into the Umkomaas valley to inspect his brother's cotton farm. 'There is no doubt that this is one of the most beautiful valleys in the colony',[8] he gushed. With those words, Rhodes must have hoped to soften the impact of the news that had to follow. The farm itself was a disaster. Herbert's accommodation was no more than 'a large Kaffir hut ... [but] it is a very nice size. It is circular, consisting of one room. I like the appearance.'[8]

The next point could not be glossed over so easily if Rhodes was to make any sense of his request for the remainder of Aunt Sophy's grant. Herbert had been misleading the family with his glowing reports from Natal. In truth, his first year as a cotton farmer had been a 'dead failure'.[8] He had only cleared 20 acres (8 hectares) and, hoping to squeeze the maximum from this land, had ignored local advice and planted the rows too close. In the rich virgin soil the cotton had grown into a matted and impenetrable mass, making it virtually impossible to keep the ground clean. Boreworms, aphids and caterpillars had played havoc with the crop. 'A few bales were harvested, but not of sufficient value to defray working expenses.'[9] No matter! A valuable lesson had been learnt. Other settlers, who had planted their rows at the proper distance apart, had been 'most successful, and the proof is they are all going in for it, and all the land is nearly taken up'.[8]

It is touching to find Rhodes trying to balance conflicting loyalties to his brothers. Arthur, the next youngest, was seriously thinking of following him to Natal. For Herbert's sake Rhodes had to minimize the bad news from the farm. For Arthur's sake, he must not oversell. The compromise was perfectly judged: 'I don't believe in the very sanguine results Herbert held out, but I do believe that a very nice living can be made out of it, and that it is by far the best thing in Natal ... but I should hate Arthur to come out before we can say for certain ...'.[8]

It is hard to believe that this is the voice of a 17-year-old, trying to put the best gloss on the misrepresentations and blunders committed by a brother eight years his senior.

The temptation to give up the farm must have been strong. Diamonds were the talk of the colony. One of the Sutherlands' many visitors was a Captain Rollerston, who had gone to the river diggings with a party of officers from the 20th Regiment[9] and returned with a parcel of diamonds, which he showed off at the dinner table. Rhodes was agog.

> To hear Rollerston talk and to see his diamonds makes one's mouth water ... People out here talk of nothing but diamonds ... News came down yesterday of three more 'whoppers' being found, one worth £8,000, another £11,000 and another £7,000. There are already 6,000 people up there, and every day hundreds more pour in. They say it will be the capital of Southern Africa. In another month, there will only be old men, children, women and men holding government appointments, left in the colony.[2]

Not quite. Even at this young age Rhodes knew the importance of having 'one great idea, one great object, which is to be accomplished, and ... never [giving] in until you have achieved it'.[10] He had not come to South Africa to be a diamond digger but to prove himself as a cotton farmer, 'and cotton requires you to stick to it entirely'.[2] Be that as it may, he continued to debate the pros and cons in letter after letter for the next 12 months.

> Of course, it is not all gold that glitters, and you may go up there and dig and dig for months without finding anything, though it is an acknowledged fact that these diamonds are the richest and the best that have ever been known.[2] ... The diamonds are an undeniable fact.[8] ... You cannot understand what an awful excitement the diamonds are.[11]

From his first days in Natal, Rhodes used every opportunity to experience the country and establish newfriendships. Although the Sutherland home remained his base, he would sometimes invite friends to stay with him in the hut on the farm or join him on long cross-country rides. He relished the African landscape:

> I never saw such an extraordinarily beautiful place in my life ... It was one immense natural fernery, and there hundreds of feet below us stretched out

the whole valley with our huts looking like specks, and in the distance there were hills rising one above the other, with a splendid blue tint on them. I often wish that I was able to sketch; I have seen lately such wonderful scenery.[12]

Rhodes established an easygoing relationship with the local Africans, sleeping in their huts and sharing their suppers 'of chicken and milk, with some mealie porridge'.[12] Apart from a brief reference to fleas, there is no hint of disdain in Rhodes's descriptions of life in an African kraal. What he does reveal, though, is a remarkable eye for detail and an intense interest in the way everything functioned.

A Kaffir hut is exactly like a beehive, and a kraal is a collection of huts, with an enclosure for cattle. It is somewhat like this … [His mother is now provided with a sketch] The outer line is a fence all round them. The dots are the beehive huts, and the inside line represents another fence within which they kraal the cattle. A hut has one little hole as entrance, which you crawl in at, and once in, you see all the Kaffirs sitting on their haunches round the fire, which is lighted in the middle of the place. There is no chimney, and the entrance hole is wonderfully small, so that the smoke sometimes is rather overpowering, and you have to bolt for the entrance hole to get a little fresh air.[12]

By the first week of October Rhodes had cleared another 40 acres (16 hectares) of dense bush and was already planting the new crop.[3] Some time in the middle of the month, Herbert rode in. He had been no more successful as a diamond digger than he was as a cotton farmer, 'having only one or two diamonds, worth five to ten pounds'.[12]

It is fascinating to read Rhodes's account of his brother's return. After assuring the family that Herbert was in good health, Rhodes focused on the essentials. 'We had a talk over money matters, and Herbert agreed to go equal shares with me in the land and profits. In fact we are *partners*.'[12]

It is not difficult to guess who initiated this discussion, nor does one have to search far for evidence of Rhodes's tact. As long as the terms were clearly understood, he was more than willing to protect an older brother's pride, and always referred to *Herbert's* farm and *Herbert's* achievements, both in Natal and later in the diamond fields: 'With proper weather, Herbert ought to have from four to five hundred pounds worth of cotton.'[12] 'Diamonds only have to continue at a fair price, and Herbert's fortune is made.'[13]

It is obvious who was the dominant force in this partnership. These early letters also give important clues to Rhodes's working methods, methods he must have used in his later, successful years when we no longer have the evidence of frank, personal letters.

Natal landscape.

At the early age of 17, Rhodes understood that success depended on keeping abreast of the latest scientific and technical developments. He had brought with him the best New Orleans seed[14] and an English hand-operated gin to separate the fibres from the boll. This machine was slow, but it produced cotton of a higher quality than the rough stuff the colonists were getting from their crude saw-gins. Rhodes also came armed with the latest technical literature, and would continue to pester his family for more of the same throughout his time in Natal.[15]

There are other clues to the later Rhodes in this correspondence. He had already developed the salesman's gift for sounding authoritative, even on subjects of which he had no knowledge. When Frank showed a serious interest in diamond digging, Rhodes informed the family: 'Winter would be much the best time to go up, it being beautifully cool and all the game up country ... and the locusts are up there in the summer.'[16]

Six months later and with no less authority, Rhodes wrote: 'You in England cannot understand that all transport here depends on ... oxen and the oxen depend on the grass. [Winter] is the worst time of the year for going up, as there is no grass at all.'[17]

These qualities are obvious pointers to the man Rhodes became, but the letters reveal other facets to his character that are seldom associated with future multi-millionaires. One of these was blind loyalty to those he loved, no matter how worthless they proved themselves to be nor how many times they let him down. This would be a running theme throughout his life and

A Zulu with his wives.

the cause of his greatest political disaster. In Natal, we see the earliest evidence of it in his relationship with Herbert.

At the busiest times, the older brother would be away horse-racing in Pietermaritzburg and the nearby village of Richmond or playing cricket in matches that could drag on for a week. He seldom bothered to write home, leaving the task to Rhodes. But there were no complaints in the letters. On the contrary, descriptions of Herbert's sporting activities were there to illustrate his popularity and success – 'Herbert coming in first by a neck amidst ringing cheers'[14] is a typical climax to one of the sporting stories. The justification given for all the cricket-playing was particularly charming:

> It is astonishing what a lot of useful knowledge you pick up at one of these matches. There are no market days here, and it is the only chance one has of hearing about each other's cotton, and the experiments each has tried, and how they have succeeded, for though you may live only 3 or 4 miles from each other, yet the hills are so impassable, that it is quite an undertaking to ride to another plantation.[14]

A typical day on the farm began at sunrise (approximately 5.30 a.m. in the summer). At 9.00 a.m. there would be a break for a meal 'prepared by a capital cook called Chinguzo'.[12] Rhodes usually bathed after breakfast, and relaxed during the heat of the day. Work resumed in the afternoon and would continue until sunset.[3] Sunday was always respected as a day of rest; working clothes 'with more holes than patches' would be set aside, and the brothers would ride four miles to the Anglican mission dressed in something 'respectable'.

One the most fascinating aspects of these letters is the evidence of Rhodes's relationship with his African workers especially in the light of his later career. Rhodes had 30 Africans working for him. For reasons no one can fathom, they called him 'U'Twasi', which means 'salt' in Zulu. Herbert was known as 'Umbila' or 'green mealie' because of his fondness for unripe maize.[9]

Ever since the abolition of slavery in the 1830s labour had been a problem in the African colonies. Most blacks were still self-sufficient. The land provided all their needs, and until whites devised ways of destroying their self-sufficiency there were few incentives for Africans to sell their labour for cash. One that will feature strongly in the later story was the African demand for guns. Another was created by the colonial practice of imposing a hut tax in rural areas. Although this would become an important *additional* stimulus once land and cattle had been expropriated, it was less effective now, when the means of survival were still largely intact.

In the early 1870s a tax of 10 shillings was levied on every African hut in the colony of Natal. The going rate for a labourer varied between 5s. and £1.00 a month. Provided that a working family had the resources at home to feed, house and clothe themselves for the rest of the year, they could discharge their 'debt' to the white man after only a few weeks' work. In these circumstances, it is hardly surprising that the labour supply was erratic.

Rhodes, as we have seen, enjoyed an easy, unprejudiced relationship with the local Africans. He was always intensely interested in them (as he was in everything) and quickly appreciated the value they placed in a man's trust. Before long, he had applied that understanding to the labour problem and introduced the revolutionary scheme of paying his workers in advance. Furthermore, he wrote, 'I make it a rule, if I can, never to refuse a Kaffir labour, and if I know anything about him, never refuse to lend him money.'[15] To the sceptics he laughingly replied that Africans were 'safer than the Bank of England'.[15]

Of course, it all worked to Rhodes's advantage, but at this stage of his life one can believe in something beyond self-interest – as his dilemma over the African chief's land clearly shows (see p. 14 of the introduction).

By mid-December, the planting was finished. Rhodes wrote a triumphant letter home: 'There is a fine show of cotton over the land. It is all thinned and hoed, and is in splendid condition ... There is no doubt cotton does splendidly in these valleys, the greatest sceptic would be obliged to confess it.'[14]

Rhodes seemed to have resolved his conflict. Cotton was 'trumps', diamonds a disaster.

> The accounts of the diamond fields are rather gloomy; oxen dying by the hundreds, no food for the cattle, as there has been a plague of locusts up there, which have eaten up everything, even the tents and clothes of the diggers ... There are, too, hundreds of men up there who are totally without money, and glad to work for a shilling a day, many of them having been in good positions in the Cape and elsewhere.[16]

This was myth. The truth was that the diamond saga had entered an important new phase during the three and a half months that Rhodes had been in Natal. By the end of 1870 the original river diggings had been eclipsed by important new finds in open country some 20 miles (32 kilometres) south of the Vaal river. In the same month that Rhodes arrived in Durban, diamonds had been found at Dutoitspan (Dutoit's pond) on the farm Dorstfontein. The Boer owner tried to keep his discovery secret, but within a very short time 20,000 people were swarming over his property. Diamonds were even found in the mud walls of the farmhouse, which was then pummelled to the ground. Unsurprisingly, the owner sold out for £2000 and moved away. Within a month of this discovery diamonds were found on a neighbouring farm called Bultfontein, owned by another Boer, Cornelius Du Plooy. He sold out for £6000.

In March 1871, just as the cotton was due to be harvested, Herbert abandoned the farm to his younger brother and, taking their best oxen, returned to the diamond fields.

Tales of locust swarms and destitution were quite forgotten in Rhodes's rush to defend Herbert's decision: 'I daresay you will think it very foolish of Herbert to abandon the cotton in this way, but when you consider that the cotton can't hurt, and will be picked up as well in his absence, I think it really would have been throwing a chance away, if one of us had not gone up.'[18]

From March to early May Rhodes was a whirlwind of activity, harvesting and ginning the cotton. He had hoped to gin a significant proportion of the crop with the slower 'McCarthy' machine that he had brought with him from England, but with Herbert absent he was forced to borrow a cruder but faster gin-saw from a neighbour. Eventually he baled fifty 50-pound (23-kilogram) bags, which were sold at well below the price he had expected. There was one small compensation, though Rhodes did not see it in that light. At the annual show of the Pietermaritzburg Agricultural Society on 25 May 1871, his was the only cotton entry from the Umkomaas valley. According to a press report, 'Mr. Rhodes came close behind the winner of the £5 prize. He had tried to gin a whole bale with the small McCarthy gin, which would most certainly have taken the best prize had there been the requisite quantity.'[19]

It was the sad tale of the perfectionist who misses his deadline, though in Rhodes's case this was not entirely his own fault.

While the young cotton farmer was drawing up pages of figures and estimates in the hope of convincing his family (and himself) that his next season would be a triumph, there were two sensational developments in the diamond fields. In May 1871, diamonds were found on the farm Vooruitzigt three miles (five kilometres) northwest of Bultfontein, where the first discoveries had been made. Vooruitzigt was owned by two brothers named De Beer. Unable to cope with the stampede of fortune-hunters, they sold out for £6000 and moved away, but their name remained and became legend. By July 1871 some 10,000 diggers were already working the De Beers mine when a 'Hottentot cookboy called Damon' found diamonds on low hill a mile or so from the original De Beers' farmhouse.[20] This proved to be the most sensational discovery of all. Originally known as 'New Rush', it would in time receive the more dignified title the Kimberley mine.

In each of the four sites diamonds were concentrated in a small area, roughly circular in shape. The first diggers assumed that all their finds would be near the surface – such had been their experience at the river sites – but the miracle here was that however deep the diggers went they still found diamonds. Although they did not understand this at first, they had struck true diamond mines – 'pipes' of long-extinct volcanoes with well-defined containing walls, which continued down to unknown depths.

Bultfontein, Dutoitspan, De Beers and New Rush were clustered within a radius of two and a half miles, and in this remote and unlovely spot 40,000 men and women had come together by late 1871.

Cecil Rhodes finally abandoned his cotton farm in October of that year. He made the 400-mile (645-kilometre) journey in a Scotch cart drawn by a team of oxen. For luggage, he had an unlikely miscellany – biscuits, flour, tea, 'that wonderful box of lozenges father sent me', diggers' tools and several volumes of the classics, including Plutarch's *Lives* and a Greek lexicon.[21]

———— FIVE ————

DIAMONDS

*When we see many giving up good situations, and even
leaving their wives and children with little resources, we begin
to think that diamond hunting is becoming a dangerous
madness ... All classes are on the road ... Some are trekking
on foot, some in ox-wagons and some in mule carts.*

CAPE ARGUS, 6 SEPTEMBER 1870

Between those two wide, brown, sluggish rivers – the Orange and the Vaal – lies an immense plain, thinly sprinkled with coarse grass and twisted thorn trees. Only an occasional rocky outcrop relieves mile upon mile of flat monotony.

In the dry season the wind whips the red earth into a thick, choking dust. When it rains, the tracks are turned into strips of glutinous red mud. In summer the place is like an oven, with temperatures rising well into the hundreds. Winters can be vicious. An early visitor limited his description of the place to one dismissive sentence: 'Her Majesty possesses not, in all her empire, another strip of land so unlovely.'[1] Rhodes, once his youthful optimism had cooled, told his Aunt Sophy, 'Really this country is without change and is merely a Dead Sea Plain.'[2]

Only the sky has majesty. In the cloudless winter months it is a dome of pure cobalt that reduces everything beneath it to insignificance, while all year round sunrise and sunset have a savage beauty.

To this place they came in their thousands, by stage-coach, Scotch cart and Cape cart, by lumbering ox-waggon, on horseback and on foot. The nearer they drew, the greater the flow of human and animal traffic, as routes converged from Cape Town, 700 miles (1126 kilometres) to the south, from Port Elizabeth, the nearest sea port, 400 miles (645 kilometres) to the east, and from the Boer republics to the north and east.

The first indication these travellers had of their distant destination was the sight of a massive plume 'of fine dust, ascending heavenward'.[3] A few miles further and they could just make out a white sheen on the horizon

66

beneath the column of dust. 'A few yards more and the sight was lost behind a dip in the plain. Another rise, and it was seen again, defined more clearly. So on, lost and regained alternatively …'[4] Finally, the white sheen took the shape and form of a distant encampment:

> Many a heart beat faster as the Diamond City of the Plains became less and less indistinct, and those whose everything depended on the success of their expedition watched the ghost-like series of tents grow whiter and whiter as they outlined clearer … Hardly a word was said.[5]

In a letter to his mother Cecil Rhodes described that same moment, when he gained his first clear impression of the distant 'Diamond City': 'Fancy an immense plain with right in its centre a mass of white tents and iron stores, and all mixed up with the camp, mounds of lime like ant-hills …'.[6] At this distance it became clear that 'the dusty pall observed from afar was occasioned by the continual sifting and sorting of thousands of busy diggers and their vast army of native helpers'.[3]

The first thing to assault the traveller was the smell of the place – and the flies:

> The flies are far more aggressive than the European insect … They are particularly fond of plunging into the corners of your eyes, and sticking there if you will let them, or into your ears, nose etc … Dishes and drink choked with them. They actually bit our flesh and drained our mortal juices … [and] when one reflects that there are outside the camps, hundreds of carcases of cattle which have died in different stages of putrefaction and that … the public latrines [are] huge open trenches, lying in many cases in the midst of the tents, the horror felt at the contact of a fly can easily be imagined.[7]

Dead animals were always taken for granted in the scenery of the diamond fields. Exhausted pack animals would be left to die where they fell, and the road into camp was lined on either side with 'a hedge of bones and horns and rotting carcases'.[8]

> Mostly they lie just in the shape they fell in, with limbs out-tossed and heads extended. Some have been picked clean by dog and bird and their bones still hang together; others have dried up as they lay, no one having taken the trouble to skin them; the bones of some are scattered in queer dissection, head and fore-quarters here, hind legs and spine two yards away.[8]

When Cecil Rhodes first arrived at the diggings there were two main settlements three miles (five kilometres) apart. Dutoitspan served the mine of the same name and nearby Bultfontein, while a second settlement was fast expanding between De Beers mine and New Rush, where Herbert Rhodes now owned three claims. Although Dutoitspan had superior pretensions, the traveller to either settlement would have passed through the same confusion of tents, 'pitched together all anyhow or higgled [sic] piggledly',[9] before reaching stores, rooming houses, canteens and a central market square.

From a number of contemporary accounts, we gain a vivid impression of the sights and sounds that must have greeted Cecil Rhodes as he entered New Rush for the first time.

> Nearer and nearer we came. Canvas shelters were everywhere ... The only wooden buildings seen were made of packing cases, though dismal-looking iron shanties intermingled with mud-heaps, wells and washing apparatus were on view by the score ... Unwashed diggers popped their heads out to see us pass. Naked Kafirs and dogs appeared in plenty ... Diggers in woollen shirts and sombrero hats [were] standing without the canteens or drinking inside, and Coolies arrayed in white turbans and linen suits [were] ringing bells outside the eating houses ...[5]

There were saloons and gambling dens with names like The Hard Times, The Perfect Cure and The Red Light and, at the very centre, a market square surrounded by stores. Here the Boer farmers brought their produce by the waggonload – hundreds of springbok at a shilling each; blesbok and wildebeest at half-a-crown; vegetables, firewood, mining equipment and household utensils. 'A blazing sun poured its whitest and strongest light upon the scene. The footsteps of the ceaseless crowd, the trampling of horses and the whirl of wheels, threw up the sand in clouds of finest dust; a noise of eager voices and loud laughter filled one's ears.'[10]

On one side of the square claims were bought and sold in the 'Griqua-land Share and Claim Exchange', a barn of a building clad in corrugated iron. From here, the cries of the auctioneers buying and selling diamond claims mingled with the shouts of the hawkers in the square outside: 'Do I have me? Do I have me? A quarter claim in the old De Beers ...' 'You know what a potato is; a pomme de terre, a murphy! Twenty-three shillings – twenty-four – twenty-five ...' 'Here's a nice little pick, a sweet little pick, a diamondiferous little pick ...'[11]

From the square it was just a short ride along Main Street to the New Rush mine which, at first sight, appeared to be huge mound of debris dumped at the end of the street. Carts and gangs of labourers were in continuous motion up and down the slopes.

The climb to the top revealed a scene that was 'beyond every expectation'. Anthony Trollope described it as 'one of the most remarkable [sights] on the face of the earth'.[12] The top of the mound was, in fact, a plateau measuring 180 yards by 220 feet (165 by 67 metres) – equivalent to four football pitches. Ten thousand people were working in that space.

The plateau was subdivided into 600 claims, each measuring 31 feet by 31 feet (9.5 by 9.5 metres). These were serviced by 14 parallel roadways running the full length of the plateau, which were permanently choked with carts and people. By the time Rhodes arrived, some of the claims had reached depths of 50 feet (15 metres) and more, and from the margin of the mine these would have looked like a series of bottomless trenches running alongside the unfenced roadways. In a letter home he wrote: 'There are constantly mules, carts and all going head over heels into the mines below, as there are no rails or anything on either side of the road, nothing but one great chasm below.'[6]

Another new arrival described his first attempt to look down into the claims from one of the roadways:

Holding to one of the posts by which buckets are hauled up and down, you crane your neck over the edge, and look down into the gulf. You draw back in amazement, with an exclamation! There is another world down yonder,

Diamond sorting, New Rush, 1872.

The New Rush mine, 1871.

sixty feet below! ... The crowd is almost as great as that around you ...
Naked blacks, diminished to the size of children, are shovelling, picking, and
loading – hundreds of them, in that cool, shadowed, subterranean world.
They fill buckets with crumbling earth, and endlessly haul them up and
down on pulleys. Some are swarming to the surface on rope ladders. There
is an endless cry, and laugh, and ring of metal below. Buckets rise and fall
with the regularity of a machine. On the top, they are detached and emptied
in a heap, ready for conveyance to the sieve ...[13]

The crumbling earth was transported away from the claim by mule cart,
wheelbarrow or a bullock's hide sewn to two poles to any patch of ground
the claim-owner could find near the mine.

> Here, under awnings of various kinds or rugs, blankets etc, placed on four
> props, round the [sorting] table, sit men and many ladies too, with a scraper
> in one hand and sometimes a horse's or wildebeeste's tail in the other for
> flicking flies away. ... [The ground] is first put through fine wire sieving
> which sieves all the lime-dust away. What remains is put on the sorting
> table. ... The sorter ... armed with an iron scraper ... detaches a convenient
> quantity of the heap of stuff on the table, spreads it out before him, exam-
> ines it carefully but quickly, detaches the diamonds when there [are] any,
> and throws the rejected stuff away. This is done with great speed and almost
> mechanical regularity and skill ... To avoid eye-strain, some of the richer
> diggers [leave] sorting to their native servants.[14]

Caught in this manic routine of digging, carting, loading and sorting was a
cross-section of 'every conceivable cast and colour of the human race'.[15]
There were women diggers.[16] There were child diggers.[17] There were seasoned veterans from California, Bendigo and Ballarat, resplendent in their
checked flannel shirts, wide-brimmed felt hats, corduroy trousers and broad
piratical belts.[18] There were ship's deserters, still wearing their nautical
'ducks' of white sailcloth. There were 'darkey swells'[19] – African and
Coloured claim-owners whose flamboyant dress sense was already exciting
the envy of less successful white competitors. There was a huge force of
naked and near-naked African tribesmen, who performed most of the heavy
physical work on the mine. There were entire families of Boer diggers.
There were aristocrats, professional hunters and common criminals. There
were corduroy suits, moleskin breeches, military jackets, pith helmets, slouch
hats festooned with feathers, crimson puggrees (turbans), silk cummerbunds
and sashes, green veils and blue veils, white, orange and yellow parasols and
hatbands of zebra skin and fox fur.[20]

Diamond sorting.

Cecil Rhodes fell into the routine of the mine at once. He had to. Within two weeks of his arrival the erratic Herbert had departed for England, leaving Cecil in charge of his three claims. For some inexplicable reason, when the middle brother, Frank, suggested a short spell at the diggings prior to taking his army commission, Herbert felt it necessary to escort him all the way from Bishop's Stortford to New Rush.

Rhodes was not daunted by the sudden responsibility and, in an exuberant letter to his mother, boasted that he was now averaging 'about £100 a week'[6] – at least £2750 by today's values.[21] A fellow digger gives us an early impression of young Rhodes on the mine: 'I was working for some time near Rhodes's ground, and the picture of this tall delicate figure crumpled up on an inverted bucket, as he sat scraping his gravel surrounded by his dusky Zulus, lives in my memory.'[22]

Conditions during Rhodes's first summer at the diggings were daunting, even for the toughest and most experienced. Characteristically, Rhodes gave few indications of these hardships in his letters home, and we must rely on other writers for a proper sense of the daily cycle of suffering, catastrophe and death. One recalled that the summer storms dislodged 'avalanches of shale ... with persistent and fatal regularity',[23] while another notes, 'Every day there [were] accidents and an accident means death'.[13]

73

The precarious roadways were threatened by a lethal combination of greater mining depths and human avarice:

> Greedy and reckless diggers have undermined [the roads] in every part, and landslips more or less severe have been the consequence. Some have already given way in mass, and were bridged over; nearly all were supported by causeways of plank … Not a day passed without its accident. Now a mule-cart fell over, and now a landslip crashed headlong down upon the workers underneath … One of the richest roads has toppled over, parting in the middle, and left a chasm of fifty feet.[13]

As well as mining hazards, there was the weather to contend with. 'Tropical lightning and rain flattened tents, and sometimes the weaker hovels.'[24] There were dust storms that blew up at a moment's notice, ripping the bell tents away from their pegs and lifting the canvas over the pole, 'like a big umbrella, turned inside out'.[25] Lionel Phillips, who would play a significant role in the later story, gave a vivid description of one of these storms:

> In a perfectly still air one could see a distant wall rise far away on the plain. In a few minutes it would be on us with a roar, darkening everything, filling one's eyes, nose and ears, stinging one's face, forcing one to turn one's back upon it … Often sheets of galvanized iron were torn from roofs of verandas and hurled about like leaves of paper… A diamond buyer's little office, a wooden frame and canvas affair, lifted some ten feet in the air, while some hundreds of pounds worth of diamonds that were being sorted there were scattered far and wide and mostly lost.[26]

But the worst danger was disease. The shortage of water, the open latrines, the rotting carcasses and plagues of flies contributed to severe outbreaks of typhoid and dysentery in the summer of 1871–72. Scurvy, brought on by a lack of fresh fruit and vegetables, raged through the camps. The flies and the all-pervading dust caused serious eye infections and turned 'a slight break in the skin into a villainous wound'.[27] 'There were no hospitals and nurses were unknown.'[28]* To make matters worse, most diggers were barely earning enough to make ends meet. The lucky ones were those who found large stones; they celebrated by 'firing off a shot for each carat of the diamond'.[30] But such moments were rare. Diggers working in the Dutoitspan and Bult-fontein mines were compelled to abandon hundreds of claims every month through not being able to pay the licence fee of 10s. per claim.[31]

---

*In fact, there was no attempt to build a hospital until the end of 1874. The first building was destroyed by fire before it could be completed and was only partially serviceable by the end of that year. By comparison, the speed with which churches sprang up (from 1870 onwards) 'was one of the wonders of the diggings'.[29]

**Major Drury's encampment. Cecil Rhodes is standing centre right.
Frank Rhodes is on his left, leaning against a chair.**

Rhodes never experienced these extreme privations. Whether by luck or
good judgement, Herbert had bought into the richest sector of the richest
mine. Although there were no spectacular finds in his three claims, a list of
early returns from New Rush includes a reference to 'Mr. Rhodes of Natal',
who had found '110 carats, including stones of 14, 16 and 28 carats'.[32]
Certainly there was sufficient to maintain Rhodes's average weekly profit
of £100.

Although the diggers often boasted of their egalitarian and democratic
values, this was a highly stratified society. Rhodes was fortunate enough to
have the means (and the background) to place himself in the upper stratum
of army and university men 'labelled gentlemen as plainly as an eighteen carat
gold ring is hall-marked'.[33] He and five others lodged with Major Drury,
formerly of the Cape Mounted Rifles, who was soon to serve with a cavalry
regiment in India.[34] The major's mess was popularly known as 'the West
End'.

The contrast between these upper-class establishments and conditions
elsewhere in the camps was striking:

> The tents of some of our richer diggers, round de Beer's and the Colesberg Kopje especially, are very comfortably arranged inside and out ... A large well-furnished tent stands in the middle of a big enclosure, fenced in with thorn bushes, containing also a tent or 'kraal' for the Kafirs, and little corral for horses, mules or cattle. Any good-sized trees standing near the tent will generally be used as a larder, its branches tastefully hung with legs of mutton and other joints of meat, so that it looks like a very substantial Christmas Tree.[35]

This may or may not have been a reference to Major Drury's establishment, but there can be no doubt about the following description or the identity of the 'tall fair boy' who attracted this visitor's attention.

> I lit upon a little cluster of tents and beehive huts, set around an old and gnarled mimosa tree: a Zulu was chopping wood and an Indian cook was coming out of the mess tent with a pile of plates ... Alongside of him was a tall fair boy, blue-eyed, and with somewhat aquiline features, wearing flannels of the school playing field, somewhat shrunken, with strenuous rather than effectual washings, that still left the colour of the red veld dust ... The burly man of later years was at this time a slender stripling, showing some traces of the delicacy that had sent him to the Cape ...'[22]

Under Major Drury's military regime, one imagines formal dinners and strict routine rather than festering carcasses and open latrines, although even the good major was powerless to deal with flies, dust storms and torrential rain.

In January 1872 Herbert returned to the diggings with Frank. 'We found Cecil down in the claim, measuring his ground with his lawyer and in a tremendous rage with another man in the next claim to him, who had encroached on his ground ... I know that Father will be horrified at the idea of Cecil going to law.'[36]

Thanks to William Scully, who joined Drury's mess when Herbert was collecting Frank, we have the benefit of several fascinating sketches of the three brothers during those early digger days.

> Herbert Rhodes ... was a tall, lean, hatchet-faced man of, I should say, about twenty seven. Although sparsely built, his strength was considerable, and he was a splendid boxer ... [He] was generally away on some adventure or another ... [and] appeared to be one of those men to whom constant change was an imperative necessity.
>
> Cecil Rhodes was long and loose-limbed, with blue eyes, ruddy complexion, and light, curly hair ... [He] had a rusty-brown pony named 'Brandersnatch' ... and one of the strangest-looking dogs I have ever seen. It had

no vestige of a tail, and generally it bore a strong resemblance to an exaggerated guinea-pig.[37]

Scully made several references to Rhodes's acts of kindness to him, but added:

> We never became really intimate. While Rhodes was already a man in mind and body, I was still a boy. With Frank, whose age was nearer than mine I was more in sympathy … I have never met any one possessing such charm of manner as did Frank Rhodes at this period … He was, I fancy, a year or so younger than his brother Cecil.[37]

In fact, Frank was almost two years older, but Scully can be forgiven the mistake. Rhodes's letters reveal him to be far wiser than his years. Not only must he have seemed more mature than Frank, but he was already assuming the mantle of the senior brother, accepting responsibilities and making decisions on behalf of 27-year-old Herbert.

There was something else about Rhodes that intrigued Scully:

> After dinner it was his wont to lean forward with both elbows on the table and his mouth slightly open. He had a habit, when thinking, of rubbing his chin gently with his forefinger. Very often he would sit in the attitude described for a very long time, without joining in whatever conversation happened to be going on. His manner and expression suggested that his thoughts were far away, but occasionally some interjection would indicate that, to a certain extent, he was keeping in touch with the current topic. Indeed, it often seemed to me that the larger part of his brain was dealing with something of which no one else had cognizance.[37]

Scully lived with the Rhodes brothers for many months, and one trusts the accuracy of his observations. Unfortunately, writers have felt it necessary to exaggerate these early impressions, turning the thoughtful young man of Scully's memory into an abstraction, a solitary and friendless dreamer 'leaning moodily with his hands in his pockets against a street wall, [who] hardly ever had a companion, [and] seemingly took no interest in anything but his thoughts'.[38]

Once again, we have to turn to the marvellous Sarah Gertrude Millin for a convincing rebuttal:

> It is strange that Rhodes should be so constantly reported as a solitary. He seems always to have had friends and to have loved and trusted them … The loneliness of Rhodes, the spiritual solitude, is mere romanticism. Isolation seems to fit the character of a great man, that is all.[39]

For all the pensiveness, Rhodes could be fun-loving and gregarious. Close to Drury's mess there was a tin church, with a rather discordant bell. Scully described how, returning to camp one night with the Rhodes brothers after a mild spree, 'My companions threw me onto the roof and forced me, under stress of pelting stones, to climb up the steep pitch and ring the bell. When the indignant inhabitants of the surrounding tents swarmed out my friends decamped, leaving me stranded.'[37]

On another occasion Herbert returned to camp in a waggon he had borrowed from Scully and wrecked. Naturally, it fell to Rhodes to pay the compensation, but when he and Scully failed to agree a fair price, Rhodes produced a pack of cards and suggested they should decide the issue over a game of euchre. Sitting on the ground, with a mealie-bag as a table, they played for 'best of three'. Rhodes lost.[37]

Rhodes was an exuberant dancer, and it was said that he would always pick out the plainest girl in the room. Some biographers have attributed this to his 'characteristic kind-heartedness';[40] others have found such behaviour gauche and absurd. According to one account, 'when the boys laughed at his taste in women, he would redden and flash back: "Just an enjoyable exercise … Just an enjoyable exercise".'[41]

This picture of shyness and social ineptitude is unconvincing. Young Rhodes was blessed with charm, and the women were as susceptible as the men. Mrs Sutherland, the wife of the surveyor-general of Natal, would be the first in a long line of officials' wives, farmers' wives and governors' wives who succumbed to the legendary Rhodes charm. Indeed, it was a frequent tactic of his to approach the men through their wives. There was never a suggestion of physical intimacy with any of these (generally older) women, not because Rhodes lacked the power to attract, but because physical intimacy with a woman was not something Rhodes appeared to want; and sadly, as the years advanced, Rhodes only focused his charms on those who could give him exactly what he wanted.

Even at this early and relatively innocent stage, Rhodes was concentrating on two men who, in their very different ways, would be crucial to his future.

Charles Dunnell Rudd was nine years older than Rhodes. He had been educated at Harrow and Trinity College, Cambridge, where he had distinguished himself as an athlete. Like Rhodes, Rudd had originally come to South Africa to recuperate after an illness, but in spite of this he had led a roving, adventurous life in Africa for nearly five years before acquiring two claims adjoining Herbert's on the New Rush mine.

Rudd cut an imposing figure. He was tall and lean, with thick hair and a well-trimmed beard. Though not blessed with great imagination, he was conscientious, steady and thoroughly businesslike. He also had important family and financial connections in England.[42]

Early in 1872, during one of Herbert's many absences, Rhodes took it upon himself to form a partnership with Rudd and link their adjoining claims. It was the first small step on the long road towards amalgamation and monopoly but, even at this early stage, it was a practical step that enabled the two men to rationalize their labour and equipment. It was also the first clear demonstration of one of Rhodes's greatest talents – his ability to recognize gifted men and win them to his cause.

If Rhodes looked to Rudd to help him lay the foundation of his business career, it was John X. Merriman who first encouraged him to consider a parallel life in politics.

Merriman was 12 years older than Rhodes and a regular visitor to Major Drury's mess. The son of the fiery Bishop of Grahamstown, Merriman was both a serving member of the Cape Parliament and a diamond digger – an unlikely combination until one realizes that members of the colonial legislature were unpaid in those days. Merriman was over 6 feet 4 inches (1.9 metes) tall and very thin. He was also respected as a man of principle, qualities that are beautifully combined in Millin's description of Merriman as 'a man like a knife – true, long, shining, sharp'.[43]

Merriman may not have been a success as a digger, but he was probably the first man on the fields to recognize Rhodes's great potential. 'Mr. Merriman praises Cecil up to the skies', Frank enthused in a letter to his mother. 'He says Cecil is such an excellent man in business; that he has managed all the business in Herbert's absence wonderfully well, and that they are all so very fond of him … He says most young fellows when they get up here and do well get so very bumptious, but that Cecil was just the contrary.'[44]

Merriman and Rhodes would take long rides together, discussing, 'the affairs of the [diamond] fields and South Africa, the classics and universal history. Mr Merriman still recalls his companion's remarkable interest in politics.'[45] It was on one of these rides that Rhodes made a pact with Merriman that he would eventually join him in public affairs.

At the age of 18 it seemed that Rhodes's future was set. And then disaster struck. In July 1872, shortly after his 19th birthday, Rhodes suffered his first heart attack.

---SIX---

'A FATEFUL CORNER'

It often strikes a man to inquire what is the chief good in life;
to one the thought comes that it is a happy marriage,
to another great wealth … To myself thinking over the same question,
the wish came to render myself useful to my country.

CECIL RHODES (AGED 23) IN HIS 'CONFESSION OF FAITH'

R hodes's first heart attack is invariably described as 'mild'. Be that as it may, it would take him away from the diggings for almost eight months.

As soon as Rhodes could face the journey Herbert took him north, leaving Frank and Rudd in charge of the claims. The two brothers travelled by ox-waggon, the slowest and most comfortable form of transport. While Herbert hoped that the long, leisurely journey across the veld would restore Rhodes to health, he had another purpose.[1] In the north, far beyond Pretoria, capital of the Boer republic of the Transvaal, gold had been found at Tati on the edge of the African kingdom of Matabeleland and at Marabastad in the mountainous country round the headwaters of the Limpopo. Herbert had dreams of a second New Rush, this time built on gold.

The northern journey was one of the turning points in Rhodes's life. He deepened his knowledge of South Africa, its land and its people. It is said that he would sit on the *stoeps* (verandahs) of the Boer farmhouses during the evening hours, drinking coffee with the old men and learning about their customs and their history. Although there are no letters from Rhodes describing these encounters, they are certainly consistent with his earlier experiences in Natal, when his friendliness and unfeigned interest in people took him into Zulu villages where he would observe the details of African life and share their food and hospitality.

Gordon Le Sueur, Rhodes's young secretary from the mid-1890s, believed that it was this northern journey that first inspired his imperial ambitions, and he credited Herbert with imbuing Rhodes with 'his great ideas of acquiring the hinterland … for the British Empire'.[2]

Certainly, the eight-month trek gave Rhodes valuable time to reflect. He was 19 years old and had made a success of everything he had turned his hand to. By some estimates, he was already worth £5000[3] (£135,000 by today's values) … *but to what purpose?* It was a theme that would recur again and again in his writings through his late teens and early twenties: 'What is life worth at my present mode of existence with no object, no aim?'[4]

As a young man, Rhodes had a strong religious sense. He believed (or needed to believe) in a power beyond himself and in purposes transcending mere money-making. The answer did not seem to lie in Christianity. 'Modern research' he wrote 'had pulverised the authority of the Bible'[5] and, besides, he had already experienced enough in the diamond fields to cause him to question the Christian faith. In a letter to Frank, he concluded a moving description of the slow death of a friend ('He died by inches') with the observation that 'One's belief in anything to come gets very weak out here when as you know nearly every mortal is an atheist, or next door to it.'[4]

Rhodes had the solace of his beloved volumes of the classics, and they travelled with him on that eight-month trek. His favourite works were Marcus Aurelius's *Meditations*, with its stress on virtue and the brevity of human life, and Gibbon's *Decline and Fall of the Roman Empire*. He was also fond of the sayings of Aristotle, which impressed upon him 'the importance of having an aim sufficiently lofty to justify spending your life endeavouring to reach it'.[5]

Powerful contemporary writings would soon be added to this repertoire and help shape a creed that Rhodes would eventually articulate when he was 23 years old. At this early stage he was content to pen some initial reflections and write a will, in which he left his worldly goods to be used for the extension of the British Empire. He also purchased a 3000-acre (1210-hectare) farm in the Transvaal, which qualified him as a burgher – a property owner with voting rights in the Boer republic.

When the brothers reached Marabastad the gold was already washed out, but the diggers there were talking of another great find in the eastern Transvaal.[6] That was enough for Herbert, and within days of the brothers' return to New Rush he had sold his diamond claims to Cecil and was off to take part in a new adventure. The two brothers would never see each other again. After a spell as a gold digger and a prison term in Mozambique for gunrunning, Herbert came to an untimely end in Nyasaland (today's Malawi) in 1879. He had set up camp on the banks of the Shire river and was pouring out a demi-john of home-brewed gin when an ember from his pipe ignited the spirit. The demi-john exploded, setting fire to his clothes. He rushed to the river and jumped in, but succumbed to his injuries shortly afterwards.[2]

Rhodes eventually heard of his brother's death from the famed hunter, Frederick Courtenay Selous. According to Le Sueur: '[He] felt Herbert's death very keenly, and in after years had a tombstone erected to his memory over his grave in Central Africa.'[2]

We do not know why Herbert was so determined to make the switch from diamonds to gold. It may have been nothing more than the habitual restlessness, or he could have had more solid reasons. Certainly there had been dramatic and worrying changes during the brothers' eight-month absence from the diamond mines.

By 1873 all the roadways on the mines had collapsed, leaving huge open pits. Men and materials were now transported from claim to surface in iron or leather buckets that ran on a network of fixed cables, flying, as one observer wrote,

> … like shuttles in a loom up and down the vast warp of wires, twanging like dissonant harp-strings, with a deafening din of rattling wheels and falling ground… So thickly were these lines set that the whole face of the pit seemed to be covered by a monstrous cobweb, shining in the moonlight as if every filament was a silver strand … The encircling wreath of the chasm rose sheer and black like the walls … of a demon's cauldron.[7]

As the separate claims were all being worked at different levels, the floor of the mine was broken up into hundreds of separate blocks 'as though a diabolically ingenious architect had contrived a house with 500 rooms, not one of which should be on the same floor, and to and from none of which should there be a pair of stairs or a door or a window'.[8]

At these levels mining operations were complex and costly, with an ever-increasing risk of landfall and flooding. To add to the diggers' woes, prices were falling as an uncontrolled supply of South African diamonds saturated the world markets. There was also the perennial problem of IDB – illicit diamond buying. At every stage in the process, from digging to loading to sorting and even during delivery to the ports, somebody had an opportunity to steal diamonds. The disposal of uncut stones was not a problem. Anyone who could afford the 10s. licence fee could register as a diamond-buyer, and the fields were swarming with them. There was also the alternative of selling stolen gems to unscrupulous claim-owners, who could resell them as genuine finds from their own claims.

Instead of getting to the root of these problems, the diggers preferred to look for scapegoats. And scapegoats were not hard to find.

It is a remarkable and little-known fact that a high proportion of the original claim-owners were non-white. Virtually the only blacks that feature in the (white) digger literature were the 'naked', 'laughing', 'singing' 'Kaffir' labourers who performed the menial heavy work on the mines and were often recruited from tribal areas far outside the territory. Apart from an occasional disparaging reference to 'darkey swells', the literature (including every biography of Cecil Rhodes) makes no mention of an aspiring black middle class. In fact, the diamond diggings were a focal point for the ambitions and aspirations of hundreds of Africans and Coloureds from different parts of the Cape and beyond who shared common interests, values and experiences as a result of education at the hands of the Christian missionaries.[9] On one mine, Bultfontein, blacks owned 80 per cent of the licensed claims.[10]

At this crucial moment, when South Africa was on the verge of an industrial revolution made possible by her newly discovered diamond wealth, blacks and whites stood ready to cross a threshold together, but this was not to be. Although white diggers were only too grateful for the cheap labour supplied by tribesmen, African claim-owners were another matter: 'It would be almost impossible for white men to compete with natives as diggers; there were differences between their living expenses ... The difference between their general wants, necessities, character and position of the two races utterly forbid it.'[11]

That was the nub. 'For the first time, the black man was seen not only as

The Kimberly mine (formerly the New Rush mine) in 1874.

83

the white man's servant, but as his economic rival. A fateful corner had been turned.'[11]

On the pretext that every black was a potential participant in the IDB racket, whites took the law into their own hands, disqualifying black claim-owners and herding black labourers into compounds, where they could be strictly controlled. A curfew was enforced, and any labourer found outside his quarters after the 10-o'clock bugle received 15 lashes.[12] Savage punishments were meted out to blacks found 'guilty' of IDB, often on the flimsiest evidence.

For a time there was was no authority with the power to intervene, for the simple reason that the ownership of the diamond territory was in dispute. For years there had been bickering over the fuzzily mapped boundaries of the Boer republics and neighbouring black territories. Theoretically, both the Free State Boers and the Griquas, a mulatto people, had a strong claim to the region. With the discovery of diamonds, the Transvaalers and the Cape authorities entered the fray. It would take years to resolve the dispute, but in the early stages the Griqua chief Waterboer (or, to be more exact, Waterboer's adviser David Arnot) took the initiative.

Arnot was a handsome and extremely able Cape lawyer. Son of a Scots father and a Cape Coloured mother, he was dedicated to British expansion in Africa and, although he chose to deny it, passionately anti-Boer.[13] He argued that the Griquas had the legitimate claim to the territory and proposed that 'Griqualand West' should be given the status of a separate crown colony with its own lieutenant-governor. Unsurprisingly, this was a solution that appealed to Sir Henry Barkly, British governor of the Cape.

In June 1873 a proclamation appeared declaring that 'the encampment and town heretofore known as De Beers New Rush, the Colesberg Kopje No. 2, or Vooruitzigt, shall henceforth be and be designated the town of Kimberley'. This was in honour of Lord Kimberley, secretary of state for the Colonies. Ten years later a posthumous tribute was paid to Benjamin Disraeli, when Dutoitspan was renamed Beaconsfield.

By digger custom, the respect shown to new arrivals at the diamond fields was measured by the distance people were prepared to ride out 'and give them first cheer'.[14] Accordingly, an immense crowd had gathered at Alexanderfontein, a tiny hamlet seven miles (11 kilometres) outside Kimberley, half an hour before the new British administrators were expected.

At 4.00 p.m. precisely the imperial party arrived. Sir Richard Southey, the new lieutenant-governor, was accompanied by Lady Southey, 'his young and dark-eyed pretty wife',[14] John Blades Currey, the portly colonial secretary, Mary Currey, and the Curreys' 10-year-old son, Harry. This was a family that would play an important part in Rhodes's life.

The splendid Sir Richard had arrived in his full imperial regalia (plumed hat, lavishly embroidered tunic, top boots), and the crowd responded by giving him a resounding cheer before escorting him into town.

> Every inch of [the veld] was covered with well mounted horsemen and well laden vehicles, and ... when his excellency arrived, before and behind him was one mass of living people ... The run into town was at splitting pace ... The square was fairly packed with people, and the Lieutenant Governor and Mrs. Southey ... met with good wishes from every one. The display of fireworks was a blazer, for the people in charge of the rockets, the Roman candles and catherine wheels, had placed the box containing the bulk of the stock under the platform from whence the display took place; a spark fell into the box, and the whole was ignited, and blazed, crackled, fizzed and went off together.[15]

But the general exuberance was short-lived. Southey made it clear from the start that he was here on behalf of Her Majesty's Government to restore the full rights of her black subjects. When the digger leaders requested a meeting in the hopes of achieving a compromise, Southey simply refused to see them. There was nothing to negotiate. There was only right and wrong.

Southey's unbending principles were clearly set down in a letter he wrote to the governor of the Cape:

Sir Richard Southey.

> The objects aimed at by the leaders of the opposition are to exclude persons of Colour from the exercise of the franchise and to grant privilege to white persons purely because they are white ... As until recently nearly all the land in the Province belonged to persons of Colour ... there is great injustice in attempting to deprive them.[16]

Southey restored the rights of black claim-owners. Kangaroo courts and the 10-o'clock curfew were abolished, as were the residential restrictions white diggers had imposed on blacks.

Black claim-owners and labourers were not the only beneficiaries of Southey's liberal policies. The new lieutenant-governor was a

85

passionate champion of the ordinary man, regardless of colour. He recognized that insecurity of tenure and the fear of rising rents were the principal causes of anxiety among the ordinary diggers, some of whom owned no more than a fraction of a claim.[17] Already, these small-timers were being squeezed by powerful consortia, whose members began to press Southey to lift all restrictions on the number of claims that could be purchased in the name of a single owner. Their arguments in favour of consolidation were sound, and Southey was no fool. He knew that the trend towards greater monopoly and control would help to stabilize the price of diamonds and bring enormous benefits to a few, but he also foresaw that tens of thousands of small-time diggers would be wiped out in the process. This was a price Sir Richard Southey was not prepared to pay. In recognition of the greater complexity of deep-level mining, he did eventually raise the limit on individual ownership to ten claims, but unrestricted rights were out of the question.

Southey had made his most dramatic move on behalf of 'the little man' even before he arrived at the diggings. When his appointment was first announced in the Cape, the syndicate that had originally bought the De Beers brothers' farm informed him that they intended to raise the diggers' monthly licence fee from 10s. to £10. To their utter astonishment, Southey replied that they were not entitled to any fees at all as they had only purchased the surface rights to the farm.

Once he was installed and his opinions had been legally confirmed, to the diggers' delight Southey not only refused to allow the syndicate to collect further fees but demanded a refund of the money they had already received. After a long legal tussle, the syndicate finally gave in and sold the farm to the government for £100,000.[18]

Sadly, the benefits brought by this heroic man were virtually annulled by forces beyond his control. Flooding and landslip continued on the mines. At one stage thousands of pounds worth of claims on the Kimberley (formerly New Rush) mine were buried in debris. World depression followed the collapse of the Austrian Bourse in August 1873, sending the price of diamonds spiralling down still further until the mines were scarcely able to pay their way.

The greatest blow of all was the discovery of 'the blue'. After digging for almost three years through a friable yellow soil, the diggers suddenly reached a hard, compact, blue-coloured ground. According to one account, the first man to strike 'the blue' believed he had hit 'rock bottom' and that the mine was played out. He quietly paid off his labourers, leaving a few inches of yellow ground covering the floor of his claim, and sold out.

The new owner soon discovered the same hard bluish looking floor of the claim he had bought. It was not many hours before he was telling everybody how he had been tricked into buying the claim. His news spread fast and a panic amongst diggers resulted. Tests conducted all over the now very deep claims revealed the presence of this same blue ground. Fear was seen in every face, and in the canteens men sat despondently consoling one another while wondering what to do ... The Governor at the Cape was bewildered at the sudden collapse of the miraculous treasure pits, for what had happened in the Kimberley Mine would happen to others. Hundreds of thousands of people in South Africa having some or other connection with the diamond fields were in despair ... Within a year at most, or so it seemed to everybody ... the mine would close down. It would not be long before the other three would follow suit. The news that the wondrous diamond-strewn yellow ground in the Kimberley Mine was becoming exhausted was flashed around the world. Those on the diamond fields, those still on their way to the diggings, those who were still planning to go to the South African diamond fields were stunned. What now?[19]

Rhodes kept his nerve. In later life he would take sole credit for understanding that the diamonds must have been forced up from below. 'Who was right about the blue ground in Kimberley?' he used to say. 'Me or the experts?'[20]

Whether he had the geological knowledge at the age of 19 or was acting on instinct, Rhodes 'and a limited circle of friends' were convinced that the blue ground was as rich in diamonds as the yellow. While thousands of diggers were selling out at knock-down prices and deserting the fields, Rhodes and Rudd bought all the claims they could afford and established a strong footing in the De Beers mine. If they had had the capital and the laws of ownership had allowed, they could have acquired the entire mine for £6000 – two big 'ifs' that Rhodes would regret for years to come.

Rhodes's faith in the blue ground was soon justified. Not only was it richer in diamonds than the yellow ground but, when exposed to air and sunlight, it slowly disintegrated and could eventually be worked.

At this crucial juncture, when the partners were finally on their way, Rhodes made the surprise announcement that he intended to leave Kimberley to read classics at Oxford. His reasons were both mystical and practical. Because he lacked a degree, he believed he had become too cautious and that caution was hurting him, as he explained in a letter to Rudd:

> On a calm review of the preceding year I find that £3,000 has been lost because, owing to my having no profession, I lacked pluck on three occasions, through fearing that one might lose and I had nothing to fall back on as a profession ... By all means try and spare me for two years and you will find I shall be twice as good a speculator with a profession at my back.[21]

New Rush, 1872.

But there was another side to Rhodes's yearning, which would have made less sense to a business partner. Rhodes believed that Oxford cloaked its off-spring with a mystical mantle of greatness. "'Have you ever thought", he said to Bishop Alexander, "how it is that Oxford men figure so largely in all departments of public life? The Oxford system in its most finished form looks very unpractical, yet, wherever you turn your eye – except in science – an Oxford man is at the top of the tree.'"[22]

It has also been suggested that another factor in Rhodes's sudden decision to go to Oxford at this time was the news that his beloved mother was seriously ill.

On 30 July 1873, Rhodes and Frank set sail for England. During the voyage they passed the *Anglian*, a steamer bound for Cape Town. On board was 21-year-old Barnett Isaacs, the son of a Jewish shopkeeper from Whitechapel. In his luggage he carried his sole capital, 40 boxes of inferior cigars, the result of many years savings, which he hoped to sell at a profit. From these unlikely beginnings emerged the man who would one day be locked with Rhodes in a titanic struggle for control of the world's diamonds.

SEVEN

'DREAMING SPIRES AND PIRATE FLAGS'

I have that inner conviction that if I can live,
I have thought out something that is worthy …
The fear is shall I have the time and the opportunity?

CECIL RHODES[1]

As soon as he arrived in England, Rhodes took the train to Bishop's Stortford for his first reunion with the family in three years. Both parents were now a cause of concern. His mother looked 'so very thin in the face …', he told his aunt, 'she must have had a most severe attack by all accounts. They prayed for her in church.' The nature of this attack was not stated.

His father was also in poor health and away from home taking 'the cure' at nearby Woodall Spa, where the visits of the 19-year-old diamond digger would not be forgotten. He is said to have surprised patients and visitors by presenting them with uncut diamonds, which he carried about in his waist-coat pocket.[2]

It was during his stay at Bishop's Stortford that Rhodes finally made the decision to abandon the cotton farm in Natal. In concluding his letter to Dr Sutherland, the surveyor-general, he wrote:

> I go up to Oxford next week. Whether I become the village parson, which you sometimes imagined me as, remains to be proved. I am afraid my consti-tution received rather too much of what they call the lust of the flesh at the Diamond Fields to render that result possible.[2]

That final sentence is significant. Unless we can accept that there was a side to Rhodes's life that has escaped the notice of everyone who knew him or has ever written about him, we have to assume that this 'confession' was bogus. Rhodes had given much more convincing reasons for his rejection of Chris-tianity in the letters he wrote from the diggings,[3] and he was not one to share personal confidences with someone outside the family unless there was a purpose. The only interpretation that makes sense of Rhodes's 'confession' is that Dr Sutherland was a broad-minded man who expected the young to

The Rhodes family and servants, 1873. Cecil Rhodes (right foreground) in front of Aunt Sophy. Rev. Francis Rhodes (upper left). Louisa Rhodes sitting in front of him.

indulge their sexual appetites and Rhodes was claiming the role most likely to impress him.

Rhodes's correspondence from this time onwards supports other evidence of his increasing tendency to play the part best calculated to serve his interests. The contrast in the style of his personal letters is sometimes startling. In two of these, written at virtually the same time, we hear a sweet, unworldly boy talking to his Aunt Sophy[4] and a hard-boiled, middle-aged businessman pressing Merriman to use his parliamentary influence in support of the construction of the railway line to Kimberley.[5] These letters read like the work of two people with nothing in common; whether in age, outlook or literary style.

Rhodes's intention at Oxford was to gain a place at prestigious University College, and he arrived with a letter of introduction to the master, G.G. Bradley. When he explained that he did not intend to read for honours but was only looking for a pass degree, Bradley turned him down, although he did agree to write a letter of introduction to the provost of Oriel College, 'where they are less particular'.[6]

> The Provost, says Rhodes, read the letter while he waited. He stared down at the table in hostile silence, and, afraid for his dream, Rhodes waited. 'All the colleges send me their failures,' said the Provost at last.
>
> In this way Rhodes was admitted to the college of Raleigh, the first Chartered Empire-Builder, and to Oxford. He did eventually matriculate.[7]

During his first term Rhodes suffered a double tragedy. On 1 November 1873 his beloved mother died and he left Oxford to attend the funeral at Bishop's Stortford.

Shortly after his return, Rhodes caught a severe chill while rowing on the Isis. The college doctor was sufficiently concerned to seek a second opinion from Dr Morell Mackenzie, a London chest and throat specialist, who 'found his heart and lungs affected' and insisted that Rhodes return to the hot, dry climate of Kimberley at once. Mackenzie entered in his casebook a prophesy: 'Not six months to live.'[2]

Without explaining how this could have happened, the biographer Sarah Gertrude Millin tells us that Rhodes read the diagnosis in the specialist's casebook.[8] It is certainly true that he would be obsessed by a sense of his own mortality for the rest of his life[9] and, if Millin is correct, she has also provided a convincing explanation for the sudden moral shift that took place soon after Rhodes's return to Kimberley. Ambitious young men who believe they are under sentence of death might be expected to cut corners.

Rhodes boarded the steamer *Asiatic* at Southampton on 15 December 1873. In two tender letters to the Rev. Francis Rhodes he described his condition during the voyage and the overland journey to Kimberley, taking care on both occasions to reassure his father that the worst was now over. In fact, Rhodes suffered a serious relapse during his first few days at sea and engaged a steward as full-time nurse. He was so afraid of what might happen during the waggon journey to Kimberley that he asked the man to leave ship at Cape Town and accompany him to the fields. 'If I get there alright, I shall give him a claim to work, and if I do not he will look after me. I still suffer at times from my lungs, but nothing at all like I used to.'[10]

There is no record to tell us what happened to this steward, but we do know that Rhodes was cared for in Kimberley by the family of the colonial secretary, J.B. Currey. In the words of a living descendant, 'Great-grandmother adored Rhodes, mothered him ... treated him like a son.'[11]

When Rhodes returned to Kimberley in January 1874, the situation in the mines was still precarious. No sooner had the blue-ground crisis been resolved than another took its place. Water was beginning to seep into the claims and the deeper they were sunk, the worse the menace became. All four mines were flooded during the heavy rains of February 1874 and work was brought to a virtual standstill.

Sir Richard Southey had appointed mining boards to handle the overall management of the mines, and Rhodes was quick to recognize an opportunity. In spite of his poor health and limited capital, he approached the Kimberley mining board with a bid for an exclusive contract to pump the mine. To help raise the necessary finance to purchase machinery, Rhodes and Rudd took on two new partners.

It would have been a shrewd move – if it had worked. Control of the pumps meant virtual control of the mine. In wet weather the diggers would be dependent on the pumping contractors to keep their claims workable. In the dry weather, they would be equally dependent for a continuous supply of water for diamond-washing.

Unfortunately for Rhodes, the Kimberley bid failed. He and Rudd then turned their attention to the smaller Dutoitspan mine, and this time they were successful. The problem was that they had no machinery to their names. They had decided to secure the contract before risking their money on pumps, but by the time the deal was confirmed the wet weather had already set in. The Dutoitspan board expected work to begin at once. They were certainly not prepared to wait for pumps to be ordered from England and brought up from the Cape.

The solution to this problem has become a Rhodes legend.

He had heard that a suitable pumping plant had been imported from England by a farmer called Devenish, who intended to use it to irrigate his lands in the Karoo. Rhodes hired a Boer transport driver to take him on the eight-day ride to the farm, where he tried to persuade Devenish to sell the machinery to him. He argued that the farmer could make a profit on the deal and would have plenty of time to bring in new equipment before the start of the dry season when it would be needed. Devenish was not interested in the proposition.

Rhodes returned to the farm day after day, and still Devenish refused to budge, but Rhodes was not discouraged. He was using these visits to build a relationship with the farmer and, sure enough, within a few days he was invited to eat with the family. Once inside the home Rhodes was able to turn his attentions from the man to the wife and win Mrs Devenish to his side. Wearied by war on two fronts, the farmer eventually succumbed, but at a high price. Rhodes was forced to part with all the cash he had – £1000. Money, though, was not the issue. What mattered to Rhodes was his

Early mechanisation in Kimberley. Horse whims to draw loads out of the mine (1875).

reputation in Kimberley. 'I may tell you,' he is quoted as saying to Devenish, 'I meant to stay and keep at you till I got your plant.'

Even then, Rhodes's troubles were not over. He had to transport the machinery and, during the days of bargaining, the rains had turned the tracks into mud. The transport driver was now insisting that they wait until conditions improve, but Rhodes could not afford any further delays without jeopardizing his contract with the mine. He pleaded with the man, who refused to risk his waggon and the lives of his oxen. Rhodes then tried to buy him out. He offered £120 – another exorbitant figure by the standards of the time – and the driver agreed. Rhodes, of course, was now out of cash, but he managed to persuade the man to accept a cheque written in pencil on a scrap of paper. This implicit trust, Rhodes would say whenever he described the incident, gave him a renewed respect for the Afrikaner race.

I hope the story of Devenish's pump is true.[12] It certainly illustrates all the Rhodes qualities – pertinacity, resourcefulness and an astonishing ability to charm those who stood in his way until he was able to extract anything he wanted from them. It was also an early confirmation of his famous maxim that 'every man has his price'.

By fulfilling his contract, Rhodes had secured his first pumping mono poly. He was now out of the ranks of the small-time diggers. On his triumphant return to Kimberley, it is said that he greeted his partner with the words 'We're a force, Rudd; a force to reckon with!'[13]

In spite of his recent illness, Rhodes drove himself hard in this new venture.

> Fuel was a great difficulty, the radius of wood supply was steadily retiring before the increasing demand and at that date there was no coal; but Rhodes had a shaggy Basuto pony and an old yellow cart in which he scoured the country before sunrise to waylay the great Boer wood waggons as they lumbered to the Kimberley market.[14]

The partners missed no opportunity to keep their machinery busy, even manufacturing ice-cream as a sideline.

> You can imagine the great Cecil Rhodes, standing behind a white cotton blanket, slung across a tent, turning a handle of a bucket ice-cream machine, and passing the finished article to Rudd to sell from a packing-case at one of the corners of the diamond market. The ice-cream was retailed at sixpence a wine glass-full, with an extra sixpence for a slab of cake.[15]

A story that the older Rhodes loved to tell about himself is set in this time and appears in various forms in the biographies. Once, when it was his turn to mind the pumping engines, Rhodes was so absorbed in his thoughts that he failed to notice that the boiler was running dry. In several versions, Rhodes was only brought to his senses by the ensuing explosion. In another variation, 'He suddenly heard the engine safety-valve hissing, and after one look, he turned and fled for his life, leaving the engine to its fate.'[16]

These stories of the absent-minded youth, preoccupied with higher thoughts, were circulated in later life when Rhodes was deliberately cultivating the image of himself as the great visionary. However, the evidence suggests that the young Rhodes was highly practical and a clear-eyed pragmatist with his eye to the main chance. As soon as he had secured the Dutoitspan contract he approached the board of the De Beers mine, where he was already a substantial claim-owner. At first he was unsuccessful. The board preferred to buy their own machinery and organize the pumping themselves, but, when they failed to clear the mine, Rhodes took on a new partner and secured the contract.

Since his return from Oxford, Rhodes had been quick to read the signs. In spite of Southey's efforts, the days of the small-time diggers were numbered. Mechanization and large-scale organization were now essential if mining was to remain profitable at deep levels. Apart from the problems of landfall and flood, there was the hard blue ground to contend with. This could not be worked with bucket and spade and, once extracted, had to be left to weather for several months before it could be broken and sieved. The rules were changing, and those who still hoped to get by on a day-to-day basis would soon be out of the game. A man needed capital and professional expertise to survive.

Those, like Rhodes, who were now in the ascendancy were heavily outnumbered by the men who had failed. The mass exodus from the diggings continued throughout 1874,* and the small-timers who remained were quick to blame their declining fortunes on the very man who had tried to defend their interests. Once again, the familiar scapegoats were paraded. Illicit diamond buying was held up as the cause of all financial woes. The blacks were accused of being the chief culprits and Southey was blamed for freeing them to resume their nefarious trade. As one observer caustically observed, 'The only point on which the malcontents join issue is niggers being allowed to hold claims.'[17]

As the atmosphere thickened, racist propaganda took a broader sweep. With or without the IDB slur, blacks were damned as dangerous and inferior beings:

> Ruin, financial ruin for the whites, moral ruin for the natives, these are the results of the attempt to elevate in one day the servant to an equality with his master ... Class legislation, restrictive laws and the holding in check of the native races, till by education they are fit to be our equals is the only policy that finds favour here.[18]

The man who wrote this editorial for a Kimberley newspaper was Alfred Aylward, 'alias Rivers, alias O'Brien, alias Nelson',[19] a convicted killer and Fenian who had the unlikely sideline of acting as Kimberley correspondent for the London *Daily Telegraph*. Aylward had pretensions and liked to be addressed as 'doctor' by virtue of his experience as a medical orderly at the Bultfontein hospital.

In January 1875, Aylward delivered a fiery oration in the Kimberley Hall. His cheering followers were exhorted to 'assemble with their weapons in the name of Heaven and the Country'[20] and to prepare to rise in rebellion as soon as a black flag was hoisted on the mine.

---

*The process continued through the 1870s. According to a reliable estimate, the population of the diggings shrank from a peak of 60,000 in 1871 to 18,000 in 1877. See *Early Diamond Days* by Oswald Doughty (London 1963), p. 106.

More meetings were called. Some of the rebels were pressing for an independent digger republic. Others wanted to join the territory to the Orange Free State, where the Boers' treatment of Africans was more to their liking. Although these crucial issues remained unresolved, a council of war was established in March 1875 and the movement was put on a military footing. According to one account, a thousand men were organized into seven distinct battalions with squadrons of cavalry, officered by Prussian and Irish-Fenian army men, and were drilled openly in the market square. 'Sometimes, when ordered to "right about face", they would, in a menacing and derisive manner, point their rifles at the Government Offices.'[19]

Southey issued a proclamation warning all people against 'taking illegal oaths or assembling in arms'. The rebels issued a counter-proclamation and Southey began to organize his defences. He sandbagged the legislative council rooms, public offices, magistrate's court, police barracks and powder magazine.[21]

The crisis came to a head at the beginning of April when William Cowie, a canteen keeper, was charged with supplying guns to Alfred Aylward without a permit. This gave the militants the pretext they had been waiting for. They issued a threat that any attempt to convict Cowie would be resisted by force of arms.

The case was heard in the resident magistrate's court on the afternoon of 12 April 1875. Cowie was found guilty and sentenced to pay a £50 fine or serve three months' hard labour. No doubt acting on the advice of the rebels, Cowie chose to serve the prison term.[22]

As soon as sentence was passed, Aylward rode with the black flag towards the Kimberley mine.

> I shall never forget on this memorable revolutionary occasion being in the Main Street, when suddenly I saw a man of Satanic bearing come galloping down it, waving a black flag in one hand and shouting valorously as if he were leading a heroic charge of cavalry. By his side a huge General Boom sabre dangled … This burlesque of Murat was a fair-sized man with luxuriant black curly hair and beard and moustache, which brought into prominence his thick sensual red lips and bright, though dissipated, bloodshot eyes. The Rouge et Noir on horseback was none other than the redoubtable Irish-Fenian Alfred Aylward, a fellow of tremendous composition, and he was on his way to see hoisted the piratical emblem which might have brought murder and chaos to many.[19]

Once Aylward had reached the mine, he was prudent enough to order one of his followers, 'a silly young man called Albany Paddon',[19] to hoist the banner and commit the act of treason. On the signal, some 300 armed men charged down Main Street towards the magistrate's court. They were met by a handful of constables, who held them in check with drawn revolvers.

Four justices of the peace were immediately summoned to accompany Cowie and his police escort to the jail, some 250 yards (230 metres) from the court. They were overtaken by the rebels, 'who barred the entrance to the jail with a wall of 300 armed men'.[21] At that moment police reinforcements arrived armed with rifles with fixed bayonets and positioned themselves in front of the rebels. It was a tense moment. A crowd of some three thousand people was milling about in front of the jail. If either side had opened fire, it would have resulted in mass slaughter.[22]

Alfred Aylward.

The situation was saved by the coolness of the resident magistrate, who refused to be intimidated even when a revolver was fired close to his ear. With the rebels jostling him on all sides, he calmly asked the leaders to identify themselves, and then offered to take them to see the lieutenant-governor. Characteristically, Southey refused to receive them, but J.B. Currey was more pliant. After discussing the matter with the magistrate and Sidney Shippard, the acting attorney-general, Currey agreed to release Cowie on receipt of a cheque for £50, not to be cashed until the sentence had been properly reviewed. The canteen keeper was set free and the crowd dispersed.

Alfred Aylward was not there to witness this temporary truce. As soon as the black flag was raised, he and Albany Paddon had fled the territory and gone into hiding, where Aylward tried to cover his tracks. 'From a Transvaal farmhouse, where he had secreted himself, he sent a notice of his death to the newspapers.'[21]

In spite of Currey's initiative, the dispute in Kimberley was far from settled. The rebels refused to disarm, and Southey appealed for volunteers to act as special constables. One of those who came forward was Cecil Rhodes.[23]

True to his principles, Southey made it clear that whites and non-whites would be equally welcome to serve in this new force. This 'insanely injudicious step of beginning to arm natives'[24] inflamed rebel passions still further, and Southey was threatened with violent retaliation unless he disarmed his black constables. Southey refused to do anything of the sort and instead appealed to the Cape Government for troops to deal with the threat. They arrived in Kimberley on 30 June 1875 after an exhausting march across country. Cohen recalls:

> I well remember seeing the men march up Du Toit's Pan Road, tired and dusty, straining their eyes for the sight of the diamonds they expected no doubt to see in heaps ... The next morning five of the loud-voiced rebels were arrested, an operation effected on them as easily as if they were goats. A bleat or two and all was over.[19]

The last flickerings of revolt had petered out.

There is an interesting footnote to the 'black flag rebellion' in the form of a police report prepared for Southey, which showed that no fewer than 13 of the rebel ringleaders had criminal records and that seven of them were suspected of, or had actually been imprisoned for, illicit diamond buying.[25] If ever proof was needed that the campaign to stamp out IDB was merely an excuse for oppressing blacks, one need look no further.

The digger revolt against Southey had a significance out of all proportion to its comic-opera ingredients. It was a clash of ideologies that would be central to the ensuing South African tragedy. In time, when the stakes were far higher and the consequences more devastating, Rhodes would become the major player in this conflict, but not on the side of the Richard Southeys. The cause Rhodes chose to serve was Alfred Aylward's.

The position taken by the 21-year-old Rhodes comes as no surprise to anyone who recognizes that at this early age he had already adopted his lifetime strategy of ingratiating himself with those who could be useful to him. In 1875 the British administrators in Kimberley were clearly in this category, and Rhodes's efforts to establish good relations with them were more than successful. As we have seen, he was invited to live with the family of the colonial secretary, where he was loved and – more to the point – trusted and respected. According to Currey's own account, when he was asked by the governor to draw up new anti-gambling legislation, he consulted 'young Cecil Rhodes'. One Sunday afternoon, the two men sat down together and between them drafted a document clause by clause.[25] In the same spirit, Rhodes immediately responded to the governor's call for volunteers to take up arms on his behalf, but there was no real commitment to Southey's cause, as Rhodes made clear in a letter to his brother Frank.

> The Government called out volunteers and we had to guard the gaol and offices for nearly three months while the troops came up. It was a frightful

nonsense, but still there was some grounds for it as the other side had about 300 men under arms ... One could not help sympathising on certain questions with them.[23]

In the end, things went badly for Southey. Military intervention had cost the imperial government in London £20,000. In a long dispatch to Lord Carnarvon, the colonial secretary in London, Sir Humphry Barkly, Governor of the Cape made it clear that he did not consider morality and justice to be worth such a high price. While the arrested rebel leaders were acquitted in state trials, Southey, Currey and the entire executive council were dismissed for their handling of the rebellion. The post of lieutenant-governor was abolished and a less highly paid official appointed to administer the territory. He was Colonel Crossman, and he had firm views on Africans. 'They must be treated as children,' he wrote in an official report, 'incapable of governing themselves.'[26] Here was a man who could be counted on not to cause offence to the diggers.

At the time of Southey's departure Rhodes had troubles of his own to con0tend with. In bidding for the De Beers contract, he had overreached himself. By the middle of 1875 it was clear to everyone that Rhodes lacked adequate equipment to keep the mine dry. He was summoned before a full meeting of the De Beers mining board and told that he had failed to honour his contract. The board now intended to appoint their own engineer and revert to their former plan of organizing the pumping operations themselves.

We do not know what arguments Rhodes used to mollify his accusers, but one witness to his performance was an old friend from the Natal days, who wrote: 'I have never forgotten the way in which he, still quite a youth, handled that body of angry men and gained his point.'[27]

The 'point' Rhodes gained was remarkable. Before the meeting was over, he had persuaded the board to agree to handle pumping on an interim basis only. As soon as Rhodes could bring in new equipment from England the contract would revert to him.

The engineer appointed to supervise the board's temporary pumping operations was a 35-year-old Mauritian called Heuteau, and he performed well. The mine stayed dry during the wettest months at the end of 1875 and operating costs were held well below Rhodes's contract price. Why, people began to ask, was it necessary to change this happy state of affairs in order that the contract could revert to a man who had already failed at the job and whose pumps were still on a ship somewhere out on the Atlantic?

These critics received their answer on 26 December 1875. On that day, Heuteau's pumping operation failed spectacularly and the mine flooded. On close inspection it was discovered that 'the plunger, gland and collar of the pumping engine [had been] removed, sabotaging the engine and flooding the claims'.[26]

Understandably, there was fury in the mine, but the means of retribution were at hand. As part of the new British policy of reconciliation, Crossman had already agreed to set up a commission of inquiry to hear digger complaints – white digger complaints, that is. In Crossman's book, 'natives' had nothing to complain about.

On 5 January 1876 the session opened in the Kimberley Hall. Almost immediately the issue of sabotage was raised. Heuteau was called and under cross-examination, made the astonishing admission that he had been offered £300 by a 'speculator' to damage De Beers' equipment. When asked to name the villain, he refused. Threatened with legal action, he pleaded for a compromise. He would write the name down on a piece of paper and hand it to the royal commissioner. This, of course, was a pointless gesture. As soon as Crossman read the paper, he called out in a loud voice for Mr Cecil Rhodes to step forward.[28]

> There was not a moment lost before Mr. Rhodes was sent for. Character was at stake, and the Royal Commissioner did all in his power to prevent Mr. Rhodes remaining under the stigma longer than was unavoidable if the statement was true. Unfortunately Mr. Rhodes was not within reach ... But a matter so serious is not to be disposed of by pitting word against word, and both Heuteau and Mr. Rhodes were summoned to appear in Court on Friday morning.[29]

At the Friday hearing Rhodes dismissed the story as 'fictitious'. He had taken legal advice and now announced that he intended to hand the matter over to the public prosecutor and charge Heuteau with perjury. The case was out of Crossman's hands.

The preliminary hearing took place in the resident magistrate's court six days later. Then, mysteriously, Rhodes dropped the charges and made no further attempts to clear his name, but perhaps that was not the primary purpose of this legal manoeuvre. By threatening criminal proceedings, Rhodes had effectively put a stop to any further investigation by the court of inquiry.

The historian Brian Roberts was the first to expose the bribery charges (in 1972), and he concluded that Heuteau's accusations were probably false. The main reason he gave was that the engineer had nothing to gain from destroying his own work.[30] Nevertheless, £300 (approximately £8000 by today's values) was a substantial sum for a man on a temporary contract. However, there are other, stronger grounds for questioning Rhodes's innocence. Since the departure of the Curreys he had been sharing quarters with the three leading members of the British legal establishment in the colony, and was particularly close to one of them, the acting attorney-general Sir Sidney Shippard. (In later years, this Shippard would be a willing collaborator in three of Rhodes's more unsavoury schemes.)

The historian Rob Turrell builds a persuasive case against Rhodes.

> [In spite of his conclusion] Roberts did regard the refusal of Shippard to prosecute the suit of perjury that Rhodes brought against Heuteau as suspicious. Rhodes messed with Sidney Shippard, Advocate Halkett and Recorder Barry, who presided over the High Court, and it was probably their idea to file a case against Heuteau, which effectively quashed any public discussion of Rhodes's conduct. The fact that his honour was not pursued to legal judgement in a litigious society where such concepts were important and under advice from men at the hub of colonial law is very damning. This combined with the possible loss of the contract swings the scale of doubt decisively against Rhodes.[31]

If Dr Turrell is right, and it is hard to disagree with this analysis, Rhodes committed his first criminal act at the age of 23. If Mr Roberts is right, we must conclude that Rhodes 'crossed the line' at some later date. Neither interpretation changes one's view of Rhodes's later career.

One thing, though, is certain. Rhodes did not suffer financially from the scandal. Although a majority of claim-holders voted at a public meeting to have his contract annulled if his pumps did not arrive within a month, Rhodes was able to mollify his critics by offering a guarantee that he would have his pumps on the mine in time or forfeit £100. The gamble paid off and in March 1876 Rhodes finally secured the De Beers contract. After all that had taken place, this was a considerable personal triumph.

With the contract secured, Rhodes decided to return to Oxford and continue to work for his degree. He had come a long way during his two-year absence from the university, but his reputation had been damaged. Reflecting from Oxford, he wrote: 'My character was so battered at the Diamond Fields that I like to preserve the few remnants.'[32]

A month after Rhodes's departure from Kimberley the Crossman commission announced its recommendations. All restrictions on the number of claims that could be owned by a single consortium should be lifted. Africans should be barred from owning claims or washing debris. All these recommendations were adopted.

Company mining was now inevitable, and in future Africans would only have one status on the mines: that of labourer.

EIGHT

A CONFESSION OF FAITH

*There is a destiny now possible to us, the highest ever set before
a nation to be accepted or refused. We are still undegenerate in race;
a race mingled of the best northern blood ... Will you youths of
England make your country again a royal throne of kings, a sceptred
isle, for all the world a source of light, a centre of peace ... This is
what England must either do or perish: she must found colonies as
fast and as far as she is able, formed of her most energetic and
worthiest men; seizing every piece of fruitful waste ground she can set
her foot on, and there teaching these her colonists that their chief
virtue is fidelity to their country, and their first aim is to advance the
power of England by land and sea ...*

JOHN RUSKIN'S INAUGURAL LECTURE AT OXFORD UNIVERSITY, 1870

Rhodes would keep all terms at Oxford for the next two years, only returning to Kimberley for the long vacations. His correspondence and the recollections of his contemporaries combine to give a flavour of his curious double life – as an undergraduate and as a growing power on the diamond fields. One existence had him ordering pumping machinery, visiting Hatton Garden diamond merchants, alternatively exhorting Rudd to be cautious ('Do not plunge for more at the fields'[1]), or boosting his partner's flagging morale when times were bad: 'Don't be low-spirited ... All I can say is I envy you. I never was so happy as when in bills up to my neck and pump breaking down.'[2]

In his other life, Rhodes played polo, rowed or kept his neighbours awake at night by practising on a hunting horn. (This was 'to acquit himself with credit' in his new role as master of the Oxford drag hunt.)[3] He also became a member of the exclusive Bullingdon and Vincent's clubs, 'which only accepted men of wealth, dandies and bon vivants'.[4] Oscar Wilde was a member of Bullingdon's at the time, as was Rochfort Maguire, who would one day perform a valuable service for Rhodes in Matabeleland. The club was 'a sodality of cheerful young gentlemen who were wont to wear grey bowlers and on festive evenings to parade the High Street with horsewhips and hunting cries.'[5]

Rhodes was older and considerably more experienced than most under-graduates. This gave him self-confidence and a sense of detachment from the day-to-day concerns of the majority. He seldom bothered with lectures, and when reprimanded for non-attendance replied airily, 'I shall pass, which is all I wish to do.'[6]

On the face of it, a regime of hunting, rowing, polo, skipped lectures and bowler-hat parades seems an unlikely choice for someone as driven and puri-tanical as Rhodes; someone so obsessed with the 'sin' of wasted time. The choice becomes less surprising when one understands Rhodes's view of the university and his purpose in being there. At Oxford, he had the opportunity to join the society of England's future leaders, young men from landed and titled families brought up in the expectation that they would be the future leaders of government, the Civil Service, the army and the Church. Accep-tance at this level meant more to Rhodes than academic or sporting distinc-tion, and if hunting, polo and bowler-hat parades were the price of admission, he was happy to pay. Once inside the charmed circle, Rhodes could enjoy the rewards of shared confidences and ideological debate such as he loved. At Oxford he developed friendships and contacts that he would use

Oriel College, Oxford. Rhodes is on the extreme left.

for the rest of his life. Writing years later, a tutor described Rhodes and the company he kept during his undergraduate days:

> He belonged to a set of men like himself, not caring for distinction in the schools and not working for them, but of refined tastes, dining and living for the most part together, and doubtless discussing passing events in life and politics with interest and ability.[6]

These discussions were crucial to Rhodes. In Britain, the 1870s were a time of intellectual ferment, when attitudes to empire, Africa and the rest of humanity were changing. Oxford was central to this debate.

To understand the context, it is necessary to go back 40 years and evoke the moral climate in Britain when slavery was abolished 'in all lands subject to the Crown'. It was a time when the British people were recoiling from the crimes their countrymen had committed in Africa with feelings of self-disgust and guilt.

> What was the state of Africa? Why it was one universal slaughterhouse ... What was its trade? A trade in the bodies of its inhabitants ... Thousands were destroyed in the nightly combustions which took place – thousands fell by day travelling the burning sands; and as to a slave-ship, it was impossible to describe, except in the words of the scripture, which said: 'A pestilence walketh upon the waters'; nay, the very shark knew the slave-ship to be a barque of blood, and expected from it his daily sustenance.[7]

Those rousing words were delivered by Thomas Buxton, the man who had succeeded William Wilberforce as leader of the crusade against slavery. The occasion was the first anniversary meeting of the Society for the Extinction of the Slave Trade and for the Civilisation of Africa. The venue was London's Exeter Hall. The date, June 1840.

London had never seen an occasion like it.

> It was a warm summer's day ... and London was fairly bursting with a zeal and an excitement and a righteous self-assurance ... From early morning the streets around the Strand had been crowded with people anxious to get a good view of the high and mighty, as they made their way by carriage to Exeter Hall, though the doors would not be open until *10 o'clock* and the first speech was not due until after *11*. The demand for tickets had been so great that days before large sums of money had been offered by those hoping to gain admission ...[8]

Among those present at this great gathering were Prince Albert, Robert Peel, William Gladstone, the French ambassador, a dozen peers of the realm, seven bishops and 'somewhere down in [the] audience ... a man who was destined much more than anyone else ... to exemplify the spirit which was now being proclaimed and released as a benison upon degraded Africa'.[9] This man was an unknown medical student at Charing Cross Hospital called David Livingstone.

One by one, the Exeter Hall speakers called for what amounted to a new contract with the peoples of Africa. They wanted to establish industry,

The Missionary.

agriculture and commerce. Above all, they wanted to claim the 'dark continent' for Christ: 'It is the Bible and the plough that must regenerate Africa. The profiteers in human flesh and misery would have their trade undercut by the introduction of a commerce based upon Christian standards and Western commodity.'[10]

In the late twentieth century, this creed may seem patronizing, even offensive. It placed little or no value on African achievement and culture and assumed that the greatest gift that could be bestowed on the black man was the opportunity to work, live and pray as a white man. Yet, for all its shortcomings, this was an enlightened creed by comparison with the ideologies that would supplant it. In the spirit of the Gospels, men like Buxton believed that all human beings were of equal value and potential. In their view, history and geography had conspired against Africa and excluded her people from the influences that had shaped European civilization. It was now the duty of British Christians to guide the peoples of Africa along paths of wisdom and righteousness until they were ready to take their rightful place in the civilized world.

According to Thomas Buxton, this meant signing treaties with local chieftains and carrying out explorations into the agricultural and commercial potential of Africa under the *temporary* protection of the British flag. Buxton was very clear on that last point ,saying, 'I entirely disclaim any disposition to erect a new empire in Africa.'[10]

Emotions reached a climax in Exeter Hall when Buxton delivered a resounding finale to his 30 minute address. The British people, he told his audience, now had the opportunity to dedicate themselves to an 'illustrious, noble and pure' ideal that would bring them more glory than their triumphs at Trafalgar and Waterloo.

> To arrest the destruction of mankind, to throw a blessing upon a continent now in ruins, to give civilisation and to spread the mild truths of the Gospel … was a higher and nobler road, and his desire and prayer was that Her Majesty might tread it (cheers) and that, crowned with every other blessing, she might:
>
>> 'Shine the leader of applauding nations,
>> To scatter happiness and peace around her,
>> To bid the prostrate captive rise and live,
>> To see new cities tower at her command,
>> And blasted nations flourish in her smile.'[11]

The missionary legacy was, to put it charitably, a mixed blessing for Africa.

At their worst, the missionaries became paid agents of colonial expansion and contributed to the destruction of African family life through their attacks on traditional domestic institutions. Some groups, such as the Church of Scotland missionaries in Nyasaland, gained temporal as well as spiritiual powers over Aficans, and went about their task with sadistic relish. A hundred or more lashes was the usual punishment they meted out for relatively minor offences, such as fornication or the theft of a loaf of bread. Serious offenders were executed in the most horrifying ways after trials that were a travesty of justice.[12]

All this, of course, was absolutely contrary to the spirit of Exeter Hall, which continued to exert a benign influence on the thinking of the early governors of the Cape and subsequent advocates of colour-blind policies, such as Richard Southey. It also helped to establish the principle (never abandoned by some) that Britain's proper role in Africa was that of temporary protector, not occupier.

Contemptuously dismissed in later years as 'Exeter Hall negrophiles', the better missionaries also provided education and avenues of advancement for thousands of Africans when other options were closed off by racist legislation.

Although the original ideal would never be extinguished, the public mood in Britain had swung in another direction by the time Rhodes entered Oxford. In 1872, Gladstone's Liberal Government had been defeated by the Conservatives under the romantic and ebullient Disraeli, who had frequently criticized his political opponents for their neglect of the glorious Empire. Under Disraeli's leadership, the years 1872–78 saw a surge of Imperial activity with the annexation of Fiji, Garnet Wolsey's campaigns in West Africa, the acquisition of Cyprus and the Suez Canal purchase, which would ultimately lead to British occupation of Egypt. In 1877, Queen Victoria was delighted to be made Empress of India and, to Gladstone's dismay, all these measures enjoyed popular support. Soon 'Exeter Hall' antipathy to empire-building in Africa, or anywhere else, no longer seemed desirable or popular.

While these transformations were taking place at the centre, attitudes were changing in the Colonies. Rhodes, travelling between Oxford and Kimberley, would have been subjected to a double influence.

In the Cape there was an increasing tendency to regard non-Europeans as an inferior species incapable of attaining the same standards as whites, and therefore unworthy of equal treatment. This development was closely related to the issues of land and labour. As we have seen, blacks on the diamond mine were unwelcome competitors, but essential labourers. The same reappraisal would take place throughout the colony when labour was required for the construction of railways, harbours and other major projects financed by diamond wealth. White labourers (including some especially imported for the purpose) proved too 'independent, unreliable and expensive'.[13] African labour was another matter. Indeed, the colonists were now discovering that they possessed 'a great raw material': 'What an abundance of rain and grass was to New Zealand mutton, what a plenty of cheap grazing was to Australian wool, what the fertile prairie acres were to Canadian wheat, cheap native labour was to [South Africa].'[14]

In his excellent study of racial prejudice Dr Bickford-Smith notes the massive increase in racist propaganda and institutionalized racism in the Cape from the mid-1870s, a period that exactly coincided with the expansion and enrichment of the colony, following the discovery of diamonds. He suggests that this was not coincidental: 'Racism justified the conquest or suppression of African people ... It could explain unequal social, political and economic relationships with Blacks after conquest as well as conquest itself.'[15]

In this time of imperial expansion, moral justification was just as important to the British people as it was to the colonists.

The Boers had found sanction for expropriation and enslavement in an obscure reference to the 'sons of Ham' in the book of Genesis. In the 1870s, a more credible authority was needed. It would be supplied, almost exactly when required, by Charles Darwin. His two major works, *On the Origin of Species* (1859) and *The Descent of Man* (1871), challenged every philosophical and religious assumption man had made about himself, his gods and his place in creation. Darwin's world of natural selection was 'a horrible, ruthless, savage world'[16] where 'the weak go to the wall, and the strong receive the title deeds to the future' and 'the law of Murder is the law of Growth'.[17]

Darwin's work was a gift to the new prophets of racism. Indeed, they seem to have been ready and waiting for him. In Cole's *The Cape and the Kafirs*, written in 1852 (a full seven years before the publication of *On the Origin of Species*), we read: 'The fate of the Black man ... [will be that] his race is exterminated. The Kafir's time is well-nigh come.'[18]

Once Darwin had published, these arguments could be given a pseudo-scientific gloss. The different tribes and races were said to occupy higher or lower positions on the evolutionary scale. The Australian Aborigine and South Africa's indigenous Khoi-San were placed 'among the lowest on the scale of the negro races'.[19] Their extinction would be no loss to humanity as 'even the lovers of the lower orders will admit' (*Cape Times*, 1879).[20]

In 1875, the *Cape Argus* suggested that Africans would serve well as 'labouring machines'.[20] A few years later, the argument was taken a stage further by the editor of an Afrikaans newspaper, who wrote that 'the lower people are in the scale of humanity, the more will they be taught by working, obeying and submitting.'[20] It was only one small step from ideas like these to the notion that members of the 'lower races' who would not accept the disciplines of work, obedience and submission should be exterminated. Indeed, by the 1890s that option was frequently mentioned in Cape newspapers and periodicals, but the idea was rejected on practical, rather than moral, grounds.[21]

Unsurprisingly, whites placed themselves at the top of the evolutionary scale, their confidence hugely boosted by recent technological achievements. In previous centuries, Europeans might have questioned such an assumption as they encountered the civilizations of Asia and the Middle East, but in this new age of railways, telegraphs and powerful weapons of war, the white man (and particularly the white man in Africa) believed that his superiority was self-evident.

The point has to be made that all the racist theorizing (which historians would subsequently dignify with the label 'Social Darwinism') rested on a misapplication of Darwin's theory. There is no scientific basis to racism. Natural selection does not choose between races, or any other large groupings for that matter. It chooses between individuals.[16] Darwin himself was normally clear about this, but even he was not immune to the racism endemic to his times, and some of his writings lent themselves to misuse by propagandists. What they took from Darwin was the message that life had evolved through a 'savage' mechanism that eliminated the weak and promoted the strong. By constructing bogus scales of human development, it was possible to rework Darwin's theory of evolution into a new doctrine of *racial* evolution, which accorded the white race the first position on the scale of 'physical and human evolution'.[22] It was even possible to add a further refinement, and invent an evolutionary scale for whites, which had the English in top place and granted them 'the title deeds to the future'. Ludicrous though this reasoning may sound, it was not far from the position Rhodes adopted during his second year at Oxford.

Apart from Darwin, Rhodes would claim other important influences that helped to shape his ideology during his university years. A name he frequently mentioned was John Ruskin, Slade Professor of Art at Oxford. 'Listening to Ruskin while at Oxford his lectures made a deep impression on one. One of them in which he set out the privileges and opportunities of the young men in the Empire made a forceful entry into my mind.'[23]

John Ruskin would exert a profound influence, not only on Rhodes, but on a whole generation. An extract from his inaugural address at Oxford

University is quoted at the head of the chapter. It was actually delivered in 1870, but 'was still ringing in the ears of the University'[23] when Rhodes first went up to Oxford three years later and, no doubt, he would have read the published text. The timing of Ruskin's address, so close to the dawn of Disraeli's new imperial age, was also crucial.

Ruskin's text was strongly influenced by Social Darwinism – 'We are still undegenerate in race; a race mingled of the best northern blood', etc. – but was remarkable for one important omission. No mention was made of the *people* who might already be living on those 'distant plots of land' which Ruskin's youths were being asked to seize on England's behalf. The issue is skilfully avoided in the phrase 'every piece of fruitful waste ground' (an obvious contradiction in terms). Colonists (that is, those whites who had already settled in these parts) *did* get a mention, and 'the youths of England' were under an injunction to teach them fidelity to their mother country, but no guidance was given about their responsibilities towards the indigenous people. Indeed, the existence of such people was not acknowledged.

This was a long way from the spirit of the Exeter Hall meeting, and yet there were striking similarities between Ruskin's address and Buxton's speech 30 years earlier. Both men were appealing to a spirit of idealism and asking their listeners to dedicate themselves selflessly to a cause that would bring glory to England. It was this aspect of Ruskin's address that meant so much to Rhodes: 'All that I ask of you is to have a fixed purpose of some kind for your country and for yourselves, no matter how restricted, so that it can be fixed and unselfish.'[24]

Those closing words from the inaugural address echoed the sentiments expressed in Rhodes's favourite classical texts, and were crucially important to him at a time when he was still agonizing over the purposelessness of his life, as in this letter to his brother Frank: 'What is life worth at my present mode of existence with no object, no aim? I cannot help feeling I was made for better things.'[25]

Another significant influence on Rhodes was Wynwood Reade, whose major work *The Martyrdom of Man* first appeared in 1872. Rhodes read the book shortly after

John Ruskin.

publication and described it as 'creepy'. He would also claim that 'it made me what I am'.

In 1872, England was not ready to welcome *The Martyrdom of Man*; indeed the book received no favourable review until 1906, but it was impossible to ignore. By 1924 it had gone through 24 editions and numerous reprintings.[26] It is seldom read today, but those who do take the trouble might be impressed by its vivid language and prophetic insights.

Reade foresaw 'the discovery of a motive force that will take the place of steam ... the invention of aerial locomotion ... the manufacture of flesh and flour from the elements by a chemical process in the laboratory' and the end of all wars: '... [when] science discovers some destroying force, so simple in its administration, so horrible in its effects, that all art, all gallantry, will be at an end, and battles will be massacres which the feelings of mankind will be unable to endure.'[17]

Reade also prophesied in 1872, that 'Disease will be extirpated; the causes of decay will be removed; immortality will be invented. And then, the earth being so small, mankind will cross the airless Saharas which separate planet from planet and sun from sun.'[17]

Reade was one 'Darwinist' who did not take a racist message from *On the Origin of Species*. Instead, it led him to the conclusion that all man's religions (including the 'Syrian superstition' of Christianity) were false, and that a 'God of Love', a God who cared about human beings, was an absurd concept: 'The law of Murder is the law of Growth. Life is one great crime ... Pain, grief, disease and death, are these the inventions of a loving God? That no animal shall rise to excellence except by being fatal to the life of others, is this the law of a kind creator?'

Reade did not deny the existence of God, but his 'Supreme Power' had no relationship with individual men and women. Human beings were merely the 'corpuscles' in the larger organism of mankind. Their lives and deaths were of no significance. What mattered to the Creator was the perfection of the 'body' as a whole: 'If we take

Rhodes at Oxford.

the life of a single atom, that is to say of a single man ... all appears to be cruelty and confusion; but when we survey mankind as One, we find it becoming more and more noble, more and more divine, slowly ripening towards perfection.'[17]

History has taught to us to be wary of those who devalue individual life and liberty in the interests of some larger cause, but to Rhodes this thinking was a revelation. His political and business speeches would be peppered with 'Readisms' throughout his life – 'We human atoms may divide this country, but Nature does not, and the Almighty does not'.[27] At its basest level, it was a view of history that would give Rhodes sanction to rob and slaughter those who stood in civilization's way – but that lay in the future. For the present, a 'truth' had been revealed to the 20-year-old that satisfied his religious yearn-ings and filled the void left by the loss of his Christian faith. He now under-stood that evolution was not simply some blind force operating in a meaningless universe, but an expression of the Divine Will. It was God's plan for the human race.

One last experience should be mentioned in this context, not because it had a bearing on Rhodes's intellectual development, but because it suggested a course of action to him.

On 2 June 1877, Rhodes became a life member of the Masonic Order. At the celebratory dinner that followed his initiation, he angered some of the members present by 'revealing the cherished secrets of the craft'.[5] Clearly, Rhodes did not take the Masonic Order very seriously. 'I see the wealth and power they possess, the influence they hold ... and I wonder that a large body of men can devote themselves to what at times appear to be the most ridiculous and absurd rites *with no object, with no aim.*'[28]

But might it not be possible to form another secret society, that *would* be prepared to use its wealth, power and influence in the service of a great object, a great aim ...? On the same day he joined the Freemasons and betrayed their confidences, Rhodes felt ready to commit his personal mani-festo to paper. He was 23 years old.

> The idea gleaming and dancing before one's eyes like a will-of-the-wisp at last frames itself into a plan. Why should we not form a secret society with but one object, the furtherance of the British Empire and the bringing of the whole uncivilised world under British rule, for the recovery of the United States, for the making the Anglo-Saxon race but one Empire?'
>
> [It] would be a society not openly acknowledged but which would have its members in every part of the British Empire ... placed at our universities and our schools ... in every Colonial legislature. The Society should attempt

to have its members prepared at all times to vote or speak and advocate the closer union of England and the colonies, to crush all disloyalty and every movement for the severance of our Empire. The Society should inspire and even own portions of the press for the press rules the minds of men.

What a dream, but yet it is probable. It is possible.[28]

The principal points of interest in this extraordinary document (which would be known as Rhodes's 'Confession of Faith') are his unqualified statements regarding the supremacy of the 'English race' and his comments on life's objectives, where he seems to acknowledge that marriage is not a possibility open to him.

It often strikes a man to inquire what is the chief good in life; to one the thought comes that it is a happy marriage, to another great wealth, and as each seizes on the idea, for that he more or less works for the rest of his existence. To myself, thinking over the same question, the wish came to me to render myself useful to my country ... I contend that we are the finest race in the world, and that the more of the world we inhabit the better it is for the human race ... Added to this, the absorption of the greater portion of the world under our rule simply means the end of all wars ...[28]

A final paragraph was added some months later, when Rhodes was in Kimberley, in which he wrote: 'For fear that death might cut me off before the time for attempting its development, I leave my worldly goods in trust to S.G. Shippard and the Secretary for the Colonies at the time of my death to try to form such a Society with such an Object.'[28]

This, of course, was the same Shippard who had steered Rhodes through certain legal difficulties in Kimberley. The secretary of state for the Colonies at the time was Lord Carnarvon, and one wonders how His Lordship would have risen to the challenge, if asked.

Although Rhodes never rewrote his 'Confession of Faith', his five subsequent wills are regarded as revisions of the Rhodes manifesto. A final edition exists in the form of 'The Last Will and Testament of Cecil John Rhodes', edited by his friend W.T. Stead. It is intended to be a synthesis of the wills, as well as many conversations and an extensive correspondence between the two men. As such it stands as Rhodes's personal manifesto in the last years of his life; it is remarkably similar in tone to the earlier document. There is the same obsession with a secret society, although the Jesuits, rather than Masons, are now given as the model. The only significant development is that God has now been worked into Rhodes's master plan, and in a manner that indicates Wynwood Reade's lasting influence.

What follows is a faithful summary of this second 'confession' by Cecil Rhodes.

> I have considered the existence of God and decided there is an even chance that He exists. If He does exist, he must be working to a Plan. Therefore, if I am to serve God, I must find out the Plan, and do my best to assist him in it's execution.
>
> How to discover the Plan? First, look for the *race* that God has chosen to be the Divine instrument of future evolution.
>
> Unquestionably, that is the *white* race. Whites have clearly come out top ... in the struggle for existence and achieved the highest standard of human perfection. Within the white race, English-speaking man, whether British, American, Australian or South African, has proved himself to be the most likely instrument of the Divine Plan to spread Justice, Liberty and Peace ... over the widest possible area of the planet.
>
> Therefore, I shall devote the rest of my life to God's purpose, and help Him to make the world English.[29]

Apart from W.T. Stead, most biographers have had difficulties with Rhodes's Last Will and Testament. 'The Confession of Faith' was more or less excusable as the work of a 23-year-old, but what were they to make of this second document? Whether they ranked among his detractors or his admirers, serious biographers have generally acknowledged Rhodes's organizational genius, his extraordinary ability to persuade and inspire, his grasp of new technologies and his strong aesthetic sense. How could the juvenile statement put together by W.T. Stead possibly represent the guiding ideology of such a man?

If the reader will forgive me for closing this chapter on a personal note, I have to say that I do not share these difficulties. Perhaps this is because mine has not been an academic life, but one that has allowed me to move about the world, mixing with all kinds of men and women, including those who hold (or held) positions of great power. Within that group are – or were – several notorious dictators, as well as the heads of crime syndicates, religious denominations and sects, 'terrorist' organizations and multinational corporations. Happily, I have usually had the time (and the motivation) to form close relationships with such people and been given surprising opportunities to share personal thoughts. Knowing my obsession, the reader will not be surprised to hear that I also felt I was learning more about Cecil Rhodes through these experiences.

Very early on, I discovered that all men in positions of great power need to construct a personal ideology that makes sense of their actions and decisions – both to themselves and to others. (Sadly, I have only met one woman among the ranks of the very powerful, so do not feel qualified to make generalizations there). The need for moral justification seems equally compelling whether the activity is religious, political, commercial or criminal. Let me be clear, though, that I am not referring to the foot soldiers in this context, but to the men at the top: men with the gift to lead and inspire; men like Cecil Rhodes.

The second discovery I made was that these otherwise intelligent and highly capable individuals often become simpletons when they attempt to describe the principles that guide them. Their seriousness at such times is real, as is the impact of their words on their immediate entourage. Nevertheless, an uncommitted observer often finds that the guiding ideologies of great men are based on a set of astonishingly naive assumptions and beliefs.

Another common observation is that these personal ideologies are elastic. This is particularly apparent among prominent politicians and civil servants in times of radical change. (It is also true, of course, of broadcasters and journalists, although I would not include them among the ranks of the very powerful.)

I remember once spending an evening with a man who was running the security services of a country that had recently experienced revolutionary change after a long and bitter civil war. The interesting fact about him was that he had held the same job under the previous regime, and was now destroying the terror apparatus he had so carefully constructed on behalf of his former employers. This meant assisting the new military establishment to fight an all-out war against the men and women who had formerly been on his payroll. I can only say that he went about his task with gusto.

During our evening together, the security chief spent a long time imparting his own 'confession of faith'. I no longer remember the exact content, but I do remember that it offered him a perfect rationale for all his actions and decisions.

Another example that comes to mind is less sinister, but in many ways more telling. A couple of years after my evening with the security chief, I had an opportunity to observe a very successful Christian evangelist, both on and off stage. At the time, he was running a lucrative television network in the United States and had plans to expand worldwide. A few months later he would suffer a spectacular fall from grace, but when I knew him he was at the peak of his power and popularity.

While I was watching one of his broadcasts, someone in the invited studio audience stood up and described a homely encounter he had had with an angel. The evangelist was sceptical at first, but quickly realized that this position was unpopular with the audience. Indeed, some of those present were soon on their feet, contributing angelic experiences of their own, to the evident delight of the crowd. Without turning a hair, the evangelist gestured for silence, and capped all their stories with a particularly moving description of his own personal encounter with an angel. In no time at all his audience was applauding and in tears.

'Hypocrisy' is a threadbare word to use in these situations. The point is that the evangelist had the gift to inspire and motivate others. He gave meaning to their lives. It takes a strong and highly principled individual to stop short and ask himself searching questions when he discovers he has talents like these. More often than not, events seem to move forward under their own momentum, and the temptation is to let them roll.

Rhodes had the evangelist's talents and many more besides. He was also a young man in a hurry. At the age of 20, he had been given only six months to live.

If it is still difficult to accept the idea that a sensitive, loyal and unprej udiced youth could have turned into the person Rhodes became, let me say that I have plenty of evidence that men with darker reputations than his shared similar virtues and ideals when they were young. These qualties sometimes endure, but only in the limited context of the 'great man's' inner circle. Here, he may continue to be a man of principle, maintaining the high standards of his youth in all his dealings with close and trusted associates. While he may be loathed and feared outside the circle, the fierce loyalties of those on the inside are often based on genuine trust, affection and respect, rather than fear. This is especially true of some dictators and underworld bosses. It would always be true of Cecil Rhodes.

In my more pessimistic moments, I have sometimes felt that the only thing that separates good and evil is opportunity. This, of course, is a partial truth, but what I know for certain is that popular writers and dramatists usually fail in their attempts to portray evil. Evil, real evil, often has a famil iar and attractive face. In its presence, one often finds oneself thinking, 'There but for the grace of God and my own limitations …'

———— NINE ————

THE PURSUIT OF POWER

*[Mr. Rhodes's] life and his interests seem to be mapped out into squares;
and the man who is concerned with Square No. 6 must know
nothing of Square No. 7.*

HARRY CURREY, SECRETARY TO CECIL RHODES[1]

On April Fools' Day 1880, Rhodes, Rudd and four other partners floated the De Beers Mining Company Limited with a capital of £200,000; their stated aim was to regulate the production and marketing of diamonds.[2] Rhodes was 26 years old at the time, and prudently decided to let one of the older partners assume the mantle of company figurehead. Accordingly, Robert Graham, a solicitor, was appointed first chairman of De Beers, while Rhodes was content to accept the position of company secretary. A note of bathos was struck at the end of the historic inaugural meeting, when Rhodes had to request a cheque for £5 as an advance against his salary as secretary.[2]

No doubt, the partners had taken the name of the mine as a statement of their ultimate objective. For months previously, the six of them had been working independently and sometimes secretly to secure as many properties in the De Beers mine as they could lay their hands on. By the time the new company was formed, the partners owned 90 claims between them,[3] but were still a long way from their goal. Altogether, there were 622 registered claims in the De Beers mine.

The dream of amalgamation – of a single company controlling the entire output of the mines – was almost as old as the diggings themselves. As early as 1872, Frederick Boyle, a visitor from England, had grasped an obvious fact. The only sure way to keep the price of diamonds artificially high was to restrict production. This meant creating a monopoly.

> You cannot drown the market with an article only appertaining to the highest luxury ... without swift and sudden catastrophe. These things require the most delicate manipulation ... They need a hand to hold them back or loose them as occasion asks ... By royal monopoly alone, or by means of great and powerful companies can jewel digging be made a thriving industry.[4]

117

Richard Southey believed that the survival of the independent diggers overrode those considerations, but with his dismissal and the removal of restrictions on claim ownership there was an inexorable move towards amalgamation. The increasing complexity of deep-level mining hastened the process still further, but by 1880 there was a third factor.

Since the days of Professor Gregory, South African diamonds had received a bad press overseas. Not only was Kimberley regarded as a dangerously unstable place, but it was frequently suggested that the South African diamond was not the genuine article. By 1880, these myths had largely been dispelled. Banks were now more ready to give credit and digger syndicates were able to attract foreign investment by turning over their claims to joint stock companies.

As always, Rhodes was quick to sense the trend, but he was also very careful. De Beers had issued 2000 shares of £100 each. Only 100 were offered to the public. The rest were held by the partners. As things turned out, this was a wise decision.

Within months of the formation of the De Beers Mining Company, another group moved aggressively against them, and 'secured the key to the De Beers Mine'. The man who headed this rival consortium was F.S. Philipson-Stow, a prominent Kimberley lawyer. According to his account, 'We had succeeded in cutting off the firm of Rudd, Rhodes, Graham, Alderson and Dunmore from the East and West. Besides holding this last position strategically, our claims were among the richest.'[5]

Philipson-Stow was immediately approached by Rhodes. For some inexplicable reason, he capitulated to his weaker rival and effectively agreed to be taken over by the De Beers Mining Company. The methods Rhodes used to secure this victory have never been revealed.

Rhodes was now in the dominant position in the De Beers mine, but that did not put him ahead of the field. The Kimberley mine, where Herbert had bought their first three claims, was richer by far. In 1880, when the average value of a claim in the De Beers mine was £1333, Kimberley values were nearly three times higher at £3681.[6] The man in the dominant position on the Kimberley mine was Barney Barnato.

Barney's story is one of the great South African legends. Born Barnett Isaacs, he was the grandson of a rabbi and the son of a second-hand clothes dealer in London's East End. He was exactly one year older than Rhodes. They shared the same birthday, 5 July, but that was all they had in common.

Barney's education had taken him no further than the Jew's Free School in Bell Lane, Whitechapel, which he left shortly after his 13th birthday. Already 'a huxter in embryo'[7] – it is said that he used to 'trade among his

Barney Barnato.

schoolfellows in liquorice, lace, toffee, brass buttons and a variety of beer-bottle labels salvaged from refuse bins at Truman's brewery[7] – Barney soon graduated to the streets, where he hawked everything from birdseed to headache powder from the back of a barrow. He was irrepressibly cheerful, with a sharp cockney wit. He was also intelligent and shrewd and could play the part of helpless innocent to great effect.

Barney had 'a funny brussels sprout of a nose ... but as good a pair of grey-blue eyes as ever flashed through a pair of glasses.'[8] According to one biographer, his 'butter-yellow hair ... and chubby pink cheeks seemed to hint at some remote Baltic ancestor …'[7] Since childhood, he had been afflicted with poor eyesight. He was always small for his age, never growing to be over five foot three inches (1.6 metres), but was solidly built and exceptionally strong.

Barney had an elder brother and sister, Harry and Kate. Their father, Isaac Isaacs, taught his boys how to use their fists, and imparted one piece of advice that Barney would never forget: 'If you have to fight, always get in the first blow.'

Shortly after Harry was taken on as a barman in the King of Prussia, a spit-and-sawdust gin palace[7] owned by Kate's husband, Joel Joel, Barney joined the family firm as a bouncer and tapster, whose job it was to heave barrels up from the cellar. It was at the King of Prussia that the brothers came to know the performers from the Cambridge Music Hall, where Barney soon made himself popular as an unpaid scene-shifter. Harry was more ambitious, and honed his skills as an amateur conjurer until he was considered good enough to perform publicly. Anxious to expand his repertoire, he worked up a mock-tipsy juggling act which required a stooge, and so it was that Barney began to appear at his brother's side, wearing a false moustache and a pair of baggy pantaloons.

Harry regarded himself as the main attraction and hogged both the act and the applause, but one night a kindly stage-manager signalled to the wings and called out, 'and Barney, too!'. The brothers liked the sound of that. 'Barneytoo' had a certain ring to it and was altogether more exotic and professional than 'Isaacs' for a juggling comedy act. Within a few weeks, 'Barnato Brothers' had begun to appear in small print near the bottom of music-hall bills.

The boys' cousin and sparring partner, David Harris, was the first member of the family to be touched by diamond fever. He left for South Africa early in 1871, and although he was no success at the diggings, sent glowing reports in his letters home. Harry was easily persuaded, and left for South Africa in September 1872. Barney hesitated until his cousin made a dazzling reappearance in London. David Harris had had an astonishing stroke of luck. Just as he was beginning to lose heart at the diggings, he had strayed into a bar which was offering free whisky, snacks and cigars to anyone willing to try his luck at the tables. In a single incredible hour, David Harris scooped £1400 at the roulette table. He took the next boat home. That was enough for Barney.

Barney gave up smoking and took any odd job he could find until he had saved enough for his passage and expenses. Joel Joel then persuaded him to part with most of his cash, so that the two of them could go halves on 40 boxes of 'Finest Quality Coronas', which his brother-in-law was sure would yield a handsome profit at the diggings.

On 5 July 1873, Barney's 21st birthday, the *Anglian* steamed out of Southampton on her maiden voyage. Barney was travelling steerage. Some time during the voyage he passed another ship, heading north. On board and travelling first class from Cape Town to Southampton was Cecil Rhodes. Ahead of him was that tragic first term at Oxford, when he would have to cope with the loss of his mother and read his own death sentence in a doctor's casebook.

Within a week of Barney's arrival in Cape Town, he left for Kimberley. He could not afford a seat on a waggon, but for £5 arranged to have his luggage transported, while he followed on foot. It was a 700-mile (1125-kilometre) walk.

When Barney arrived in Kimberley, Harry's theatrical career was in decline and he had been reduced to staging sparring exhibitions with an ex-policeman in the market square.[9] Barney's next disappointment was to discover that Joel Joel's cigars were unlikely to become the basis of a fortune. Indeed, one angry buyer swore that the 'Finest Quality Coronas' were made of gunpowder and demanded his money back. Undaunted, Barney went to work as a labourer, hauling sacks of produce and making deliveries on behalf of the Boer farmers who came daily to the market square in their waggons. After enjoying a brief success as a clown, performing for a visiting circus, he felt ready to enter the diamond business. He had scraped together enough money to pay for a licence and the tools of the *kopje-walloper's* trade – a bag, a set of scales and a magnifying glass.

Kopje-wallopers (literally, hill-bashers) were the lowest form of diamond-buyers. Too poor to rent an office of their own, they wandered the diggings in search of sellers on the spot and could only afford to buy the smaller, cheaper stones. It was a desperately hard way of earning a living, as Barney's first partner, Louis Cohen, graphically described: 'You can hardly realise what it is, as wet with perspiration one minute, and the pores of your skin clogged with deadly dust the next, you toil from mound to mound under the glaring sun. And this to a man with rather defective sight.'[10]

Cohen was a recent immigrant from Liverpool, and as gullible and inexperienced as Barney when the two of them first came together, but they were quick to learn from early mistakes. Before long, they could afford the guinea-a-day rent for an 'office' – a tin shanty at the edge of the Dutoitspan mine, where they worked, slept and ate.

According to Cohen, Barney's big break came when another *kopje-walloper* advertised that he was leaving the diggings and offering his entire stock, which included his pony, for £27 10s. Barney had been watching this individual, and noticed that he enjoyed 'splendid connections' with the Boer diggers.

> The Boers were always the best to buy from, because, to be plain, they were the most ignorant, and consequently the simplest to trade with. But, strange as it may seem, it was a difficult job to find among the wilderness of tents, huts and debris heaps the domiciles of the more prosperous Boers.[11]

Barney had noticed that this particular buyer rode with a loose rein, and left it to the pony to find its own way among his Boer contacts. Barney bought the pony. It was an inspired move. 'When the man was parting with the animal, he was virtually selling the list of people with whom he traded. The pony was introduction enough to get into conversation with the Boers, and we made much money out of Barney's inspiration.'[11]

Before long, the partnership was amicably dissolved, but Barney went from strength to strength. 'Sharp competition honed his bargaining instincts, but he was also blessed with a natural jollity which bubbled within him and brimmed over. The Dutch farmers, the diggers and even his fellow-hucksters all reacted to his sparkle.'[12]

In the meantime, Harry had been working in a relatively lowly capacity for an established firm of diamond-buyers. At Barney's suggestion, he quit his job and the two brothers went into partnership. Early in 1875, 'Barnato Brothers, Dealers in Diamonds and Brokers in Mining Property' were open for business.

The brothers not only held fast during a difficult year, but added to their capital. Although they owned an office of sorts, Barney never lost his *kopje-walloper* instincts, and continued working his way around the claims. He developed a loyal clientele, who preferred the ebullient cockney to the frosty Germans working for most of the established firms in town. Barney often picked up bargains but, more importantly, 'he developed an up-to-date, almost hour by hour, intelligence service about the output in each sector until he knew every twist and turn of the reef like his own hand'.[13] He was soon convinced that the richest claims were at the centre of the mine and, like Rhodes, believed that diamonds would continue to be found at greater and greater depths.

In the early months of 1876, when values were still uncertain, Harry heard a rumour that two brothers named Kerr were anxious to sell their four adjoining claims in the central sector of the Kimberley mine. After much haggling, a price of £3000 was agreed, which all but emptied the Barnato coffers.

The claims were soon yielding £2000 a week. By the end of their first year the brothers had extracted £90,000 worth of diamonds, making them among the richest men in the fields. Harry was tempted to sell while the going was good, but Barney overruled him. He was equally insistent that they should not deal with the German and Dutch brokers who were now offering to send their output to Europe. The Barnatos would mine *and* sell their own diamonds, building up sufficient capital reserves to be in a position to buy every claim that became available.

Diggers cast envious eyes at the Barnatos. It was often hinted that they had bought the Kerr claims from IDB proceeds, and were now using them as a cover to move stolen diamonds on to the market. The gossip intensified when Harry took over the London Hotel, a favourite rendezvous for 'illicits'. Barney, who was always sensitive to criticism, reacted angrily. 'Every form of slander and insinuation was heaped upon me,' he would say of those early years. 'Men of the diamond fields, you can never know the bitterness they caused me.'

No charges were ever brought against the Barnatos, and rumour, however hurtful, was powerless to stop them. Before Rhodes's De Beers Mining Company existed, the brothers had already amalgamated with former rivals in the Kimberley mine and created the powerful Barnato Mining Company. While Rhodes and his partners were relishing their victory over Philipson-Stow, the Barnatos were in London raising capital to finance their next move. They returned to Kimberley at the end of 1880, bringing two of their nephews, Isaac and Solly Joel, with them. A third nephew, Wolf Joel, had come out to South Africa earlier and was already an experienced diamond-buyer. Barnato's was going to be a family concern.

In March 1881, the brothers floated four new companies, and each was a remarkable success.

Apart from the Barnatos, there were at least six other syndicates in a position to block any moves Rhodes might try to make to capture the dominant position in the diamond industry. Amalgamation was still a very distant prospect. Faced with the certainty of a long and bitter struggle, Rhodes made a move which, to a superficial observer, must have seemed like a sideways step. He decided to stand for election to the Cape Parliament.

By October 1880, the long dispute over the legal status of the diamond territory was finally 'resolved' by an act passed in the Cape Parliament. The arguments on which Britain had based her original claim to the territory were now conveniently forgotten, and the land of the Griqua people was formally handed over to Cape Colony. Two new parliamentary constituencies – Kimberley and Barkly West – were created, each to be represented by two Members of Parliament.

J.B. Robinson, 'the Buccaneer', immediately put his name forward as a candidate for Kimberley. His connection with diamonds went back to the days of the river diggings. He had served on many of the important digger committees since the early 1870s and had an inflated view of himself as Kimberley's leading citizen.

Robinson was feared and respected, but never liked. Quarrelsome, mean, litigious and insanely jealous, he could be terrifying when provoked, as Louis Cohen discovered when he dared to include this description in his book, *Reminiscences of Kimberley*:

> Robinson was never a popular man with anybody in Kimberley; he had no personality, no magnetism, but resembled a mortal who had a tombstone in his soul ... Sour-visaged and unsympathetic, he looked as yellow as a bad apple, and green with spleen like a leek ... As for charity, nobody ever connected his name with that.[14]

Robinson brought a libel action against Cohen and, after wringing the then colossal sum of £2800 out of him, continued to pursue him through the courts on a private charge of perjury. He also succeeded in getting Cohen's book banned.

In 1882, Robinson's Standard Company was a serious rival to De Beers, and throughout Rhodes's career 'the Buccaneer' never lost an opportunity to try to thwart his younger opponent. Very wisely, Rhodes decided not to get involved in the fight for the Kimberley seat and put his name forward as a candidate for Barkly West, the original centre of the river diggings. As this activity declined, Barkly West had reverted to its former status as a rural community of Griquas and Boer stock farmers.

Rhodes campaigned with enthusiasm and loved to remind his Boer constituents that his own ancestors were also 'keepers of cows'. According to one account, he also used the services of his 'friends' to drum up support.[15]

Rhodes's campaigning efforts proved unnecessary. For reasons never explained, a third candidate dropped out of the race,[16] leaving the field open to Rhodes and Francis Orpen, the local surveyor-general. Both were returned unopposed.

It was one of the marks of Rhodes's character, a sign of the loyalty he could inspire, that the Boers of Barkly West would continue to return him, despite Raid and war, for the rest of his days.

Rhodes entered the Cape Parliament as the junior Member for Barkly West on 7 April 1881. Black clothing was the form among MPs, but Rhodes breezed into the House dressed in his Oxford tweeds. 'I think I can legislate in them as well as in sable clothing,' he said. In Sarah Gertrude Millin's

The members for Barkly West – Francis Orpen and Cecil Rhodes (1881).

words, 'Rhodes's Oxford tweeds really meant a new way of life in the governing of South Africa ... South Africa was soon to know it.'[17]

Rhodes liked to give his English supporters the impression that his decision to enter parliament was motivated by a pure desire to secure the hinterland of Africa for the British Empire. If one attempts to apply that standard, his political career is a bewildering series of tactical switches and reverses. However, if one accepts the view of some contemporary historians that Rhodes's first loyalties were always to his commercial and business interests,[18] the lines become much clearer.

Rhodes appreciated that all decisions made in the Cape Parliament – whether over 'native' policy, transport policy, colonial policy, external or internal relations between English and Afrikaner – affected the mining industry, and he was tired of pleading with the likes of Merriman for their support in an Assembly that seemed incapable of taking the diamond industry seriously. One of his many causes of frustration was Parliament's failure to authorize the extension of the railway line to Kimberley, while allowing resources to be wasted on 'branch lines to farmers' to attract country votes. It was high time that Rhodes grasped the levers of power himself.

There was another important consideration for 27-year-old Cecil Rhodes. He was now no longer content to hide behind frontmen like Robert Graham. He needed recognition in his own right. Parliament could give him status and authority so that when the time came, as it most surely would, Kimberley would look to him for leadership and guidance as the diamond industry moved towards a monopoly.

Rhodes received mixed reviews during his first months as an MP. One commentator wrote:

> He is an exceeding nervous speaker; there is a twitching about his hands, and he has a somewhat ungainly way of turning his body about… He is in a continued state of restlessness, whether sitting in his seat or standing on his legs. He is never still from the time he enters the House, until he leaves it.[19]

Another observer remembered Rhodes as 'a fine ruddy Englishman, with no graces of oratory … He was at times boyish to the last, and had a trick of sitting on his hands and laughing boisterously when amused.'[19] Although finding Rhodes 'nervous in speech and blundering in manner', the same commentator went on to say that Rhodes 'soon emerged as the most effective speaker in the House', adding ominously, 'but he never gave the House in those days an inkling of his great plans. No doubt he feared to alarm both parties.'[19]

The *Cape Times* complained of Rhodes's disregard for parliamentary etiquette – he would frequently refer to the other members by name, instead of by constituency – but put this down to his 'youth and inexperience'.[20] The *Cape Argus* took Rhodes more seriously. While noting his tendency to 'jump up and down in his seat with delight at the discomforture of a troublesome opponent', the paper went on to prophesy that Rhodes would soon emerge as 'the undisputed leader of the Diamond Fields Party'.[21]

Saul Solomon, the Cape Parliament's boldest liberal and philanthropist, was in no doubt. 'Watch that man,' he said when Rhodes first took his seat. 'He is the future man of South Africa and possibly of the world.'[22]

As soon as he was established in Cape Town, Rhodes began to secure contacts and influence both inside and outside the House. Sir Richard Southey and J.B. Currey made him welcome but they were both retired and of limited use. More important to Rhodes at the time was his old

Oxford chum, Frank Newton, secretary to Sir Hercules Robinson, High Commissioner* and Governor of the Cape. Robinson would soon become a valuable ally.

Operating in great secrecy and through an intermediary, Rhodes paid £6000 to buy a controlling interest in the *Cape Argus*, the leading newspaper in the colony. For the first, and certainly not the last time, he was acting on his belief that 'the press rules the minds of men'.[23]

Inside Parliament, he assessed the situation with a cold, clear eye. The prime minister at the time was Gordon Sprigg, who headed a cabinet of seven. There were 72 MPs, with English speakers in the majority but not organized on formal party lines. Rhodes was unimpressed:

> The 'English' party in the house was hopelessly divided and individually inca-
> pable. And it had no policy beyond that of keeping office. On the other side
> was a compact body of nominees of what afterwards came to be called the
> Afrikander Bond, who acted all together at the dictation of Hofmeyr.
> Hofmeyr was, without doubt, the most capable politician in South Africa.[24]

This 'compact' and disciplined body was certainly worth courting, even though their objectives were worlds away from those that Rhodes had set down in his Confession of Faith.

The Afrikander Bond had been formed two years before Rhodes entered parliament, with the stated aim of preventing 'the sacrifice of Africa's inter-est to England or those of the Farmer to the Merchant'.[25] The party's founder, the Rev. S.J. du Toit, was aggressively anti-British and republican. He recruited from the ranks of 'poor white' Afrikaners, who attributed their hardships to English discrimination, and he established his pan-Afrikaner credentials by setting up branches in the Boer republics of the Transvaal and the Orange Free State. Du Toit represented a political tradition that went back to the disaffected Trek Boers of the eighteenth and early nineteenth centuries and would continue forward to the Nationalist Party of Malan, Strijdom, Verwoerd, Vorster and P.W. Botha.

By the time Rhodes entered the Cape Parliament, the leadership of the Bond had been captured and transformed by J.J. Hofmeyr, who represented the more patrician interests of Afrikaner merchants and commercial farmers. Merriman disliked the man for his underground tactics, giving him the nick-name of 'the Mole – an industrious little animal … You never see him at work, but every now and then a little mound of earth, thrown up here or there, will testify to his activities.'[26]

*The title of High Commissioner tended to be used more frequently after the Colony was granted responsible government in 1872.

This was someone Rhodes could do business with.

Rhodes's maiden speech was on the subject of guns. In April 1880, colonial troops were involved in a costly attempt to disarm the Sothos, who, after decades of conflict with Zulu, Boer and Britain, were refusing to give up the protection of their weapons without a struggle.

The Sotho nation was the creation of a remarkable chief, Moshesh, who had successfully united a collection of warring tribes and reigned over them from 1815 to 1870. From the late 1850s, his people had been driven further and further into their mountain strongholds by the Boers. Moshesh was only able to put an end to the threat by appealing for British protection, which was granted in 1869. Three years later, and without consulting the Sothos, Disraeli handed the Sotho homeland (Basutoland) to Cape Colony. The Sothos were now subject to Cape laws, including an Act of 1877 forbidding Cape Africans to own guns.

Rhodes's position was straightforward. He was opposed to any attempts to disarm the Sothos, who provided a significant proportion of the labour force in the mines. Their main purpose in being there was to earn the money to buy guns. If that incentive were removed, there were few other reasons why a tribal African would wish to sell his labour for cash.

Apart from the labour issue, Basutoland was an important source of Kimberley's wood and grain. Hostilities were disrupting supplies and forcing up prices.[18] That, too, was bad for the mining industry.

Troops had been sent to Basutoland by Sprigg's government, but in the face of strong opposition from the House. MPs were not concerned with the issues that were of primary importance to Rhodes, but objected to the cost of the campaign, which was placing a huge financial burden on the colony.

Rhodes planned his strategy carefully. In his maiden speech, he declared his opposition to the policy of disarmament, but in terms that were relatively mild and excited little comment.[27] He then approached Sprigg privately and threatened to deliver the four votes of the 'Diamond Fields Party' to the opposition unless he got his railway extension to Kimberley.[28] Sprigg refused to horse-trade and on 25 April Rhodes delivered a devastating attack against the government's disarmament policy. He made no reference in the speech to his primary concerns, but concentrated instead on the issue that mattered most to the House – the cost of the campaign:

> Are we a great and independent South Africa? No, we are only the population of a third-rate English city, spread over a great country ... Can we afford to go on spending an amount on defence which is equivalent to England spending 200 millions a year?[29]

Rhodes could not deliver Robinson, but three votes were enough to wipe out the government's slender majority and Sprigg was forced to resign. He was succeeded by Thomas Scanlen, a quiet and dependable country lawyer, who was virtually unknown outside the House.

At the end of the parliamentary session, the four members of the 'Diamond Fields Party' were invited to a banquet hosted by the mayor of Kimberley. The dinner was intended to be a celebration of their return, but Robinson roused the passions of the guests by accusing Rhodes of bringing down the government he was elected to support. His speech was so inflammatory that Rhodes was reported to have been 'received with cries of "rat" and mingled cheers and hisses'[30] when he stood up to reply. There is no record of the speech he gave, so we can only guess how he was able to convey the intricacies of his strategy to his critics. We do know, though, that he won them over to his side.

Having secured his first political victory, Rhodes left for England to keep his last term at Oxford and take his degree. When he returned to South Africa in January 1881, the Basutoland question was still unresolved.

In his crucial speech to Parliament, Rhodes had told his fellow MPs they should cut the knot and hand the territory back to Britain: 'I much prefer that native races outside our border should be subject to Imperial rule.'[29]

Sprigg's successor Scanlen was opposed to the suggestion, and hostilities continued while he pursued a vague policy 'to bring about the restoration of law and order'.[20] Finally, General Charles Gordon offered his services as mediator.

Gordon was a popular Victorian hero who was believed to have a mystical affinity with 'backward people'. He had virtually eradicated slavery in the Sudan during his time as governor-general, and he had led the Imperial Chinese forces to victory against the Taipeng rebels. In 1882, he was 'between missions of glory and excitement'.[31]

In a letter to Scanlen, Rhodes suggested that Gordon should be assisted in his task by various Cape luminaries with a knowledge of Sotho affairs. Although he did not say so in as many words, he strongly hinted that he would like to be included in this commission.[32] Scanlen agreed on both points.

Gordon's little band had a formidable task ahead of them in Basutoland. Not only were they required to bring an end to hostilities by persuasion, they also had to deal with the delicate question of compensation for those Sothos who had suffered losses for collaborating with the colonial authorities; a group quaintly know as 'the loyal Basutos'.

The whole exercise ended in failure. After agreeing the main points of a settlement with the Sothos, Gordon fell out with the Cape Government and resigned. In the end, the only practical solution was the one that Rhodes had originally proposed in his speech to the Cape Parliament, and in 1884 the territory became a British protectorate once again. The Sothos kept their guns.

The months Rhodes had spent in Basutoland were not wasted. He had had time to traverse the country, valuing trees for export to Kimberley.[18] He had also formed a close relationship with General Gordon. Although these two remarkable Victorians were separated by 20 years and held very different views, Gordon was so impressed with Rhodes that he 'urged the young man to throw in his lot with him'.

> Rhodes, however, had already thought out his life and was not to be moved. 'There are very few men in the world,' added Gordon, 'to whom I would have made such an offer, but of course you *will* have your way. I never met a man so strong for his opinion; you think your views are always right.'[33]

A favourite Rhodes story is set in this time. On one of their many walks together, Gordon told Rhodes that the Chinese Government had offered him a roomful of gold as a reward for his services. The principled Gordon had refused. Rhodes's famous reply was: 'I'd have taken it, and as many roomfuls as they offered me. What is the use of having ideas for the benefit of mankind if you haven't the money to carry them out?'[34]

That story was often repeated by Rhodes. It gave the interpretation to his career that he wanted – the accumulation of wealth, but only in the service of a great cause. There were no witnesses to the conversation, and readers must make of it what they will.

Two and a half years later, General Gordon died a hero's death in Khartoum. When Rhodes heard the news, he said, 'I am sorry I was not with him'.

After his successful intervention over the issue of Sotho guns, Rhodes performed another great service for the mining industry. In March 1882, he helped to steer the Diamond Trades Act through the House.

It was a time when the industry was again in serious trouble. The great share boom of 1880 had encouraged unscrupulous operators to play the market. Some of them had attracted investors by salting worthless claims with diamonds. Others had floated companies without owning any claims at all. By the middle of 1881, the banks had become nervous and were refusing to make any more advances *on scrip* for mining companies. The rush for shares was immediately thrown into reverse. By the end of the year most of the dubious companies had been wiped out, while the share values of the reputable concerns were in sharp decline.

As if that were not enough, Kimberley experienced one of its worst storms early the following year. Mine buildings were flattened and machinery destroyed. The storm was followed by a series of disastrous landfalls that brought all work at the centre of the Kimberley mine to a standstill.[35]

Just has it had done 10 years earlier, financial crisis brought the issue of IDB back on the boil. Once again, it was the African labourer who would suffer most in consequence.

There is no question but that IDB was a genuine menace. It is also true that labourers working in the claims were among the first in the production process with the opportunity to steal diamonds. However, IDB depended on a whole network of illicit buyers, smugglers and sellers, and this network was in white hands.

Barney Barnato's first partner, Louis Cohen, had no doubts who the real culprits were. In his highly entertaining *Reminiscences of Kimberley*, Cohen devoted pages to some of the more celebrated IDB scams, and his cast of characters was exclusively white. He also accused the established diamond-buyers and mine-owners of gross hypocrisy.

> Nobody bowed more obsequiously than the important buyer as a notorious I.D.B. entered his office … Many of the claimholders … commenced their diamond field life as professors of the same art … and when they themselves became mine-holders, then they discovered, to their intense horror and indignation, the heinousness of a crime which they had practised themselves so successfully … And yet these persons, on hearing of some starving outcast's downfall would turn up the whites of their hypocritical eyes and ejaculate: 'Serve the scoundrel right.'[36]

The colourful Louis Cohen was certainly not the most reliable of historians, but neither was he alone in suggesting that the diamond laws were treated with disrespect by the citizens of Kimberley. The mine-owners themselves were sufficiently aware of the problem to demand the abolition of the jury system in IDB cases. Those Kimberley men of property who qualified for jury service could not be relied upon to convict.

Alfred Aylward and his followers had used the issue of IDB to justify the disqualification of black claim-owners and the strict control of black labourers. Ten years later, the black claim-owner was a vanished species, but the issue of control was more important than ever. With vast amounts of capital now tied up in equipment necessary for deep-level mining, stoppages could be ruinous. There had to be a constant and reliable supply of black labour to sustain production, but as the mine-owners discovered to their cost, their hold over the labour force was tenuous. Their attempts to club together and force down

African wages during the 1881 crisis came to nothing. Black workers either deserted the mines or moved over to companies outside the cartel.[37]

The most effective way of dealing with this problem was to impose a compound system, whereby Africans could be contacted for fixed periods and confined to closed compounds linked to the mines by tunnels or fenced walkways. A crude prototype had been built as far back as 1875,[38] but now the mine-owners wanted legal sanction to perfect the system.

In March 1882, a brief truce was declared between Rhodes and J.B. Robinson, who were both determined to push the Diamond Trade Act through Parliament. This draconian bill was presented to the House as an essential measure to save the industry from catastrophe. Nearly all the arguments turned on the IDB menace, with clause after clause designed to improve security and discourage the illegal trade. Workers would be strip-searched daily as they left the mines. Diamond thieves would be flogged and the jury system abolished in IDB trials.

Rhodes and Robinson fought their bill through Parliament clause by clause. The only proposal that was rejected outright was one that retained flogging as a punishment for buyers as well as thieves. A later provision authorizing strip-searching of white mineworkers was hastily abandoned after a series of disastrous strikes in Kimberley.

From photographs and contemporary accounts[39] we gain a clear impression of the 'native' compound, as perfected by Rhodes's De Beers Mining Company. Over 11,000 African labourers were housed 20–25 to a room in corrugated-iron barracks, set out in a square and surrounded by a 12-foot fence (3.6-metre), which was patrolled by company police with dogs. The whole area was roofed over by double-meshed wire netting and guard towers with searchlights were placed at each corner. At the centre of the compound there was a cook-house, consisting of four strips of tin roofing supported by wooden posts. A concrete pool was provided for communal bathing.

When the workers returned to the compound at the end of their shifts, they had to discard the sacks they wore in the mine and file naked into a tin shed, where they were subjected to a full body search:

> [The guards] ran fingers through their woolly hair, pressed their flat nostrils, felt inside their mouths, under their tongues, in the ears, and up their rectums. Then the native had to lift his arms, stretch apart his fingers, and 'jigger' (jump), so that any diamonds concealed by muscular contraction would drop on the floor.[40]

At the end of their terms of contract, the workers were shut in a 'detention house' where they remained 'in a perfectly nude condition, save for a pair of

De Beers compound (1896).

fingerless leathern gloves, which were padlocked to their hands, for some ten days.'[39] Their excrement was collected and examined daily.

In spite of the emphasis on theft prevention, the underlying importance of the Diamond Trades Act was its provision of the first systematic disciplining of a large black labour force, enforced by law. It also offered a model for future industrial and agricultural employment. Closed compounds, pass laws, fixed periods of contract, strict disciplines and controls would become common features of an economy increasingly dependent on black labour as it expanded and diversified.

Rhodes's mining interests had moved him a long way from his original instincts and much closer to the position that Afrikaners had taken towards blacks. It now suited his larger ambitions to close that gap entirely. By the early 1880s, Rhodes was already looking beyond his immediate ambitions in Kimberley to a future that would depended on close co-operation between Englishman and Afrikaner. And if the blacks had to pay the price for white unity, that was a small consideration compared to the great issues that were now turning in Rhodes's mind.

TEN

THE RACE FOR AFRICA

'Africa is still lying ready for us. It is our duty to take it.'

CECIL RHODES[1]

It was said that Rhodes's northern journey with his brother Herbert first excited his interest in the African interior.[2] Whether this is true or not, Rhodes would have heard stories of the lands between the Zambesi and the Limpopo from the missionaries, hunters and traders who were continually passing through Kimberley in the 1870s. These travellers described sights previously unseen in sub-Saharan Africa – groves of lemons and pomegranates, ancient mines and an abandoned city, magnificently designed and built entirely in stone. For centuries, the Arabs and Portuguese had obtained gold from this territory and in the 1860s, Carl Mauch, a young German schoolmaster-turned-explorer, found several specimens of gold-bearing reef while travelling through the country with the hunter Henry Hartley.

Those who were romantically inclined believed that this land was once the kingdom of Ophir, the fabled site of King Solomon's mines, the source of the queen of Sheba's riches. It was situated at the southern tip of a high fertile plateau, stretching cool to the equator, cool to the Sudan: 'a country', to use Rhodes's own words, 'for white men and for their families'.[3]

There were other considerations that were just as important to Rhodes as his power was growing in Kimberley. The territory to the north offered both the promise of gold and the threat of new diamond discoveries.[4] In the wrong hands, those diamonds could destroy Kimberley. There was also the perennial labour question. From the late 1870s, recruitment of Africans from the north had become increasingly important to the diamond industry.

It is clear that Rhodes had already set his sights on the African hinterland when he wrote his Confession of Faith. Indeed, at that time the only great 'untaken' lands in the world were in Africa. The timing of Rhodes's Confession was significant in another respect. The English, under Disraeli, were in the mood for expansion. Only two months before Rhodes had committed his great manifesto to paper, the imperial government had annexed the Transvaal and accepted financial responsibility for the bankrupt Boer republic. In 1877, Rhodes could believe that his cause and England's cause were one.

By 1880, the position was radically changed. Disraeli had been defeated and the Liberals, under Gladstone, were once more back in power. The new government had far less enthusiasm for empire-building and the financial responsibilities that went with it. There was ideological resistance as well. The spirit of Exeter Hall was still alive in the Liberal Party and among its friends.

The Transvaalers were the first to test Britain's will in those changing times. Three weeks before Rhodes took his seat in the Cape Parliament, Boer commandos routed a small English force at Majuba and killed the general in command. Britain quickly made peace, restoring self-government to the Transvaal and limiting its control to 'native and frontier policy'.

Rhodes was disgusted with the compromise. To make matters worse, Britain was revealing her weakness and lack of resolve at the very time when her European rivals were becoming increasingly active on the continent. France was beginning to push out her colonial frontiers in north Africa and along the west coast. The Belgians, led by the explorer Stanley, were in the Congo. Portugal was awakening from four centuries of slumber and claiming vast territories in the southeast and the southwest. The Italians already had their eyes on the Red Sea coast and, most serious of all, German traders were busy in East Africa and the coastal territory bordering the northwestern Cape.

Despairing of Britain's commitment, Rhodes now calculated that the backing he needed would have to come from the Cape. To achieve this, he must unite the white colonists behind him. Once he had secured the trust of the Cape Afrikaners he could then move on to form alliances with the Transvaal and Free State Boers. In time, he would create a federation of South African states, strong enough and powerful enough to support his ambitions in the north. The 'native question', which had been the prime cause of the rift between Englishman and Afrikaner since the first British administration, must no longer be allowed to stand between them.

Just as the elements were beginning to come together, Rhodes's 'grand design' was threatened by developments in Bechuanaland, the vast territory to the north of Kimberley.* Most of that country was desert, but on Bechuanaland's eastern border, where it met the Transvaal, there was a strip of comparatively fertile land known as the English or missionary road to the north. Rhodes had travelled the road with Herbert and was acutely aware of its importance to his future plans. The Transvaal Boers also had their eyes on the territory, but were restrained by the terms of their recent treaty with

---

*The territory was subsequently divided (see p. 145). Today the southern sector is part of South Africa. The northern sector is the nation of Botswana.

Britain. However, late in 1881, they were given a sudden opportunity. War broke out between two sets of minor chieftains to whom this land belonged. One faction appealed to the Cape and Britain for support, and were largely ignored. The other side appealed to the Boers, who were only too keen to enter the fray. They had no interest in 'kaffir' quarrels, only in the land they could claim as a reward from their black 'allies' or as punishment from their black 'foes'. To relieve their government of any legal difficulties with Britain, hundreds of Boers renounced their rights as Transvaal citizens and moved into Bechuanaland. Their declared intention was to carve out two new Boer republics, which were given the names of Stellaland and Goshen before they had even been established.

Rhodes responded immediately. From his perspective, there was only one possible solution. He must persuade the Cape Parliament to claim the territory for the colony, and he must obtain all-party support. Any actions taken in defiance of the Bond would destroy his carefully laid plans for white reconciliation. It was essential for Rhodes to carry Hofmeyr with him.

In July 1882, Rhodes made his first appeal to the Cape Parliament. He warned the House that 'Boer filibusters' were preparing to create two new republics, and stressed the financial losses to the colony if the Cape's trade to the interior were blocked. He also issued dire warnings about the risks of cattle raids into the colony should the 'filibusters' be allowed to settle along the Cape's northern border.[5] For once, the appeals to self-interest failed. Ties of blood were stronger, and Hofmeyr's Bondsmen refused to countenance any action against their fellow Boers. The English-speaking MPs were confused. The previous year, Rhodes had denounced Cape involvement in Basutoland in scathing terms. Why was he now reversing his policy, and demanding intervention somewhere else?

At this early stage of his parliamentary career, Rhodes's colleagues can be forgiven for failing to grasp the underlying logic behind the apparent twists and turns. Basutoland was of no strategic importance to Rhodes, nor did it hold out any promise of mineral wealth. He had said so in as many words: 'It is not as if white colonists would go there … The land would simply be peopled with native races.'[6] As long as Basutoland continued to supply Kimberley with labour, wood and grain, Rhodes was happy to leave it alone. But his 'Suez Canal to the North' was another matter.

Rhodes was now faced with a number of dangerous possibilities. If his fellow MPs continued to be apathetic, two new Boer republics would certainly be established across the road to the north. Worse, the Transvaalers might then persuade an irresolute British Government to lift the restrictions imposed on their borders and permit them to unite with these new states.

There *was* a third possibility. Rhodes might be able to prevail upon the imperial government to expel the 'filibusters' by force; a course that was also fraught with danger. The Exeter Hall faction now had a strong influence at Westminster. Any troops sent with the approval of Gladstone and his colonial secretary, Lord Derby, might be under orders to restore the territory to the blacks. If Rhodes was thought to have initiated that action, the Cape Afrikaners – never mind the Transvaalers – would not forgive him.

Rhodes's approach to the crisis was remarkable. Indeed, if we only had this one episode from which to judge his methods, it would be sufficient.

Rhodes persuaded Prime Minister Scanlen to send him north. For six weeks he moved backwards and forwards across the disputed territory, dealing with Africans and Boers. He persuaded Mankurwane, the principal pro-British chief, to accept the protection of the Cape. At the same time, he promised the Boer 'filibusters' legal title to the farms they had carved out of Mankurwane's lands. On this occasion, self-interest did prevail, and the 'freebooters' assured Rhodes that if he really could give them the security of land titles backed by Cape law, they would accept annexation in preference to independence or Transvaal rule. They made it clear, though, that they would not come out openly in support of the Cape until he had proved he was able deliver on his promises.

Rhodes bombarded Scanlen with letters and telegrams. He needed the prime minister's authority. He needed Parliament's authority. If they could provide him with the necessary guarantees, he could deliver the territory to the Cape 'without costing you a sixpence',[6] and just as important to Rhodes, without ruffling Bond feathers.

Scanlen dithered. Rhodes sent more dispatches, hammering his points over and over again:

> Let me press upon you, you must act at once. The key to the position is to stop Lord Derby from giving the Transvaal the right to extend; secondly have the courage to take it for the Colony …
>
> If Transvaal get them, Cape Colony entirely shut out from interior trade, and our railways to Kimberley comparatively useless …
>
> Stellalanders want secured title, and though the Transvaal is at the bottom of the whole thing, they would join the Cape Colony to-morrow to get security …
>
> Don't part with an inch of territory to the Transvaal. They are bouncing. The interior road runs at the present moment on the edge of Transvaal boundary. Part with that, and you are driven into the desert.[7]

Not an inch... Not an inch... Not an inch...

The cautious Scanlen would not be stampeded. After six weeks in Bechuanaland, Rhodes returned to Cape Town and appealed directly to the House to give the Boer intruders the guarantees they had asked for. The speech he made was, in the main, tactful and conciliatory, especially towards the Transvaal. He used the occasion to outline his vision of a future 'United States of South Africa', where each member would be 'practically an independent republic ... with all the privileges of the tie with the Empire'. He concluded: 'Possibly there is not a very great divergence between myself and the honourable member for Stellenbosh [i.e. Hofmeyr], excepting always the question of the flag.'[8]

It was a brave attempt, but it did not win him the support of House, and as soon as it was clear to the Stellalanders that Rhodes was unable deliver on his promises, they declared their new, independent republic. The Goshenites were not far behind.

Rhodes tried again. It was one of his most important speeches. His 'grand design' was now crystal clear.

> You are dealing with a question upon the proper treatment of which depends the whole future of this Colony. I look upon this Bechuanaland territory as the Suez Canal of the trade of this country, the key of its road to the interior ... The question before us really is this: whether this Colony is to be confined to its present borders, or whether it is to become the dominant state in South Africa – whether, in fact, it is to spread its civilisation over the interior ...
>
> The people of Stellaland have offered to come under our rule ... Some honourable members may say that this is immorality ... 'The lands,' they may say, 'belong to the chief Mankoroane [Mankurwane]. How improper! How immoral! We must not do it.' Now I do not have these scruples. I believe that the natives are bound gradually to come under the control of the Europeans ...
>
> We want to get rid of the Imperial factor in this question, and to deal with it ourselves, jointly with the Transvaal ... If we do not settle this ourselves, we shall see it taken up in the House of Commons ...
>
> I respect the Transvaal, but as politicians we have to look to our position as the future paramount state in South Africa ... I claim the development of the interior as the birthright of this Colony ... and I have learned how great are the prospects of the territory beyond the Transvaal [i.e. the territory which is now Rhodesia].[9]

That final, significant comment was added by the Rev. John Verschoyle (nomme de plume, Vindex), the grey-eyed Ulsterman and muscular Christian who faithfully compiled all Rhodes's speeches. In passing, one might also note the contrast between Rhodes's tactful references to the Transvaal in his speeches to Parliament and the strident language he used in his communiques to Scanlen. That, too, was part of the strategy – be all things to all men if it serves your purpose.

For all his passion and clarity, Rhodes was still unable to win Parliament to his side. He now turned to Sir Hercules Robinson for support. The High Commissioner was already in Rhodes's web and compromised with De Beers shares, offered at very favourable rates.

In spite of the risks involved and his assurances to Parliament, Rhodes now pressed Sir Hercules to play the Imperial card. Scanlen concurred, and both High Commissioner and prime minister used what influence they had to try to persuade the British Government to intervene in Bechuanaland. It is doubtful whether they would have succeeded had not Fritz Lüderitz unwittingly come to their aid. In April 1893, the German trader raised his country's flag in Angra Pequena, a small harbour on the Atlantic coast 150 miles (241 kilometres) north of the Cape border. The British Government was finally jolted into action, and invited a Transvaal delegation to London in February 1884, in the hopes of reaching an amicable settlement over the Bechuanaland question. Heading this delegation was the Transvaal's new president, Johannes Paulus Kruger.

Lord Derby, the colonial secretary, offered important concessions, including the cancellation of Britain's power of veto over the Transvaal's 'native policy', thereby abandoning 750,000 Africans to a regime that forced them to carry passes and reside outside the towns, and even forbade them to walk on the pavements. Derby's offer was gratefully accepted by the Transvaalers. In return, Kruger agreed to a frontier line which left most of Stellaland and Goshen outside the Transvaal's boundaries. He also accepted the principle of British protection over the two territories.

While this happy compromise was being stitched together, the missionaries were hard at work, denouncing Boer treatment of Africans and gaining influence and support. Prominent among them was the Rev. John Mackenzie, 'a grizzled and intense Scottish missionary'[10] who had given years of his life to Mankurwane's people. Mackenzie was cut from the same cloth as Sir Richard Southey. Principled, uncompromising and tactless, he embodied the spirit of Exeter Hall.

In London, Mackenzie engaged the sympathies of the powerful Aborigines Protection Society, who bent Lord Derby's ear. Mackenzie was duly appointed deputy commissioner of Bechuanaland.

Rhodes was horrified and made his objections known. Mackenzie contemptuously dismissed his opponent as 'an inexperienced store-keeper at Kimberley'.[11]

The missionary went about his task with zeal. Before British protection had been ratified, he raised the Union Jack in Stellaland in the faces of the furious Boers. He informed the Goshenites that their farms were now the property of HM Government pending a proper investigation of titles. He signed an agreement with Mankurwane, guaranteeing the return of the chief's lands, and he demanded that a contingent of police should be sent to enforce the terms.

Rhodes's worst fears had now been realized, but once again Sir Hercules Robinson was able to come to his aid. Mackenzie was dismissed, and in his place Robinson appointed Cecil Rhodes. The news was received in London with disbelief. During a debate in the Commons, Lord Randolph Churchill made a scornful reference to 'some cypher' who had been appointed by the High Commissioner to take Mackenzie's place.[12] Of course, the true nature of the Rhodes–Robinson relationship was the exact reverse of the one His Lordship had suggested.

Rhodes left for Bechuanaland, where he found – in his own words – 'a pretty kettle of fish'. Stellaland was his first port of call. Unarmed and alone, he walked into the camp of their leader, van Niekerk, whom he had successfully dealt with two years earlier. The old patriarch was still receptive, but his lieutenant, an enormous backvelder called 'Groot' – 'big' Adrian de la Ray, would have none of it. 'Blood must flow', he roared. Rhodes smiled back. 'Give me my breakfast, and then we can talk about blood.' Rhodes stayed with de la Ray for a week, and became godfather to his grandchild.[13] In return for these favours, the Stellalanders were allowed to extend their borders well beyond the limits set in London and into African territory.

'I have never,' Rhodes would often say, 'met anyone in my life whom it was not as easy to deal with as to fight.'[14] Although much had changed in Rhodes's life, his power to win hearts and minds, his power to seduce, was as potent as ever, but now that he was in a position of power that great gift had its dangers, for Rhodes as well as for others.

One can only reach people in the way Rhodes was able to reach them by appearing to share their aims and values. Men like de la Ray are not given to conferring great honours on strangers, unless they believe they have encountered a kindred spirit. Yet there were so many others who fell under Rhodes's spell; men and women, with vastly different interests and backgrounds, who were all persuaded that they had found in Rhodes a champion as well as a kindred spirit. One day these contradictions would be exposed and inevitably there would be anger and a widespread sense of betrayal. So far, however, Rhodes's tactics were working, even though a few of his oldest and closest friends were beginning to worry. Among them was John Merriman, who wrote: 'His wretched compromise with the Stellalanders was a bitter pill to swallow and surprised all those who looked upon him as a strong Imperialist.'[15]

Confident of success after his dealings in Stellaland, Rhodes moved on to Goshen, where he was given a very different reception. Van Pittius, the leader of the Goshenites, had brought in volunteers from the Transvaal and, in Rhodes's presence, launched an attack on Montshiwa, one of the pro-British chiefs. Rhodes protested that this was in breach of the London convention, but his warnings were ignored. He returned to Stellaland, where he heard the news that Montshiwa had been forced to cede most of his lands to the Boers. Kruger then broke the London convention himself by proclaiming a protectorate over Montshiwa's territory. Du Toit, the founder of the Afrikander Bond, immediately raised the Transvaal flag in the enlarged republic of Goshen.

Rhodes returned to Cape Town at once. On his advice, Sir Hercules Robinson appealed to the British Government to clear the road to the north by force. Once again it was the Germans who gave Rhodes and Robinson an opportunity to press their case. On 24 April 1884, a year to the day after Fritz Lüderitz had raised the flag in Angra Pequena, Bismarck declared a German protectorate over the whole of southwest Africa (today's Namibia). Rhodes and Robinson warned London that Kruger would push his frontiers westwards until he had linked his territory with Germany's. Transvaal's dependence on Britain would be drastically reduced and, worst of all, the road to the north would be permanently barred.

The Rev. John Mackenzie had not been idle during this crisis, and for once the missionary and the Kimberley 'store-keeper' were working with a common aim. Mackenzie convened a mass meeting in Cape Town's Commercial Exchange. As he mounted the platform with the lord mayor at his side, 'there was a torrent of cheering, and the vast audience joined in singing "Rule Britannia".'[16] The spirit of Exeter Hall had briefly descended on Cape Town.

In that cheering audience was 18-year-old Frank Johnson, a recent immigrant from England. According to his own account, 'Mackenzie's eloquence moved me profoundly'.[16]

An Empire League was formed. Resolutions were passed, demanding that Her Majesty's Government should expel the Boer intruders by force and 'fulfil its obligation towards the native tribes in the Protectorate of Bechuanaland.'[16]

In November, the British Government agreed to send General Sir

Charles Warren to South Africa to head a British and colonial force. His orders were to clear the road to the north and assert British supremacy. London undertook to meet the costs of the campaign, which eventually totalled £1,500,000.

Frank Johnson quit his job with the Cape Fire Brigade and volunteered for service in the Bechuanaland Field Force. In a few years' time that same Frank Johnson would lead a very different body of men with a very different purpose.

Rhodes persuaded prime minister Scanlen to grant leave of absence to his handsome young secretary, Harry Currey.[17] There was a bond between Rhodes and this young man that went back to the old Kimberley days when Harry was just 10 years old and his parents had nursed Rhodes back to health.

In mid-December 1884, Warren left for the north with a force of 4000 men consisting of British garrison troops, colonial regulars and volunteers. Rhodes, Harry Currey and Frank Johnson rode with them. To Rhodes's astonishment 'and unspeakable chagrin',[18] the Rev. John Mackenzie came along as well.

From a military standpoint, Warren's expedition was an unqualified success. The Stellalanders offered no resistance, and the belligerent Goshen-

On Sir Charles Warren's expedition. Rhodes (far left). Standing (left to right) Col. Carrington, Rev. John Mackenzie, Warren. Front centre holding hat, Gordon Sprigg.

ites slipped away across the Transvaal border without firing a shot. Kruger had been humiliated and agreed to meet Warren at Fourteen Streams on the Vaal river.

By this time Warren and Rhodes had fallen out. Officially, Rhodes was still the Deputy High Commissioner of Bechuanaland, but his appeals for a tactful and conciliatory approach to the Boers were brushed aside. When Warren discovered that Rhodes had enlarged the frontiers of Stellaland, he repudiated the agreement. One night, when Rhodes and Harry Currey were dining with the general and his brother officers, everyone at the long table listened eagerly as Rhodes endeavoured to explain the importance of a diamond monopoly. Everyone, that is, except the general, who interrupted Rhodes with: 'I hate monopolies of all kinds, and if I had my way I would hang every monopolist.' With that, according to Currey, 'The discussion on the diamond industry was concluded.'[19]

A short while later, Warren was able to deliver a calculated insult to the Deputy High Commissioner. Rhodes had invited van Niekerk to a private supper. In the middle of the meal, Warren's men surrounded the hut and ordered van Niekerk outside. In Rhodes's presence, the 'President of Stellaland' was informed that he was under arrest on a murder charge.[19] A furious Rhodes returned to Cape Town and offered his resignation, but Sir Hercules prevailed upon him to go back and maintain a presence during the negotiations with Kruger.

Warren rode to this meeting with an escort of 200 dragoons. The president of the Transvaal was accompanied by a handful of shabby artillerymen. A point had been made.

Rhodes had repeatedly warned Warren that Mackenzie's presence would be an unnecessary provocation, but the general ignored the protests and rode towards Kruger with the missionary at his side. Rhodes tagged along behind, 'wearing a big slouch hat, the shabbiest and most ragged of coats and a very dirty pair of white flannel trousers, with old tennis shoes as footwear'.[20]

It was the first time Rhodes and Kruger had been brought together. They would cross each other's paths frequently and fatally in the coming years.

Rhodes was 31 years old in 1885, but in experience, achievement, habit, thought – and body too – he was already a middle-aged man. Kruger was 60. He was also a man of experience, but a very different experience. He had married at the age of 17, become a widower at 21, remarried twice and fathered 16 children. During his entire life, he had only had three months' schooling. He read the Bible and no other book. When he was 14 he had gone on his first commando raid and also shot his first lion. After that, he

Paul Kruger.

went to war again and again. He was a ferocious hunter, an expert horseman and a powerful swimmer and diver. Once, when he was hunting rhino, his rifle exploded in his hands. Calmly he sat down, pulled out his pocket knife and cut away what was left of his thumb. With his stubbornness, his tremendous voice and his ever-open Bible, Kruger was to become Rhodes's most formidable adversary.

As he now watched Rhodes, hovering at the edge of the meeting, sometimes contributing a conciliatory phrase, sometimes accusing, forever balancing, Kruger observed: 'That young man will cause me trouble if he doesn't leave politics alone and turn to something else.'[21]

Outgunned and shackled with a bankrupt treasury, Kruger was forced to accept Warren's terms. African rights would be confirmed over the northern sector of Bechuanaland, a vast area of 225,000 square miles (583,000 square kilometres), which would be known as the British Protectorate of Bechuanaland (today's Botswana). The southern sector would be declared a crown colony, with the stipulation that only settlers of English descent would be permitted to reside there. As a direct result of Rhodes's manoeuvres and stratagems more than 300,000 square miles (777,000 square kilometres) had been added to Britain's empire in Africa.

In the long term, the imperial solution benefited Rhodes. The Germans and the Transvaalers had been stopped in their tracks and the road to the north had been kept open. His friend and trustee Sir Sidney Shippard was appointed first resident commissioner of the Bechuanaland protectorate, and within 10 years Rhodes was able to prevail upon the imperial government to hand the crown colony over to the Cape.

In the short term, however, Rhodes had to perform some difficult footwork. To preserve his relations with the Cape Afrikaners, he had to disassociate himself from Warren, from missionaries and from 'the Imperial factor'.

In June 1885 he delivered a passionate speech to Parliament, attacking Mackenzie's 'Exeter Hall position'[22] and describing the missionary's appointment as 'one of the direst misfortunes that ever happened to this country'. He accused Warren of making a dishonourable settlement and, in his conclusion, cleverly suggested that his own pro-Boer policy was in the best interests of Britain.

> The proposed settlement of Bechuanaland is based on the exclusion of colonists of Dutch descent. I raise my voice in most solemn protest against such a course, and it is the duty of every Englishman in the House to record his solemn protest against it. In conclusion, I wish to say that the breach of solemn pledges and the introduction of race distinctions [by this he meant distinctions between Englishman and Afrikaner] must result in bringing calamity to the country, and if such a policy is pursued it will endanger the whole of our social relationships with colonists of Dutch descent, and endanger the supremacy of Her Majesty in this country.[22]

Rhodes had effectively squared the circle but, just in case there were any misunderstandings in London, he added a carefully worded postscript to a letter written to Lord Harris, the under-secretary of state for India: 'P.S. – Do not

John X. Merriman in later life.

be led away by the assertion that I am pro-Boer in my sympathies. I had to consider the best mode of permanently checking the expansion of the Boer Republics in the interior. The only solution I can see is to enclose them in Cape Colony ...'[23]

These subtle twists and turns were lost on Rhodes's old friend Merriman, who complained to his wife Agnes: 'I cannot make out Rhodes's proceedings ... I disapprove most strongly but cannot say so owing to friendship. Politics are very disheartening, all the men one seems to lean upon and trust give way.'[24]

Merriman would have plenty of future opportunities to 'make out Rhodes's proceedings'. What he was perhaps slow to appreciate was that Rhodes's methods and his goals had been firmly set by the time he was only 31 years old.

ELEVEN

'HOME FIRES'

*I like doctors for my work, because their calling gives them
such an insight into humanity ... And besides, when there is
blood-letting to be done, they are less squeamish.*

CECIL RHODES[1]

Since his earliest digger days Rhodes had shown a remarkable talent for recognizing men of ability and winning them to his cause. Once secured, they remained bound to him by strong ties of loyalty, taking responsibility in their particular fields and freeing Rhodes to pursue his many other ambitions.

While he had been ranging across the political stage, Rhodes's Kimberley interests had been well looked after by the other De Beers partners – the original six, plus Philipson-Stow and the two partners he had brought with him into the company. This 'little band of Englishmen'[2] worked according to a well-defined plan. Operating separately and in different parts of the mine, they bought individual claims or controlling interests in rival companies. All their purchases were brought to the pool at the prices they had paid for them. 'None but themselves ever knew the plan of campaign; and they could trust one another absolutely.'[2]

By early 1885 the partners had secured the majority of claims in the De Beers mine (360 out of a total of 622), yet their efforts paled by comparison with the gains the Barnatos had been making in the richer Kimberley mine. In 1885, when Rhodes's income was estimated at £50,000, Barney earned £200,000 – and Barney's partners were his family. (His nephew Woolf was already a millionaire before he came of age in November 1884.)[3]

These private fortunes were amassed in the teeth of disasters that wiped out rival companies and triggered a spate of suicides in Kimberley that Rhodes described in a letter to Merriman as 'an epidemic' and a 'mania ... seizing the community'. Almost nonchalantly he concluded: 'I do not despair of the place, as the wealth in diamonds, if regulated, must eventually become a source of profit to the holders.'[4]

In fact, only men with nerve and deep pockets could stay the course. Following the financial crash of 1881–82, the great storm of 1883 and the landslides that followed, there was another massive fall of reef early in 1884 which buried most of the claims in the Kimberley mine. The consequences were so serious for Kimberley MP J.B. Robinson that he had to abandon politics and appeal for a huge loan from the banks. Most of the Barnato claims were buried at the same time and the brothers came close to dissolving their company. The following year, nearly five million cubic feet of rubble fell into the De Beers mine and stopped all work for six months. In March 1886, a great fall in Dutoitspan killed 18 men. This was followed by a series of landfalls in Bultfontein that buried every single claim in the mine. The only solution was to sink shafts through the rock at the edges of the mine or vertically through the fallen rubble. In 1885 the Barnatos were among the first to reach blue ground by these methods, and a year that had begun disastrously for them with the crisis of buried claims eventually gave Barney his incredible personal income of £200,000 – over £9 million by today's values.

The contrast between the few high earners and the majority in Kimberley was now more striking than ever. Africans had become contract labourers, permanently confined to compounds. Those small-time white diggers who had survived into the 1880s formed a distinct working class, employed in manual jobs that were barred to their black co-workers – diamond sorting, machine operating, the 'supervision' of labour. In this respect, the diamond industry established the future pattern of white employment in South Africa just as surely as it had done for blacks. From henceforth poor whites would always be protected from the competition of even poorer blacks by formal job discrimination.

In the early 1880s conditions in the town of Kimberley reflected the extreme contrasts at the opposite ends of the social scale. The place was still an untidy shambles of corrugated iron shacks. It was still dusty, fly-blown and cursed with a high mortality rate (twice as high for blacks as it was for whites).[5] The short, crooked streets were full of pot holes; water was scarce and the state of the drains defied description. The conditions in the hospitals – and particularly the 'out-house set aside for Kaffirs' – were appalling. Yet Kimberley was also the first town in the southern hemisphere to have electric street lighting (in 1882) and the first town in South Africa to experiment with an electrically powered tramway. From the early 1880s, magnificent buildings began to appear among the shacks. The Barnato Stock Exchange, which opened for business in 1882, was a substantial brick and stone structure, built at the then unheard of cost of £10,000. Here and there, ornate cast-iron pillars graced public and private buildings and the turrets of lavish private homes peeped above screens of blue gum trees, specially imported from Australia because of their rapid rate of growth. When the railway eventually reached Kimberley (in 1885), the cost of building material was substantially reduced and the élite could indulge their architectural passions to the full.

One of the most notable early buildings was the Kimberley Club, a two-storey red-brick structure which opened in 1882. Seventy-four leading citizens (including Cecil Rhodes) had each pledged £100 to create an environment that would rival anything the famous London clubs could offer. One visitor described the Kimberley Club as 'stuffed with money – more millionaires per square foot than any other place in the world'.[6]

Another early description was less brusque:

> It beats anything of the kind I was ever in. We have our dinners and dances – one finds oneself in evening dress every night. It's ruination to health and pocket. And then our Club is such perfection. Electric bells wherever you like to touch. Velvet pile and Turkey carpets to walk upon and then one loses oneself in the luxurious lounge. This reminds me of an advertisement I remember seeing at home: Call a spade a spade, but call our new velvet lounges the very essence of luxury and extreme comfort.[7]

The young man who extolled the virtues of the Kimberley Club with such childlike enthusiasm was Neville Pickering. He was to become the greatest love in Rhodes's life.

The Kimberley Club

149

Neville Pickering

Like Rhodes, Pickering was a clergyman's son. His father had first come to South Africa with the British army when he was a young man and had returned with his wife, Frances, and four young children to take the position of rector of St Paul's Church, Port Elizabeth. Neville, the last child, was born on 29 October 1857, six months after the family settled in South Africa.

When he left school at the age of 18, Pickering was apprenticed as a clerk to Messrs Dunnel Ebden and Co., a leading firm of merchants based in Port Elizabeth. This was the same firm that had originally bought the farm Vooruitzicht from the De Beers brothers and subsequently made the grave mistake of informing Richard Southey that they intended to raise diggers' licence fees. Although they lost the battle and were forced to sell the farm to the government, they still held substantial interests in Kimberley, where Pickering was transferred early in his career. The young man seemed to have enjoyed universal approval. Gregarious, fun-loving and easy-going, he was described as 'beloved by both men and women alike'. To Merriman, who fondly called him 'Pickling', he was 'a remarkably pleasant and promising fellow with everything before him'.[8]

Shortly before he entered parliament for the first time, Rhodes relinquished the secretaryship of De Beers. Some time later that year (the exact date is uncertain) Pickering was appointed to take his place. He was then 23 years old. We cannot be sure that Rhodes was responsible for his appointment (although this seems likely) and we have no idea of the circumstances in which they first met. We do know, however, that a close relationship developed between the two men immediately after Rhodes returned from Oxford with his degree in January 1882. Almost at once, Rhodes moved out of his bachelor quarters – a British mess locally known as the 'Twelve Apostles'[9] – and set up home with Pickering in a humble corrugated-iron cottage opposite the Kimberley cricket ground.

Graham Bower, Sir Hercules' deputy in Cape Town during the 1880s and 1890s, described the relationship between Rhodes and Pickering as, 'an absolutely lover-like friendship'.[10] In the words of Basil Williams, an early biographer, Rhodes 'never loved anyone so well' as Neville Pickering.[11]

In October 1882, when Rhodes and General Gordon were in the midst of their negotiations with the Sothos, Rhodes rushed back to Kimberley (a three-day ride) to be with Pickering on his 25th birthday. It was during this visit that Rhodes wrote his third will, stating: 'I, C.J. Rhodes, being of sound mind, leave my worldly wealth to N.E. Pickering'. The next day, almost as an after-thought, he drafted a letter which he handed to Pickering together with the sealed will. It read: 'Open the enclosed after my death. There is an old will of mine with Graham, whose conditions are very curious, and can only be carried out by a trustworthy person, and I consider you are one ... You fully under-stand you are to use interest of money as you like during your life.'[12]

Robert Graham was the first chairman of De Beers, and if Neville Pickering had ever read the will in Graham's possession he would have dis-covered that he had been entrusted to use Rhodes's money to make the world English.

Pickering was a conscientious company secretary. Though described as 'not particularly intelligent',[13] he was highly regarded by the De Beers directors for 'his strict probity and unfailing attention to detail'.[14] However, his importance to Rhodes transcended the qualities of a virtuous and reliable company secretary. For probably the first time in his life, Rhodes was personally fulfilled and happy. When in Kimberley, he would always be seen in Pickering's company: 'They shared the same office and the same dwelling-house, worked together, played together, shot together.'[15]

Although there were only four years between them, in appearance they were a generation apart. Rhodes had always seemed older than his years, and the slender youth who had landed in Durban 12 years earlier now had the body of a middle-aged man, 'heavy in stance, heavy in seat; big, thick, square'.[16] On the evidence of the one photograph that has survived from his Kimberley days, Picker-ing was still a fresh-faced youngster, not

Dr Leander Starr Jameson

particularly handsome but clean-cut, attractive and open. One biographer has suggested that Rhodes 'saw in Pickering a link with the boyishness he had never totally abandoned.'[17] Although this is speculation, one does sense a strong element of nostalgia in Rhodes's relationship with Pickering and a succession of uncomplicated, frank and trustworthy young men; a nostalgia not simply for his lost youth, but for the values he held in his youth, for a lost innocence.

Under Pickering's influence, Rhodes softened and became more sociable. The two of them would go to the bachelor's balls at the Kimberley Club Pickering cutting a dashing figure with the ladies, Rhodes dancing vigorously with the plainest in the room.

In June 1884 tragedy struck. While the two men were riding together, Pickering was thrown into a thorn bush. No bones were broken, but thorns pierced both legs below the knees and were difficult to extract. A chronic infection set in from which Pickering never fully recovered. When not confined to his bed, he was forced to hobble about on crutches. During the young man's many relapses Rhodes was a devoted nurse.

The doctor Rhodes called in to treat Pickering was Leander Starr Jameson. He would soon become the most important person in Rhodes's life.

Jameson was five months older than Rhodes, and had arrived in Kimberley early in 1879. He was a first-class surgeon and the most highly qualified doctor in Kimberley, with a reputation that soon extended beyond the diamond territory. When President Brand of the Orange Free State was seriously ill, Jameson was called for, and it is certain that Rhodes would have chosen him as his personal physician long before Pickering's illness. According to one account, their friendship dated back to the 'Twelve Apostle' days, when Jameson would drop by 'to gossip, drink, play cards and smoke Boer tobacco'.[9]

Jameson was the youngest of 11 children. He was born in Edinburgh on 9 February 1853, and moved with his family to London when he was seven years old. Educated at Godolphin School in Hammersmith and the University of London, he was an outstanding student, qualifying as a Doctor of Medicine and a Bachelor of Science. He also became a Member of the Royal College of Surgeons, where his abilities were immediately recognized: 'Those who watched him at work say that never was touch more light, hand more confident, or eye more sure. Why then did he chose to exile himself in a Mining Camp in a South African wilderness?'[18]

Biographers have suggested several answers, including 'the overpowering restlessness of [Jameson's] Northern blood',[18] his impatience 'for daring physical action', dreams of Imperial glory inspired by his hero, Clive of India,[9] and a reason that 'was the same as Rhodes – to cure a weak lung'.[19]

Perhaps, the simplest answer has been overlooked. By coming to the 'diamond capital' with qualifications that put him far ahead of the competition, Jameson was assured of a generous income. In his first year in his new practice he earned £5000, and although one hates to repeat these comparisons, it is worth pointing out that this represented an income of £196,000 by today's values.

Jameson was hugely popular in Kimberley, where he soon earned the affectionate nickname of 'Dr Jim'. In appearance he was unimpressive, but everyone seemed to respond to his generous, flamboyant personality. Prematurely bald and described as 'small in stature, very light and slim of body',[20] he was nevertheless 'great in spirit and energy'.[21] Writing years later, another witness made the same point with a vivid description of Jameson, who was a regular visitor at her father's house when she was a young girl in Kimberley:

There was something so warm and friendly about him that, even though I never dared to speak lest I be banished, whenever his dark, wide-set eyes rested upon me, I felt that I was an integral part of the group. Actually, Dr. Jim was thin and insignificant in appearance, with just a fringe of dark hair below his shining bald dome, but no one ever thought about his looks, so big was his heart, so inspiring his enthusiasm, so great his charm.[22]

An addicted gambler, Jameson was soon famous in Kimberley for his 'reckless zest in life' and his 'brusque yet winning manner'.[23]

His humorous prescription to a fanciful patient who complained of a pain in her back – 'rub it with a brick' – became proverbial in the camp.

He used to drive – in a billycock hat – a very smart victoria with two very fast black horses. He performed miraculous operations, and effected marvellous cures. He was wonderfully kind to the poor, and indeed to everybody. He gave famous dances, and boxing matches at which he was a bottle holder, and was renowned for his skill and daring in the game of poker.[24]

In one game of poker he is said to have staked everything – his horse, his carriage, his furniture – lost them all and won them all back in a single night ... Sometimes Jameson played bridge with Rhodes, the Doctor's wild bidding often leading him into trouble. 'Well, Jameson,' Rhodes remarked after a rubber, 'you went out skirmishing, but the enemy swooped down on you and annihilated you.'[25]

According to Jameson's biographer, Ian Colvin, 'Neville's sickbed clinched the intimacy' between Rhodes and Jameson.[26] ('Intimacy', that is, in the Victorian sense of a very close friendship). There is overwhelming evidence to support this statement, and to suggest something else. As young Pickering was languishing on his sickbed, his doctor and his attentive nurse were colluding in 'the greatest medical scandal in the long and honourable history of British medicine',[27] playing – to borrow Dr Turrell's vivid phrase – 'the politics of death'.[28]

Pickering's riding accident occurred at a time when the mining industry was experiencing yet another crisis. On this occasion, the danger was not falling reef, flooded claims or flattened buildings, but an epidemic of smallpox.

There had been a serious outbreak in the Cape two years earlier, and it was feared that if the disease spread to Kimberley, the mine workers 'would bolt as one man into the African veld'.[29] Boer farmers and transport riders would also stay away, for 'no people feared the disease more than the Boers'.[30] Cut off from crucial supplies of labour, food and fuel, the diamond industry would die.

In the face of this threat, 'an unseen hand' had moved swiftly to defend the mines. Police were ordered to block all the approach roads from the south and to divert incoming traffic to one particular crossing on the Modder river, where a quarantine station and a 'disinfecting chamber' had been set up.

> The disinfecting chamber was a closed shed, filled with the fumes of burning sulphur, in which the hapless traveller was confined for the space of three asphyxiating minutes. As a great concession white men were allowed to put their heads through a hole in the wall, thus avoiding suffocation; but the Kafirs were denied this privilege on the grounds that 'infection may lurk in their woolly locks', and were dragged out at the end of their three minutes of Hades often more dead than alive, choking with the sulphurous acid. Whether the process had any effect on the microbe was a matter of doubt, but it was nearly fatal to man.[31]

Travellers who refused to submit to this 'savage ceremony' and could not show proof of a recent smallpox vaccination were compelled to spend six weeks in the quarantine station before they were permitted to travel to Kimberley.

The young man in charge of this operation was Dr Hans Sauer, scion of a wealthy and well-connected Afrikaans family and a recent graduate of Edinburgh University. Sauer had been given his job and his instructions by Denis Doyle, Kimberley's sanitary inspector, and was assisted 'by a company of mounted police and by a goodly number of Doyle's Redbreasts or Zulu sanitary police'.[32]

In his personal account, Sauer readily acknowledges that he was acting without any legal authority. Although ordinary mortals submitted to these indignities, the 'coach passenger class' which included 'Judges of the Assize ... lawyers ... [and] men and women of the world ... had some idea of what their rights were'.[33]

> There were, of course, many who objected violently, but force was always employed to make them submit, with the result that at one time I had as many as nineteen actions for assault, battery, and interference with persons on the Queen's highway, but somehow none of these actions came to anything; they all mysteriously faded away and died out.[33]

It was some time before Hans Sauer discovered that the unseen hand that 'squared' every case before it could come to court was that of Cecil Rhodes.

> It was Rhodes, and Rhodes alone, who had conceived the plan, and who had persuaded all the important factors in the Fields to back the adventure. As always, Rhodes displayed his extraordinary ability for pulling the strings while keeping entirely out of sight. On my return to Kimberley from the Modder I met him for the very first time and got to know him very slightly but even with the little knowledge I had of him I felt that he had a remarkable power of attraction for his fellow-men, so that one became fond of him without exactly knowing why.[34]

This first meeting between Rhodes and Sauer took place after the Cape smallpox threat had receded and the quarantine station had been closed. Sauer could then boast that 'no case of smallpox got through to Kimberley'.[33]

After his success, Sauer went on a long hunting trip, travelling through the Transvaal and Mozambique. He returned via the eastern Transvaal gold fields, where Herbert Rhodes had been prospecting six years earlier. There had been a recent flurry of activity after the discovery of 'the great and rich Sheba reef' near the town of Barberton. Dr Jameson was already in the area and Sauer soon caught gold fever, but his dreams of a prospector's life were shattered when he rashly challenged Jameson to a game of poker. Sauer lost everything he possessed – 'my wagon and oxen, guns and outfit, and finally a pair of top-boots ... I rose from the table broke to the wide world. Jameson kindly returned me the top-boots and my surgical instruments.'[35] Jameson would not be so chivalrous at their next meeting.

Six months after smallpox had subsided in the Cape there were fresh outbreaks in Portuguese East Africa (Mozambique) and the Transvaal. Shortly after his ignominious withdrawal from the gold fields, Sauer was summoned back to Kimberley by Dennis Doyle. As his coach was nearing the town centre, he noticed a number of small boys distributing pink slips of paper to people in the streets. One of these was thrust into his hand as he stepped off the coach. It read: 'The disease at Felstead's farm is not smallpox, it is a bulbous disease of the skin allied to pemphigus'. It was signed by Drs Jameson, Matthews, Crook, Rutherfoord Harris and Wolff.[36]

Sauer had no idea of the significance of Felstead's Farm, but he was sufficiently experienced to know that pemphigus was an extremely rare skin disease.

He had made arrangements to stay in Kimberley with his sister, Mrs Caldecott. Her husband was a lawyer in partnership with Philipson-Stow – the same Philipson-Stow who had mysteriously succumbed to Rhodes's advances and was now 'a large holder in the De Beers mine ... with great influence in the town'.[36] When Sauer arrived at the Caldecott house, Philipson-Stow was already waiting for him. After the usual greetings, Sauer was handed another pink slip and asked for his comments. It is not clear what Philipson-Stow hoped to gain by sounding out the young doctor, but Sauer managed to turn the interview round and extract enough information from the lawyer to confirm his suspicions about the 'pemphigus' diagnosis. Sauer knew from his earlier experience that Rhodes and the other mine-owners believed that if smallpox reached Kimberley and this fact were known, African labourers, Boer farmers and transport riders would keep away. Kimberley was an artificial island in the middle of the veld. Cut off from the outside world, it would die. Sauer learnt that Felstead's was a farm and trading store nine miles (14.5 kilometres) outside Kimberley where a number of Mozambique Africans had been detained by the police, who suspected smallpox. Jameson and the other pink-slip doctors had been sent for and, on their return, Jameson had told Philipson-Stow that 'the disease was undoubtedly smallpox'.[38] Now, it was pemphigus, which bore no resemblance to smallpox. Sauer was extremely suspicious: 'I asked [Stow] point-blank what he thought of the pink slip ... Stow, who was a man of few words, and extremely cautious, smiled sardonically and said nothing, showing me that he knew more than he cared to tell.'[37]

Sauer acted swiftly. The next day he rode out to Felstead's with Doyle and confirmed that the disease on the farm was smallpox. Now that his presence in Kimberley was known, he was contacted by doctors who had not signed the pink slip and told them that smallpox was already in the compounds. Confirmed cases were immediately sent to a new isolation centre, hastily constructed three miles out of Kimberley.

It struck Sauer as 'curious' that none of the compounds 'under the care of the pink slip gentlemen produced any cases at all'.[38] So curious, in fact, that he forced his way into some of these compounds with escorts of armed police, only to discover case after case of smallpox. Prudently, he stayed away from the De Beers compounds.

By the end of 1883, hundreds of cases had been reported and the death toll continued to rise. Jameson and the pink-slip doctors still clung to their pemphigus diagnosis, even though 'they were carefully vaccinating all their private patients, Dr Jameson himself taking the lead in this'.[39]

Sauer knew that these doctors were putting thousands of lives in danger. There was only one way to deal with smallpox and that was to acknowledge the disease, isolate suspected cases and inoculate the entire population. He appealed to George Wolff, a Kimberley merchant and member of the Cape Parliament, who was considered unsympathetic to the diamond magnates. He wrote to his brother J.W. Sauer, the member for Aliwal North, and to many other prominent Cape politicians, including John X. Merriman. They were slow to respond, but in the middle of 1884 a Public Health Act was eventually passed in Parliament, that empowered Sauer to enter any house, building or compound and vaccinate at his discretion. He was vilified for his pains. People 'simply spat when I passed'.[40]

Shortly after the Act was passed, Sauer was approached by a very distressed young Irishman who told him that a close friend and fellow countryman 'was lying dead in the Kimberley Hospital, that he had died of the prevailing disease, and that before he died he had been operated upon by Drs Jameson and Wolff [Jameson's partner]. He further informed me that there were several other dead bodies lying in the hospital ... satisfied with the veracity of my informant's story, I sent for Doyle and instructed him to draw a cordon of police round the hospital at dawn on the following morning, and not to allow any human being either to enter or to leave it before my arrival.'[41]

As soon as he reached the hospital, Sauer informed the sister-in-chief, the formidable Henrietta Stockdale, that he intended to make a full inspection of the wards and the mortuary, and would begin by examining all the nursing staff. 'On her continual refusal I was obliged to inform her that unless my orders were carried out, she and the whole nursing staff, male and female, would be carted off to the lazaretto as suspected persons who had been in contact with cases of smallpox.'[42]

Sister Henrietta gave way, and Sauer discovered that the entire staff had been carefully vaccinated. He then moved to the wards. Before he had reached the third bed, Dr Wolff arrived and ordered two male nurses to throw the intruder out. Sauer called for his police escort and it was Wolff who was 'ignominiously ejected from the ward'.

Sauer was horrified at what he found. There were several smallpox sufferers, all diagnosed with different diseases and kept in the same wards as

157

the other patients. In the mortuary he found the body of the young Irishman, who had died of a severe attack of confluent smallpox. Worse, Jameson and his partner Wolff had performed a tracheotomy shortly before the man's death in order to bypass 'air passages blocked by the pustular eruptions'.[43] Sauer believed that this was the first time in medical history that such a procedure had been used to treat someone suffering from smallpox: 'The operation was useless, needless, and verging on criminality.'[43]

Sauer presented a full report. Its publication 'created a sensation not only on the Diamond Fields but throughout the whole of South Africa'.[43]

Jameson issued a writ for libel in the High Court, and was imprudent enough to accuse Sauer of diagnosing smallpox to make money. Sauer issued a counterclaim, and the Kimberley court awarded each party £2000 damages against the other. It was a highly unfair judgment as the charges against Jameson were 'true in substance and in fact' but, as Sauer noted wryly, the judges 'were not men of sufficient character to be proof against the influence of the diamond trade'.[44]

Shortly after the hospital scandal, Sauer was called to treat a young pregnant woman called Mrs Sarsfield. She was suffering from severe confluent smallpox and had no hope of recovery. Sauer learned that Mrs Sarsfield's close friend and neighbour had been one of Dr Wolff's patients until her recent death from 'pneumonia'. During this woman's illness, Mrs Sarsfield had seen the doctor leaving the house, and asked whether it would be safe for her to visit her friend. She was particularly anxious not to take any risks while she was carrying a child. Wolff had assured her that his patient was only suffering from a mild attack of pneumonia and 'that she would not run the slightest risk' if she went to the house.

> On entering the bedroom of the sick woman, Mrs Sarsfield was so affected by what she saw that she dropped to the floor in a dead faint ... Of all known diseases, a bad case of confluent smallpox is the most loathsome to look upon ... the entire surface of the skin being covered with purulent pocks so close together that the face is simply a large suppurating mass, swollen to such an extent that the eyes of the patient are hardly visible ... The disgusting smell from the body of the sick patient adds to the horror of the scene.[45]

Sauer discovered that 12 days had elapsed between Mrs Sarsfield's traumatic visit and her first smallpox symptoms ('the classical period of incubation in smallpox being 12 days in practically every case'). He made a successful application to have her friend's body exhumed, and verified that 'she had died of confluent smallpox of the most severe type. The certificate of death issued by Wolff was criminally false.'[45]

On Mrs Sarsfield's death, Sauer presented his evidence to the Kimberley's public prosecutor, who was unwilling to act until Sauer threatened to put his evidence before parliament. Wolff was arrested and charged with the murder of Mrs Sarsfield, but once again, Kimberley justice was diamond justice, and Wolff was discharged.

It was not until 1885, nearly two years after Sauer had been handed his first pink slip, that the Cape Government declared Kimberley an infected area, and steps could be taken to inoculate mine workers and the town's population. According to the official figure (generally believed to be an underestimation), 751 people died in this epidemic.[46] Most of these deaths could have been avoided if prompt action had been taken as soon as the first cases were discovered in the compounds. The attempt to conceal the disease was not only a crime, it was an act of gross stupidity. Once it was known that effective measures had been taken to deal with the disease, neither Africans nor Boers stayed away from Kimberley.

Of the five doctors who had put their names to the notorious pink slip, Jameson was the most culpable. The others, as Sauer caustically observed, were graduates of second- and third-rate medical colleges. Jameson had a first-class London degree, and his opinions carried weight.

The question has to be asked why Jameson should have risked his reputation and his career by persisting with a false diagnosis that led to so many deaths. The mine-owners certainly believed they had strong reasons for concealing the true nature of the disease, but the doctors had nothing to gain and everything to lose by participating in a cover-up.

Biographers have been strangely reluctant to link Rhodes to this crime, but the evidence – both actual and circumstantial – is overwhelming. J.B. Robinson certainly believed that Rhodes had orchestrated the cover-up, but he can be discounted as an enemy and a rival. Other evidence may not be dismissed so easily. We know that a very close bond had been established between Rhodes and Jameson at the time of the smallpox outbreak. It is hard to find any reason for Jameson's actions apart from his devotion to Rhodes and to Rhodes's cause. And if this seems far-fetched, it is worth considering the many future occasions when Jameson would commit serious crimes at Rhodes's behest and subsequently shield him by taking the blame.

The other names on the pink slip are telling. After the smallpox scandal, the sinister Rutherfoord Harris would embark on a new career as Rhodes's accomplice in the crimes of blackmail and gunrunning and his agent in the most secret and sensitive deals. Dr Wolff would be one of the key conspirators in the Jameson Raid (see Chapter 19). Dr Matthews, who excelled himself during the epidemic by declaring that pemphigus was 'infectious and contagious to Kafirs but not to white men',[47] was crippled with gambling debts until Rhodes offered him an additional source of income as medical controller of the De Beers compounds.[48] Another accomplice, whose name did not appear on the pink slip, was Dr Smith. Smith was one of the first doctors to diagnose the disease as smallpox.[49] According to his daughter's account, '[My father] said, "Mr. Rhodes, I am sorry to tell you that smallpox has broken out in the compounds." Mr. Rhodes was furious and replied, "Don't be a fool, it's chicken-pox."'[50]

Dr Smith then accepted an offer of £600 a year to join the De Beers medical staff. In return, he 'reported what he took to be a case of chicken-pox'[47] at Felstead's and no longer played any public role in the attempt to stamp out smallpox.[50]

The most intriguing testimony was that of Dr Sauer. In his account of the interview with Philipson-Stow, he clearly implicated De Beers in the cover-up, but was much more careful with his references to Rhodes. In the Modder river context, Sauer described Rhodes as 'the hidden hand' in Kimberley, the one man with the power to block off roads and elicit the help of the local police to commit an illegal act. He had marvelled at Rhodes's extraordinary ability for 'pulling the strings while keeping entirely out of sight' and went on to to credit Rhodes with 'squaring' all the cases brought against him by furious travellers.

Two years later when the epidemic had spread to Kimberley, Sauer again discovered a hidden hand at work, corrupting doctors, hospital staff and the judiciary. But this time, Sauer kept to generalizations. It was 'the influence of the diamond trade' that perverted the course of justice and 'the mining magnates' who concocted the pemphigus diagnosis. Rhodes's name was never mentioned, but can one fail to read between the lines?

Sauer's discretion should be seen in context. Only months after the smallpox epidemic was formally acknowledged, the young doctor needed Rhodes's money and his support to embark on another great adventure.

----- TWELVE -----

'GOLD'

When I am in Kimberley, and I have nothing much to do,
I often go and sit on the edge of the de Beers mine, and I look
at the blue diamondiferous ground, reaching from the surface,
a thousand feet down ... and I reckon up the value of the
diamonds in the 'blue' and the power conferred by them. In fact,
every foot of blue ground means so much power. This I cannot
do with your gold reefs ... I cannot see or calculate the power.

CECIL RHODES TO HANS SAUER[1]

For more than 30 years men had dreamt of a great gold discovery in South Africa. There *were* finds, in the Tati region and in both the northern and eastern Transvaal, and although these were of no great significance, they kept the dream alive and sustained the restless search for gold in the South African veld. Briefly in 1884, it seemed that faith had been rewarded. The discovery of a spectacularly rich quartz vein in the Barberton area of the eastern Transvaal prompted an immediate gold rush. Investors in Britain and South Africa clamoured for mining shares. Sauer and Jameson both visited the area and played their famous game of poker.

The excitement was short-lived. The Barberton fields only contained pockets of payable gold, and thousands lost their savings. The great South African gold field was still a mirage.

The Struben brothers were not discouraged. Fred and Willi, two amateur geologists, were convinced that gold would be found in an area known as the Witwatersrand (White Waters ridge), a great tract of undulating veld south of the Transvaal capital of Pretoria. Here they had found surface outcrops of quartz and gravel, compressed and cemented into solid masses. The local Boers called this material 'banket' after a favourite sweet of the same name, which they made by binding clumps of nuts and spices with melted sugar.

When the Strubens dug around these outcrops they found that the layer of banket continued below ground, falling away from the surface at an angle of 40–50 degrees. The brothers surmised that this conglomerate had once been the gravel floor of an ancient lake or inland sea and was likely to contain rich deposits of gold.

Early in 1886, they were proved correct. There are several versions of the story of the first gold find on the Witwatersrand, some of them involving a Boer prospector called Bantjes, others giving credit to George Walker, variously described as an assistant to the Struben brothers, an itinerant farm worker and a tramp. All we know for certain is that the first discovery of gold-bearing banket was made on the farm Langlaagte, owned by the widow Van Oosthuizen. Whoever made this find had struck a layer of gold that came to be known as the 'main reef', and, within months, prospectors would follow it for 30 miles (48 kilometres). Ultimately, men would understand that the Witwatersrand finds were in just one sector of 'the richest, the largest, and the most permanent' gold field on earth,[2] a huge elliptical bowl 170 miles by 100 miles (274 by 161 kilometres), buried beneath the soil of the Transvaal and the Orange Free State.

Dr Hans Sauer was one of the first in Kimberley to hear of the Witwatersrand finds. After the resolution of the smallpox crisis he had started a private practice in the town, but decided to drop everything and leave for the Transvaal. On entering the coach, he was surprised to find that Rhodes's adversary J.B. Robinson had already taken his seat. Robinson had been deeply in debt since the calamitous landfalls in the Kimberley mine two years earlier, but unbeknown to Sauer, he now had a secret backer.

Sauer and Robinson tried to deceive each other into believing that their destination was Pretoria, but when the two men left the coach at the town of Potchefstroom, they found they had both booked a place in the same country cart that took travellers to the Witwatersrand.

They spent their first night on the Rand together, as guests of the widow Van Oosthuizen. Robinson offered to buy her farm for £1500 but, after her land had been surveyed, found that the acreage was slightly less than that shown on her deeds and accordingly deducted a proportionate amount from the price.

When Sauer wrote his account 50 years later, he estimated that the mines that were established on the widow's farm had produced a revenue of 'anything from one hundred to two hundred million sterling'. He noted drily, 'This action of Robinson's cannot be called generous'.[3]

Sauer, who was an impecunious doctor in 1886, bought no land but, with the widow's son as his guide, spent the next two days following the line of the reef for 10 miles (16 kilometres), taking samples as he went. He then hurried back to Kimberley, determined to find a backer. His brother-in-law, H.S. Caldecott, advised him to approach Cecil Rhodes.

When Sauer arrived at Rhodes's cottage the following morning, the diamond magnate was still in bed. Sauer received a cool reception, but after he had given his account, was told to come back with his samples later in the day. On his return he found Rhodes, Rudd and two Australian miners waiting for him in the back garden of the cottage. The Australians had brought pestle, mortar and a gold-panning dish and within a short time were able to assure Rhodes and Rudd that every sample contained payable gold.

Sauer was told to go back to the Witwatersrand at once to buy properties on Rhodes's behalf. He pleaded for time to settle his affairs in Kimberley and to find someone to take over his practice, but Rhodes had anticipated his needs. A locum had already been arranged. After some hesitation, Sauer agreed to leave the following morning. When asked what share he expected in the venture, Sauer proposed 20 per cent. Rhodes offered 15, and wrote out a cheque for £200 to cover immediate expenses. 'That cheque for £200 [Sauer wrote] was the most remunerative Rhodes ever signed, as it led to the making of millions. He amassed a far greater fortune out of the Witwatersrand Gold Mines than he ever got out of diamonds.'[4]

Sauer was told that he must not board the Transvaal coach in Kimberley, but should wait at the first stage outside the town. 'It is better not to excite curiosity,' Rhodes told him.

The next morning, Sauer walked 20 miles (32 kilometres) and waited as he had been instructed. When the coach eventually arrived, he was amazed to find 'Rhodes and Rudd both comfortably seated in the two corner seats, with their backs to the driver. No explanation was offered by either of them.'[5]

Sauer's month on the Witwatersrand with Rhodes and Rudd was a time of extreme frustration. Rhodes knew little about gold and the cautious Rudd knew less. When Sauer obtained the option on a very promising section of the reef, Rudd refused to believe the evidence of the pannings and insisted that the ground had been salted. Rhodes was persuaded not to buy. Robinson then stepped in and purchased the property, eventually establishing a mine which was valued at £15 million five years later. Other blocks of claims, where Sauer held the options, were also refused by Rudd, including a mile- (1.6-kilometre) long section of the reef which, in time, would support six highly profitable mining companies. To make matters worse, Gardner Williams, an American mining expert, joined the party shortly before his formal appointment as general manager of De Beers. 'Dr Sauer,' he said, 'If I rode across these reefs in America I would not get off my horse to look at them. In my opinion they are not worth hell room.'[6]

Sauer was not always overruled and eventually succeeded in persuading Rhodes to take options on a number of properties, including a portion of the farm Doornfontein, which was adjacent to the site that the Transvaal Government had already set aside for a township, soon to be know as Johannesburg. Sauer secured his option for £250. In two years' time, that same piece of ground would have a municipal valuation of over £3 m.

Sauer pleaded with Rhodes to close the Doornfontein deal and secure his other options before they expired, but Rhodes's mind was elsewhere. News had just reached him that Neville Pickering was dangerously ill.

Pickering had never recovered from the after-effects of his riding accident. For the whole of the previous year he had suffered from severe inflammation of the lungs and was said to be 'drooping slowly from month to month'.[7] It seems very likely that Rhodes's concern for Pickering was a major cause of his uncertainty and lack of resolve on the Rand. When Rhodes left for the Transvaal, Pickering had been with his family in Port Elizabeth but, 'at his own earnest request',[7] had now returned to Kimberley.

Rhodes was desperate to leave at once, but all the seats on the evening coach were taken. Such was his distress that his usual persuasive powers deserted him. No-one was prepared to give up their seat to the ranting, pathetic creature who begged to be allowed to travel to Kimberley. Eventually Rhodes persuaded the driver to allow him to ride on top with the mail bags. To be at Pickering's side, Rhodes was prepared to make a 300-mile journey through the dust and the heat in conditions a modern traveller can scarcely imagine.

> The discomfort was so extreme and the fatigue produced by the continuing effort of maintaining your position on top of the mail bags was such that I have seen strong men, used to knocking about the African veld, weep from sheer exhaustion ... You constantly ran the risk of being flung from your perch on to the hard ground ... when the wheel ... struck a large boulder, an ant-heap, or a deep rut ... Your misery became acute during the night, the desire for sleep, the fatigue, and the feeling of insecurity becoming almost unbearable.'[8]

Rhodes nursed Pickering for six weeks. Sauer sent telegram after telegram but received no answer. Rhodes lost the farm Doornfontein and other options that might still have made him master of the world's greatest source of gold.

On the night of 15 October, Rhodes and Pickering's brother, William, were keeping vigil in the cottage. At 1 a.m. Pickering went into a sudden decline. Rhodes sent William to fetch Dr Jameson, but nothing could be done. Pickering lingered until 7 a.m. Finally he whispered to Rhodes, 'You have been father, mother, brother and sister to me', and died in his arms.

In the heat of a Kimberley summer, the dead were buried without delay.

That same afternoon 'all the leading citizens of the Diamond Fields'[9] attended the funeral at the Dutoitspan cemetery. Rhodes, dressed 'in his usual outfit of crumpled stained flannel trousers, Norfolk jacket and grey slouch hat',[10] alternated 'hysterically between laughter and tears'.[11] Barney Barnato, most sentimental of men when his heart was touched, was also there, weeping copiously. After the funeral Rhodes turned to him and said, 'Ah, Barney, he will never sell you another parcel of diamonds!'[11]

A few days later, Sauer's brother-in-law, Percy FitzPatrick, came unexpectedly upon Rhodes and William Pickering in a back office of De Beers. Both men were crying and FitzPatrick noticed that they were sliding something back and forth between them across a bare table. '"All I heard,"' FitzPatrick wrote, was "No, you are his brother," and "No, you are his greatest friend."'[12] It was Neville Pickering's watch.

Rhodes never returned to the cottage he had shared with Pickering. On the night of the funeral, he moved into Jameson's little one-storey, corrugated-iron-roofed and verandahed bungalow,[11] which became his permanent Kimberley home.

From that day Pickering's name was never mentioned again. Once, when someone foolishly broke the taboo, Rhodes snapped back, 'A detail, only a detail!' As his biographer William Plomer astutely observed, Rhodes covered his grief with an increasing 'hardness and even a brutality of manner'.[13]

The Witwatersand, 1889.

Pickering's death seemed to trigger an extraordinary outburst of energy – and indeed brutality – as Rhodes moved ahead on five fronts at once: politics, diamonds, railways, gold and 'my north'.

Rudd was sent to England to secure financial backing in the City, while Rhodes returned to the Witwatersrand with Sauer, Caldecott and young Harry Currey.

Currey had seen very little of Rhodes since the Warren campaign. During the intervening two years he had worked as a minor bureaucrat in the office of the commissioner of Crown Lands and Public Works and had managed to save a little money. In December 1886 he had been planning a trip to England and was surprised to receive a telegram from his father, John Blades Currey, stating: 'Mr Rhodes is going up to the Transvaal and he suggests that you accompany him instead of wasting your time and money on a trip to England'.[14]

When Rhodes's party arrived on the Rand, the place was swarming with would-be prospectors. The future city of Johannesburg was already a sizeable mining camp, as rough and raw as New Rush in the early days. There was one street of 'reed shanties'. Liquor flowed freely and, on his first afternoon, Harry witnessed six fights.[14]

Rhodes had lost his chances in the central sector of the main reef but now moved aggressively to secure properties on the east and the west Rand. He was his old self again, decisive and thorough. On one occasion he spent a whole evening coaching Sauer how to conduct negotiations with a farmer he was due to meet the following morning. Rhodes played the part of the Boer, and Sauer was not allowed to go to bed until Rhodes was satisfied that he was competent to deal with his canny opponent.[15]

Rhodes formed his claims into the Gold Fields Company of South Africa. The trust deed gave Rhodes powers to acquire, develop, or explore for any kind of mineral, anywhere. It was a taste of things to come.

Harry Currey had only been on the Rand a few weeks when he received a telegram from the Crown Lands office ordering him to return to his job in Cape Town. Rhodes asked him how much he earned. 'One hundred and fifty pounds per annum,' came the reply. Rhodes offered him the job of Gold Fields company secretary at £450 a year, and Harry gratefully accepted.[16] It was an echo from the past.

During their time on the Rand, Rhodes informed Sauer that he had invited Jameson to join them. The two doctors hadn't spoken to each other since the smallpox crisis and Rhodes now wanted them to shake hands and 'let bygones be bygones'. Sauer, 'being of a forgiving disposition', did as his paymaster required.[17]

Rhodes had lost the primary position on the Rand to Robinson but, as

Sauer had observed, that first cheque for £200 eventually brought a handsome return. After six years, the capital of the Gold Fields Company had been increased by a million and a quarter; by 1895 the dividend was 50 per cent, and for several years Rhodes drew an income of between £300,000 and £400,000 a year from the company.

On the political front Rhodes moved swiftly to seal his Faustian pact with the Afrikander Bond. He supported a Bond motion to stop Sunday trains running in and out of Kimberley in contravention of the Lord's eighth commandment. A passionate Free Trader, he was suddenly converted to the cause of protection for agricultural products. However, his greatest opportunity came in June 1887 when the Voters Registration Act was debated in the House.

Until this time British administrators and Cape liberals had prided themselves on the colony's 'colour-blind' franchise. To qualify as a voter, a man had to own property worth at least £25 or earn a minimum of £50 a year, or £25 plus room and board. Although these conditions may not seem particularly onerous, the figures have to be multiplied 49 times to give the equivalent values today. Their effect was to disenfranchise a few whites and large numbers of blacks – but not large enough to satisfy the Afrikander Bond. The Bondsmen objected to the black vote on practical as well as 'ideological' grounds. Colonists of Dutch descent were still in the majority but if significant numbers of blacks were allowed to vote, they would be able to swing the electoral balance against them.

These concerns were magnified in 1885 when the Transkei (formally part of British Kaffraria) was incorporated into the colony. This territory between the Cape and Natal had a black population of 500,000, and although only 2500 were qualified to vote[18] under the existing provisions, that was 2500 too many for the Bond and their supporters.

The Voters' Registration Act sought to disqualify voters if any part of their land was communally owned. Traditionally, all African land was communal, and the purpose of this sly measure was transparently clear.

Rhodes delivered a blatantly racist speech in support of the Act. It was a shameless attempt to curry favour with the Bond and promote a future South African Union on the Bond's terms.

For over an hour, he repeatedly hammered his points.

> Does this House think that it is right that men in a state of pure barbarism should have the franchise and the vote …? Treat the natives as a subject people … Be the lords over them … The native is to be treated as a child and denied the franchise … If I cannot keep my position in the country as an

Englishman on the European vote, I wish to be cleared out, for I am not going to the native vote for support ... We must adopt a system of despotism, such as works so well in India, in our relations with the barbarians of South Africa.

Why should we not settle all these grievances that exist between Dutch and English ...? This is the crucial question, and ... the native is at the bottom of it. Does the House think for one moment that the Republics of the Transvaal and the Free State would join with the Colony with its native franchise ... The way has got to be cleared for South African union. That union is impossible under our present native system ...[19]

Merriman was outraged. He described the Act as 'a miserable sham' and opposed it on grounds of truth, liberty and justice. 'We have no right to take away the rights that have been conferred upon the natives' he told the House.[20] He was particularly upset by the shallow opportunism of his former friend and protégé, but had already seen the signs a year earlier when he wrote to his wife Agnes:

I remember when Rhodes used to propose to maintain British influence by using the native vote – now he descants on the theme of the integral race difference between black and white and I should not be surprised to find him an ardent advocate for the restriction of the franchise.[21]

To Merriman's disgust, the Act was passed, and 20,000 black voters (about a quarter of the Cape's black electorate) were removed from the electoral rolls.[18]

Rhodes was well rewarded. A year later, Hofmeyer supported his demands for an extension of the railway line northwards from Kimberley towards the African interior, and in 1889 he backed Rhodes's scheme to take over the territory between the Zambezi and the Limpopo in the name of the Chartered Company.

Politics, gold, railways, 'my north' – and finally diamonds. After 15 years of scheming and dreaming, the time had come to move against Barney Barnato and amalgamate the Kimberley mining companies into one great monopoly. To support him in this titanic struggle, Rhodes had secured a powerful ally.

THIRTEEN

'THE MOST POWERFUL COMPANY THE WORLD HAS EVER SEEN'

Every man has his own pleasure. My pleasure has been beating them all round, and I want no sums of money.

CECIL RHODES AT THE FIRST ANNUAL GENERAL MEETING OF
DE BEERS CONSOLIDATED MINES LTD

Alfred Beit was six days younger than Dr Jameson. His entry into the story completes the trio of confirmed bachelors, all born in the year 1853, whose close collaboration would have such devastating consequences in southern and central Africa.

Beit was born in Hamburg, the son of a Jewish trader who was dogged by ill health and barely able to support his family.[1] Beit's cousins were gem importers and 'little Alfred' was promised a position in their firm, Lipperts of Hamburg, when he had learnt the diamond trade. After serving his apprenticeship as a clerk to a diamond dealer in Amsterdam he joined Lipperts, which already had branches in Cape Town and Port Elizabeth. In 1875, when he was 22 years old, Beit was sent to South Africa to represent the family firm in Kimberley.

Like Barnato, Beit started as a *kopje-walloper*,[2] toiling through the heat and dust of the mines in search of sellers on the spot; unlike Barnato, 'little Alfred' did not owe his early success to a flamboyant, winning personality. He relied on knowledge.

'When I reached Kimberley,' he said in an interview he gave many years later, 'I found that very few people knew anything about diamonds; they bought and sold vaguely, and a great many really believed that the Cape diamonds were of an inferior quality. Of course, I saw at once that some of the Cape stones were as good as any in the world.'[3]

Beit was able to offer some of the best prices in the fields and his success was virtually guaranteed. After a short while he left Lipperts and joined the

Alfred Beit.

far more prestigious firm of Jules Porges and Company, one of the largest and richest diamond merchants in the world. His next move was to form a partnership with the company's representative in Kimberley, an imposing ex-Prussian dragoon called Julius Wernher. From 1880, Porges's interests in Kimberley were represented by the firm of Wernher, Beit & Co.

Contemporary admirers heaped praise upon Alfred Beit. His 'genius in finance' and his knowledge of diamonds were said to be unrivalled in Kimberley. According to one story, an attempt to sell him stolen diamonds was foiled when Beit recognized the stones at once 'as having passed through his hands some seven years earlier'.[4]

Like Rhodes, Beit enhanced his early reputation by showing trust. A bag of silver was kept open on the counter of his office to help diggers who had difficulty finding coins to pay the weekly wages to their African labourers. 'As each digger asked for change either for a sovereign or for stones sold, Beit would simply say, "Help yourself" and leave the counting of the change to the digger. This unexpected gesture of trust ... won their hearts.'[5]

One of Beit's partners recalled an occasion when a little girl came into his office with a note from her destitute and widowed mother, asking for £250 to set up a small shop. 'Beit questioned the little girl, and, satisfied that the story was true, handed the child a cheque for £250. He had never seen the woman, and knew nothing about her.'[6]

Lewis Michell remembered Beit for 'his singleness of aim, his kindness of heart, his princely but unobtrusive generosity'.[7] Percy FitzPatrick went even further and declared that 'there was something Christ-like about Alfred Beit'.[4]

Beit was, in fact, a complex and neurotic man. Short and dumpy with bulbous eyes, receding hair and chin, he was painfully shy with a mass of nervous mannerisms. One writer described how he would tug at his collar, twist his moustache and bite the corner of his handkerchief. 'With strangers he could never relax. Embarrassed himself, he would embarrass others. Nothing could be done to put him at ease.'[8] An earlier biographer attributed Beit's mannerisms to a nervous condition which began in Kimberley and afflicted him unceasingly to the end of his life.[9]

'Little Alfred' had a touching obsession with size. Although he was no horseman, he chose 'the biggest horse in the place, a great bony chestnut of over sixteen hands',[10] which he could barely control. When dancing at the Kimberley Club, Beit selected 'the tallest and biggest women' as his partners. 'These towered above him, and he, instead of dancing with them, spent his time running round them'.[11]

Big men attracted him too, men like the huge and handsome Julius Wernher; men like Cecil Rhodes.

Beit's mother Laura was the only woman he ever loved. Whatever pressures he might be under, 'every week, almost without exception, he set aside a quiet time in which to write to his mother'.[12] On his first return visit to Hamburg, he delighted her by taking her for a ride in a carriage.

> As they were nearing their home ... he asked if she liked first the carriage, then the horses, and finally the coachman. She answered in the affirmative to each question. Whereupon he said to her: 'Mother, when I was a boy I always hoped that one day I should have enough money to give you a carriage and a pair of horses, and now my dream has come true, and all these, the carriage, horses, and coachman, are yours.' ... Rhodes was right when he said, 'all that Beit wanted was to be rich enough to give his mother £1000 a year'.[13]

Rhodes and Beit knew of each other, but had no dealings during their early years in Kimberley. There is a famous account of their first meeting, which probably took place in 1880. Beit was an obsessively hard worker, rising before six and often staying at his desk until after midnight. Late one evening Rhodes saw the lighted windows of Wernher, Beit & Co and decided to look in.

> 'Hello!' said Rhodes: 'do you never take a rest?' 'Not often,' said Beit. 'Well, what is your game?' said Rhodes. 'I am going to control the whole diamond output before I am much older,' said Beit. 'That's funny,' said Rhodes, 'I have made up my mind to do the same; we had better join hands'.[14]

Several years would pass before there was any joining of hands. As late as March 1884, Beit led a delegation protesting the undue influence of Rhodes's company in the De Beers mine. Four out of the seven members of the mining board were Rhodes's nominees, and Beit complained that the needs of the smaller companies and private holdings were being ignored.[15]

There is no record to tell us how Rhodes dealt with Beit and his objections, but it will come as no surprise that the next time the two men were seen together in public was at a meeting of Rhodes's De Beers Mining Company, which Beit attended as a shareholder.

Rhodes made such a profound impression on Beit that he eventually renounced his German citizenship to become a British subject.[16] He would be Rhodes's staunchest supporter, both in the diamond fields and in his African adventures. Rhodes's banker, Lewis Michell, doubted whether Rhodes's 'far-reaching aspirations' would have become fact without 'the intellectual and financial aid of his loyal friend'.[7]

> Between them reigned a complete mutual trust ... Beit, with his extraordinary knowledge of and memory for diamonds and his calculating practical mind, would bring Rhodes just what he most wanted. Beit could steady without discouraging; no man knew better what was and what was not possible in the world of diamonds. 'Ask little Alfred' became a catch phrase in Rhodes's circle.[17]

By the beginning of 1887 the battle for control of the diamond industry was narrowing down to a struggle between two main protagonists – Rhodes and Barnato, each firmly established in different mines.

Some biographers have given the contest the flavour of a glorious poker game between 'the Anglican clergyman's son and the Whitechapel Jew'.[18] In stressing the inherent drama of a struggle between two men of such different character and background, they have perhaps overlooked the fact that amalgamation was a serious business which affected the lives of many. Admittedly, the creation of the De Beers monopoly required breathtaking deceit, bluff, counterbluff and unheard of sums of money, but hundreds would lose their lives in this 'game' and thousands more would be thrown out of work or see their savings wiped out.

When the battle began in earnest early in 1887, Barnato seemed to be in the dominant position. He was far richer than Rhodes, and the Kimberley mine where he was firmly established was (by his own reckoning) worth 'three of De Beers'.[19] However, the Barnato Company had four powerful rivals in the Kimberley mine – the Central Company, J.B. Robinson's Standard Company, W.A. Hall & Company and La Compagnie Française des Diamonts du Cap, colloquially known as 'the French company'. The Kimberley mine had also suffered three years of virtual paralysis after the landfalls of 1884 and was only returned to full production with the development of underground mining.

In the De Beers mine, shafts had also been sunk through the debris, but the landfalls there had occurred much later and the mine was not saddled with anything like the same debts as Kimberley mine. Rhodes had several other advantages. By 1887 there was only one significant rival left in 'his' mine, the Victoria Company, a public corporation registered in London. He had also gathered a loyal and experienced corps of directors and engineers around him and perfected the most ruthless and sophisticated system of labour control and exploitation in Kimberley. He also had the backing of Alfred Beit.

When the Kimberley mine came 'on stream' Rhodes was determined to keep pace with its output in order to convince investors (especially European bankers and financiers) that De Beers was still the best base for the unification of the diamond industry. From the beginning of 1887 his company 'picked the eyes' out of the mine and, in an official report, was accused of 'burrowing regardless of ultimate consequences into the rich veins', of adopting a 'hand-to-mouth policy' and of showing 'reckless disregard of human life'. That report was prophetic. In that year, 202 miners lost their lives as a direct result of Rhodes's push for greater production.[20]

In February 1887 Barnato secured his first major victory in the 'war'. For over a year he had been softening J.B. Robinson's Standard Company for a takeover. Reports had appeared in London and Cape Town claiming that the company's underground workings were 'a danger to life and limb' and Standard shares had tumbled.[20] The Cape of Good Hope Bank, which was holding Robinson's own shares in his company as security against his overdraft, began selling. Robinson suspected that Rhodes and Beit were behind the plot. 'One day he came into my office,' Beit told an interviewer years later, 'and said that he had lost all his money: that Rhodes and I had ruined him, and wanted to know would I give him something to go to Johannesburg with and make a fresh start.'[21]

That was Beit's version, and if true, it was doubly ironic. Robinson walked out of that meeting with a cheque for £20,000, which laid the foundation of his vast fortune in gold and, at the next shareholders meeting of the Standard Company, he discovered that it was Barnato and his crowd who had manipulated the markets and now held majority shares in his company. A merger was forced between the Standard and the Barnato Company, with the new consortium taking Standard's name.

Rhodes had not been idle in the meantime. When the directors of the Victoria made it clear they entertained no thoughts of amalgamation, Rhodes and Beit plotted to take their company by stealth. Beit left for England and secretly purchased 6000 Victoria shares on the London market. By April 1887 Rhodes was able to advise the De Beers board that 'the time had arrived to inform the Victoria that we [are] their largest shareholders'.[22] Rhodes now held all the companies in the De Beers mine and was ready to move into Barnato's territory.

His first assault ended in failure. Sir Donald Currie, the man who had built up the Castle Steamship Line, had a majority shareholding in the Hall Company. Two of Rhodes's agents were instructed to join a ship that was taking Currie to England and to persuade him to part with his shares. The shipping magnate wavered but, when they docked at Lisbon, he discovered that the quoted market price of his shares was higher than Rhodes's offer. 'You young thieves,' he is reported to have said, 'had I listened to you, I should have sold at a loss'.[23] The 'two young thieves' cabled Rhodes, who promptly beared the market by selling his minority holdings in the Hall Company. When the ship arrived in Plymouth, Currie discovered that the value of his shares had plummeted. He was so angry with Rhodes for this blatant manipulation that he refused to have any further dealings with him. Two months later, Currie sold to Barnato, who in the meantime had secured another victory.

After outwitting Robinson the Barnato brothers had left for London, where they persuaded the British shareholders in the Central company to accept amalgamation. The brothers then returned to Kimberley, where Barney addressed meetings of Standard Company and Central Company shareholders that his nephew Woolf had set up on the morning and afternoon of the same day, 7 July 1887. Barnato carried both meetings and the companies were formally amalgamated under the Central name. In celebration, dynamite charges were set off that evening all around the Kimberley mine.

One company now stood in Barnato's way. The 'French' owned a line of claims, separating the holdings of the Central and the former Standard Company. It was controlled by a board of directors in Paris, whose Kimberley interests were represented by Wernher, Beit & Co.

Rhodes knew that he had no hope of blocking Barnato unless he could acquire the French company outright. He was a rich man, but his money was tied up in shares he dared not release. He needed to negotiate a massive loan.

While Barnato had contacts in the City, Rhodes had none, but through Beit he obtained an introduction to Nathaniel Rothschild, head of the biggest financial house in Europe. The day before Barnato set off his triumphant cacophony of dynamite blasts, Rhodes and his general manager, Gardner Williams, sailed for London. Williams, who had originally come to South Africa as Rothschild's advisor on South African minerals, had prepared a comprehensive report on the diamond industry and its future prospects if amalgamation went through.

Nathaniel Rothschild was impressed with Rhodes and his report. At the close of the interview, he offered to back Rhodes if the directors of the French company would agree to sell.

De Beers directors, 1893. Rhodes (front centre), Jameson is on his right, Rutherfoord Harris (back row, extreme left).

Rhodes left for Paris that evening. Beit had already prepared the ground and the French directors were receptive. A sale price of £1.4 million was agreed. Rhodes intended to borrow £750,000 from Rothschild and to find the balance by issuing 50,000 De Beers shares to a consortium of French and German financiers Beit had put together; he had not reckoned on Barney Barnato, who owned one-fifth of the French company shares.

As soon as he heard of Rhodes's offer, Barnato announced that he was prepared to pay £1.7 million – £300,000 more than Rhodes – for the French company. Rhodes and Beit hurried back to Kimberley, where a meeting of the company's South African shareholders was scheduled for 21 September 1887. Barnato took the chair and told his audience that the directors in Paris knew nothing about the Kimberley mine and had sold them short in a deal that had been hurried through in 24 hours.[24]

By the terms of the French company's trust deed, the directors in Paris were entitled to sell, but Barnato had found a legal loophole. If it could be shown that the directors stood to gain from this transaction 'by as much as one share', they could be held liable for 'every sixpence' the shareholders might claim they had lost. A long and messy legal battle now seemed inevitable, and with it, the risk that Nathaniel Rothschild might pull out altogether.

Faced with this prospect, Rhodes appeared to surrender. He told Barnato that if he was allowed to purchase the French company without interference, he would sell it back to the Central Company for £300,000 in cash and the remainder in Central shares. Barnato was delighted to accept, and the deal was finalized in October 1887. The Kimberley mine was now safely in Barnato's hands – or so it appeared.

From this point, the intrigue and deception becomes almost impenetrable. There is an 'orthodox' version of the events that took place during the next hectic five months, and it is supported by popular legend as well as the accounts given by both Rhodes and Barnato. According to this version, Rhodes's acquisition of Central shares was a brilliant Trojan-horse manoeuvre that gave him a one-fifth stake in the Kimberley mine. A 'council of war' was held in Kimberley in December 1887. This is Rhodes's version of what took place:

> We decided ... that we would buy a sufficient number of Kimberley Centrals to give us control. That was a big undertaking, and it meant two or three millions of money. But we said, 'If only we have the pluck to undertake it we must succeed. Don't let us go to the shareholders. If we fail they can only make us personally liable!' I said at first, 'Where's the money to come from?' But Mr. Beit only said, 'Oh we will get the money if we can only buy the shares.' And so the thing was done.[25]

Kimberley (1888). The Barnato building is on the right.

According to Rhodes, he and Barnato fought each other for every Kimberley Central share that came on the market. Prices did indeed climb dizzily from £14 in the middle of February to £49 a month later. At the same time, Barnato forced the pace of production in order to demonstrate the Kimberley mine's superiority to De Beers. Diamonds flooded the market, prices were forced down and the disparity between share and asset values widened still further.

Again according to Rhodes, Barnato's crowd could not resist the temptation to sell when share prices soared to these unrealistic levels, while Rhodes's enthusiastic supporters remained loyal and 'were always increasing their holdings'.[26]

> When I came back from the gold-fields, I met Mr Barnato again. I said to him, 'Well, how are we getting on now? He replied. 'Why, you've bought a million pounds' worth of Centrals.' I said, 'Yes and we'll buy another million pounds' worth.
>
> 'And now', I said further to him, 'I will tell you what you will find out presently, and that is you'll be left all alone in your Central Company.'[26]

One of the most famous amalgamation stories is supposed to have taken place at this time. According to Barnato's biographer, Stanley Jackson, Rhodes was spending so heavily that he started to run out of the cash he desperately needed to continue buying Central shares. To resolve the crisis, he offered to sell 220,000 carats of De Beers diamonds for £750,000, and invited Barnato and other leading buyers to the boardroom to inspect his stock.

Barnato would have interpreted such a move as an act of surrender. Only he could afford to buy diamonds in that quantity. If he refused to deal, Rhodes's scheme to buy his way into the Central Company would come to an abrupt end. If he bought, he could flood the market and inflict massive damage on De Beers.

According to the story, the Barnato brothers and their experts arrived in the De Beers boardroom where they found the stones 'laid out on tissue paper in 160 piles and graded according to size, shape and quality. They rested on a long trough running down one entire side of the room.'[27]

Rhodes asked Barnato and the other buyers to decide amongst themselves what proportions they wanted to take. As expected, the Barnato brothers agreed to purchase the largest share. After a careful inspection and a lot of haggling, the deal was agreed, whereupon Rhodes raised one end of the trough and tipped the stones into a bucket concealed at the base. Barnato understood the significance at once. It would take six weeks to re-sort the diamonds, and in the meantime Rhodes had £700,000 (mostly Barney's money) to fight him with.

It was a superb bit of *chutzpah* (Yiddish: cheek) which Barney appreciated rather more than his fellow-merchants. Indeed it gave him a new respect for a man whom he had too long despised as a priggish amateur in business. This was worthy of any 'Peruvian', and Barney enjoyed telling the story against himself. 'Rhodes only beat me once,' he used to laugh. 'Over those diamonds in that bucket of his. But I didn't mind – it pleased him. Just a bit of sugar for the birds.'[27]

The story ends with Rhodes lifting the bucket and saying to Barnato, 'I have always wanted to see a bucketful of diamonds. Now let's walk down to your office with it and make people stare.'[27]

The other famous story is set in the Kimberley Club, where Barnato had long been regarded as a social leper. Rhodes invited Barnato to lunch, with the provocative 'I'll make a gentleman of you yet'.[27] Barnato behaved outrageously, talking in a voice as loud as his checked suit and helping himself to liberal pinches of snuff to make his sneezes heard. The club committee protested. Rhodes ignored their objections and invited Barnato again and again. During one of these lunches, Rhodes and Barnato hammered out their final agreement. Barnato would join forces with Rhodes on condition that he was made a life governor and the largest shareholder of the new company. In addition, Rhodes had to use his influence to secure Barnato a seat in the Cape Parliament and membership of the Kimberley Club.

Entertaining though these stories are, they should be treated with caution. Rhodes and Barnato were masters of deceit and it suited them both to pose as champions of the ordinary shareholders, prepared to battle tirelessly and to take enormous personal risks on their behalf. 'Mr Barnato fought me tooth and nail,' was how Rhodes described the contest in public.

The historian Rob Turrell has uncovered evidence that suggests both men had already made their peace long before the legendary struggle was supposed to have begun, and thereafter colluded in a scheme to manipulate the amalgamation battle and enrich themselves at the expense of the shareholders.

In a remarkable letter sent to Philipson-Stow in October 1887, Rhodes wrote: 'The great comfort I feel now is that the goal is reached. Barnato who has 8000 De Beers and 1500 one hundred Centrals or roughly £600,000 of parent stock [£3.5 million] *is working in everything with me and has given his pledge to go to the end with me.*'[28] (My italics.)

That letter was written two months before the December 'council of war' when Rhodes and Beit supposedly agreed to risk millions of their own money in order to buy their way into Barnato's Central Company. In November, according to Dr Turrell, 'when the De Beers Company decided to buy Central shares, it used the excellent services of both Barnato and Beit in the share market. *There was no share struggle between Rhodes and Barnato: Barnato was buying shares for De Beers* ... Just how much Barnato made out of this speculation it is impossible to tell. He made the claim to the manager of the Standard Bank in Kimberley that he realized £750 for each of his £100 shares, but it is not clear how he calculated this vast profit.'[29]

If Dr Turrell's findings are correct, they indicate the extremes that Rhodes and Barnato were prepared to go to in order to deceive the public.

Whatever happened during and after October 1887, the end of the 'war' was announced in March 1888. Barnato had agreed to give up his interests in the Central Company in exchange for De Beers shares. In return, he became a life governor and the largest shareholder in the new corporation, De Beers Consolidated Mines Ltd. The other life governors were Rhodes, Beit and Philipson-Stow. For the record, Barnato also became a member of the Kimberley Club and the Cape Parliament.

In return, Rhodes had obtained one vital concession from Barnato. The trust deed of De Beers Consolidated Mines Ltd gave him exceptional powers. The company could control and manage 'railways, tramways, roads, telegraphs, canals and harbours'; it could raise armies, form secret services 'without submission of vouchers' and 'acquire any tracts of country in Africa or elsewhere, and expend such sums of money as may be deemed advisable in the development and government thereof.'[30] As one commentator wryly observed, you could do anything with that document 'except turn a man into a woman'.

Barnato had originally refused to agree to these outrageous proposals. He was a businessman, not a politician. There is no accurate record of the arguments Rhodes used to convince him during their all-night session in Dr Jameson's cottage, but it is safe to assume that Rhodes wasted no time appealing to Barnato's idealism and patriotism, but spoke as one business-man to another. And the business arguments were compelling. Here was Kimberley, source of virtually all the world's diamonds. Only 300 miles (480 kilometres) northeast was the Witwatersrand, the greatest gold field known to man. How could they be sure there were not another fifty Witwatersrands, another hundred Kimberleys in that vast African hinter-land? Where would their precious monopoly be then?

At 4.00 a.m. an exhausted Barney Barnato finally gave way. 'Some people have a fancy for one thing and some another,' he is reported to have said. 'You have a fancy for making an empire, and I suppose I must give it to you.'[31] The fate of millions of Africans had been sealed over stout and sand-wiches in a corrugated-iron cottage in Kimberley.

The first Annual General Meeting of De Beers Consolidated Mines Ltd was held on 31 March 1888. The new corporation owned the whole of the De Beers mine, three-fifths of the shares in the Kimberley mine and the controlling interest in both Bultfontein and Dutoitspan.[32] In a bullying, arrogant speech, Rhodes told the shareholders in the remaining companies that they had no alternative but to surrender. 'We are the leading contingent ... whether we obtain the balance of the shares or not.'[33] The remaining Central shareholders were offered one De Beers share in exchange for two Centrals.[33]

Rhodes ended his speech on a triumphant note: 'We are prepared to continue as directors of your Company, for our ambition is to make it the richest, the greatest, and the most powerful Company the world has ever seen.'[34]

He was given a standing ovation by the De Beers directors and shareholders, and a motion was passed awarding him a bonus of £10,000, but he waved the gift aside. 'Every man has his own pleasure,' he said. 'My pleasure has been in beating them all round, and I want no sums of money.' He could afford to be generous. Rhodes had 4000 shares in the new company (against Barney's 7000). In addition, the four life governors were entitled to an equal share of all profits in excess of £1,440,400. This meant that they would each receive a bonus of £120,000 in the first year, rising to £316,000 five years later, when these rights were exchanged for a settlement of £3 million worth of De Beers for each life director.[35] (That is £148 million at today's values.)

These figures seem all the more outrageous when one considers that this wealth was largely created by African labourers whose working and living conditions were described by John Merriman as 'a scandal and a disgrace to everyone whose moral sense is not blunted by the habit of looking at them as mere working animals'.[36]

Within months of that triumphant inaugural meeting, Bultfontein and Dutoitspan fell into Rhodes's net. However, the Central shareholders refused to surrender without a fight. In August 1888 they brought an action in the Cape Supreme Court, charging that amalgamation of the Central Company with the new corporation was illegal. By the terms of its trust deed, De Beers was not a 'similar company'. 'Since the time of the East India Company, no Company has had such power as this.'

De Beers lost the case, but Rhodes had a ready, if crude answer. He controlled the Central company and immediately put it into liquidation. All the assets were offered to De Beers, and a single cheque for £5,338,650 (£264 million by today's values) closed the deal.

The effects of amalgamation were immediate and dramatic. Costs of production fell to 10s. a carat, which sold at 30s. on the world market.[37]

Approximately a quarter of the white labour force was immediately made redundant. There are no accurate figures for black employees, but estimates run as high as 50 per cent.[38]

Rhodes and Barnato were now so unpopular that they had to be given police protection in Kimberley. In June 1888 a twilight procession of unemployed white and Coloured workers marched from Dutoitspan to Kimberley. As an effigy of Rhodes was burned outside the new De Beers company headquarters, the demonstrators intoned:

> We ... now commit to the flames the last mortal remains of Cecil John Rhodes, Amalgamator General, Diamond King and Monarch of De Beers ... a traitor to his adopted country, panderer to the selfish greed of a few purse-proud speculators, and a public pest. May the Lord perish him. Amen![39]

Rhodes was 35 years old. He controlled all South African and thereby 90 per cent of the world's diamond production. He now had the resources for his next great ambition. He was ready to take Africa.

FOURTEEN

'THE PLACE OF THE KILLING'

The Matabele King ... is the only block to Central Africa ...
Once we have his territory, the rest is easy.

CECIL RHODES TO LORD ROTHSCHILD[1]

In the 1880s the route of expansion from the Cape to the African interior passed through lands that had been claimed 50 years earlier by the Matabele, one of the most formidable warrior nations on the continent. If the missionary road, which Rhodes had fought so hard to keep open, was the 'Suez Canal to the north', the land of the Matabele was the Red Sea.

It had not always been so. The people who were indigenous to the country – Shona-speaking Africans – were settled and peaceable and regarded as no threat to European expansion. Their glories belonged to other ages, when they had created two great African empires in the lands between the Zambezi and the Limpopo.

Shona power was finally broken in the 1830s when Zulu armies entered their territory. The first of these slaughtered, looted, burned and moved on. Some eight years later a second army invaded. This time the Zulus settled.

The man who led the second incursion was Mzilikazi, chief of the House of Khumalo, a minor Zulu clan. From 1818 he had helped Shaka establish and consolidate his great Zulu kingdom but, after a quarrel over the distribution of loot, had fled north with 300 followers. This little band crossed the Drakensberg mountains and reached the high veld, where the Sotho tribes went down one after the other before their onslaught. Mzilikazi's victims named his warriors the *Amandebele* – the people of the long shields – subsequently anglicized to 'Matabele'.

In the fertile Marico valley they found rich grazing land and settled – they hoped, for good. By now, their numbers had risen to some 60,000 after they had been joined by more fugitives from Zululand and had forcibly incorporated captured Sotho youths for their regiments and desirable Sotho maidens as concubines and wives. But their sojourn in the Marico valley was short-lived. In 1837, the Boers entered the territory on their 'Great Trek' and inflicted a devastating defeat on the Matabele regiments during a nine-day running battle. It was during this engagement that Paul Kruger, then a boy of 14, got his first taste of combat.

Mzilikazi took his defeated people further north, crossing the Limpopo river and settling in Mashonaland. Two years after his death in 1868, Mzilikazi was succeeded by his son, Lobengula – 'He that drives like the wind'[2]. His capital was at Gubulawayo, or 'The Place of the Killing'.[3]

The Matabele were not so much a tribe as a standing army. Their towns were regimental kraals, closely packed together within a 40-mile radius of Gubulawayo.[4] From here they launched raids deep into Shona territory, slaughtering adults, capturing cattle and grain, and bringing back youths and children who would serve as *amahole* (slaves) until they might be favoured by assimilation into the new nation. Sometimes, but not always, Shona chiefs could buy peace by agreeing to pay tribute to the Matabele king.[5]

In a written report an early missionary described what he saw when he entered a Shona village after a typical Matabele raid:

> Fastened to the ground was a row of bodies, men and women, who had been pegged down and left to the sun's scorching heat by day and the cold dews by night; left to the tender mercies of the pestering flies and ravenous beasts. To add to their agonies a huge fire had been lighted against their feet, and the ashes of it were still warm.[6]

Other reports, ostensibly based on interviews with Matabele warriors, contained equally horrifying descriptions of mass slaughter by the spear[7] and by fire, after dry grass saturated with fat had been tied around the naked bodies of the victims.[8]

Yet there was another strand in the accounts of these early hunters, missionaries and traders. However cruel the Matabele might have been, whites could not help admiring their extraordinary courage, stoicism and dignity. 'Magnificently, one might say almost painfully arrogant' was how one traveller described them. He continued 'I think, honestly that there were no people like them in the world ... There was something about a pure Matabele which was outwardly very attractive. Their placid brute courage was very perfect.'[9]

By all accounts Lobengula, the Matabele king, was an awesome figure. Described as over 6 feet tall and weighing close to 300 pounds, 'he was an enormous and majestic man, with his waxed head-ring and a plume of crane's feathers. Naked apart from some skins hanging from his waist, he yet maintained a regal appearance.'[10] A French explorer declared him to be, 'the most imposing monarch he had ever seen, except the Tsar Alexander',[11] but perhaps the most vivid description was provided by Rhodes's agent, Frank Thompson:

> In age [Lobengula] is forty-eight to fifty. He walks as I have seen no other man walk, before or since, moving his elephant limbs and planting his feet one after the other as if he were planting them for ever, and rolling his shoulders from side to side and looking round him in a way which is dreadful to see. He has great bulging, blood-shot eyes, and when he rolls them to look you up and down, in his lordly way, I tell you it's enough to scare a man off-hand.[12]

As Lobengula made his royal progress with his long staff in his right hand, all the men around him shouted his praises:[13] 'Eater of Men!', 'Stabber of Heaven!' and 'Thunderer!'[14] No-one dared approach the king except on their hands and knees.[12]

Lobengula ruled his black Sparta with the help of his senior *indunas* (councillors). Estimates of the number of his wives vary between 60 and 200;[15] but whatever the true figure, there were enough to ensure a royal presence in each of the 40 regimental kraals, where they acted as the king's eyes and ears.

Lobengula's capital, Gubulawayo, stood on a dome-shaped summit overlooking the Umguza river. It was a huge military encampment, roughly circular in shape and half a mile (0.8 kilometres) in diameter, surrounded by a strong stockade of mopani poles and thorn bushes. Immediately inside this outer ring was a circle of tightly packed grass huts, six rows thick and built in the traditional beehive shape. These housed the king's attendants and his royal regiment and looked beyond an inner barrier on to a large parade ground some 200 yards across. At its centre were Lobengula's private quarters, enclosed in yet another stockade and containing two large brick houses, the royal waggon, the huts for Lobengula's wives and the king's goat kraal – soon to become 'the focal point of interest in Africa among those who moved in the splendid world of courts and chancelleries in Europe'.[16] Here the king performed his religious rites and 'all the plans were concocted for smelling out and killing people, when the sacrifices had to be made for rain'.[10] No-one dared enter these sacred precincts, death being the penalty:[17]

> The inhabitants of [Gubulawayo] lived an ant-heap sort of life. There was no such thing as privacy; their souls were not their own; they were oppressed by a great fear of offending the elephantine King or his witch-doctors, and everybody moved like a puppet twitched by his will.[18]

Since the late 1850s, white hunters had been permitted to enter Matabele

Gubulawayo (the original site)

territory for limited periods. The first Europeans who were allowed to settle were the missionaries, thanks to the good relations Robert Moffat of the London Missionary Society (LMS) had established with Mzilikazi during the time of the Matabele diaspora. In 1860, the LMS was given permission to build the first mission station in Matabeleland.

Over the next 25 years, three more LMS missions and a Jesuit community were established but, during all that time, not one Matabele was converted to Christianity.[19] Frank Johnson had a ready explanation:

> [Lobengula] rather cleverly decided to acquiesce in the residence of the missionaries in his country, but he saw to it that their, to him, poisonous doctrines, based on the acceptance of a 'word' more important than his own, should never take root. If, therefore, any convert was reported to him ... [the man] simply disappeared ... The tolerated missionaries had to acquiesce, and agreed to teach only the elements of carpentry, etc.[20]

It did not occur to Lobengula until it was far too late that his 'ready acquiescence' to the missionaries would contribute to his death and downfall.

After the missionaries were allowed to settle, a few white traders and hunters were permitted to reside outside the Gubulawayo stockade. Lobengula referred to them as his 'white dogs'. C.D. Rudd was more charitable. They were 'a rum lot', he wrote.[21]

185

James Fairburn was the natural leader of this outlaw community. He owned the only trading store and had custody of Lobengula's seal, which bore the image of an elephant and was used to validate all royal documents. Fairburn's partner was Jimmy Dawson. The group included Tainton, an old hunter, who lived in a waggon with his African wife; George 'Elephant' Phillips, an intinerant trader; Bill Usher, whose occupation is not known, and an old Yorkshireman, known only as 'Johnny Ugly', who did odd jobs of repairs to the waggons of visiting hunters. Some of these names would take on a special significance during the dying days of the Matabele nation.

Other Europeans were permitted to pass through the territory for limited periods. There was the artist Thomas Baines. There were the famous white hunters – Hartley, Finaughty, Leask and Selous. There were dozens of Boers, who left no written records, but who would be seen travelling to Gubulawayo with their families to seek the king's permission to hunt in the north.

These requests were seldom refused, but no man was given permission to mine in the territory claimed by Lobengula. Karl Mauch had obtained his gold samples by attaching himself to a hunting expedition, and as long as Lobengula stood astride the road to the interior, no-one could hope to profit from Mauch's discoveries.

In 1887 the pressure on Lobengula started to build. The men who now pestered the king for permission to dig were no longer lone prospectors but the agents of well-funded consortia. One of the first in the field was Frank Johnson. After serving in General Warren's force he had joined the Bechuanaland Mounted Police, where he found the life 'monotonous'.[22] He obtained his discharge and travelled to Cape Town where, at the tender age of 20, he put together a consortium of leading citizens, including the mayor, two of his councillors and the managing directors of four banks and finance houses. In May 1887 Johnson arrived in Gubulawayo with a letter signed by his backers seeking the king's permission to search for 'gold, silver or other minerals as well as precious stones' and requesting 'sole right of digging or mining for same'.[23]

Hard on Johnson's heels came a German party, followed by the 'Grahamstown syndicate', which the Kimberley press described as 'the finest expedition that ever went into the interior'.[24] Lobengula refused them all.

Private speculators could be dealt with foreign governments were another matter. In 1887, the Portuguese claimed Lobengula's territory. The Germans then sent an agent to Gubulawayo, but the first country to make a decisive move was the Transvaal. Emboldened by the recent gold discoveries in the Witwatersrand, Kruger was now in the mood for expansion. In July

1887, his agent, Pieter Grobler, a horse-dealer and notorious confidence trickster, persuaded Lobengula to put his mark to a 'treaty of friendship' with the Transvaal. It was an extraordinarily one-sided document guaranteeing hunting and trading rights in Matabeleland to any Transvaaler issued with a permit by Kruger's government and forbidding entry to anyone else. In addition, Lobengula was obliged to provide troops whenever requested and to accept the presence of a permanent Transvaal consul in his capital.

It is certain that Grobler mistranslated the terms of the written agreement Lobengula had signed with his mark. As the king would say later, how could he have agreed to give away his country to the Boers?[25] The horse-trader may have been the first white man to take advantage of a king who could neither read nor write. He would certainly not be the last.

Whatever Grobler and Kruger hoped to gain from this fraudulent agreement, they decided on secrecy, no doubt fearing the reaction of Britain, or more precisely, of Cecil Rhodes. Then, in early December 1887, news of the 'treaty' leaked.

Rhodes immediately summoned his old friend Sidney Shippard, the Commissioner of the Bechuanaland protectorate, and together they rushed to Grahamstown where Sir Hercules Robinson was spending the holidays. The matter was considered so urgent that his Excellency was forced to attend to it on Christmas Day.

Rhodes was in the middle of his complicated manoeuvres to take over the diamond industry. He needed time to amass the resources that monopoly would bring but, above all, he needed the powers that would be conferred on him by the trust deed of the amalgamated company; the power to raise armies and secret services, the power 'to acquire any tracts of country in Africa or elsewhere'.[26] As he wrote to Shippard, 'My whole success in the interior depends on my getting my trust deed right here in order to have the sinews of war for our plans.'[27]

Our plans. That is significant. Shippard had been an accomplice since 1876 when, as acting attorney general in Griqualand West, he had steered Rhodes through certain legal difficulties arising from the sabotage of pumping equipment. Robinson was also a close ally, and his appointment of Shippard to the key Bechuanaland position three years earlier had been crucial to Rhodes's long-term strategy.

These three men had been acutely aware of the mounting dangers in Matabeleland throughout 1887 and another accomplice was now waiting in the wings in readiness for any unwelcome developments in Lobengula's capital. This 'fourth man' was John Moffat, brother-in-law of David Livingstone and the son of Robert Moffat, the missionary whom 'Mzilikaze had

187

loved ... and trusted ... as far as he could trust any European'.[28] The Matabele had known 'u-Joni', as they called him, since childhood.[29] He had the right credentials.

In June 1887 Robinson appointed Moffat assistant commissioner for the Bechuanaland protectorate, a post that hitherto had not been considered necessary. Moffat's real purpose was to represent Rhodes/Robinson/Shippard interests in Matabeleland as and when required. One hesitates to describe these as British interests since Moffat himself seemed to have been aware of a distinction when he wrote:

> The British Government is a poor master to serve these days in out-lying places of the world. It seems to me there is a want of nervous energy in John Bull's extremities. If it goes on much longer in this way, it will be better soon for him to drop his colonies to sink or swim for themselves.[30]

On Boxing Day Shippard sent his instructions to Moffat, who was already in Gubulawayo on an exploratory visit, his first for 22 years. Moffat received his orders at the end of January and arranged an immediate meeting with Lobengula, who denied the terms that were rumoured to be contained in the Grobler treaty (the British still had no copy of the text). Two weeks later, on 11 February 1888, Moffat concluded a treaty of 'peace and unity' between the 'Great White Queen' of England and the 'Mighty Elephant' of Matabeleland, which bound Lobengula 'to refrain from entering into any correspondence or treaty with any Foreign State or Power or to sell, alienate, or cede ... any part of the Amandabele country under his chieftainship'.

In private letters, written before and after the signing of this agreement, John Moffat expressed intentions that were far removed from any thoughts of peace and amity:

> 'I fear there will be no change for the better until there has been a breaking-up of the Matabele power and a change in the whole regime';[30] 'It will be a blessing to the world when they are broken up ... I am sure their days are numbered.'[31]

Robinson sent a copy of the treaty to London, where Her Majesty's Government dithered until mid-April. It was feared that the treaty would offend Portugal and might commit Britain to the defence of Lobengula, if ever he were attacked. It was only through the personal intervention of Lord Salisbury, the Conservative prime minister, that Robinson was given the authority to ratify the treaty on 25 April 1888. (This was just four weeks after Rhodes had chaired his triumphant inaugural meeting of De Beers Consolidated Mines Ltd.)

When the text of the Moffat treaty was made public, Grobler was already on his way to take up his appointment as the Transvaal's first consul in Gubulawayo, but before he could cause any embarrassment he was attacked by tribesmen in Bechuanaland and mortally wounded. In his memoirs Kruger wrote: 'There is no doubt whatever that the murder was due to the instigation of Cecil Rhodes and his clique'.[32]

For once, the charges against Rhodes appear to be unfounded. There was no advantage in eliminating Grobler at this stage and all the evidence suggests that Grobler's attackers had been victims of one of the horse-trader's earlier swindles.[33]

With the signing of the Moffat treaty, Rhodes had achieved his first objective. Foreign powers had been warned off. His next objective was to gain a concession from Lobengula granting him exclusive mineral rights in all the territory claimed by the Matabele. Armed with such a document, Rhodes would then be in a position to petition Her Majesty's Government for a royal charter; in effect, a legal guarantee of those rights, backed by an Act of Parliament.

Chartered companies were not an original idea. The British East India Company had provided a highly successful early model and in the 1880s the British East Africa Company and the Royal Niger Company were operating on a similar basis elsewhere in Africa. The great advantage from Britain's point of view was that chartered companies offered colonies on the cheap. The companies themselves had to bear the costs of administration and infrastructure. Only when a territory had proved itself profitable was the British Government prepared to step in, 'raise the flag, claim [the country] as a British possession and exercise governmental control'.[34] The Germans and the French operated on the reverse principle – government followed by exploitation and trade. Writing in 1896, an American admirer of the British system estimated that colonial occupation had already cost the French $750 million (over £8 billion at today's values), while each German colonist had cost his home government $1750 (equivalent to £8000 today).[34]

A chartered company, operating in territories as rich in mineral wealth as the lands of the Matabele and the Shona were reputed to be, held out the prospect of enormous profits, but there were also serious risks attached. Nobody had yet conducted a proper survey of these territories and, at some stage, an expensive military campaign would be necessary to eliminate the Matabele threat. Rhodes, Shippard, Robinson and Moffat were already agreed on that point. The gamble was only worth taking if Rhodes could obtain *exclusive* rights to all the territory claimed by Lobengula. He had no intention of sharing the spoils.

The trouble was that other powerful groupings now had similar ideas. The Moffat treaty may have eliminated rival governments but had left the road wide open for rival entrepreneurs. Almost as soon as it was ratified, three consortia moved in for the kill. The most serious contender, from Rhodes's point of view, was the aptly named Bechuanaland Exploring and Exploiting Company, controlled by Lord Gifford and 'a shadowy London stock-broker, share-jobber and social climber'[35] called George Cawston. Gifford and Cawston were altogether in a different league from the groups that had petitioned Lobengula the previous year. Indeed, one of their first moves was to take over Johnson's Cape Town syndicate, thereby acquiring the mineral rights the young adventurer had obtained in Bechuanaland after Lobengula had turned him down. Although Rhodes had the De Beers millions behind him as well as the support of Robinson and Shippard, Gifford had one great advantage. He was a leading member of the English Establishment. He had the ear of Lord Knutsford, the colonial secretary, and other influential aristocrats and power-brokers. Rhodes was merely a clergyman's son with a seat in a colonial parliament. In the circles that mattered those credentials meant nothing.

In June 1888 Rhodes paid a hurried visit to England and laid his plans before Lord Knutsford, who was non-committal. Gifford and Cawston immediately scented danger and cabled Cape Town where their agent, Edward Maund, had just arrived from London: 'Rhodes seen Secretary of State for Colonies. Object is you anticipate Lobengula. Proceed immediately to Matabeleland.'[36]

Rhodes rushed back to Cape Town and planned his strategy with Sir Hercules Robinson. It was agreed that Shippard should detain Maund in Bechuanaland while Moffat would return to Gubulawayo immediately to pave the way for Rhodes's agents.

Three men had been selected by Rhodes for the important task of securing exclusive mineral rights throughout Lobengula's domains – Charles Rudd, Frank Thompson and James Rochfort Maguire.

Thompson, the former De Beers compound manager, was obviously well qualified for the job. This 'bronzed, hardened-looking'[37] frontiersman spoke several African languages and understood African custom and etiquette. Rudd was an experienced and trustworthy colleague, but Maguire seemed a curious choice, at least to Thompson. 'As far as I ever knew,' he wrote, '[Maguire] came with us to Matabeleland ... for want of something better to do.'[38]

Maguire was an old Oxford chum whom Rhodes had just brought out with him from England. Described as 'an effete snob' and 'a spoiled child of fortune',[39] he seemed the last person one would want as a companion on a trek into the African interior. Travelling with his 'tooth brushes and hair-brushes and nail-brushes and pomade and scent',[40] Maguire would be a continual liability in the wild, and so impractical that Thompson could not trust him to open a tin of salmon.[41]

Yet Maguire had a value to Rhodes that a colonial like Thompson could not have appreciated. This Oxford scholar, double-first and fellow of All Souls had important social connections. He was Rhodes's counter to Lord Gifford and everything Gifford represented and Rhodes lacked. A former secretary to the governor of Hong Kong and a member of the English Bar, Maguire could also be relied upon to couch the concession document in the turgid language of the Inns of Court.

Charles Dunell Rudd.

At first light on 15 August 1888 Rhodes's agents slipped out of Kimberley in two waggons. The party consisted of Thompson, Maguire, Rudd, his young son Frank, Frank's friend Denny and six servants, including George, a black American.[42] Inquisitive bystanders were told that it was a hunting expedition but, unlike most huntsmen, this party travelled with £10,000 in gold sovereigns,[43] presents for Lobengula (including a barrel organ) and an official letter, bearing the Queen's stamp and Sir Hercules' signature, commending them to the king. Rhodes had insisted on this favour. Anything that could help his agents pose as the Queen's official representatives was bound to have an influence on Lobengula, but Sir Hercules had been nervous of the implications. To cover himself he had written to the colonial secretary seeking permission to issue the letter, but had taken care to send his request by (sea) mail rather than by telegraph. By the time Sir Hercules received Lord Knutsford's reply forbidding him to 'favour one company against another',[44] it was already too late. Rhodes's agents were on their way.

The official letter would prove its value long before Rudd and party reached Gubulawayo. On entering the Bechuanaland protectorate they were told that Chief Khama was absent from his capital and had left orders that no white man should pass through his country until his return. However, when the wife of the local missionary saw 'that most formidable-looking letter ...

bearing the Queen's stamp ... and addressed in the best official style' she per-suaded Khama's deputy to let the party through.

After seven more days of hard and difficult travelling Rhodes's agents reached the Matabeleland border. Ignoring protocol, they entered Loben-gula's territory without waiting for his permission.

On 20 September they reached Gubulawayo, but the king was residing in Umvutcha, a comparatively small kraal seven miles to the north. Here Rudd and his party found some 30 white concession-hunters 'settled down in separate jealous little groups in a scene that must have been vaguely reminis-cent of a gypsy encampment'.[45] Although Rhodes had temporarily disposed of the problem of Maund, agents representing other syndicates were already in place. Among them was E.R. Renny-Tailyour, representing Edouard Lip-pert of Hamburg, who was said to hold a strong grudge against Alfred Beit, since his cousin had deserted the family firm. These whites would be in per-manent opposition during the weeks and months that followed, 'always egging [the king] on, prompting him to ask nasty questions, and twisting round the answers so as to make him angry'.[46] The atmosphere would become even more poisonous in the first week of October, when a furious Edward Maund arrived after being detained by Shippard for a whole month in Bechuanaland.

On their first day in Umvutcha, Rudd, Thompson and Maguire pre-sented their credentials and a gift of 100 gold sovereigns to the king. Thompson was highly entertained by the sight of the dapper Maguire, 'the ex-attaché, the Fellow of All Souls, squatting in Homeric dung'[37] at the feet of the king, as Matabele court etiquette demanded; but Rudd was not amused. He found the royal kraal at Umvutcha 'the most dirty miserable affair' and Lobengula's eating habits 'altogether very much like a wild beast'.[47]

After their first meeting the party had to wait on the King's pleasure, but they wasted no time in preparing the ground. During their first two days they had long discussions with Moffat and the Rev. Charles Daniel Helm, the senior LMS missionary in Matabeleland and the king's trusted interpreter. Helm accepted a payment of 200 gold sovereigns and within a fortnight was writing to the LMS directors in London recommending their support for 'a strong company to work the Mashonaland gold fields and keep out others'.[48] 'Helm is our man' was the triumphant entry in Thompson's diary some time later. 'He has worked through thick and thin in our interests.'[49]

There is no doubt that Helm's willingness to deceive the king and his own superiors in London would be crucial to Rhodes's eventual success. Two hundred pounds seems a paltry sum to pay for 'favours' of that magnitude and one can only assume that this misguided man of God believed, as John Moffat did, that the end of Matabele power would bring a rich harvest of converts to the Lord.

Finally, Rudd and Thompson worked on the king's own councillors. Lotshe, 'who occupied among the Matebili [sic] a position equivalent to that of Prime Minister', and Sekombo, another senior *induna*, were 'promised gifts if they assisted us'.[42]

Here too one would like to believe that material reward was not the prime consideration. During their discussions with the *indunas*, Rudd and Thompson held out the promise of a gift that meant more to the Matabele that anything the rival concession hunters had dangled before their eyes. If they were granted the concession, Thompson told the *indunas*, they would be prepared to supply a thousand Martini-Henry rifles and ammunition.[42] No independent (and belligerent) black nation had ever been offered arms in this quantity by whites.

On 27 September Rudd, Thompson and Maguire had a second meeting with the king and his senior *indunas*. Thompson assured the gathering 'that we were not Boers, and were not seeking for land, but only the right to dig for the gold of the country'.[50] The rifles and ammunition were now discussed openly. The Matabele, Thompson told the king, were like 'a dish of milk that was attracting flies'[50] – That is, Boers, Portuguese, Germans. With rifles, the Matabele would soon scatter those flies.

Lobengula needed time to reach a decision, and for days Rudd, Thompson and Maguire languished in the squalid white encampment waiting to receive the king's word. Thompson wrote:

> Nobody can conceive the weariness of the ensuing days. For reasons of his own Lobengula did not wish to be hurried. He was willing enough to meet us, but did not wish to discuss a concession. We were reduced to spending every day in our little camp, most of the time playing backgammon or reading. We did not dare to go far afield in case we might be called by Lobengula.[51]

Rudd hated the wait and found it a 'continual strain to be civil' to Lobengula, but a more perceptive observer understood that the king was in a 'most difficult and precarious' position.

> He has to consult all the great *indunas* on all public questions affecting the whole country and the dominant Matabele race; he has to consider the feelings and wishes of the *indodhas* [the married warriors] who form the second line of defence; he has to stave off by all possible means the threatened

193

rebellion of the *Matjaha* [the young warriors]; he has to deal with a steadily increasing influx of European concession hunters who are becoming a source of serious anxiety to him and whom he can now scarcely protect from the bloodthirsty *Matjaha*...; and lastly he has the perpetual dread of an inroad of Boers ... He knows all about *Majuba* [the Boer defeat of the English; see p. 139] and the retrocession of the Transvaal ... He knows how England, after the fairest promises, handed over 750,000 unwilling natives to the Boers whom they dread and detest [see p. 139] ... He is sharp enough and farsighted enough to understand that the English alliance might be his best card if only he could trust the English, but there's the rub. England has a bad name in South Africa for breaking faith with the natives.[52]

To illustrate Lobengula's fears of the English, the writer went on to quote a discussion that must surely contain one of the most moving and perceptive observations ever made by a doomed monarch. During a private meeting with Helm, Lobengula had looked straight at the trusted missionary and asked:

Did you ever see a chameleon catch a fly? The chameleon gets behind the fly and remains motionless for some time, then he advances, very slowly and gently, first putting forward one leg and then the other. At last, when well within reach, he darts out his tongue and the fly disappears. England is the chameleon and I am that fly.[53]

Sad to say, the writer who reported this conversation and showed such understanding and sympathy for Lobengula's predicament was none other than Sir Sidney Shippard. It was to him that Rhodes and Sir Hercules now turned to break the stalemate in Gubulawayo.

On 16 October 1888 an official delegation arrived at Lobengula's capital with an escort of Bechuanaland mounted police, commanded by Major Goold-Adams. Also included in the party were Shippard, Moffat and, for reasons best known to Rhodes, Dr Knight-Bruce, the Anglican bishop of Bloemfontein.

Although it was the hottest season of the year, Shippard advanced to meet the king across the carpet of goat dung wearing a tightly buttoned black frock coat (on which he had pinned the Star of the Order of St Michael and St George), a solar topi, patent leather boots and kid gloves. He certainly had no intention of grovelling before the Matabele King and insisted his servants should carry chairs to the meeting.[54]

While appearing to be scrupulously neutral over the merits of the rival concession seekers, Shippard made it clear to the king that Rudd's party represented a group with substantial resources, while Maund and Renny-Tailyour were 'speaking falsely' when they implied that they were acting on behalf of the Queen's government.[55] He scored an easy diplomatic point over the land-hungry Boers by portraying the English as a nation of shopkeepers who only wished to mine and trade. It was, he assured Lobengula, England's desire to maintain a peaceful and friendly alliance with the king.

This was clever, but not honest. Shippard was as keen as Moffat to see the Matabele nation destroyed and expressed his opinions with brutal clarity in a letter written a fortnight later to Rhodes's old Oxford friend Francis Newton, now the colonial secretary in Bechuanaland: 'I must confess that it would offer me sincere and lasting satisfaction if I could see the Matabele ... cut down by our rifles and machine guns like a cornfield by a reaping machine ...'[56]

Lobengula should have trusted the judgement of his own people, who had long called Shippard 'marana maka', father of lies, but it was not to be. Shippard's visit had exactly the effect intended and, within a week of his departure, Lobengula called an *indaba* (a grand council) of his *indunas* to discuss the merits of the Rudd concession. According to custom, the king did not attend this gathering, which was presided over by Lotshe. Helm was present during the entire proceedings.

Thompson repeated his promise of the guns and the parable of the milk. The Matabele were also offered a steam boat on the Zambezi (that was Rhodes's idea). When the *indunas* accused Thompson of greed for refusing to share the mineral rights with other concession-seekers, he had a ready answer: 'I told them I was not going to have two bulls in one herd of cows'.[57]

The meeting dragged on into a second day. At one point Rudd weakened and told the gathering that he would be prepared to share the mineral rights, but Maguire pulled him down by his coat tails and Thompson refused to translate.[57] After more arguments and accusations Thompson finally jumped to his feet and declared that he and his companions were about to leave: 'I said, "Yes, Indunas, your hearts will break when we have gone. And you will remember the three men who offered you moshoshla (Martini rifles) for the gold you despise in this land."'[58]

This had the desired effect. Lotshe told Thompson to follow him to the royal enclosure, where he was asked to repeat to the king everything he had said to the *indunas*. Thompson obliged, but Lobengula still needed to be reassured that 'the big one' (Rhodes) had no aggressive intentions. Would we arm the Matabele, Thompson asked the king, if we intended to attack them?

> This made an obvious impression on the king, and after pondering it for a few moments he exclaimed, 'Give me the fly-blown paper and I will sign it.'

I then said that according to our customs we three brothers should all be present when the document was signed ... He asked, 'Are you brothers?' I replied, speaking in the usual metaphorical style, 'Yes, there are four of us. The big one (Rhodes) is at home looking after the house, and we three have come to hunt.'[59]

Thompson hurried out to collect Rudd, Maguire – and Helm. They returned to find the king sitting on a brandy cask in a corner of the goat kraal, and squatted in a semi-circle at his feet.[60] Lobengula now seemed 'much hussled [sic] and anxious', and for the next half-hour he refused to sign.[60]

According to Helm's account, a promise was made to the king that no more than 10 white men would be brought in to dig in his country and, furthermore, that digging would not be permitted near the towns, 'but these promises were not put in the concession'.[61] According to Rudd's account, he assured the king that all white miners would 'be bound to fight in defence of the country if called upon', another assurance that was not written into the concession document.[62] But still the king hesitated.

I had almost made up my mind to try the clearing-out business again when [Lobengula] suddenly said to Helm, 'Hellem, tele lappi' – Helm, give it me – and there and then he signed.

As he did so Maguire, in a half-drawling, yawning tone of voice, without the ghost of a smile said to me, "Thompson, this is the epoch of our lives." ... I asked Mr. Helm to certify on the back of the Concession that all things had been done in conformity with the customs, laws and usages of the Matabeli [sic] nation in full Council and after full consideration, and that the Concession had been fairly and honestly obtained.[63]

Helm was happy to oblige, even though no attempt had been made to explain the real meaning and purpose of the concession. In fact, Lobengula had been deceived into putting his mark to a document that granted Rhodes 'complete and exclusive charge over all metals and minerals situated and contained in my Kingdom, Principalities and Dominions, together with full power to do all things that they may deem necessary to win and procure the same ...'. It also authorized 'the grantees' to exclude all rival concession seekers from Lobengula's 'Kingdom, Principalities and Dominions'.

In return, Lobengula would receive a stipend of £100 a month, 1000 Martini-Henry rifles, 100,000 rounds of ammunition and 'a steamboat with guns suitable for defensive purposes' to be delivered on the Zambesi river.

In spite of the many verbal assurances given by Thompson and Helm, Lobengula had effectively signed away his country. Not only did this

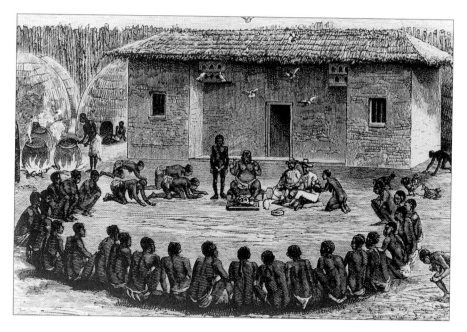

Lobengula holding court inside his royal enclosure.

document give Rhodes the right to mine anywhere he chose (he could dig in the royal enclosure, if he so desired) but the phrase 'all things that they may deem necessary to win and procure the same ...' conferred powers that were open to virtually any interpretation Rhodes might choose to give.

Certainly no-one had explained to Lobengula that the purpose of a chartered company was to run the government, levy taxes, maintain a police force and, when necessary, try a man for his life.

That was not all. The concession was a fraud built upon a fraud. It had suited Rhodes, his agents and Her Majesty's Government to accept Lobengula's claim to be 'undisputed ruler over Matabeleland and Mashonaland'.[64] This meant that they had only one authority to deal with. However, Lobengula's claim was a fiction. The Matabele had settled a compact area centred on Gubulawayo. They did not rule the Shona – they raided them or exacted tribute – and there were still vast areas of Mashonaland that the Matabele *impis* (regiments) had never reached. When Lobengula put his mark to that document he was signing away his own country and a great deal else besides.

Lobengula was given as little time as possible to change his mind. The document had been signed at midday, and by 4.00 p.m. Rudd was on his way south by mule cart – the fastest conveyance on the road. Thompson and Maguire were left behind 'to hold the fort'.

On the road Rudd caught up with Bishop Knight-Bruce, Shippard, Goold-Adams, the policemen and the boys, Frank and Denny, who had left Gubulawayo with Shippard's party. They all celebrated with a champagne lunch. Rudd then raced on, but his haste was almost in vain. In the Bechuanaland desert he lost his way in a sandstorm. Dehydrated and exhausted, he buried the concession, his money and a farewell letter to his wife in an 'ant-bear' (aardvark) hole, but had not gone very far when local tribesmen came to his rescue. The hidden items were recovered and Rudd completed the journey to Kimberley in record time. He and Rhodes then boarded the train to Cape Town for an immediate audience with Sir Hercules Robinson.

Rhodes's position was now precarious, and would remain so until he had obtained a royal charter. In Thompson's words, 'the mere signing was a trifle – all hung on the history of the next few months'.

It would seem that the logical first step would be to forward the concession to London as proof of Rhodes's right to Lobengula's territory: logical, but, in the circumstances, impractical. Before Her Majesty's ministers caught sight of that document, they had to be persuaded that it was necessary and desirable to arm a warrior nation whose lands bordered a British protectorate. With or without their approval, the arms would then have to be shipped out of the Cape Colony, in contravention of an act passed in the Cape Parliament expressly forbidding the supply of firearms to African tribes outside the colony's borders. After that, the rifles would have to be taken through the Bechuanaland protectorate, whose chief, Khama, was Britain's ally and the last person on earth who would approve a gift of 1000 Martini-Henry rifles to his arch-enemy Lobengula. The alternative route through the Transvaal was obviously out of the question.

Lobengula's acceptance of those rifles would, in Rhodes's view, seal the transaction but, until then, he could neither prospect nor pretend to realize the concession. There was also the danger that Lobengula might repudiate the agreement at any time. There were certainly enough whites in Gubulawayo (not to mention the king's own warriors) who would do anything in their power to make that happen.

When it came to persuading Her Majesty's Government over the question of the rifles, the Rev. Helm's assistance proved invaluable. The missionary wrote a report in which he declared that, 'the substitution of long-range rifles for the stabbing *assegai* [a light, strong spear] would tend to diminish the loss of life in the Matabele raids and thus prove a distinct gain in the cause of humanity'.[65]

Helm's report was enthusiastically endorsed by Shippard, who informed his superiors that it would be 'sound policy for us to furnish Lobengula with the means of maintaining his authority';[65] a strange sentiment from a man who looked forward to seeing the Matabele nation cut down by machine-guns.

Knight-Bruce, the Anglican Bishop of Bloemfontein, took a very different view when he discovered that the concession had been obtained with the promise of guns. In a well-reported speech, given in the second week of December, he declared: 'Such a piece of devilry and brutality as a consignment of rifles to the Matabele cannot be surpassed ... Everyone must know that it would be used to assist in the murder of hapless innocents.'[66]

Rhodes made short work of the bishop. On Christmas Day he was able to write to Rudd: 'Without telling you a long story I will simply say I believe [the bishop] will be our cordial supporter in the future. I am sorry for his ... speech ... but he has repented.'[67]

The methods Rhodes used to persuade the bishop have not been recorded, but it is worth noting that Knight-Bruce would be appointed the first Bishop of Mashonaland and would also be present when Rhodes's mercenaries fulfilled Shippard's dream and machine-gunned the Matabele in their thousands.

Just as Rhodes seemed to be succeeding with the rifles, things started to go badly wrong in Gubulawayo. In November Rhodes had felt it necessary to warn off his rivals. Rudd was asked to prepare a bowdlerized version of the concession, which was approved by Rhodes and Sir Hercules before its publication in both the *Cape Argus* and the *Cape Times*. Much was made of Helm's endorsement and the 'great favour' with which the concession was viewed by 'all the local missionaries'. Two days later, Rhodes added a further flourish in the form of a notice, published in the *Cape Times* (supposedly on Lobengula's instructions), which warned:

> All the mining rights in Matabeleland, Mashonaland and adjoining territories of the Matabele Chief have been already disposed of, and all concession-seekers and speculators are hereby warned that their presence in Matabeleland is obnoxious to the chief and his people.[68]

Copies of all these articles eventually reached Gubulawayo, which, by now, was awash with rumours about the contents of the Rudd concession. Thompson and Maguire were both under tremendous pressure from the young warriors and the rival concession-hunters. The 'white dogs' had also joined the opposition as it had now dawned on them that they might be subject to British law if Rhodes succeeded. One of their number, the old hunter

Tainton, translated the Cape articles to the king. Although Rudd had been careful with his revisions of the text, Tainton added a gloss of his own which, surprisingly enough, turned out to be an accurate interpretation of the uncensored document. He told Lobengula that: 'He had in fact sold his country, [and] the Grantees could if they so wished bring an armed force into the country; depose him and put another chief in his place; dig anywhere, in his kraals, gardens and towns.'[69]

Thompson was hauled before the king, who demanded to know whether he had a brother called Ulodzi (Rhodes), who 'eats a country for breakfast'.[70] Lobengula then showed him the articles and asked him to tell him plainly whether it said that he had given his country away to Rhodes. Thompson attempted one of his poetic explanations, comparing Matabeleland to a 'fine, sleek, cow ...: If she calves, the calf is your's [sic]. If she dies, the skin is your's. All he asks is the milk, which, as the king knows, is fit only for children. Not for men.'[71]

Lobengula's next move came as a complete surprise, although it is probable that Maund had already sown the seed in the king's mind. Lobengula summoned two of his *indunas*, Babayane and Mtshete, and gave them unwritten instructions which they were forbidden to divulge to anyone. He then ordered Maund to take the *indunas* to London and present them to Queen Victoria.

According to another *induna*, who confided in Moffat some months later, Lobengula's words to Babayane and Mtshete were: 'There are so many people who come here and tell me that they are sent by the Queen. Go and see if there is a Queen and ask her who is the one whom she has really sent.'[72]

According to Maund, the *indunas* were also instructed to deny that Lobengula had 'given away his country' to Rudd, and may even have been told to repudiate the concession in the Queen's presence.[72]

Renny-Tailyour offered his own interpreter, Johann Colenbrander, to accompany Maund. Colenbrander, described by a female admirer as 'six feet two inches tall ... and one of the handsomest brutes I have ever seen', was a Natal frontiersman, fluent in Ndebele.[73] For the moment, the German party and Lord Gifford's consortium were prepared to unite against the common enemy.

Maund, Colenbrander and the two *indunas* took a circuitous route through the Transvaal to avoid any possible difficulties with Shippard. When they reached the railhead at Kimberley, Maund decided to look in on the club. He had not been there long before Jameson arrived and informed him that Rhodes would appreciate a visit. 'Scenting trouble [he wrote] I went and found Rhodes lying on his bed (a favourite thinking and scheming place of his), and Jameson sitting on edge of bed in a small room of quite a small house just close to the club.'[74]

Rhodes questioned Maund closely. Why had he gone through the Transvaal? Had he seen Kruger? Why didn't he take the Bechuanaland route? Maund was then informed that the Rudd concession was 'a solid certainty, signed and sealed, and now in the hands of the [British] government'. It would be in his best interest to forget about Gifford and join Rhodes. Maund replied drily that he was not a man 'to let a pal down'. The meeting ended acrimoniously, with Rhodes threatening to telegraph Sir Hercules in Cape Town that 'an adventurer called Maund' was on his way 'with a couple of niggers he had picked up in the veld' and should be put under arrest.[74]

In Cape Town, Sir Hercules did indeed obstruct Maund. Although he had no authority to prevent the *indunas* travelling to England, it was in his power to recommend that they should be given no official recognition once they arrived. Maund and the *indunas* were subjected to three long interrogations, with Sir Hercules present on two of these occasions. Colenbrander was not trusted to interpret, and an independent translator was brought in.

Babayane and Mtshete consistently refused to disobey Lobengula's command and divulge the message they had been asked to take to the Queen. The impasse was eventually broken when Maund received a telegram from his principals in London. Unbeknown to him, the wires between Kimberley and London had been busy while he was being obstructed in Cape Town. Lord Gifford now informed his agent that he was close to a deal with Rhodes.

Everyone suddenly was on the same side; everyone, that is, except the *indunas*. Sir Hercules immediately changed his tune and Colenbrander, who was not a man to let his obligations to Renny-Tailyour and Lippert spoil his chances, welcomed the opportunity to join this powerful new alliance.

It was agreed that the *indunas* should go ahead with their visit to England and Sir Hercules undertook to commend the party to the colonial secretary. It was clear to them all that they would only raise the temperature in Gubulawayo if they frustrated the king's wishes. Anyway, 'the old savage' was paying for the trip, and it seemed safe to assume that no-one at court spoke Ndebele and that all discussions would have to be filtered through Colenbrander. As things turned out, this was a serious miscalculation.

Graham Bower, Sir Hercules' deputy and a solid Rhodes supporter, had an uncomfortable feeling that Maund would use the *indunas* as a pawn in the final negotiations between Rhodes and Gifford. If Rhodes's terms were acceptable, Lobengula's message would be suppressed, but if not, Bower was in no doubt that 'the messages which are now being held back will be brought forward'.[75]

On 6 February 1889 Maund's party sailed out of Cape Town on the *Moor*. They did not to know until they were already out at sea that Frederick Selous, 'the blue-eyed hunter', was also a passenger. Selous had his own agenda. The previous October he had negotiated an important concession with two Shona chiefs for exclusive mineral rights in a large tract of land in their country. On hearing of the Rudd concession, he had written several articles stating that Lobengula's claim to Mashonaland was fraudulent and consequently that Rhodes had no legal rights in that country.[76] At this stage, though, Rhodes had more pressing concerns. He needed to be in London as soon as possible but, before he could leave, one vital task had to be accomplished.

Throughout January, the situation in Gubulawayo had deteriorated still further. Thompson believed that Matabele opposition to the concession was now so great that Lobengula's own position was threatened. To make matters worse, Maguire had caused grave offence by bathing and then cleaning his teeth in the king's sacred fountain. Matabele witnesses had seen him 'foaming at the lips, and ...[turning] the water into milk'.[77] Before he had a chance to put on his clothes, Maguire was dragged before the king and accused of witchcraft. The very next day Lobengula's mother died, and Maguire's accusers claimed this as proof of their charge. Thompson had to use all his poetic skills to persuade the king that Maguire was innocent, but the incident nearly cost both men their lives.[77]

Shortly afterwards Lobengula dictated a letter denying that a concession of any kind had been granted to Rudd, Thompson and Maguire. It was sent to a number of newspapers in the Cape, where Rhodes, of course, had the power to suppress publication, but he could not stop the letter appearing in the *Bechuanaland News*.

It was now crucially important to get the rifles to Gubulawayo. Only then could Rhodes claim that he had clinched his deal with Lobengula. Rudd was asked to accompany the shipment, but refused, claiming ill health. Who could Rhodes trust to handle such a delicate mission in Rudd's place?

The obvious candidate was a man whose loyalty, charm and brazen courage were already beyond question – Dr Leander Starr Jameson. For days Rhodes applied all his persuasive talents until Jameson was persuaded to resign his practice to the care of a partner and join Rhodes in his great adventure.[78] The doctor's decision would have momentous consequences for him as well as southern Africa.

As a first stage, two traders were entrusted with the task of smuggling the rifles across the Cape border into Bechuanaland. No permits had been obtained from the Cape authorities and when Gordon Sprigg, the prime minister, heard the rumours that were circulating, he immediately wrote to

Shippard, who feigned ignorance. The High Commissioner's complicity was beyond dispute. According to Rudd, in a letter written to Thompson and Maguire, 'We have been very anxious about the guns, because the thing is now quite public. Shippard has behaved like a brick and sent them through Bechuanaland ...'[79]

On 3 February 1889, when the first consignment of rifles was safely inside Bechuanaland, Drs Jameson and Rutherfoord Harris set out from Kimberley. (Harris will be remembered as a co-signatory to the notorious pink slip during the smallpox epidemic.) Like Rudd six months earlier, Jameson let it be known that they were on a hunting expedition.

Somewhere inside Bechuanaland, Jameson and Harris collected the first batch of 500 rifles and half the ammunition. Maguire was waiting to meet them on the Matabeleland border.

Anti-Rhodes feeling was strong in Gubulawayo, but it is said that Lobengula was quickly won over by Jameson's charm and fearless sense of humour. The king was nevertheless careful not to touch the rifles and ammunition, which remained stacked in their tin-lined cases in Thompson's camp. Evidently he shared Rhodes's belief that acceptance of the shipment would confirm the concession.

When Jameson and Harris departed from Gubulawayo, Maguire slipped out with them, leaving Thompson to deal with the Matabele and white opposition on his own.

By this time, Rhodes was sailing for England. He now faced the most formidable challenge of his life. He had to penetrate the closed ranks of the English Establishment, deal with Liberal and 'Exeter Hall' opposition and persuade Her Majesty's Government to endorse his vaulting ambitions in Africa. And all this had to be achieved in the minimum time to prevent the situation unravelling in Gubulawayo.

At this crucial juncture in his life Cecil Rhodes was only 35 years old.

FIFTEEN

CONQUEST

I would annex the planets if I could.

CECIL RHODES[1]

South Africa was suddenly fashionable in the year 1889 and the visit of Lobengula's *indunas* was the sensation of the London season.[2] Babayane and Mtshete were received by Queen Victoria at Windsor Castle, and society hostesses vied with one another for the privilege of adding this exotic duo to their guest lists. The British press and public were at their silliest, hanging on to the *indunas'* every word and move during their hectic round of engagements.

Her Majesty's Government had arranged an evening at the ballet for the *indunas* and a visit to London zoo, where 'Babayane tried to attack a caged lion with his umbrella' – or so it was reported.[2] Lobengula's envoys were shown the 'White Queen's treasure house' in the vaults of the Bank of England where (again, according to reports) Mtshete let it be known that distinguished visitors who were taken to see *their* king's wealth of cattle always received a gift of a beast or two. The hint was not taken up.[3]

The *indunas* also witnessed 'the firing of the big guns from a man-of-war'[3] at Portsmouth and a military display at Aldershot, where the programme included a demonstration of the British army's newest and deadliest weapon – the Maxim machine gun.

As *The Times* smugly reported, Babayane and Mtshete were suitably impressed by British might and majesty:

> It appears that many of Lobengula's people have been led to believe by the Boers that since the defeat of the English at Majuba Hill, the power of England has been broken and that the Great White Queen has passed away.
>
> They now say that their eyes have seen her and their ears have heard her voice ... Their answer to her when she inquired whether they felt cold was characteristic, for they said 'How can we feel the cold in the presence of the Great White Queen?'[4]

**Cartoonist's grotesque depiction of Babayane and Mtshete
in the presence of Queen Victoria.**

The *indunas'* visit had serious implications for Rhodes. From the moment Maund and Colenbrander discovered that Frederick Courtney Selous was travelling with them on the *Moor*, they knew they would no longer be able to censor exchanges between Lobengula's envoys and the representatives of the 'Great White Queen'. Selous was fluent in Ndebele. To make matters worse, he was something of a celebrity in Britain and America thanks to his bestseller, *A Hunter's Wanderings in Africa* (1886). This book had been followed two years later by Rider Haggard's immensely successful *King Solomon's Mines*, which not only excited public interest in Mashonaland and the legend of Ophir but added extra lustre to Selous's image. In spite of Haggard's denials, it was generally assumed that his hero, Alan Quartermain, was modelled on the author of *A Hunter's Wanderings in Africa*.

It came as no surprise, therefore, that Selous had been added to the guest list when Maund and his party were invited to meet the 79-year-old Queen at Windsor.[5] As Mtshete delivered his verbal message from Lobengula, Selous was listening intently and Colenbrander had no alternative but to provide an accurate translation: '... Lobengula desired [the Queen] to advise him, as he was much troubled by white men who came into his country and

205

Mtshete   **Maund**

asked to dig for gold. There was no one whom he could trust, and he asked the Queen to send someone from herself.'[6]

In reply Lord Knutsford, the colonial secretary, read a statement on the Queen's behalf, welcoming the messengers from Lobengula and promising a written response. This came three weeks later in the form of a Colonial Office letter, which contained two paragraphs potentially lethal to Rhodes:

> In the first place, the Queen wishes Lo Bengula [sic] to understand distinctly that Englishmen who have gone out to Matabeleland to ask leave to dig for stones have not gone with the Queen's authority, and that he should not believe any statements made by them or any of them to that effect ...
>
> It is not wise to put too much power into the hands of the men who come first, and to exclude other deserving men. A King gives a stranger an ox, not his whole herd of cattle, otherwise what would other strangers arriving have to eat ...?

For good measure, Her Majesty also provided the departing *indunas* with a picture of herself and a gold bracelet inscribed 'Babyan [sic] from the Queen'.[7]

Rhodes arrived as the *indunas*' visit was coming to an end. According to his own account, Maund immediately advised Rhodes of 'the Queen's letter', but that was only part of the problem. The *indunas*' visit had made a profound impression on the British public, rekindling the Exeter Hall spirit and focusing opposition to the Rudd concession. Indeed, the odds could not have been stacked more heavily against Rhodes. He had no clout in government circles – for a while, Lord Knutsford confused him with Graham Bower, Sir Hercules Robinson's deputy – and the little that was known about Rhodes

Colenbrander   Babayane

tended to be uncomplimentary. 'Rather a pro-Boer MP in South Africa, I fancy' was the view of the Prime Minister, Lord Salisbury.

To add to his difficulties, Rhodes's old adversary, the Rev. John Mackenzie, had been marshalling the forces against him. Sir Thomas Buxton, who had chaired that electrifying meeting in Exeter Hall half a century earlier, was still a power in the land, and his Aborigines Protection Society now swung behind Mackenzie. The society was determined both to thwart Rhodes in London and undermine his position in Gubulawayo. A second warning letter was handed to the *indunas*, exhorting Lobengula to 'be wary and firm' in resisting all concession-hunters.

An even greater threat to Rhodes was the South Africa Committee, chaired by Joseph Chamberlain and activated by Mackenzie. Among its powerful and titled members were Lord Grey; R.W. Thompson, secretary of the London Missionary Society; the Earl of Fife; W.T. Stead, editor of the influential *Pall Mall Gazette*, and many other prominent Liberals. Thomas Buxton also served on this committee and the principle that drew these men together was a commitment to justice for the people of Africa.

If all this were not enough for Rhodes to deal with, his most important channel to the Colonial Office had been shut off (albeit temporarily) when Sir Hercules Robinson was forced to resign as High Commissioner of the Cape. Rhodes's close and trusted ally had overstepped the mark in a speech he had delivered in the Cape, denouncing 'the amateur meddling of ... ill-advised persons in London which would turn many a colonist from an imperialist into a republican'.[8]

In a little over three months, Rhodes would overwhelm all the forces lined up against him. It would be the most breathtaking accomplishment of his career, vindicating his cynical judgement of the human condition – 'every man has his price' – time and time again.

Rhodes's first concern was to prevent Babayane and Mtshete delivering the damaging letters to their king. The 'letter from the Queen' was bound to create a profound impression on Lobengula and was a much greater threat to Rhodes than the warning issued by the Aborigines Protection Society.

From all the conflicting accounts, it is virtually impossible to be certain of the methods Rhodes used. According to one historian, Babayane and Mtshete were put on a slow boat to Cape Town – a *very* slow boat indeed, since its first port of call was Rio de Janiero.[9] According to Maund, Rhodes ordered him to go straight back to the Colonial Office and insist that the two offending paragraphs be removed from the letter. When the attempt failed, Rhodes suggested that Maund should toss it overboard.[10]

However this was achieved, the outcome is perfectly clear. The Colonial Office letter was dated 26 March 1889. If the authorities in Cape Town and Bechuanaland had been co-operative, the full text could have reached Gubu-lawayo (via telegraph and runner) within two to three weeks. Babayane and Mtshete could certainly have delivered the letters personally to the king before the end of May. In fact, the *indunas* arrived in Gubulawayo, accompanied by Maund, on 5 August, by which time it was already too late.

Another of Rhodes's early priorities was to 'square' Gifford and Cawston (see p. 190). Although Gold Fields had funded the Rudd/Maguire/Thompson mission and technically owned the concession, Rhodes and Rudd transferred this precious asset to a newly minted shell, called the Central Search Company. Gifford and Cawston were bought off with a large block of shares. Other rivals, men with the flimsiest claims who had vowed to expose the fraud against Lobengula, were also silenced with shares. Sir Hercules Robinson was not overlooked when the spoils were handed out.

At the same time, Rhodes picked off the members of the South Africa Committee, one by one. The Earl of Fife, shortly to become son-in-law to the Prince of Wales and a duke of the realm, agreed to be vice-chairman of Rhodes's new company. Lord Grey, a highly respected Liberal peer with a long record of public service, accepted a position on the board and a large block of shares. Grey, who had been one of Mackenzie's closest associates, was a priceless asset. R.W. Thompson, secretary of the London Missionary Society, was promised official backing in the land of the Matabele. He soon succumbed.

Initially, W.T. Stead had held out against Rhodes, even refusing requests to meet him. He was eventually persuaded by a mutual friend, who deliberately left the two men alone together. After three hours, a gift of £2000 (to settle a libel judgment) and the promise of a £20,000 contribution to the *Pall Mall Gazette*, Stead was 'converted'. Immediately after the meeting he wrote to his wife:

> Mr. Rhodes is my man ... He is full of far more gorgeous idea [sic] in connection with the paper than even I had. I cannot tell you his scheme, because it is too secret. But it involves millions ... He took to me; told me things he has told to no other man, save X ... It all seems like a fairy dream ...
>
> His ideas are federation, expansion and consolidation of Empire ... On my expressing my surprise that we should be in such agreement, he laughed and said – 'It is not to be wondered at, because I have taken my ideas from the *Pall Mall Gazette*.'[11]

Stead, a 40-year-old intellectual heavyweight, was responding to Rhodes in the language of an infatuated schoolgirl. He had not merely been 'squared', he had been seduced.

Stead's letter is a testament to the force of Rhodes's personality. It is also a confirmation of Rhodes's extraordinary powers of perception, his ability to judge a man's character and use that great gift of insight to maximum advantage. To us, the flattery used on Stead – 'I am trusting you with a confidence I have placed in no other man except X; I have taken all my ideas from [your writings]' – may seem obvious, if not crude, but from Stead's reaction we can see that it was perfectly judged. Rhodes knew not only how to flatter his erstwhile opponent but also how to intoxicate him with talk of astronomical sums of money (Stead was under great financial pressure at the time).

Writers who have suggested that Rhodes's conquests were achieved by crude bribery underestimate the man and his opponents, as Stead's experience makes clear. Of course there were many men 'whose only desire was filling money bags', and Rhodes made quick work of them. The exciting challenge, though, was to persuade 'men of principle', men burdened with a conscience or a great reputation, to accept his gifts of money, land or preferment. The technique was invariably the same. First, Rhodes had to convince them that their cause was also *his* cause. Once that had been achieved, bribery took on a different complexion. It was a just reward for risks taken in pursuit of a noble aim.

There were a few, very few, who would not be deluded. Men like Mackenzie and Buxton knew that Rhodes's cause – the cause of the capitalist and the colonist – threatened the interests of the African people they were determined to defend. Even Joseph Chamberlain was able to hold out against Rhodes in the year 1889, but success on other fronts was spectacular.

The press could not resist Rhodes. After the seduction of Stead he turned his attention to *The Times*, which had published several unfavourable articles. Moberley Bell, the managing director, and Flora Shaw, the influential colonial correspondent, soon came under Rhodes's spell. The *St. James Gazette* also reversed its hostile policy after Rhodes had spent a little time with the editor, the eminent Sir Sidney Low. The Rev. John Verschoyle, deputy editor of the *Fortnightly Review*, and Sir Charles Dilke MP, an important contributor to that journal, were secretly placed on Rhodes's payroll and became life-long supporters.

Another crucially important conquest was Sir Harry Johnston, the man responsible for overseeing the African Lakes Company, which operated in a vast area between the Zambezi and the African lakes. Originally founded by Scottish missionaries, the company was now in serious financial difficulties. Rhodes's offer of a subsidy of £9000 a year seemed unbelievably generous, but it was money well spent. Johnston had direct access to Lord Salisbury, the prime minister. At the same time, Rhodes was acquiring a stake in another huge slice of Africa. The parallels with the Kimberley amalgamation are not hard to see.

Rhodes did not, of course, reserve all the plum positions on the board of his new company for the eminent Liberals on the South Africa Committee. He was careful to spread his largesse to both sides of the House. The Duke of Abercorn, a wealthy Tory peer with vast estates in Donegal and Scotland, accepted the chairmanship. With Grey on one side and Abercorn on the other, Rhodes would be relatively safe from attack by either of the great parties of State when the matter of a royal charter was debated at Westminster. That still left Parnell's Irish Party, with 85 votes and a record of implacable opposition to chartered companies; but Rhodes had already prepared the ground. The previous year he had made a gift of £5000 to party funds and pledged a further £5000 once he had received his royal charter.

Rhodes's early biographers were admirers who took pains to justify this curious alliance between Rhodes, the great British patriot, and the party of Irish Home Rule. They are supported by a high-minded correspondence between Rhodes and Parnell, in which the two men appeared to agree that the Irish Party should always maintain a representation at Westminster to preserve 'the Imperial tie'. The letters became public soon after they written – a curious fact, as party contributions were rarely divulged. Furthermore, a close examination of this correspondence reveals that Parnell had made no real commitments. It is hard to disagree with an eminent contemporary biographer, who dismissed the Rhodes–Parnell letters as 'mere verbiage', designed to obscure the fact that Rhodes had bought Irish Party support for £10,000.[12]

Within three months of his arrival in London, the obscure 'pro-Boer MP [from] South Africa' had eliminated all serious opposition and was ready to make his formal application for a royal charter. With Knutsford's blessing, a submission was made to the prime minister, who simply invited Rhodes and his associates to draft the kind of document they wanted. Rhodes proposed that the 'assets' of Central Search should be transferred to a new company, to be called the British South Africa Company, which would be authorized to operate in all territories north of the Limpopo and west of Portuguese possessions in East Africa. Although Salisbury's ministers tried to set a northern limit, Rhodes held out against them and the final document imposed no boundaries either to the north or to the west.

In this limitless territory, Rhodes's company sought:

> [All] powers necessary for the purpose of government ... the right to establish banking and other companies and associations; to make and maintain railways, telegraphs and lines of steamships; to carry on mining operations and license mining companies; to settle, cultivate and improve the lands; to preserve peace and order ... and for that object [to] obtain a force of police and have its own flag.

It is worth remembering that the 'legitimacy' of the charter was based on a document signed by an illiterate king, who had been assured (by a trusted missionary) that he was merely granting permission for ten men to dig in his country!

In July 1889 Rhodes was assured by the prime minister's office that the royal charter was secure. He could safely return to South Africa, leaving Cawston and Bourchier Hawksley, his London solicitor, to agree the fine print with Her Majesty's Government.

While Rhodes was still on board ship, Maund, Babayane and Mtshete finally reached Gubulawayo. The *indunas* had cast off their Western garb long before they reached the Matabeleland border and now stood before their king in their monkey-skin sporrans, holding warning letters from Queen Victoria and the Aborigines Protection Society. Two recent biographers have questioned why Maund should have permitted the letters to reach Lobengula at all. One of them even goes as far as to speculate that Maund might have been attempting to double-cross Rhodes. This is unlikely. The point to remember is that men like Babayane and Mtshete, brought up without knowledge of the written word, developed formidable powers of memory. Indeed Babayane, a relatively junior *induna*, was only selected by Lobengula because of his great talent in that regard. The letters would certainly have been translated to him in London and, short of committing murder, it is hard to see how Maund could have prevented Lobengula hearing 'the Queen's word' at some stage. The point is that he had managed to create a delay of at least three months. By now too many deals had been struck in London, too many great Englishmen (and women) had been 'squared'. Whatever Lobengula might do or say, there was no turning back.

As word of these letters spread, the Matabele response was terrifying, especially for Thompson, who was still 'holding the fort' on Rhodes's behalf after the desertion of Rudd and Maguire. 'Thousands came from all directions to ask the king if it were true that the white dog Thompson had bought the land. Among the Matabili [sic] I was now the most notorious person in the country, and among a section of black and white schemers the most hated.'[13]

Thompson and Lotshe were dragged before a full council of the king and his *indunas* and forced to squat 'in a broiling sun ... not being allowed to move'[14] as accusations of deception and betrayal were hurled at them. For the first time, Thompson felt that Lobengula's own position was in jeopardy, such was the *indunas*' fury that their king had allowed any deal to be struck with white men. To vindicate himself in the eyes of the *indunas* Lobengula made a decision that turned Thompson's blood cold. His friend and ally Lotshe was condemned to death for the crime of 'having advised the king to take the thousand rifles in exchange for gold'.[14] Thompson, still squatting in the heat, was forced to witness the execution.

> I saw the poor old fellow stand erect. He handed his snuffbox to a man standing near. He was taken outside the council kraal, and on kneeling down he said, 'Do as you think fit with me. I am the king's chattel.' One blow from the executioner's stick sufficed; one smart blow on the back of the head ...
>
> That night was spent by the Matebili [sic] in putting to death the men, women and children of Lotjie's [sic] family. It was the most terrible night in my experience ... Some three hundred men, women and children were killed ... Early next morning, I decided to drive over to Hope Fountain, the mission station, to discuss the turn of events with Mr Helm. I had just started when I heard a native following me ... 'Tomoson,' he called quietly, 'the king says the killing of yesterday is not over yet.'[14]

That was enough for Thompson. As a young man, he had seen Matabele raiders kill his own father by forcing a ramrod down his throat. He knew what Lobengula's people were capable of once they caught the scent of blood.

> I cut the finest horse from its traces, jumped on its back, and rode hard ... I had no saddle, only the improvised bridle from the trap harness, and in the scurry I lost my hat. After riding for hours in the blazing sun I had to make a hat by tying four knots in my handkerchief and stuffing it with grass.

Towards sundown I found myself in unknown country in the middle of the Kalahari Desert. I had neither food nor water, and I might be attacked by lions. I tied my horse, climbed into a tree and there spent the night.[15]

The next day Thompson's horse collapsed and he was forced to continue on foot, his 'tongue protruding with thirst' and his eyes 'so bloodshot that [he] could scarcely see'. On the third day he was rescued by a trader, who took him south in his waggon. As soon as he reached the first telegraph office Thompson sent messages to his wife, whom he had not seen for over a year, and to Rhodes, who had just returned to Kimberley. Thompson was 'surprised and disappointed' at Rhodes's response. He was told that he must not return home to his wife and three children. His orders were to rendezvous with Jameson in Mafeking and to travel with him back to Gubulawayo. Rhodes, who had previously assured Thompson that his share in the venture would make him a millionaire,[16] now issued an unambiguous threat: 'It seems so hard for your own future that through not seeing it through to the finish which is so near you should lose your credit and your reward.'[17]

Jameson had already proved his worth when it came to dealing with Lobengula. It was said that he was the only man who was not compelled to grovel before the king on his hands and knees. When Jameson approached Lobengula, he walked erect. According to Ian Colvin, his biographer and uncritical admirer:

> Jameson fascinated Lobengula, as he fascinated most men with whom he came in contact ... Here was a Little Man who had no fear, who laughed as no man had ever laughed before in the king's presence, a man of unprecedented frankness of speech and eye. Lobengula liked Jameson.[18]

It was not entirely a matter of the doctor's winning personality. Lobengula was suffering from gout, brought on by excessive quantities of red meat and champagne, the latter a favourite gift of concession hunters. Jameson relieved the symptoms, though not the causes, by injecting Lobengula with heavy doses of morphine, which soon turned the king into an addict. In gratitude, Jameson was made an *induna* of the Matabele nation. At his investiture he was required to stand almost naked in the great enclosure at Gubulawayo. As the paraded *impis* beat their oxhide shields and danced to their war songs, Lobengula's *indunas* placed an ostrich-feather cloak of nobility around Jameson's bony shoulders and tied ox-tail garters to his legs.

Jameson remained in Gubulawayo for eight weeks. His brief was to placate the king and his people and to obtain permission for limited digging 'so that Rhodes could say that the concession was operating'.[19] Thompson's

213

Frank Johnson in the uniform of the Pioneer Corps (1890).

brief was to convince the king that he had not abdicated land or power when he signed the Rudd concession. To make the task easier, Rhodes had agreed that Thompson should buy off the remaining concession hunters and 'white dogs' by disbursing 'a few thousand pounds'.[20] This proved to be money well spent. The white riffraff in Gubulawayo were soon happy to assure the king that 'we were wrong in all we said about Thompson'. Lobengula was not fooled. 'Rubbing his hand across his mouth he said: "Tomoson has rubbed fat on your mouths. All you white men are liars".'[20]

While this charade was being played out in Gubulawayo, Rhodes was granted his royal charter. John Moffat, who was now on Rhodes's payroll, was given the delicate task of informing Lobengula that the Great White Queen had changed her mind and decided that Cecil Rhodes should be given 'the whole herd'.

With the granting of the royal charter, the British South Africa Company (to be known as the Chartered Company) was formed and capitalized at a million pounds. The par value of the stock, £1, soon rose in the market to nearly £4, reaping a handsome profit for the company's noble directors.

Rhodes now decided that the time had come to put an end to the elaborate dance in Gubulawayo, and in December 1889 he contracted Frank Johnson to 'break up the military power of the Matabele' and deliver Lobengula to him, dead or alive.

Johnson had barged into Rhodes's life earlier that year to complain that he had been unfairly excluded from the lucrative deal that Gifford and Cawston had made when their Bechuanaland Company was taken over. At the time, Johnson was general manager of the company and expected a cut, which was refused by Gifford and his cronies.

Johnson was 22 years old in 1889 and conformed to a type that Rhodes found particularly appealing. He was handsome, aggressive and self-confident. Although his military career had not taken him beyond the rank of quartermaster sergeant in the Bechuanaland mounted police, Rhodes decided that he was just the man to lead a military expedition against one of the most formidable warrior nations in Africa. By the terms of the secret contract drawn up between the two men, Johnson undertook to raise a force of 500 colonials. If he succeeded, he would be paid £100,000 and every man in his force would receive a grant of 3000 acres of land and the right to prospect for gold in Matabeleland.

Johnson's plan was to infiltrate his force into Bechuanaland in four-man groups, disguised as prospectors. They would reassemble 'in an uninhabited part of the country' close to the Matabeleland border, and then choose a suitable 'moonlight night' to make a dash to Gubulawayo. Fortunately for all concerned, Johnson's chum Maurice Heany, an Irish-American dropout from the West Point Military Academy, boasted about the plan when drunk in the hearing of a local missionary. The matter was immediately reported to Shippard, who had no alternative but to pass the information to the High Commissioner in the Cape.

Unfortunately for Rhodes, the amenable Sir Hercules Robinson had been replaced by Sir Henry Loch, a mountain of a man in his early 60s with a grizzled patriarch's beard that came down to his chest. Apart from his formidable appearance, the problem with Loch was that he had no particular liking for Rhodes.

Johnson was swiftly summoned to Rhodes's office in Cape Town to hear that his paymaster had just returned from a grilling by the High Commissioner. Rhodes, of course, had denied all knowledge of the plot and now insisted that Johnson should return to the High Commissioner's office with him and claim sole responsibility.[21] Evidently the young man performed to everyone's satisfaction. Loch decided to take no action and when Rhodes made a more practical plan, Frank Johnson was once again 'the contractor'. This time, the idea was to raise a force of men who would avoid a confrontation with Lobengula by skirting Matabeleland and striking instead for the eastern part of the country, populated by the more gentle Shona. Under the terms of his new contract, Johnson undertook to hand over Mashonaland 'fit for civil government' by 1 October 1890 at a cost of £87,000 (with a down payment of £30,000 on signature). Johnson had drawn up the second document himself, and when Hawksley, Rhodes's London solicitor, objected on the grounds that Johnson had provided no security, Rhodes wired back: 'Have got security – his life'.[22]

Johnson had estimated that he would need no more than 250 men to take the country. On the successful completion of the mission, each man would receive a grant of 3000 acres and 15 mining claims in Mashonaland.[23] While serving in Johnson's force, their pay would be set at 7s. 6d. a day – six times that of a private in the British army.

'Pioneers'. Heany is seated in the centre with Johnson and Selous on his left.

As the intention was to skirt Lobengula's territory and take no aggressive action, there was no need for secrecy and Johnson was able to advertise for volunteers in the Cape papers. Thousands of young men responded. Rhodes had insisted on strict criteria for selection. His 'pioneers' must be 'good fighting men' with a variety of trades and skills who would be able to form 'the complete nucleus of a civil population'.[22] (The one oversight – the exclusion of women – does not seem to have occurred to Rhodes.) They had to be of both English and Afrikaans stock and limited 'as far as possible to the sons of the leading families in each district of the Cape'. When Johnson reacted to this last condition with 'amazement', Rhodes's characteristic answer was:

> Do you know what will happen to you? You will probably be massacred by the Matabele, or at least we shall one day hear that you have been surrounded and cut off! And who will rescue you do you think? I will tell you – the Imperial Factor [i.e. Her Majesty's Government] ... And who do you think will bring pressure to bear on the Imperial Factor and stir them to save you? *The influential fathers of your young men!*[22]

No sooner had Johnson drawn up his final list than Rhodes added another

12 names of his own. When Johnson refused to accept them on the grounds that each new recruit would add £500 to his costs, Rhodes settled the matter with a cheque for £6000. This little band came to be known as 'Rhodes's angels' or 'Rhodes's lambs' and included Johnny Grimmer, who would hear Rhodes's dying words in the Muizenburg cottage, and Bobby Coryndon, destined to be the governor of Northern Rhodesia.

Johnson assembled his 'Pioneer Corps' in Kimberley and then moved them to a training camp north of Mafeking. It was here that Rhodes's scheme to take Mashonaland on the cheap was compromised by the visiting High Commissioner. On questioning Johnson, Loch discovered that no plans had been made for leaving behind lines of supply. Rhodes argued that this was unnecessary as his 'pioneers' would be a self-contained community, provisioned for many months ahead. Loch accused Rhodes of extreme irresponsibility and refused to sanction the operation unless the Chartered Company provided another force of at least 400 mounted men to hold the base, and if necessary, go to their assistance. Rhodes was furious. Johnson described the scene:

> Rhodes indulged in some strong and excitable language. He foresaw ruin and every other kind of disaster for our plans; but, at the same time, he despatched a telegram to Rutherfoord Harris at Kimberley ordering him to engage the 400 mounted men at once. This was the genesis of that splendid force ... the British South Africa Police.[24]

Lieutenant Colonel Pennefather, 'a leather-tough veteran of the Zulu wars', was put in charge of this force. Sir John Willoughby, 'a keen young guardsman ... known as Johnny to his friends', was made second-in-command. (The feckless Heany, incidentally, was Johnson's second-in-command and was given the rank of captain.)

'Pioneers' and police were working under a great disadvantage. There was not a man among them who had any knowledge of the country they were supposed to occupy, let alone a way of getting there other than by the hunters' road, which went through Gubulawayo. Rhodes solved this problem in typical fashion. He approached Selous, who had been a thorn in his flesh ever since the *indunas*' visit to London. Alan Quartermain was then in Cape Town, where he sold his soul to Rhodes for £2000 in cash, a hundred De Beers shares, a grant of 21,000 acres in Mashonaland and a salary of £2 5s a day. In return for these favours he agreed to act as guide and intelligence officer (in effect, co-leader) of the 'pioneer' column. It was understood, of course, that there would be no more articles or lectures on the subject of Rhodes's 'illegitimate' claim to Mashonaland (see p. 202).

Everything was now securely in place – everything, that is, except Lobengula. Jameson paid two more visits to Gubulawayo. The second one in April 1890 was critical. Somehow Jameson had to persuade the king to accept another change to the ground rules. He was no longer asking permission to send a few diggers into the country. He wanted the king to accept a whole army.

Lobengula was in a terrible position, pressured from one side by Jameson and from the other by his young warriors, who were thirsting for blood and vengeance. Ultimately, he knew that the whites would be irresistible. All he could hope to do in the meantime was to twist and turn and play for time.

An early biographer, writing in Jameson's lifetime, provided a moving description of that last meeting between Lobengula and 'Dr Jim':

> The king ... dared not show much favour to Jameson, who saw that it was useless to remain ... He arranged to leave the next morning at daybreak, but before starting, as a final effort, went to Lobengula to say good-bye ... The old king was stark naked, somewhat agitated – an unwieldy mass of dark copper-coloured flesh moving endlessly up and down within the dim, uncertain light of [his] hut.
>
> 'Well, king,' said Jameson, 'as you will not confirm your promise and grant me the road, I shall bring my white *impi*, and if necessary we shall fight.' Lobengula replied: 'I never refused the road to you and your *impi*.'
>
> 'Very well,' said Jameson, 'then you acknowledge that you have promised to grant me the road; and unless you refuse it now, your promise holds good.' Then, as the king remained diplomatically silent, Jameson said: 'Good-bye, Chief ...'
>
> That was the last time these two saw each other.[25]

On 26 June 1890, Rhodes's 'army' moved out of base camp with 117 loaded waggons, field guns, rocket launchers, 'electric mines', Gatlings and Maxim machine guns and a searchlight with a portable steam dynamo borrowed from Her Majesty's naval station at Simonstown 'to impress the superstitious Matabele'.

The 196 officers and men of the so-called 'pioneer' force wore tunics of brown corduroy, yellow leather leggings and bush hats, pinned up at the brim. Each man carried a Martini-Henry rifle in a gun-bucket, a Webley revolver in a holster at his waist and a long-handled axe slung across his saddle.

With the 'pioneers' rode Canon Balfour and the Rev. Sturridge of the Anglican community; Frederick Selous; Arthur Hartman, a Jesuit father; Archibald Colquhoun, a retired colonial officer appointed to administer the new country; and Dr Jameson, who held Rhodes's power of attorney.

Behind the 'pioneers' rode the 500 officers and men of the British South Africa Police. A thousand 'Coloured boys and native labourers' followed on foot. The entire column stretched for two and a half miles.

Once news reached Gubulawayo that the column was on the move, the king was under tremendous pressure to unleash his warriors and wipe out the 'invaders', but he refused all demands. At the first sign of trouble, most of the traders and all the missionaries had fled the country, leaving only eight whites behind. Among them was Colenbrander, now representing the interests of the Chartered Company. A single gesture from the king or one of his senior *indunas* would have resulted in massacre, but again Lobengula refused to satisfy the warriors' thirst for blood.

On 30 June[26] the 'pioneers' crossed the Shashi river and entered Matabele territory, where they built the first of four forts. While construction was in progress, a party of *indunas* walked into the 'pioneer' camp bearing a letter written by one of the remaining Gubulawayo traders at the king's dictation. It read: 'Has the king killed any white men that an *impi* is on the border, or have the white men lost something they are looking for?'

Jameson solemnly assured the *indunas* that this was a working party, protected by soldiers, who 'were going to Mashonaland along the road already arranged with the king'. The *indunas* were not convinced, whereupon Johnson decided 'to settle the matter in a manner which ... would appeal to the native mind'.

> I gave a practical demonstration of our powers by running the searchlight and firing off our nine-pounders and machine guns. The Matabele *induna*s were so impressed with this display that they speedily returned to Lo Bengula with the most startling and hair-raising stories of our 'witchcraft'.[27]

The next 200 miles (262 kilometres) of march lay through the thick bush of the low veld and it was here that the real danger of the Matabele lay. The rate of advance was never more than 12 miles (19 kilometres) a day. One 'pioneer' troop would go ahead cutting down trees and hacking out the stumps to let the waggons pass, while Selous and his scouts fanned out, looking for Matabele. At sundown the vast column would break into several tight laagers (squares formed by waggons) and throughout the night the beam of the naval searchlight would sweep the sky and 'electric mines' would explode at regular intervals.[27]

While his private army was negotiating the dangers of the low veld, Rhodes's political career in Cape Town was also on the march. Rhodes's old adversary Sprigg had once again been forced to resign as premier. His grandiose and ruinously expensive plans to expand the whole railway network (as opposed to Rhodes's preferred option of concentrating on the line to the north) had finally cost Sprigg his job. Rhodes was now asked to form the next government. He skilfully brought together Liberals and Bondsmen in a 'cabinet of all talents'. Even Merriman was persuaded to join the team, but Rhodes's promise of balance and 'fair play' was a deception, as his old friend would find out to his cost. Hofmeyr, who had refused a cabinet position, was the real arbiter and Rhodes consulted him ahead of every political move. Whatever he might claim in public, Rhodes was running an Afrikaans government committed to Bond policies.

To borrow Geoffrey Wheatcroft's telling phrase, Rhodes was now like a gambler playing on several tables at once, and it must surely have occurred to someone to question how Mr Rhodes, the prime minister, could possibly deal with matters affecting Mr Rhodes, the diamond monopolist, or enter into contracts with Mr Rhodes, the chairman of Gold Fields, or Mr Rhodes, the railway contractor, or Mr Rhodes of the Chartered Company.

While Rhodes was relishing his triumphs in Cape Town, his 'pioneers' reached the aptly named 'Providential Pass'. A long, gentle climb took them out of the dangerous, wooded low veld into open grassland. At the crest of the pass, the 'pioneers' built another fort and named it after their queen. For some arbitrary reason, which nevertheless has an important bearing on the later story, it was decided that Fort Victoria stood on a boundary separating Lobengula's Matabeleland from Shona territory, which the 'pioneers' now claimed as their own.

Each day's march east of Fort Victoria took the column further and further from the danger of Matabele attack, and they now had another advantage as well. In open country, the superiority of Maxims and field guns over spears and single-shot rifles was absolute.

The final destination had been suggested by Selous. It was a hill he had called Mount Hamden, 'at the centre of a great grassy plain ... fertile and full of promise'. Here Rhodes proposed to establish his capital, which would be called Salisbury in honour of the British prime minister.

In this place on 13 September 1890, Lieutenant Tyndale-Biscoe of the 'pioneer' column hoisted the Union Jack on a tree. Canon Balfour offered a prayer 'and following the Royal Salute of twenty-one guns, there were three lusty cheers given for the Queen'.[28]

On 30 September Fort Salisbury was completed and the 'pioneers' were dismissed. Fired with enthusiasm, they spread out across the country to peg their gold claims and 3000-acre farms.

When he heard the news in Cape Town, Rhodes was exultant. 'Without firing a single shot we have occupied probably the richest gold-field in the world, with the acquiescence of the natives, at a cost to the Company of something like £200,000.'

Rhodes had always made it clear that once he had negotiated the Matabele 'obstacle', he would accept no limits to his African ambitions. '[Lobengula] is the only block to Central Africa,' he wrote, 'as, once we have his territory the rest is easy ...'[29] 'If we get Matabeleland we shall get the balance of Africa. I do not stop in my ideas at the Zambezi ...'[30]

Before the 'pioneer' column set out from their Bechuanaland base camp, Rhodes had held a 'council of war' in the Kimberley Club to plan northern expansion across the Zambezi and as far as the Sudan border. Among those present were H.H. Johnston and John Moir of the African Lakes Company, Maguire, Archibald Colquhoun, Grant – son of the man who, with Speke, had found the source of the Nile – and Joseph Thomson, who had already won fame by his journeys to Masailand, Nigeria and the Sudan.

As soon as the flag was raised in Salisbury, Rhodes's agents were all over the map, signing up chiefs and securing mineral and land 'rights'. Frank Lochner, aided and abetted by the French Protestant missionary François Collard, secured exclusive mineral rights to Barotseland (later part of Northern Rhodesia, today's Zambia) for a payment of £2000. In the west two more agents, Bagley and Fraser, negotiated concessions in Angola as far as the Cunene and Cubango rivers. In the east, Selous and Colquhoun signed a treaty with Mutasa, king of Manicaland, and another agent, Aurel Schulz, opened negotiations with Gungunyana, king of Gazaland. Both these territories were claimed by Portugal as their East African possessions and, for what it was worth, the claim had been recognized by Lord Salisbury's Government. But Rhodes was unstoppable.

In this incredible year of 1890, he could lay claim to a belt of territory stretching almost the whole way across Africa from the Indian Ocean to within 200 miles of the Atlantic coast, and from the Limpopo northwards to the African lakes. He was also prime minister of the Cape, chairman of De Beers and Gold Fields and managing director of the British South Africa Company.

In 1890, Rhodes was 36 years old. Seventeen years earlier he had been given six months to live, but, as Rhodes's adoring secretary Philip Jourdan wrote: 'The sheer force of his willpower would have conquered any illness at any time.'[31]

SIXTEEN

'A PRIVATE LIFE'

*I know everybody asks why I do not marry. I cannot get married.
I have too much work on my hands. I shall always be away from home,
and I should not be able to do my duty as a husband towards his wife.*

CECIL RHODES[1]

Rhodes's first home in South Africa was a grass hut in the Umkomaas valley. Since then he had lived in a succession of digger encampments, tin cottages, bachelor 'chummeries', rooming houses and hotels. He seemed to care as little for home comforts as he did for fine clothes. His money, he used to say, was there to work for him, not to pamper him. In the days when he lived with Neville Pickering, their spartan quarters in Kimberley were considered so remarkable that Robert Graham, Rhodes's trustee and the first chairman of De Beers, used to take distinguished visitors there during Rhodes's many absences. 'An outside door opened from the street into a small shabby bedroom, on the iron stretcher an old Gladstone bag sagged in the middle, served as a bolster for a dingy pillow. "That is the bed of a man worth £100,000, and I consider it one of the sights of Kimberley".'[2]

When Rhodes became prime minister, his Cape Town home was a set of noisy rooms above a bank in Adderley Street, the main thoroughfare. He shared these quarters with Captain Penfold, the harbour master, who not only introduced Rhodes to the delights of sailing but ensured that the member for Barkly West always left the premises suitably dressed.

During the first parliamentary recess after his appointment as Prime Minister, Rhodes decided the time had come to acquire a home that befitted his position. His first choice was Groote Schuur, which he leased in early 1891. Two years later he purchased the freehold for £200.

The original Groote Schuur (literally 'Big Grange') was one of three barns built by the Dutch East India Company in 1657 to store grain, wine and tithes. In 1790 the property was sold and converted into a private residence. Subsequent alterations (and a fire) eliminated much of its Cape Dutch character and, by the time Rhodes acquired the property, it had

222

been transformed into a neo-Georgian mansion acceptable to English tastes.

Groote Schuur was beautifully situated 'on the slopes of Table Mountain which to the east, west and south overlooked two oceans, and to the north that wonderful African continent'.[3] As the house was only a few miles from the centre of Cape Town, both Sir Hercules Robinson and his predecessor, Sir Humphry Barkly, had used it as a summer residence.

Once Rhodes had bought the property, he was determined to take Groote Schuur back to its roots. Cape Dutch architecture was considered raw and crude at a time when the prevalent taste tended towards clutter and fussy detail but, for Rhodes, it was style that had come to express his sense of self – 'big and simple – barbaric if you like'.[4]

To interpret his vision, Rhodes engaged Herbert Baker, a young architect who had recently arrived from England. Rhodes met Baker by chance at a dinner party given by Merriman's sister-in-law and 'took a great fancy to him'.[5] It was a fortuitous meeting. Baker was not only gifted, he was perceptive:

> It is probable that Cecil Rhodes, before he built Groote Schuur, had thought very little about art or architecture … but [now] his mind turned to the problem of art, with that wonderful power of concentration which was so strongly developed in him that it almost amounted to genius.[3]

That was certainly an aspect of Rhodes's character which had not changed since his days as a cotton farmer. Once he had decided to embark on a project, he mastered it. Groote Schuur focused his aesthetic sensibilities into a desire for clean lines and unfussy shapes. 'Breadth, simplicity and symmetry', 'whitewash and old wood', 'the subordination of ornament to a single idea' and 'nothing petty or finikin' – those became the guiding principles behind Rhodes's new creation.

Groote Schuur was gutted and massively enlarged. A whole boat-load of teak was imported from Burma and lavishly used for ceilings, panelling and floors.[5] In place of a low slate roof, Groote Schuur soon wore a crown of pitched thatch and white gables. Massive stone fireplaces appeared in the hall and principal rooms. Rhodes's bath was carved out of a block of solid granite.

With its barley-twist chimneys and colonnaded verandas, Groote Schuur was not strictly Cape Dutch. It was Cecil Rhodes. The past had been reinvented in his own image, but not long after the vision had been accomplished the house caught fire.

Groote Schuur was immediately rebuilt and, this time, Rhodes was able to impose his aesthetics even more strictly, thanks to the loss of all the original furniture, which had been bought in a hurry and in bulk from Maples of London. His agents scoured the Cape for early Dutch and Huguenot pieces 'of plain and massive character',[3] for finely-grained stinkwood chests and old Cape silver.

During both stages of building, Rhodes acquired more and more of the surrounding land until he owned an estate of 1500 acres. He laid out his great regiments of flowering shrubs, his 'lake of hydrangeas', his plantations of pines.[6] He acquired wild animals and exotic birds. He opened his estate to the public and entertained lavishly. Visiting celebrities, financiers, missionaries, politicians, military men, friends and hangers-on were all received at Groote Schuur.

When he first acquired the house in 1891, Rhodes decided that he would need a companion to share and run his home. Harry Currey was summoned to Cape Town, and although the young man warned Rhodes that he 'had neither training nor experience of running a house', he agreed to do his best.[7] Harry was to be responsible for hiring the staff and making all domestic arrangements. When it came to setting a budget to run the house, stables and gardens, Rhodes simply said: 'Let us try on £250 a month and if you want more let me know.'[7] (The sum is equivalent to £12,000 a month today.)

In addition to his domestic duties, Harry was to be Rhodes's private secretary. He would keep his position (and salary) as Secretary of Gold Fields and take on the new post of secretary to the Chartered Company, on the grounds that Rhodes would now be controlling both companies from Cape Town. Only days after Harry received this cluster of new appointments, Rhodes announced that he had to leave for London at once and wanted Harry with him.

It was less than two years since Rhodes had slipped into England, an unknown colonial MP with a formidable opposition lined up against him. Harry's account of Rhodes's reception on this visit gives the measure of the earlier achievement. At 1 a.m. on a bitterly cold March morning, the Duke of Abercorn and his entourage were waiting at Paddington Station to meet the boat train. The next day, Lord Rothschild was at their hotel before they had a chance to finish breakfast ...

> And it is no very great exaggeration to say that from that moment until we left London three weeks later there was a progression of visitors ... Society folk, politicians, financiers, newspapermen (and women) followed one another in an unceasing flow while every postal delivery brought shoals of invitations and requests of all kinds. I learnt what the expression, 'the lion of the season' meant.[7]

Harry would also learn about the foibles of the rich and privileged. Indeed, lessons began on the very first night. The Duke of Abercorn had accompanied them to the Westminster Palace Hotel, where a hot meal was waiting. Rhodes used the occasion to deliver an excited account of developments north of the Limpopo to his chairman, but the great Tory peer appeared to understand none of it. When Rhodes had finished his 'thrilling tale', there was a moment's silence before his Grace turned to Harry with a look of blank stupidity and said, 'We are having a really capital black-cock season this year and got (so many) brace.' Harry described Rhodes's face as 'a study'.

Lord Rothschild was a man of a very different stamp. As he got up to leave the breakfast table the next morning, 'he managed to slip in one last, man-to-man piece of advice: "And so remember, as I was saying, Mr. Rhodes," he remarked, as he drew on his gloves, "never allow yourself to get caught without a loose million handy".' (That's almost £50 million by today's values.)

The young private secretary's education was advancing. The story continues with his own narrative:

> The most interesting visitor of them all was undoubtedly Charles Stewart Parnell. He used to call frequently about six in the evening and wait patiently in my room until Rhodes was disengaged. And a delightful visitor he was, because though chatting to me, he might have been talking to a man of his own age. At that time he had been cited as co-respondent in the O'Shea case ... and was fighting for his political life against those in his own party who wished to oust him from its leadership ...
>
> One evening he told Rhodes 'I shall lose' and Rhodes asked 'Why do you say that?' Parnell replied, 'Because the priests are against me.' Rhodes, walking up and down the room, as he was wont, suddenly turned and asked, 'Can't we square the Pope?'
>
> One likes to think of a thoughtful Cardinal Secretary wondering just how to acknowledge the receipt of a packet, addressed to His Holiness 'with Mr. C.J. Rhodes's compliments', containing 250 De Beers Preference Shares![7]

It was Harry's job to go to Hoare's Bank and withdraw £5000 in cash – the promised second payment to Parnell. When the young man asked how he should make out the cheque, Rhodes replied 'Bearer' and in the counterfoil insert 'Self'.

Harry strolled into the bank 'trying to look as if the cashing of a cheque for £5000 was an everyday practice of mine' (£5000 is equivalent to £250,000 today).

> Without blinking an eye-lid, the teller inquired 'How will you have it?' I said, 'Well, in hundreds', and he threw me a packet of these valuable securities without so much as counting them. I put them in my breast pocket and as I did so there flashed through my mind every tale I had ever read or heard of

people being hit over the head and robbed as they came out of a Bank. I asked the Commissionaire to call me a hansom and to open the doors for me when it came up. When he announced that it was at the door I made a dash for it, jumped in, slammed the door and told the cabby to drive me to the Westminster Palace Hotel ... That evening the money was handed to Parnell.[7]

Among his many other duties, Harry had to protect Rhodes from a string of unwanted callers. He also had to organize the social diary. Queen Victoria, the Prince of Wales, Lord Salisbury and William Gladstone would all extend invitations, and although Rhodes accepted 'twenty-one luncheons and the same number of dinner engagements' during his three weeks in London, many an important host and hostess had to be refused. According to Harry, 'Rhodes was quite indifferent as to which of these lion-hunters he dined with. It was all a part of his job.'[7]

On one occasion, Harry committed the unpardonable error of double-booking a dinner engagement. The matter only came to light when Harry consulted his diary late the same afternoon. It was a private secretary's nightmare. He must either offend Lady Frederick Cavendish, 'of whom it was said that she was the keeper of Gladstone's conscience', or Baroness Burdett-Coutts, the richest heiress in England, who was rumoured to have declined proposals of marriage from both Wellington and Louis Napoleon. This hideous dilemma was resolved by Lord Chesterfield, who was with Rhodes when Harry burst in with the calamitous news: 'Lord Chesterfield gave judgement in favour of the hostess who was being honoured by Royalty that evening'. That settled the matter in favour of the 77-year-old Baroness. Harry wrote a grovelling letter of apology to the other great lady, who was, he records, 'very nice about it'.

Another of Harry's responsibilities was 'to find some good furniture shop and there place orders for the complete furnishing of Groote Schuur'. The hotel recommended Maples in Tottenham Court Road. Harry arrived with his lists but, faced with so many choices, found he was 'all at sea'. A helpful salesman suggested the firm should send 'three of everything' to the hotel, where Mr Rhodes would be able to make a selection at his convenience. The delivery arrived the next morning in a convoy of vehicles, and one of the hotel's main reception rooms was converted into another branch of Maples. 'There everything, literally everything, was displayed – "three of a kind" – salt cellars, dining room chairs, grid-irons, Persian rugs, table napkins, wardrobes.'[7]

Unfortunately, Rhodes had not yet met Herbert Baker and so had not applied that 'wonderful power of concentration' to the great questions of art, architecture and aesthetics. He simply refused to look at Maples' display and

Harry had to take the plunge. Groote Schuur was furnished 'from cellars to attic ... in about a quarter of an hour'.

The high point of the visit was the arrival of 'a large official envelope which contained a command to Mr. Rhodes to dine and sleep at Windsor Castle that night, and intimating ... that Court Dress was to be worn'. Neither Rhodes nor Harry had any ideas about court dress, and it was already mid-morning by the time Harry had completed his research. The train Rhodes would have to take to Windsor left London at 5.00 p.m., but a Bond Street tailor proved equal to the challenge: 'At four minutes to five a messenger arrived on Paddington platform with a suitcase containing everything required by a gentleman who was to dine with the Queen, including a pair of shoes with diamond buckles.'[7]

That evening Cecil Rhodes met Queen Victoria for the first time. It was less than two years since she had warned Babayane and Mtshete against him, but now she was under his spell. It is said that she asked him point-blank, 'Is it true, Mr Rhodes, that you are a woman-hater?', to which he graciously replied, 'How could I possibly hate a sex to which your Majesty belongs?'[8]

The hectic pace was maintained to the very last day, when Rhodes received an invitation to dine with Lord Salisbury. Harry raced round to the offices of the Union Steamship Company, hoping to delay the departure of their ship, which was due to leave Southampton that afternoon. The company officials regretfully informed him that they were under a contractual obligation to respect the advertised sailing times. However, there was nothing to prevent the captain dropping anchor in Southampton water and waiting there until the early hours of the following morning. A quick visit to the offices of the South Western Railway Company secured a special train, which Rhodes and Harry eventually boarded at midnight. A tug was standing by at Southampton docks, and at 2.30 a.m. they reached the mail steamer. At 3.00 a.m. they were on their way to Cape Town.[7]

Life was less arduous once they returned to Groote Schuur. Rhodes was in high form, in better health than at any time before or after. He seemed to be able to take all his responsibilities in his stride, and Harry gave him capable and conscientious support. On most days the two of them would join Merriman and Rose-Innes, his fellow Liberal in the Cabinet, for an early-morning ride. Harry's mount 'rejoiced in the name of IDB', but he did not say whether it was his witty idea or Rhodes's to name the animal after the 'scourge' of the diamond industry. In a letter written at this time, Merriman showed an understanding of at least one important aspect of Rhodes's relationship with Harry: 'Personally just now [Rhodes] is very charming ... but he trusts no one really and thinks everyone can be bought. Except Jameson and Harry, all his familiars are self-seekers and stuff him with adulation for their own purposes.'[9]

That was Rhodes's problem. His triumphs were two-edged. By his success he had proved, again and again, that 'every man has his price', but the lesson was painful. Was there anyone he could trust when he was burdened with this knowledge? There were Jameson and Harry and, of course, the late Neville Pickering, but there was more to these relationships than trust, as Harry discovered himself only four months after his return from England.

Unbeknown to Rhodes, his secretary had formed a deep attachment to a young woman called Ethel Fairbridge. The couple had originally been introduced at a dance. More than 50 years later, when Ethel was long dead, Harry recalled that first meeting: 'I can see her now in my mind's eye – wearing a white dress and round her waist a Roman sash ... She had the most beautiful blue eyes I ever saw in a human being, a pretty complexion and looked always so straight and thoroughly good in the best sense of that much abused word.'

The couple met again at dinner parties and dances, and soon contrived to see each other almost every day in Adderley Street. Harry would slip out of the nearby Parliament building, while Ethel made a point of volunteering to do all the Fairbridge family shopping. On 8 August 1891, Harry and Ethel became engaged. When Harry finally summoned up the courage to tell Rhodes, his patron 'went off the deep end at the idea of losing [me]'. Frank Johnson, who was visiting Groote Schuur at the time, described the scene:

> Everyone knew that [Harry] was engaged except Rhodes. When the news was broken, there followed an amazing scene. Rhodes raved and stormed like a maniac. His voice rose to a screech as he kept on screaming: 'Leave my house! Leave my house!' No small schoolboy, or even schoolgirl, could have behaved more childishly than he did.[10]

Harry begged Rhodes to believe that there was no question of 'losing' him and that he could still be a loyal private secretary. However, Rhodes would have none of it. 'He always used to say that no one could marry a wife and also keep secrets. "You sleep with a woman, and you talk in your sleep. A man may be perfectly honest, but he talks in his sleep".'[10]

When the initial storm had abated, Rhodes changed tactics.

> He said that he would miss me very much, that we always got on 'exceedingly well' and that had I not proposed to get married we should doubtless have continued to live together until one or another of us died. He did not know nor care whom he would get to succeed me ... Then he talked a great deal about his income, both present and prospective, and what he intends doing with it ...[7]

Rhodes was clearly forcing the young man to make a choice between his marriage and his job, and although this was not Harry's interpretation, the reader cannot fail to recognize emotional and financial blackmail. Harry was not deflected. He chose marriage and ceased to be Rhodes's private secretary. At the wedding reception, Rhodes walked up to the bride and said: 'I am very jealous of you'.[7]

Harry Currey (1897).

This seems an appropriate moment to step back from the narrative and confront an issue that seems to excite obsessive interest whenever the name of Cecil Rhodes is mentioned. Was Rhodes a homosexual? My *Oxford Dictionary* defines homosexual (adjective) as 'having a sexual propensity for persons of one's own sex'. On the basis of that narrow interpretation, one cannot say that Rhodes was homosexual. There is plenty of evidence, though, of his powerful emotional relationships with other men and an absence of anything equivalent in his relationships with women. A word of caution, though, before we invoke clichés of 'Victorian repression' and 'Victorian hypocrisy'. A vast gulf separates present-day ideas of love (and particularly love between members of the same sex) and those which prevailed in Rhodes's day. Unless one has some grasp of this, it is impossible to understand Rhodes's personal life and the importance of the relationships he formed.

Consider the following statement, written by Philip Jourdan, who became Rhodes's private secretary at the age of 24. Jourdan had been pining for the job for over a year.

> An uncontrollable desire took hold of me to be his private secretary ... It was my great secret and I did not communicate it to a soul ... Sometimes I would lie awake half the night working myself up into a state of delirious excitement, speculating on the joy and pleasure which would be mine ... when I should be always with him and would go wherever he went ... I worshipped him and had an intense desire to work for him and to please him ... I used to take long solitary walks, sometimes extending over several hours, thinking of nothing but Rhodes, Rhodes, Rhodes and my devotion towards him.[11]

Some would call this 'hero-worship'. I would call it a frank declaration of love – and it was not discovered in a secret drawer. It appears in the first chapter of Jourdan's biography of Rhodes, which was published in 1911. By that time Jourdan was married and had three children.

There is a tendency to look back on the Victorians with condescension, to think of them as either hypocrites or sexual ignoramuses. But as Robert Hyam argues in his brilliant study, *Empire and Sexuality*,[12] the Victorians perhaps showed a greater understanding than we do of the complexity and fragility of human beings. In some respects they were more tolerant. People were seldom defined by the sexual act; the idea of the homosexual as a member of a separate species is peculiar to our century and, until very recently, to our Western culture. Indeed, the word 'homosexual' does not appear in any English dictionary until 1897.

Starting in Britain in the late nineteenth century, there has been a persistent pressure to ostracize and persecute those who deviate from the repressive, Pauline prescriptions of the Protestant Church. In 1885 the Criminal Law Amendment was passed by the British Parliament. Clause XI, the notorious Labouchère amendment, made all types of sexual activity between males illegal, irrespective of the age of consent. According to Hyams, 'The new laws forced a polarisation of personal position, a rigid self-labelling of an inherently harmful kind ... By banishing male affection from normal life and experience, men in general were impoverished, even diminished ... The tendency to effeminacy was reinforced.'[12]

However, it was not until 1895 and the sensational trials of Oscar Wilde that 'the love that dare not speak its name' was brought into the public eye in England, and not until the second decade of this century that the full effects were felt in the Colonies. Philip Jourdan could still declare his feelings in 1911 and Rhodes could live his life by the standards of an earlier age when romantic friendships between men – and between women – flourished.

These were not gay relationships in anything approaching the modern sense of the word. Had they lived today, Jameson, Pickering, Beit, Harry Currey and all the young men in Rhodes's life would have had no difficulty establishing their heterosexual credentials. Jameson was a notorious womaniser[13] and Beit's 'brazen visits to brothels' were certainly no secret.[14] But what of Rhodes? One of his young secretaries wrote: 'There was one woman, a very charming daughter of a Cape family, whom ... he proposed to several times.'[15] Harry Currey once told his son in confidence that Rhodes had a sexual preference for 'low-life females',[16] and there were certainly rumours of liaisons with Coloured and Zulu prostitutes. Robert Hyams believes that Rhodes was asexual, and it is a view I share.[17] Admittedly, this is speculation, but I hope intelligent speculation, based on one's knowledge of the man.

Rhodes was capable of getting anything he wanted, including sexual liaisons with other men if that had been his wish. We know a great deal about the secret lives of some of his famous contemporaries, but in the millions of words written about and by Cecil Rhodes there is no hint of a hidden sexual life. On the contrary, the most striking thing about the books and manuscripts that have come down to us from his young men is their openness. The emotional scenes, the moments of affection, the times when they bathed together or had to share the same bed are all described, with no suggestion from these red-blooded lads that this behaviour was abnormal. If it had been, those books would have been written much more carefully.

It is my belief that in the much freer atmosphere that existed before puritan legislation had taken hold, Rhodes had all the emotional space he needed, and that his relationships, though intense and sometimes possessive, were not complicated by sexual desire.

Within Rhodes's inner circle there were both young men and older contemporaries – notably Jameson, Beit and Charles Metcalf, the big, jovial railway engineer, who is beautifully described by a visitor to Groote Schuur in the late 1890s:

> I shall never forget the first occasion upon which I dined with [Rhodes]. The only other guest was Sir Charles Metcalf, the engineer, who was, like Cecil Rhodes, a gigantic man. They both drank stout and champagne out of huge silver tankards, and looked to me like veritable Vikings.[18]

Those who were admitted into the innermost circle understood something that Harry had failed to grasp. If a man wished to stay close to Rhodes, he remained single. Marriage was seen as virtually an act of betrayal and men like Frank Johnson, who was already married when he met Rhodes, remained in the second rank. As Rhodes would often say of him, 'Johnson was lost before I knew him'.[10]

After Harry Currey's departure, Johnny Grimmer was appointed personal secretary. Born in 1867, Grimmer had been taken to the diggings in the early days of the diamond rush when he was only three years old. He had worked in the Dutoitspan mine as a boy and was later taken on as a clerk by De Beers. It is said that Rhodes was standing one day outside his office, which overlooked the company stables, when he saw Grimmer trying to mount a rearing horse. The boy was thrown several times before he managed to control the animal, at which point Rhodes turned to a colleague and said: 'That boy has grit, I must speak to him'.[19]

Grimmer was an appalling secretary. A typical letter, written on a torn half-sheet of paper, simply read: 'Dear Sir, In answer to your application, Mr. Rhodes says no. Yours faithfully, John R. Grimmer.'[20]

Grimmer was soon replaced as secretary by Philip Jourdan, but he remained close to Rhodes to the last and survived him by only two months. When Jourdan fell ill Rhodes took on another young civil servant, Gordon Le Sueur, and it was this triumvirate that remained at the centre of an expanding circle of young men.

Rhodes would receive dozens of employment applications every day, and if he liked the sound of a man, he would ask to see him. No secret was made of the fact that Rhodes was influenced by looks. Philip Jourdan wrote: 'He appeared particularly partial to people with blue eyes. On more than one occasion I heard him [say] ... about a man he had met for the first time: "I like him. He has clear blue eyes, which look one straight in the face".'[21]

Rhodes also had a particular liking for 'emphatic' young men, like Frank Johnson. When Harry Palk, an officer in the Union–Castle Steamship Line, 'rapped out a string of expletives' at Rhodes for keeping his ship waiting, he was offered a job at once. Unfortunately, the young man's decision to be with his wife when their child was born put a swift end to his new career. According to Le Sueur: 'In years after [Rhodes] said, speaking of him: "Imagine his leaving me alone ... with no one to do my letters, just because his wife was going to have a baby".'[22]

While Rhodes's relationships with his contemporaries remained constant, in middle-age his attachment to young men was more generalized. It was a broad relationship with youth – male youth. There was to be no return to the intensity and possessiveness that had characterized his relationships with Pickering and Harry Currey. Some young men joined the entourage for a month or two. Others were sent off to manage Rhodes's estates in the north or were given jobs in his companies. They continued to pass in and out of his life, like members of a large, unruly family. Even the devoted Grimmer would be away for years at a time.

The young men allowed Rhodes to retreat into an adolescent – even a child's – world. He loved to tease and be teased. There were frequent tantrums and emotional reconciliations. Sometimes Rhodes was the child, sometimes the parent. When his young men fell ill, he nursed them. When they were troubled, he seemed to bring an intuitive understanding to their problems and always offered his support. When *his* turn came to be ill or frightened, they reciprocated, often sitting with him for nights on end.

A senior figure in the De Beers Company once said to me that the current obsession with the private lives of great men and women is a modern sickness. He was, of course, being protective towards the founder of his company, and in one sense he was right. Speculation about Zulu mistresses or Rhodes's asexuality does not take us very far, but the emotional make-up of the man *is* important and has a direct bearing on his actions and decisions.

Rhodes's twelve 'apostles'. Grimmer is standing in the back row, second from right.

On several occasions Rhodes allowed his feelings for other men to cloud his judgement – with disastrous consequences in the case of the Jameson Raid (see chapter 19). Indeed, he was lucky to have avoided a similar catastrophe five years earlier when he contracted Sergeant Johnson to assassinate Lobengula. His emotional response to the sight of the young (white) casualties after the Battle of the Mambo Hills (see p. 314) had a direct bearing on his decision to make peace with the Matabele, and his extraordinary success in winning people to his cause depended, in part, on an ability to engage other men at an emotional level.

But there was more. The adolescent, almost reckless frivolity of the later relationships was the hidden side of responsibility, self-discipline and the ruthless will to succeed. Without that balance it is doubtful whether Cecil Rhodes could have continued to function.

How interesting, then, that the young men who were closest to Rhodes believed that he would have struck a perfect balance 'and risen to an even higher pinnacle of greatness' if he had married 'a good and strong-minded woman'. It was Philip Jourdan who said that Cecil Rhodes would have made 'an ideal husband'.[23]

SEVENTEEN

FAILURE AND RESOLVE

I walked between earth and sky, and when I looked down I said,
'This earth should be English,' and when I looked up, I said,
'The English should rule the earth'.

CECIL RHODES[1]

The raising of the Union Jack above Fort Salisbury in that remarkable year of 1890 was only the beginning. Rhodes had proved that a creative entrepreneur could triumph where governments had failed – or when they simply lacked the imagination and the will to proceed.

Using private capital and sound business methods, Rhodes had acquired another huge tract of Africa without asking either the British or the Cape taxpayer for a penny. Unnecessary conflict had been avoided by the imaginative use of legal documents drafted by men of the calibre of Rochfort Maguire and Bourchier Hawksley. Money had literally been conjured out of thin air, thanks to the brilliant financial strategies devised by Alfred Beit.

By tapping into the free-enterprise spirit, Rhodes had also secured a military triumph that had confounded the so-called experts. Indeed, no less a figure than Major General Sir Frederick Carrington, the officer commanding the Bechuanaland Mounted Police, had warned Rhodes that the occupation of Mashonaland would cost him a million sterling and require a force of at least 2500 men.[2] That, of course, was a civil servant speaking, but Rhodes knew better. He understood the degree to which men could be motivated by the promise of land and gold and, instead of listening to the 'experts', he had entrusted the invasion to a private contractor, who was willing to do the job for less than a tenth of Carrington's estimate.

With Mashonaland secured, Rhodes was poised to seize 'the balance of the map', but no sooner had he unleashed his agents and his fighting men into the African hinterland than Her Majesty's Government began to rein him in. Britain's treaty obligations and an outbreak of Exeter Hall 'negrophilia' back home were offered as justification.

In the north, Rhodes had acquired a stake in the African Lakes Company

234

for much the same reason as he had acquired a stake in Barney Barnato's Central Company, and he expected the same results. But the Scottish missionaries who were a power in those parts wanted nothing to do with Rhodes or his company and their wishes carried great weight at Westminster. Lord Salisbury was forced to renege on his earlier promises and declare Nyasaland a British protectorate.

Rhodes's bid to grab Katanga in the west was frustrated by King Leopold II of Belgium, whom he afterwards called Satan; but his greatest disappointments were in the east. The Portuguese, who claimed the territories of Gazaland and Manica (as well as Mashonaland), were certainly no match for Rhodes's highly motivated young men. A troop of 45 Chartered Company police was able to rout a Portuguese force 500 strong which fled towards the coast with a detachment of Company men under Lieutenant Eustace Fiennes in hot pursuit. Rhodes's lads were in reach of the port of Beira when they stumbled upon the Rev. George Knight-Bruce, who was travelling in the opposite direction. The former Bishop of Bloemfontein will be remembered for his fierce denunciation of the grant of guns to the Matabele – unsurpassed 'devilry and brutality' was the expression he had used – and also for a remarkable change of heart when he was approached by Rhodes (see p. 199). He was now on his way to take up his new appointment as Bishop of Mashonaland, but as soon as he recognized Chartered Company uniforms he felt it his duty to warn Fiennes that a certain Major Sapte was not far behind. This British officer was military secretary to Sir Henry Loch, High Commissioner of the Cape, and his instructions were to order all Chartered Company men to pull out from Portuguese territory. Sure enough, when Sapte arrived the following morning, he confirmed everything the bishop had said and Fiennes had no alternative but to withdraw. When Rhodes heard about the incident some time later, he was incensed and roared, 'Why didn't Fiennes say Sapte was drunk and put him in irons?'[3]

This bizarre encounter between a peripatetic bishop and a couple of dozen young men determined the future of 300,000 square miles of Africa and denied Rhodes a crucial outlet to the sea. As a permanent reminder of his loss, he hung the tattered colours left behind by the fleeing Portuguese on a wall at Groote Schuur.

In spite of several further attempts to provoke the Portuguese and a last-ditch effort to buy the port of Lourenço Marques, Rhodes was obliged to accept colonial borders formally agreed between Britain, Portugal, Belgium and Germany in 1892. The Portuguese kept Gazaland (today's Mozambique), while Rhodes held on to two of the three territories they had originally claimed (Mashonaland and Manica). This meant that the humid and unhealthy coastal strip went to Portugal while Rhodes took the highlands. In Le Sueur's words, 'the Chartered Company ... got the pick of the country'.[4]

All in all, Rhodes had not done badly. He had established his claim to Barotseland (today's Zambia) as well as Mashonaland and Manica to the south. This gave him a territory of 441,000 square miles (1,143,000 square kilometres) – almost five times the size of the United Kingdom.

Once the external borders had been settled, it was time for Rhodes to turn his attention inwards to his vast new empire, where things were starting to go badly.

Most of the original prospectors who had set out from Fort Salisbury were rank amateurs. They were also poorly equipped. Very few owned tents and the majority made their homes out of poles and grass and fenced them with thorn bushes to keep lions, leopards, snakes and a host of other dangerous animals at bay. In their ignorance, they tended to choose sites in shady valleys or on the banks of streams. By day, blind fly drove their oxen frantic. At night swarms of midges and mosquitoes made sleep impossible. If a prospector was unlucky enough to stray into a tsetse-fly area, he could lose his oxen within a day.

The accepted practice for establishing title to a gold claim was to peg the ground and carve one's name on the surrounding trees. In some areas there were definite surface outcrops of gold-bearing reef, but to follow the seams below ground one had to sink shafts. To work those shafts, one needed windlasses, ropes and buckets. Most of the early prospectors were only equipped with picks, shovels, pans and sieves. The resourceful improvised, fashioning ropes and buckets from eland hide and windlasses out of tree trunks, but the reward for all their efforts was limited. Most of the reefs petered out at relatively shallow depths.

There was plenty of evidence of ancient workings but here, too, the signs were troubling and a rumour soon spread that the ancients had 'picked the eyes' out of the country.

Just as it was beginning to dawn on the settlers that Mashonaland might not, after all, be a second Witwatersrand, the rains came. They were the heaviest downpours in Shona memory and they continued for five months.

Men lived and slept miserably in their sodden clothes. Bags of flour and mealie meal were reduced to dough. Clothes and blankets were constantly soaked. Boots rotted like paper. The rivers soon became impassable. Selous's dusty waggon tracks turned into treacherous channels of mud and the low-lying country became a swamp. By Christmas 1890, the pioneers were locked into the country. No new supplies – no axes, no spades, no salt, no sugar, no candles – could get through.

'Pioneers'

With the rains came swarms of mosquitoes and a plague of malaria. 'Pioneers' died in their wretched encampments, while new immigrants, trapped between the swollen rivers that crossed the waggon roads from the south, wandered 'like walking ghosts' until fever or starvation claimed them. The roads were soon lined with the bones of oxen and the skeletons of abandoned waggons. Forests of crosses sprang up along the river banks and stories circulated of men driven to madness. One fever-stricken immigrant was seen dancing stark naked in the veld, and two demented young men were discovered eating their breakfast in a tent with a corpse lying between them.[5]

In November 1890 Rhodes tried to enter 'his' country from the south, but got no further than the Shashi river, which marked the Matabeleland–Bechuanaland frontier. It was here that his 'pioneers' had built their first fort 16 months earlier, but now the river was in flood. After a journey of nearly 1400 miles (2250 kilometres), Rhodes was forced to turn back.[6] There was one compensation, though. By the end of the year 1890 it was generally agreed that Rhodes's new country should be called 'Rhodesia'. A number of alternatives had been discussed, including 'Zambesia' and even 'Cecilia', but on 1 December 1890 Jameson was able to write to his brother, Midge, confirming that 'Rhodesia' was the definite choice.[7] However, it was not until 1895 that this name was formally adopted by the British Post Office.

At the close of the rainy season in April 1891, many would-be settlers left Mashonaland for good. The news they brought back to South Africa soon changed the public's perception of Rhodes's magical kingdom of Ophir. At the same time, the finances of his Chartered Company were in desperate straits. In the period to the end of March 1891, £402,000 – nearly half the company's capital – had been spent. The principal items were Frank Johnson's fee of £87,000; £70,000 required to 'square' rival concession hunters; £50,000 spent on telegraph lines; and a massive outlay of £200,000 to support a company police force that had been largely tied down in Rhodes's private war with the Portuguese. Desperate remedies were called for.

Rhodes's first decisive move was to sack his first Administrator, Colquhoun, that 'old Indian civil servant' with an obsession for rules and regulations,[8] and appoint Dr Jameson in his place. Rhodes's parting words to his dear friend were: 'Your business is to administer the country as to which I have nothing to do but merely say "yes" if you take the trouble to ask me'.[9]

Jameson arrived in Fort Salisbury in June 1891. Rhodes's capital was in a deplorable state. The only buildings were grass huts, but the majority of settlers still lived in tents and waggons. Fever was rampant. The carcasses of dead pack animals were strewn all over the settlement and the stench was unbearable.

To make matters worse, Fort Salisbury had been sited close to a swamp, which not only exacerbated the mosquito problem but made sleep virtually impossible. A full-throated chorus of bull frogs lasted from dusk to dawn. White ants and borer beetles demolished anything made of wood and the settlement was overrun by enormous grey rats. These creatures ate anything they could get their teeth into – food, boots, clothing and, occasionally, the exposed toes and fingers of sleeping men. They even made off with Jameson's false teeth, which were discovered some days later in the roof thatch.

Spirits lifted slightly in the middle of 1891 when the first women arrived – nuns for a hospital and recruits for a brothel – but there were still no reports of any significant gold finds. Rhodes's great ambition had been built on hope, and hope was fading fast.

Undaunted, Jameson threw up an office of mud, poles and grass[10] and began his rough-and-ready administration of a territory considerably larger than the British Isles. His first move was to slash the company police force from 700 men to 40.[11] When the settlers complained that this left them virtually unprotected, Jameson calmly replied that he expected them to volunteer for police duty themselves. Although he was in no position to pay them, he did promise to provide every recruit with a horse. When the animals failed to materialize after many weeks, a second meeting was called by the angry citizens of Salisbury. Confronted by rows of sullen faces, Jameson immediately called for 'drinks for the company!'

> And then – the tension somewhat relaxed – 'Gentlemen of the Salisbury Horse' – there being at that time only one horse to the whole corps – 'I have important news for you' – the meeting pricked up its ears ... 'Gentlemen, I heard this morning' – a pause here – 'that your Bandmaster has crossed the Tuli [Shashi].'
>
> The announcement was made with such eclat and was received with so much acclamation and the fun became so fast and furious, that it was only the next day that the pioneers found the leisure soberly to reflect on the circumstance that they had not heard a word about horses.[12]

That was Jameson's style. He was the huxter, the risk-taker; witty, iconoclastic and endowed with a charm that sent women (and men) into a spin. In the words of an early settler: 'He flirted with men like a woman ... he fooled us and then laughed at us. And his laughter was so infectious that [we] usually joined.'[12]

Colquhoun had worked with a staff, but Jameson ran what was virtually a one-man administration. He was his own minister of justice, agriculture, labour, mining, defence and native affairs. He was both judge and jury in important trials and he administered justice with the same casual bravado as he handled everything else. When a drunken barman shot and killed a Shona youth who had irritated him with his drum playing, Jameson offered the man the choice of a £50 fine or a term of imprisonment. The second option was for the sake of form. There were no jails in the country, as both men knew full well. It was a source of mutual embarrassment, therefore, when the condemned man had to admit that he was unable to pay the fine. Jameson saved the situation by accepting an I.O.U.

Jameson's approach to the financial crisis was equally inventive.

To pay for services and attract outside capital, he decided to sell off the resources of the country. As there had been no significant gold discoveries, Jameson started to hand out land. Vast tracts were awarded to wealthy individuals and syndicates on condition that they spent agreed sums of money on the development of their property or imported equipment of an equivalent value. One consortium received a grant of 25,000 acres at a peppercorn rent on the curious condition that they brought 20 (white) families into Mashonaland within the first year. Sir John Willougby, second-in-command of the company police force, was awarded no fewer than 600,000 acres after promising to spend £50,000 on their development.

Five years later an eminent visitor wrote:

[Jameson] must have been off his head for some time before the Raid ... [He had] given nearly the whole country to the Willoughby's, White's and others of that class so that there is absolutely no land left of any value for the settlement of Immigrants by the Government.[13]

Immigrants apart, the shift of emphasis from gold to land was a disaster for the Shona. The point has already been made that the Rudd concession rested on two false premises – that Lobengula was the absolute ruler of Mashonaland and that the whites (10 whites, Rudd had said!) were only interested in digging for gold in his country. Just as Thompson had done two years earlier, Jameson and his 'pioneers' now took advantage of cultural misunderstandings to defraud Africans.

Amongst the Shona, and indeed the majority of pre-colonial African societies, the idea that an individual could own land was as absurd as claiming that he could own the wind or the sun. Land was where cattle grazed and wild animals were hunted. Like sunshine and rain, it had been provided for everyone. Even the village orchards and vegetable gardens were not the property of the people who cultivated them. The produce was theirs, but what possible reason could they have for claiming ownership of the soil?

The Shona believed that other men thought as they did. For centuries they had traded with outsiders who came, bartered and went away. It was only natural for them to assume that the 'pioneer' column was just another large gold-seeking caravan, which would eventually move on, as the Arab and Portuguese traders had done before them. The Shona were happy to trade with these visitors and, during the disastrous rainy season of 1890–91, many of the 'pioneers' owed their lives to local villagers who kept them in food when their own supplies had run out.

Quite suddenly, all this changed as whites began to peg out great tracts of land. Of course, these estates were of no value to the new 'owners' without men and women to work them and, before long, the Shona were being pressed to sell their labour.

Defeat by an invading force was something anyone would have understood, but this was an underhand and insidious form of conquest. The whites had arrived in friendship but, once established, they had pointed their machine guns and heavy artillery at the villages and demanded labour. When the Shona resisted, entire kraals were torched.[14] Headmen who refused to provide workers were sometimes shot. Others were flogged or forced to pay a fine of goats or cattle.[15]

The Shona were particularly vulnerable to coercion and dispossession. Since the collapse of their second great empire after the Zulu incursions of the 1830s, Shona power had fragmented into a large number of independent chiefdoms. There was now no central authority that could lead them in united resistance against the whites.

Some of the worst excesses were the direct result of Jameson's decision to replace a professional police force with unpaid vigilantes. These farmers and prospectors imposed their own rough justice, and even involved themselves in disputes between rival Shona chieftains so that they could exact a reward of cattle from the winning side.

If the police volunteers ever met serious resistance, Jameson did not hesitate to give them the backing of his remaining professionals. On one occasion, a white trader and part-time policeman was chased out of a Shona kraal when he insisted on searching for stolen blankets. In retaliation, Jameson sent out a company patrol under Captain Lendy, a particularly vicious young officer, who ordered a dawn attack with artillery and a machine gun. Twenty-one villagers were killed, including the headman and his son. According to Lendy's report, 'deeming the punishment sufficient, I did not burn the huts and left'. For good measure, he also made off with the slain man's 47 head of cattle.[16]

As a reward for this service, Captain Lendy was appointed magistrate of Fort Victoria, where he would soon have a crucial role to play.

It was not until October 1891 – almost a year after he had been forced to

Shona village.

241

turn back at the Shashi river – that Rhodes entered 'his' country for the first time. (Interestingly, he embarked on this journey immediately after Harry Currey's wedding.)

This time, instead of taking the traditional missionary road from the south, Rhodes travelled through Portuguese territory, first going by sea to Beira and then transferring to a flat-bottomed river boat for the initial stage of the inland journey. His principal companions were his manservant Tony de la Cruz, Frank Johnson and D.C. De Waal, brother-in-law to Hofmeyr and, like him, a Bondsman and member of the Cape Parliament.

Johnson had explored this route with Jameson a year earlier and now hoped to get Rhodes's backing to set up a boat and coach service linking Mashonaland to the sea. Rhodes was more interested in assessing the possibilities of a railway line.

Rhodes disembarked 70 miles (113 kilometres) up the Pungwe river, where Johnson was waiting with porters, baggage carts and ponies. Ahead of them was a gruelling 170-mile (274-kilometre) journey to the Mashonaland border which took them through swamps and bamboo forests so dense they could hardly see the sky above them. They passed abandoned waggons and animals stung to death by tsetse-fly. They were drenched by heavy tropical rains and, when the skies cleared, endured temperatures of up to 120 degrees. At night, they had to encircle their camp with fires to frighten off lions and other beasts of prey.

Rhodes, who had never shown great physical courage up to this time, insisted on sharing a tent with Johnson and De Waal so that he could sleep between them. One night Johnson was woken by the sound of Rhodes leaving the tent. Then he heard the low growl of a lion. 'Almost immediately I saw the strange spectacle of the Prime Minister dashing back towards our tent ... The trousers of his pyjamas were hanging down well below his knees'.[17]

Rhodes had not gone far on this journey before he realized that he had been deceived by Johnson. In reality, the young man's much-vaunted road to the sea was 'a wretched footpath' so steep and treacherous in places that the ponies could barely make the climb. One cart and its entire load of harnesses and furniture was lost in a marsh. The surviving vehicle had to be unpacked every time they reached swampy ground or a steep section of the track. All the loads were then carried in relays by the porters, and the cart repacked when the obstacle had been cleared. Rhodes became increasingly impatient with these delays. He wanted to see 'his' country and, before long, the second cart and all its contents were abandoned.

Eventually, the party reached the magnificent mountain range that marked Rhodes's frontier. A steep climb brought them to Fort Umtali, the company's eastern outpost. 'Here,' says De Waal, 'we met Mr Heany, Dr Jameson and some other well-known gentlemen. It was to us a moment of rejoicing when we entered Umtali camp.' As Jameson's friend and biographer, Ian Colvin, romantically observed:

> Thus Rhodes and Jameson met in the promised land. We can imagine the handgrip between these two, who now stood on the edge of the country they had won – a country half as big as Europe, stretching from the Dark Halfknown of tropical Africa and the sources of the Nile.[18]

The next stage of the journey, a 174-mile ride from Umtali to Fort Salisbury, was indeed a euphoric experience for all concerned. Rhodes's party passed through magnificent agricultural land where the Shona had laid out vegetable gardens and fruit orchards and where their cattle were deemed to be in excellent condition. De Waal was particularly excited. In his opinion the country was 'one of the most productive in all Africa. Not only is its soil extremely fertile, but the climate is healthy and delightful.'

Rhodes was amused to see his parliamentary colleague casting envious eyes over this landscape, and on one occasion rode up alongside him. 'Don't tell me anything, De Waal, and I shall tell you why you've stopped the cart ... You wish to tell me that you have here chosen ... the site of your farms.' 'Precisely,' De Waal replied, 'you have guessed well.'[17]

And why not? The land was fertile, the climate healthy and (as Rhodes pointed out to his friend) when the railway came through De Waal would have a valuable property on his hands. It was in casual exchanges like theses that the Shona came to be dispossessed of their country.

As Rhodes came nearer to his capital, he was 'just like a school boy in his spirits'. There was tremendous excitement when Johnson told him that they would be in sight of the town at the next ridge. Rhodes galloped ahead and reined up. Fort Salisbury lay below him. He was crushed.

By now a few corrugated-iron shacks had appeared among the huts, tents and waggons, but the place was still a squalid mess. When Rhodes entered his capital, Johnson was riding alongside him.

> Rhodes kept asking, 'What building is this?' 'What building is that?' He made no comment, but I could see he felt depressed on his first arrival. It was only when I pointed out to him the foundations of the Jewish Synagogue that be became cheerful once more and quite excited.
>
> 'My country's all right,' he kept on exclaiming. 'If the Jews come, my country's all right.'[17]

From the moment he arrived, Rhodes was besieged by deputations of angry

Pioneer Street, Salisbury (1892).

settlers. One crowd arrived as he was taking a bath. Never a stickler for convention, Rhodes received them wrapped in a towel and still clutching his sponge.

The settlers had much to complain of – the hardships they had endured, the cost of goods brought into the country, the company's extortionate 50 per cent tax on mining profits, the unfair privileges granted to 'the Whites and the Willoughbys', etc., etc. Rhodes countered with a homily about the great work the settlers were doing for the Empire and for posterity, whereupon the leader of the delegation, a dour Scot, snapped back: 'I'll have ye know, Mr Rhodes, I'm no' here for posterity'.[17]

During Rhodes's stay in Salisbury, a distinguished visitor arrived from London: Lord Randolph Churchill, former Leader of the House of Commons and father to Winston, then a young cadet just entering Sandhurst. His visit had been sponsored by the London *Daily Graphic* for the purpose of offering Members of Parliament and the reading public an expert opinion on Mashonaland's potential 'based upon personal inspection [and] actual experience'. Churchill was travelling with an American mining expert called Henry Perkins, and they had been criss-crossing the country since August in a vast caravan of ox-waggons. His Lordship evidently felt it necessary to travel with 40,000 pounds of supplies and a staff of servants, including valets, stewards, cooks, grooms, assistant cooks, drivers, herders and a professional hunter. The contrast between this circus and the austere lifestyle of the settlers must have been provocative, to say the least.

The first meeting between Churchill and Rhodes's party was a disaster. His

Lordship's cutting references to the 'lazy, dirty, and barbarous' Boers drove De Waal into a frenzy. Rhodes did his best to cool the row, but his real concern was not so much Churchill's prejudice as Perkins's opinion of Mashonaland. At this stage the great mining expert was non-committal, but when judgement was eventually delivered in a *Daily Graphic* article it was uncompromising:

> It cannot be denied that the high hopes which were entertained ... as to the great mineral or agricultural wealth of Mashonaland have not hitherto been justified or nearly justified ... Mashonaland so far as is known, and much is known, is neither an Arcadia nor an El Dorado.[19]

Lord Randolph Churchill had driven another nail into the Chartered Company coffin. From a peak of nearly £4, share values tumbled to 12s.

Rhodes was unaware of this impending blow as he continued his journey through Mashonaland. On 13 October the party reached Fort Victoria, which guarded the arbitrary frontier the company had set down between Mashonaland and Matabeleland. Rhodes was delighted to discover that the telegraph line was within three miles (five kilometres) of the settlement. He could now re-establish contact with the world, and spent hours in the 'telegraph office' – a waggon that moved with the advancing line.

Rhodes's last important port of call was Great Zimbabwe, one of a series of magnificent palace temples built at the time of the first great Shona empire (the Mwena Mutapa dynasty), which lasted from the eleventh to the sixteenth century. Great Zimbabwe's soaring granite walls had been intended less as protection than as a statement of Shona power and permanency. At a time when Europe was still struggling out of the Dark Ages, the Mutapas had established a stable theocratic state. Their subjects mined and worked iron and gold, farmed, carved, wove and traded with the Arabs. It was the residual evidence of these early achievements that had inspired the Victorian legends of the lost kingdom of Ophir.

In his account of the visit, De Waal wrote that 'Great Zimbabwe had been erected either by the order of King Solomon or the Queen of Sheba or else the Persians'.[20] Rhodes gave credit to the Phoenicians, a maritime people he liked to compare to the British. It is a sad comment on the prejudices of the time that neither Rhodes nor any of his contemporaries believed that blacks were capable of such achievements. Perhaps these supremely self-confident Victorians also found it harder than we do to accept the idea that a great civilization can suffer catastrophic decline.

Rhodes and De Waal trekked out of Mashonaland along the route the 'pioneers' had taken. Jameson was once again in complete charge of the country.

Since 1888, those who were close to Rhodes had looked forward to the day when Matabele power would be broken. Shippard will be remembered for confessing that he would take 'sincere and lasting satisfaction' from the sight of the Matabele being 'cut down by our rifles and machine guns', while John Moffat wrote that such a day would be 'a blessing to the world'.[21] In De Waal's account of the journey through Mashonaland there is a description of a meeting between Rhodes and a party of would-be Boer trekkers in which Rhodes made a promise that, one day, the Boers would be called upon to help him crush the Matabele and that land would be given to them as a reward.

As long as Matabele power remained intact, the Chartered Company was in an untenable position. Ostensibly, Lobengula was still the 'absolute ruler' of all the company's territory. The legality of the Rudd concession and the royal charter rested on that premise, but the white settlers were becoming increasingly convinced that Shona fear of Lobengula's authority was the principal cause of their labour problems – particularly in the so-called border area. Rumours were also circulating that the white prospectors were digging in the wrong place and that the gold fields of 'Ophir' were, in fact, in Matabeleland. Certainly, the splendid condition of Lobengula's cattle indicated that the pastures were richer over there.[22]

Rhodes was well aware of the dangers of declaring war against the Matabele. The company's finances were in a parlous state and an unprovoked invasion would cause an outcry in England and bring him into direct conflict with Loch. Before he could consider moving against Lobengula, he would have to find a convincing excuse. In the meantime, all he and Jameson could do was to bide their time and wait for the right opportunity.

In April 1893, the telegraph wire between Fort Victoria and Fort Tuli was cut and a 500-yard (457-metre) section removed. Police inquiries established that the wire had been stolen by the subjects of a petty Shona chief called Gomalla. Captain Lendy sent a detachment of police to Gomalla's kraal with orders that the chief must either hand over the culprits or pay a fine of cattle. Gomalla elected to pay the fine and the cattle were duly delivered to Fort Victoria.

Whether or not Lendy was aware of this, the cattle in Gomalla's care belonged to the king. As soon as the incident was reported to him, Lobengula sent an indignant message to Jameson in Fort Salisbury. He received a courteous reply and an assurance that, now Jameson was in possession of the facts, he would return the cattle at once and 'find the actual culprits and chastise them, or failing that ... punish Gomalla as I think fit'.[23]

There the matter might have rested had not Loch, the High

Commissioner in Cape Town, sent a dispatch to Lobengula, stressing the seriousness of the crime. The king responded by sending two of his regiments, a force of some 2500 men, to punish Gomalla's people. At the same time, the trader Dawson took down a letter at the king's dictation making it clear to Lendy that the Matabele *impis* were under strict instructions not to harm any white men. On the following day, Colenbrander, the Chartered Company's ambassador in Gubulawayo, took down three similar letters – for Moffat in Bechuanaland, Jameson in Salisbury and Lendy in Fort Victoria. All these messages were dispatched by runner and telegraph.

When the Matabele *impis* eventually reached the Fort Victoria area they launched a general onslaught against the Shona, slaughtering, burning and looting far beyond the confines of Gomalla's kraal. Although the king's orders not to harm whites were scrupulously obeyed, their servants were murdered and their cattle driven off. One Matabele contingent appeared at the gates of Fort Victoria and demanded that all the Shona men, women and children who had sought sanctuary in the fort should be handed over to them. Captain Lendy refused to comply.

Jameson in Salisbury cabled Rhodes in Cape Town, assuring him that the whites were in no danger and there was no conceivable chance of a Matabele invasion of Mashonaland. On 12 July, Rutherfoord Harris cabled the London Board of the British South Africa Company on Rhodes's behalf and a message was sent to the Colonial Office: 'Lo Bengula sent Matabele punish Mashonas near Fort Victoria at same time friendly message all Europeans. Some Mashonas killed and cattle taken ... no cause for anxiety'.[23]

The next day, Jameson started out on the 188-mile (303-kilometre) ride from Salisbury to Fort Victoria. He was suffering so much from his 'painful malady of piles' that he had to transfer to a mule cart and continue his travels leaning against the back seat in a half upright position.[24]

On completing this uncomfortable journey, Jameson changed his mind, not about the Matabele danger, but about the way he should respond. He cabled Harris from Fort Victoria:

> The labour question is the serious one. There is no danger to the whites but unless some shooting is done I think it will be difficult to get labour even after they have all gone. There have been so many cases of Mashona labourers killed even in the presence of the white masters that the natives will not have confidence in the protection of the whites, unless we actually drive the Matabele out.[25]

He went on to tell Harris that he had summoned the Matabele *indunas* to Fort Victoria. 'I intend to treat them like dogs and order whole *impi* out of the country. Then if they do not go send Lendy out with 50 mounted men to fire into them.'

On the day Jameson sent that telegram, Dr Hans Sauer arrived in Fort Victoria. Sauer had done well for himself in Johannesburg since he first introduced Rhodes to the Witwatersrand gold fields, and was now visiting Mashonaland with the idea of establishing a new mining syndicate there. On the day after his arrival at Fort Victoria, he witnessed Jameson's deliberate attempt to provoke Lobengula's *indunas* by treating them 'like dogs'.

When the Matabele responded to his summons, Jameson and Lendy were waiting to receive them, seated on two kitchen chairs in front of the fort and flanked by 50 armed men. As soon as the Matabele were in earshot, Jameson told them that he was only prepared to speak to their *indunas*, who must lay down their weapons before coming any nearer. After some hesitation, the order was obeyed, and 40 unarmed *indunas* approached and sat at Jameson's feet.

Jameson immediately demanded an explanation for the attacks on the Shona. Manyewu, the senior *induna*, courteously replied that they were acting on the orders of Lobengula, who had every right to punish transgressors in his province of Mashonaland. He pointed out that his king had not ceded government to the Chartered Company, only the right to dig for gold and other minerals.

In his description of the incident Sauer wrote: 'The old chief had correctly stated the facts, and from the legal point of view there was no answer to him.' He continued:

> When the Matabele commander sat down he was followed by a young chief, the handsomest African native I have ever seen. He was evidently an aristocrat, tall and slight, with good features and a confident bearing, and he wore a beautiful head-dress of blue jay feathers. In his speech he bluntly told Jameson that Mashonaland was part of the Matabele kingdom, that their *impis* had every right to be there and to enforce their methods of governing Mashonaland, a conquered country belonging to them. He further pointed out that they had not molested any of the white people who had come into the country ...[26]

Jameson interrupted this speech and ordered the young man to sit down, adding the deliberate insult that he 'spoke not with boys but with men'. The young man would not be silenced until he had made it clear to Jameson that the Matabele would stay where they were until they had fulfilled their duties to the king. On hearing this, Jameson leapt to his feet and declared the meeting over. The Matabele were told that if they had not crossed the nearby

Tokwe river by the time the sun was *there* (Jameson indicated a point in the sky), they would be shot.

The whites then retired for lunch. Two hours later Jameson embarked on the second stage of his plan. Lendy was sent in pursuit of the Matabele with a detachment of 38 mounted men, mostly Boer transport riders who had taken sanctuary in the fort during the troubles. There is some dispute as to how far the Matabele had obeyed Jameson's orders and what warnings Lendy gave when his men were in range. However, the essential facts cannot be questioned. Lendy's men fired at the Matabele who, in obedience to their king, offered no resistance, even though they outnumbered the whites by nearly 80 to one. Sauer estimated that some 50 or 60 were killed. Among the dead was Mgandane, the young aristocrat who had provoked Jameson. By all accounts, he had been deliberately singled out. His headdress, his shield, his genitals and possibly other parts of his body were removed and taken as trophies[27].

Emboldened by his 'success', Jameson asked Sauer to go round the Boer tents and waggons that night and ask his countrymen how many men they thought it would take to conquer the Matabele. The answer he received was from 800 to a thousand.

Jameson was now convinced that his time had come. On the following day (19 July 1893) he sent a chillingly frank message to Rutherfoord Harris for Rhodes's attention: 'Rhodes might consider the advisability of completing the thing ... We have the excuse for a row over murdered women and children now and the getting of Matabeleland open would give us a tremendous lift in shares and everything else ...'[28] In the same dispatch, Jameson suggested that the cost of the campaign could be kept to a minimum by paying the recruits in land, gold and 'loot'. Some time later, he wrote a famous description of the response he received from Cape Town:

> Rhodes, who does not waste words, wired back briefly, 'Read Luke fourteen thirty-one' ... I asked for a Bible and looked up the passage and read: 'Or what king going to make war against another king, sitteth not down first and consulteth whether he be able with ten thousand to meet him that cometh against him with twenty thousand.' Of course, I understood at once what the message meant. The Matabele had an army of many thousands. I had nine hundred settlers available for action. Could I, after careful consideration, venture to face such unequal odds?
>
> I decided at once in the affirmative, and immediately telegraphed back to Mr. Rhodes at Cape Town. 'All right. Have read Luke fourteen thirty-one'. Five words from Mr. Rhodes and eight from myself decided the question of our action in the first Matabele war.[29]

The die was cast. Jameson's plan was to advance on Matabeleland in three columns – from Fort Victoria, Fort Salisbury and Fort Tuli on the Shashi river in the south. Rhodes sold 50,000 Chartered Company shares and spent most of the money buying all the available horses in Cape Colony and sending them north (there were then only 100 horses in Mashonaland). At the same time, Jameson instructed Major Allan Wilson of the company's police force to sign up recruits. The contract of engagement prepared by Jameson guaranteed each volunteer '6000 acres of land in any part of Matabeleland and 20 gold claims'. A further clause read: 'The loot shall be divided one half to the British South Africa [Chartered] Company and the remainder to officers and men in equal shares'. 'Loot' is not a word commonly used in legal agreements, but it certainly expresses the buccaneer spirit of this particular enterprise. Lobengula owned gold, rifles and mounds of presents brought by concession hunters. He was reputed to possess buckets of diamonds smuggled out and presented to him by Shona who had worked in the Kimberley mines.[30] There were also 300,000 head of the king's cattle to be divided up.[31]

The challenge for Jameson was to find a cast-iron excuse for war that would satisfy Loch and the home government. Harris was put in charge of the propaganda campaign and circulated reports of Matabele war preparations to English newspaper editors, while Jameson did his best to provoke Lobengula into taking aggressive action. First he sent a curt note to Gubulawayo, protesting that the king had no right to send his warriors to attack Shona in the Fort Victoria area. Instead of rising to the bait, Lobengula replied contritely: 'You are quite right ... I acknowledge that I was wrong in sending my *impis* so close to white people ...'

Some days later, Manyewu's warriors returned to Gubulawayo and Lobengula heard for the first time how they had been gunned down by Lendy's men as they were withdrawing. He sent an angry message to Harris in Cape Town:

> I thought you had come to dig gold, but it seems you have come ... to rob me of my people and country as well ... You are like a child playing with edged tools ... Captain Lendy is like some of my own young men; he has no holes in his ears and cannot hear; he is young and all he thinks of is a row, but you had better caution him carefully or he will cause serious trouble between us...[32]

In spite of his anger, Lobengula still took no action to avenge the deaths of his warriors.

Jameson now turned the screw once more. On 16 August he sent a stiff note to Lobengula demanding compensation for the settlers' murdered servants and stolen cattle. This was provocation indeed. The king had been robbed of his 'province', his warriors had been slaughtered in cold blood and now he was required to pay compensation. Not surprisingly, he refused to comply and in desperation fired off messages to all and sundry, including Queen Victoria, who was told that her subjects had killed his warriors and taken his land and the people who lived there. 'Your Majesty,' he asked, 'what I want to know from you is if people can be bought at any price?'

Lobengula now wished to have no further dealings with the Chartered Company. He told Colenbrander, who provided him with his monthly payment of £100, that he regarded this stipend as 'blood money' and wanted no more of it. On Rhodes's orders, Colenbrander then left Gubulawayo. The channel between Lobengula and the Chartered Company was now closed.

Loch tried to defuse the crisis. He warned Jameson that war would be 'inadmissable' and insisted that he should send no further messages to Lobengula without first submitting the text to his office for approval. Jameson answered coolly that since relations with Lobengula had been broken there was no question of sending further messages.

Convinced that trouble was imminent, Loch then moved a detachment of Bechuanaland Police under Major Goold-Adams to the southern border of Matabeleland. One would like to believe that Loch's intention was to thwart Jameson's aggressive schemes, but subsequent events suggest that his real concern was to assert imperial authority over the country in the event of war.

On 18 September, just a few days after the Cape Parliament rose, Rhodes boarded the *German*, a coastal steamer that called at Beira. Jameson instructed Sauer to meet Rhodes and his party on the Pungwe river and escort them to Salisbury. From the moment contact was made, it was clear to Sauer that Rhodes was in a tremendous hurry to get to his destination. The party was not even allowed to pause at Umtali: 'Rhodes hustled everyone and seemed very anxious to get clear of the town.' When they were only a few hours' ride from Salisbury, Rhodes suddenly lost all sense of urgency and puzzled Sauer by asking him to find a secluded spot three or four miles off the road. Here the party established a camp and waited.[33]

By the first week of October, Jameson's force of 1400 men was fully equipped and ready for action. At this convenient time, there were reports of Matabele firing on company forces in the east and British forces in the south. According to one of Harris's dispatches, Jameson's scouts confirmed the presence of a 'large *impi*' near Fort Victoria 'by their actual footsteps through the veld'. The question has to be asked why Lobengula, after showing such restraint, should have decided to provoke the whites at a time that perfectly suited Jameson's purposes. One explanation has been provided by

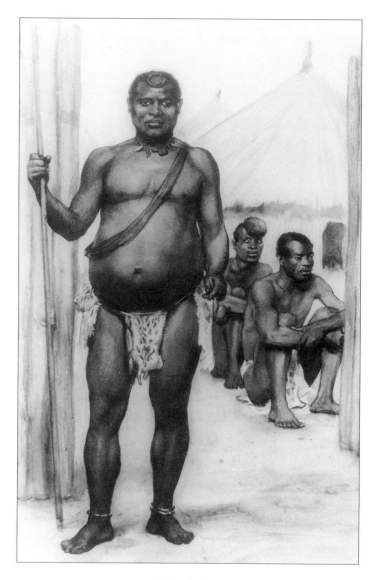

Lobengula.

the South African historian, G.S. Preller, whose biography of Lobengula appeared in 1963.

According to Preller, the facts – for which several of those in Fort Victoria who are still living in Rhodesia today can vouch – are that Jameson, 'despairing of anything approaching a real *casus belli* ... decided to make one up himself'. Preller alleges that black levies from the Cape were dressed up in the battle finery Lendy's men had taken from the Matabele they had killed in July. The levies were then sent out to a predetermined spot in the veld. Shortly afterwards, a corporal and two troopers 'specially picked from the greenest of the greenhorns in the force' were ordered to patrol the area where the levies were waiting in 'ambush'. Shots were fired in the air and the 'greenhorns' raced back to Fort Victoria 'with the report that they had been attacked by a large body of Matabele'.[34]

If Preller is right, Jameson employed tactics that Hitler would use, nearly 50 years later, to justify his invasion of Poland.

Whatever the truth, Jameson was able to inform Loch that his scouts had been attacked and that 'an enemy force of seven to eight thousand was massed in three bodies' in the Fort Victoria area. Loch wired back:

> Should the *impis* withdraw peaceably and of their own accord to a safe distance, they must be allowed to do so without interruption; but if they should resist, then I have informed you, you should take such measures as may be necessary under the circumstances for the protection of life and property.[35]

That was enough for Jameson. On 6 October he replied: 'I am now acting on your Excellency's instructions'. On 8 October the Salisbury column under Major Forbes and the larger Victoria column under Major Allan Wilson, rolled out into the veld. It was a combined force of 652 whites and a similar number of African waggon drivers and levies and they were equipped with the deadliest weapons in the arsenals of the British Army, including five Maxims, only recently perfected by their inventor in his London garage workshop, three other machine guns and two 7-pound field pieces. The whites were all mounted. Supplies were carried in 36 ox-waggons.

As soon as this force was on the move, Goold-Adams moved his detachment of police up from the south. Whatever Loch's intentions might have been, he had effectively presented Lobengula with the prospect of war on two fronts.

Jameson and Bishop Knight-Bruce rode with the Victoria column. Thanks to the bishop, the project was given a religious tone from the very start. According to one historian, the men of the Victoria column set off singing 'Onward Christian Soldiers'[36] and, from the bishop's own account, we know that several crates of hymn books were included in the deadly cargo destined for Matabeleland.[37]

The two Chartered Company columns linked up at a place they called Iron Mine Hill, 86 miles (138 kilometres) west of Fort Victoria. The fact that they were able to penetrate that far into Matabele territory without encountering an enemy force lends credence to Preller's account and exposes Jameson's report to Loch as a work of fiction.

Sauer, who was idling away the time with Rhodes, was astonished when a mounted policeman rode into their 'secret' encampment. Clearly, the authorities in Salisbury had known their whereabouts all along. Rhodes read the policeman's dispatch and immediately ordered everyone to break camp and move out. The party was already on the move when a puzzled Sauer naively asked Rhodes if the policeman had brought important news.

> He replied, 'Yes', and told me that Jameson had started for Matabeleland ... and that the combined column was far beyond the reach of the telegraph line and could not be recalled ... He further explained that he had hidden himself in the bush in order to make it impossible for him to receive orders by cable from the British Government prohibiting him from invading Matabeleland, but now Jameson had disappeared into the blue, Lord Salisbury could send as many prohibitive telegrams as he pleased, as the adventure could not be prevented.[33]

Lobengula made one last effort to secure peace and justice from the British. He sent his royal brother, Ingubogubo, the trader Dawson, and two senior *indunas* to Loch with a letter denying that any preparations were being made to attack the whites. As the party headed south, Dawson was surprised to find soldiers under Goold-Adams encamped on the Tati river, which was inside the territory claimed by Lobengula. Dawson's old friend Selous was acting as guide for this force and, instead of reporting to Goold-Adams, Dawson went off to have dinner with his friend, leaving the Matabele delegates in somebody else's charge. While he was away, one of the *indunas* was shot and the other mortally wounded with a blow from a rifle butt. The king's brother, too shocked to speak, submitted to being bound.

This highly suspicious incident was later the subject of an official inquiry which, in typical fashion, found that 'the deaths of these two *indunas* was due to a series of extraordinary mischances, for which neither the officers nor the men of the Police were to blame'.[38]

Lobengula's final peace effort had now been destroyed by a British bullet and a British rifle butt. There was no alternative to war.

The Matabele converged on Gubulawayo and unpacked Rhodes's rifles. Lobengula emerged from his royal kraal daubed with the paint of battle. In front of his assembled regiments, he raised his *assegai* and thrust the point deep into the ground. It was the traditional declaration of war. In the excitement, few noticed that the shaft of the *assegai* had broken – a dreadful omen.[39]

On the south bank of the Shangani river, Jameson's army was surrounded by 5000 Matabele. The field guns and machine guns immediately swung into action. It was the first time the Maxim had been used in battle and its effect was devastating. Five hundred Matabele were killed and the *impis* withdrew.

The battle also revealed the disservice Rhodes had done Lobengula with his gift of 1000 rifles. If the Matabele had relied on their traditional fighting tactics and rushed the enemy with Zulu ferocity, armed with *assegai* and shield, they might have overwhelmed Jameson's army in a single charge, but instead they fumbled with unfamiliar bolts and magazines and became easy targets.

Jameson's men moved on. When they had reached the Bembesi river, a little more than 20 miles (32 kilometres) from Gubulawayo, they were attacked by a large Matabele force, which included Lobengula's crack regiments. The slaughter was repeated on an even greater scale. Of the 700 men of the king's royal regiment, the *Imbesu*, 500 were casualties. Total Matabele losses were 3000. Only one white was killed. Three subsequently died from their wounds and five were slightly injured.

When the smoke of battle finally cleared that 'fidget on wheels',[40] Sir John Willoughby, solemnly declared: 'It would appear that the Umbezu [sic] and Ingubu were practically annihilated. I cannot speak too highly of the pluck of these two regiments. I believe that no civilized troops could have withstood the terrific fire they did for at most half as long.' One presumes that this Old Etonian would have wished us to include his own troops among the ranks of the 'civilized' – a questionable claim in the face of eyewitness evidence from a Boer volunteer (and other sources) that Matabele prisoners and wounded were systematically shot and their villages burned by their captors during Jameson's headlong rush to Gubulawayo.[41]

Two days after the battle of Bembesi, the troops were startled by a loud explosion from the direction of Gubulawayo. 'A great column of smoke went up towards the sky and ... spread out until it took the shape of an enormous umbrella.'[42] A scout was sent ahead and returned with the news that Lobengula's capital was in flames. Forbes ordered a Captain Borrow forward with a detachment of 20 men. When they arrived, late that evening, Gubulawayo was a smoking ruin, eerie and deserted except for roaming packs of 'kaffir dogs'. Where the king's house had once stood there was a large blackened hole.

Outside the huge smouldering ring of the Gubulawayo stockade, the shacks of the 'white dogs' were still standing, and Borrow's men were astonished to see two figures sitting on the tin roof of Fairburn's store. They rode closer. The trader, Fairburn, was playing a hand of poker with Bill Usher.

On inquiring, Borrow learnt that Lobengula had promised his protection to any white man who remained in his capital. Before leaving with his followers, the king had charged his *induna*, Sekulu, with their safety and the three men had remained behind in the deserted kraal.

When Matabele scouts reported that the column was close, Sekulu had placed all the remaining ammunition in the king's house and set fire to the thatch. 'Then he said to the white men who were at Fairburn's store: "I have obeyed the orders of the King, but now I must go lest your people slay me, for they are close at hand. And if any ill befall you, it will be from your own people and not from mine".'[43]

On 4 November 1893, Jameson's victorious men marched through the blackened shell of Gubulawayo, preceded by a pipe major of the Royal Scots Guards, who had written a special composition for the occasion. Unfortunately, the words and music of his 'March to Bulawayo' have since been lost.[44]

The flag of the Chartered Company – a lion rampant superimposed on a Union Jack – was hoisted above Lobengula's tree of justice in the centre of the great parade ground, where it had escaped the flames. Jameson's lads searched among the rubble, only to find that Lobengula had destroyed everything given to him by white men – even the portrait of Queen Victoria, her gracious gift to the *indunas* Babayane and Mtshete. For four years it had hung in a place of honour in Lobengula's brick house but, as Bishop Knight-Bruce was distressed to discover, it had since been shattered and defaced.[45]

The following day was a Sunday. The bishop unpacked his hymn books and held a special church parade. He thanked God for their deliverance.

Jameson's immediate objective was to disband his force and settle the country as quickly as possible, but that could not be done until Lobengula was captured. As long as the king remained at large, there would always be Matabele to obey him.

Jameson sent a messenger to find Lobengula and deliver a letter: 'To stop this useless slaughter you must at once come and see me at Bulawayo, where I will guarantee that your life will be safe and you will be kindly treated ... I sign myself your former, and I hope your present friend, L.S. Jameson.'[46] Some days later, Jameson received a guarded reply, but Lobengula did not turn himself in. A flying column under Major Forbes was sent in pursuit.

On 11 November, Goold-Adams and the Bechuanaland police arrived. Although they had the shortest distance to cover, they had been inexplicably delayed. Goold-Adams had orders to prevent Jameson distributing 'land, gold and loot' to his volunteers. Jameson got round the problem by distributing 'provisional land', 'provisional gold' and 'provisional loot'.

Gubulawayo burning.

With the company troops hot on his trail, Lobengula made a last, desperate bid to shake off his pursuers. He handed all the gold he had received from Rhodes's Chartered Company to one of his *indunas*. 'Tell them they have beaten my regiments, killed my people, burnt my kraals, and captured my cattle, and I want peace.'[47]

The gold and the king's message were passed to two troopers who had become separated from the rest of Forbes's column. They made off with the gold and said nothing about the message until they were brought to trial a year later. If the king's word had got to him, Forbes might have parleyed. Heavy rains had set in. His men were exhausted and mutinous but, knowing nothing, Forbes kept to his original instructions.

On 3 December, a forward reconnaissance patrol under Major Allan Wilson was sent across the Shangani river. Their orders were to find out which way the king had gone and to report back before nightfall. Wilson disobeyed his orders and pushed on through the night, determined to capture both the king and the glory. Early on the morning of 4 December he reached Lobengula's camp, where he met such heavy opposition that he was forced to retreat. He was soon surrounded. Heavily outnumbered, the entire patrol of 17 men died fighting.

Allan Wilson and his Shangani patrol became a Rhodesian legend. All 17 men were eventually buried in the Matopos hills alongside Rhodes. A

'Wilson's last stand'.

memorial to them was built at Great Zimbabwe. Wilson's last stand was celebrated in paintings, in verse, in sermons, prizes and medals. In time, the legend was embellished. Early versions had Wilson and the last survivors running out of ammunition and then springing to their feet to sing 'Nearer My God to Thee' as the Matabele hordes made their final charge. In later editions Wilson's men took off their bush hats and sang 'God Save The Queen'.

While acknowledging the courage of these men, the writer Philip Mason questions why white Rhodesians should have continued to honour them above all the brave men and women who died for King and country in two world wars. He suggests that they 'stood as a symbol for the heroic few among the barbarous many, for the supremacy of the white man's spirit even in death ...'. More to the point, he says:

> They lived on because the legend of their death was needed for this new country. The Matabele war had completed the founding of Rhodesia but it had till now been a war with few losses on the winning side. There is something in mankind deeply suspicious of a free gift, of anything too easily won, of a city not founded on a sacrifice.[48]

To borrow Joseph Conrad's phrase, the conquest of Rhodesia was 'not a pretty thing when you look into it too much'. It certainly needed to be leavened with myth but, like everything else connected with Rhodes, the legend of Allan Wilson was built on shaky foundations. Modern research suggests that there might not have been a final, defiant burst of patriotic singing in the face of the charging enemy: 'As the Martini-Henry ammunition gave out the survivors began to use their revolvers, and there is some evidence that some used their last rounds to shoot themselves.'[49]

By a strange coincidence, Rhodes made his triumphant entry into Gubulawayo on the day Allan Wilson died. No-one, of course, had any idea of Wilson's fate at the time. When Jameson welcomed his friend with a typical, 'Well, I am damned, where the devil have you come from?' Rhodes turned to one of his companions and, in a state of childish excitement, said: 'Tell him how we beat them all to get here first and give him a surprise!'[50]

As though to emphasize the fact that he was Lobengula's successor, Rhodes decided to build a cottage for himself on the ruins of the king's house. He also chose a site for 'the new township of Bulawayo' in open country three miles from the king's kraal, where excited days were spent with Jameson pegging out the business section and the parks.

On his final day in Gubulawayo, 19 December, Rhodes delivered a pugnacious speech to his troops. He congratulated them for 'the destruction of the ruthless barbarism south of the Zambezi' and made it clear he would brook no interference from London or Cape Town. The mother country, he hinted, should take care, lest Rhodes's 'pioneers' follow the example of the American colonists. He assured his men that the Chartered Company would 'deal with your grants of land without loss of time. It is your right ... You were the first to conquer this country, and the settlement must be made in a fair way and not left to the negrophilists at Exeter Hall.'[51]

With the cheers of his supporters ringing in his ears, Rhodes left Gubulawayo for Cape Town, where Harris had already started a furious press campaign under Rhodes's instructions, culminating in the threat, published in the *Cape Times*, that the British Government might find itself faced with the necessity of crushing 'a new Republic, which would cause more blood ... than the whole Matabele nation is worth.'[52] The London board of the Chartered Company were equally active in England, and the Cape Government exceeded its constitutional powers by writing a minute to the High Commissioner strongly supporting Rhodes's claims.

Inevitably, Her Majesty's Government caved in. On 18 July 1894, the Chartered Company's jurisdiction over Matabeleland was confirmed by Order in Council and the boundaries of a new state of Southern Rhodesia, incorporating Matabeleland, Mashonaland and Manica, were set down. Jameson was finally authorized to allot farmland and gold claims in Matabeleland – something he had already been doing for some eight months. Lobengula's cattle were duly handed out. 'Native reserves' were established and a hut tax was introduced.

The value of Chartered Company shares soared to £8 (from a low point of 12s). At the next Annual General Meeting of the company in London, Rhodes told his excited shareholders that they 'possessed a very large piece of the world'[53] and, he added later, 'everything within it and everything upon it except the air'.

And Lobengula? The king and a small party continued their northward trek until they were some 30 miles from the Zambezi river, where they established camp. A survivor, interviewed in the 1940s, described what happened next:

> I overheard the King speak to Magwegwe [a senior *induna*]. He said 'Do you remember your words?' Magwegwe replied 'Yes, King.' The King said again to him 'What were those words?' The reply came 'When you die so shall I.' As soon as those words had been said the King took a small bottle and drank some of the contents. Magwegwe picked the bottle up and did likewise. After about three or four hours the King and Magwegwe ... died.[54]

Magwegwe was buried nearby. The king's body was wrapped in the skin of a black ox and placed on a stretcher in a sitting position. It was then taken to a cave. Lobengula's remaining possessions were placed around the body and the mouth of the cave was sealed. 'A king is always buried in a cave,' the witness said, 'but not a commoner'.[54]

He was a king, and more. 'He was a gentleman in his way,' said John Moffat, 'and was foully sinned against by Jameson and his gang.'[55]

Moffat was not the only one who bitterly regretted the part he had played in Rhodes's schemes. The Rev. Helm wrote: 'The whole matter of this Matabele war has been so unrighteous that a searching inquiry should be made'.[56] Colenbrander described the Rhodesian 'pioneers' as white savages, 'the most terrible of men'.[56] But the last word has to go to Moffat:

> The great Rhodes is prancing around ... Everyone here is bowing down and worshipping him as the wisest of men. The popular tide is with him ... I suppose there will be a crash some day – and men will suddenly recollect that there is still such a thing as justice even to niggers'.[57]

EIGHTEEN

PRIME MINISTER OF THE CAPE

*We fight Rhodes because he means so much of oppression,
injustice and moral degradation in South Africa; – but if he
passed away tomorrow there still remains the terrible fact that
something in our society has formed the matrix, which has fed,
nourished, and built up such a man. It is the far future of
Africa ... which depresses me ... I believe we are standing on top
of a long downward slope. We shall reach the bottom, at last,
probably amid the upheaval of a war with our Native races
(then not the poor, savage, but generous races whom we might
have bound to ourselves by a little generosity and sympathy,
but a fierce and half-educated, much brutalized race who will
have come into their own). The men to come after us will reap
the fruits of our 'Native Policy'...*

OLIVE SCHREINER[1]

In the short span of five and a half years between July 1890 and January 1896, Rhodes had established the International Diamond Syndicate that fixed prices and controlled the world's supply. He had consolidated his interests in the Witwatersrand and built a second fortune in gold. He had occupied Mashonaland, waged war against the Portuguese and secured two of the three territories they had originally claimed as theirs. He had destroyed Matabele military power, added Barotseland (today's Zambia) to his company's possessions, gained exclusive mineral rights throughout Bechuanaland and effectively secured Nyasaland for Britain. He had linked his and Britain's African possessions by telegraph, pushed the railway line north from Cape Town to the Matabeleland border and, almost incidentally, revolutionized South African tastes in architecture and design.

Between 17 July 1890 and 12 January 1896, Cecil Rhodes was also running a country. He was prime minister of Cape Colony.

Rhodes's obituary in the *Cape Argus* included a long assessment of his political career, which began: 'The key to the apparently complex and

Prime minister of the Cape.

intricate character of Cecil Rhodes is to be found in his religion which [was] his devotion to his Mother Country and to his Mother Empire.'[2]

In similar vein, we are told by early commentators that Rhodes's 'broad and big idea'[3] for Africa was that 'North and South, from Cape Point to Lake Tanganyika, should form one vast federation, as large as Europe, under the British flag'.[4] Everything else in Rhodes's life was apparently subordinate to that great purpose, which he pursued without interruption to the end of his days.[5] Money was only 'the means to the end, never the end itself'.[5]

Rhodes's more sophisticated admirers realized that this view of the man as a one-dimensional patriot, working tirelessly on England's behalf, scarcely matched the facts. To begin with, there were those awkward alliances with the Afrikander Bond (pp. 167–8) and Parnell's Irish Party (p. 210–11) to explain. However, justification was at hand in the form of Rhodes's own slogans, such as his oft-repeated 'Home Rule in every part of Empire with the Imperial Tie for Defense and Trade'. It was difficult, though, to reconcile Rhodes the English patriot with the man who made such a determined effort to grab Matabeleland ahead of his 'Mother Country'; still more challenging to try to justify his threat to establish an independent republic should he fail to get his way. Unsurprisingly, that last episode was not mentioned by any commentators until the late 1960s.

There can be no doubt that Rhodes was long committed to the idea of a union of southern African states, but his methods and motives would appear to diverge considerably from those suggested by the *Cape Argus* (*his* newspaper). Indeed, on close examination, it becomes clear that Rhodes's political decisions, particularly during his time as premier, rested on a whole nexus of interconnecting deals and trade-offs calculated to benefit his business interests.

There is a famous saying attributed to Rhodes – 'I have never met anyone in my life, whom it was not as easy to deal with as to fight'.[6] Certainly it was a principle that guided his conduct of politics and business. Rhodes did not believe in open, adversarial debate. Early in his career, he had discovered that the best way to overcome dissent was to deal with opponents one by one, and in private. By that method, he seldom failed to get his way. 'He tied me up as he ties up everybody,' was how Barney Barnato described the experience. 'You can't resist him: you must be with him!'[7]

In politics Rhodes aimed, above all, for harmony and consensus. His first Cabinet, the so-called 'Cabinet of all talents', represented virtually the entire political spectrum in the colony from Bondsmen to English-speaking 'liberals' like John Merriman and Sir James Rose-Innes. At the same time, Rhodes made sure that he had the best brains and the most influential personalities in Parliament working for him – and in 1890, the year he became prime minister, brains and influence were desperately needed. The colony was facing a serious financial crisis. Over-speculation in gold shares had forced all but one of the leading Cape banks to close its doors, and the (albeit brief) slump on the Witwatersrand had badly affected trade.

Rhodes put his ablest minister, John X. Merriman, in charge of the Treasury, which was not only empty but farcically disorganized. Two years of hard and patient labour were needed to sort out the mess, balance the budget and restore the credit of the colony in the City of London. Merriman succeeded on all counts and Rhodes continued to exploit his old friend's energy and ability to the full. 'Every neglected task of government was thrust upon him, and besides doing all the work for Parliament – normally the prime minister's job – [Merriman] took over for absent colleagues and was given every new assignment.'[8]

As time went on, Merriman was less concerned with the demands that had been placed upon him than with Rhodes's style of government. Parliament, he believed, was becoming increasingly 'demoralised by the practice of underhand agreements, lobbying and caucuses'.[9]

On the evidence of Merriman and others, the biographer John Flint has argued that Rhodes's ideas of government and administration in many ways anticipated fascism:

> And though [Rhodes] never deified the state and was not impressed by military men and uniforms! he would have been at home in a one-party corporate state. He disliked the concept of opposition, and sought throughout to prevent the emergence of any coherent group on the opposite benches. To this end he kicked the leading opposition lights upstairs ... or brought them into his government.[9]

Rhodes had the instincts of a dictator. He knew his own mind and hated to waste time in debate. His secretary, Gordon Le Sueur, left a vivid impression of Rhodes in committee, and although the setting is the De Beers boardroom, Le Sueur made it clear that he might just as well have been describing a meeting of the Cabinet:

> [Rhodes] exercised a control over his colleagues on the De Beers' Board of Directors ... and over his colleagues in his Ministry to a ridiculous extent. He would walk in late ... and the minutes of the last meeting having hardly been read, he would start on the agenda and run through them, giving his own views something like this: 'Of course, what we have got to do here is so and so; I think we are all agreed about that. Just enter that in the minutes [to the secretary] as proposed and carried; and now about so and so', and the

Cape Parliament (c 1895)

same with regard to the rest. 'That's all for this morning, I think', he would add, and walk out, leaving his colleagues thinking over resolutions and amendments they intended to bring.[10]

Rhodes's idea of a parliamentary debate was to expound his own thoughts at great length and with much repetition, secure in the knowledge that any effective opposition had been stifled by prior arrangement.

It was soon clear to Merriman, Rose-Innes, Loch and others that the real business of government was being conducted through a series of backstage agreements. It was equally evident that much of this dealing was corrupt. A number of MPs were no more than De Beers and Chartered Company nominees, but the power of Rhodes's patronage extended far beyond them. As his biographer Basil Williams coyly observed, 'Some members were helped out of their difficulties by Rhodes; and by the distribution of Chartered shares, others were attached to his interests'.[11]

In fact, some 125,000 Chartered Company shares were distributed to the Bondsmen alone, and they were issued at par before they came on to the market. Rhodes also rewarded pliant MPs with great tracts of land in the north. De Waal, who accompanied Rhodes on his failed attempt to reach Mashonaland in 1890, as well as the second visit the following year, was one of a number of MPs who were rewarded with estates in Rhodesia.

With so many members of the House owning a stake in Rhodes's country and shares in his company, it is hardly surprising that the Cape Parliament exceeded its constitutional powers in 1894 by sending a written petition to Loch in support of Rhodes's claim to Matabeleland (see p. 259). Although his patronage was widely distributed, Rhodes had paid special attention to the Afrikander Bond since his earliest days in Parliament. In the year he became prime minister, he particularly needed their support for his schemes of northern expansion in preference to those of their kith and kin in the Transvaal.

Rhodes was never shy of declaring his loyalty to the Bond. Fresh from his triumphant visit to England with Harry Currey and his tête-à-têtes with Queen Victoria and Lord Salisbury, Rhodes proposed the toast at the annual congress of the Afrikander Bond in April 1991.

> The future rest[s] with the Afrikander Bond. Your ideas are the same as mine ... The people born and bred in this colony, and descended from those who existed in this country many generations ago, are much better capable of dealing with the various matters that arise than people who have to dictate some thousands of miles away ... Every question in connection with this country *we* shall decide, and *we alone*. *We* are the white men in South Africa – Dutch and English.[12]

Although Rhodes began this speech with a brief declaration of loyalty to the Queen, there was nothing else in the text to suggest his much-lauded 'devotion to his Mother Country and to his Mother Empire'. Indeed, the message to 'Mother' seems to have been: 'Keep out of our affairs. We know best.'

The leader of the Bond, J.J. Hofmeyr, had refused to serve in Rhodes's Cabinet, preferring to operate from the wings. The two men would frequently take early morning rides together to discuss the parliamentary business of the day and to work out a common strategy. Although Merriman complained of 'the mole's' undue influence (see p. 127), Rhodes ignored his objections.

The alliance between Rhodes and the Bond brought tremendous benefits to both sides. Hofmeyr backed Rhodes's plans to extend the railway northwards towards Chartered Company territory, and even visited the Transvaal to press Paul Kruger to stop any Boer treks into Mashonaland.

Rhodes repaid in kind. He removed most legal restrictions on the use of the Dutch language. He set up a commission to examine the teaching of Dutch in schools and helped to finance three new Dutch newspapers out of his own pocket. As a symbol of this new *rapprochement*, Rhodes paid for a statue of Jan Van Riebeck, the first Dutch commander at the Cape, to be erected at the foot of Adderley Street, the main thoroughfare.

It was in economic policy, though, that the trade-off between Rhodes and the Bond was particularly beneficial. The party represented the interests of the white farmers and Rhodes promised massive support for Cape agriculture on the understanding that the Bondsmen would end their opposition to De Beers. Since amalgamation, drastic cuts in the labour force had caused great hardship in the Kimberley area. In just two years (1888–91) the town's population had been halved, and there was vociferous opposition to the company, not only in Kimberley but also in the surrounding country districts. Rhodes wanted this stopped and he also wanted the Bond to drop its plan to tax diamonds.

The bargain was honoured on both sides. As his contribution, Rhodes created the first Ministry of Agriculture. He sent to America for experts who understood how to grow and package oranges and how to protect the groves from pests. He imported vine roots that were resistant to phylloxera and brought in Arab stallions and pure Angora goats from Turkey to improve breeding stocks. Most important of all, he balanced his demands for a railway line to the north with a programme of inexpensive branch lines linking the main growing areas to the ports. He even tried, unsuccessfully, to secure preferential treatment on the London market for Cape wines.

Rhodes's other great service to the Bond was his commitment to a programme of racist legislation. Indeed, this would be the most enduring and dreadful legacy of Rhodes's two terms as prime minister.

In the early 1880s, two important considerations had moved Rhodes towards a racist position – a politician's need for votes and an industrialist's need for a controlled labour force. By the end of the decade, a third factor had entered Rhodes's calculations. His dream of a federation of South African states would depend on a common 'native' policy acceptable to all participating governments. In the Boer republics of the Transvaal and the Orange Free State, no black had the vote or was ever likely to get one. The constitution of Natal, where whites were outnumbered 10 to one, had been so contrived that only 13 blacks were on the electoral rolls. The Cape, with its (limited) black franchise, was the odd man out.

Rhodes's first attempt to pass racist legislation had very little bearing on these larger issues. Some months before Rhodes became prime minister, a Bondsman had tabled an amendment to the Masters and Servants Act, that would have given rural magistrates powers to sentence blacks to flogging for trivial misdemeanours, such as disobedience or insolence to their employers. Since these charges would be difficult to prove, the word of the white master (or mistress) would be regarded as sufficient evidence.

Rhodes supported the Bill, but there was vehement opposition in the House. One member pointed out that children might be flogged as no age restriction had been specified in the amendment. Others described the measure as a return to slavery and called it a disgrace. It was rejected by a substantial majority.

Soon after he had assured the Bond that 'your ideas are the same as mine', Rhodes attempted to reintroduce the flogging amendment. Merriman was appalled and threatened to resign. 'Possibly,' he wrote to his wife Agnes, 'this may be a way out of a very ignominious position and with honour, too.'[13]

The Bill was withdrawn after a second reading and Merriman stayed in the Cabinet. What appears to have been a stupid miscalculation on Rhodes's part was, in fact, a typically Machiavellian manoeuvre. The Bondsmen were grateful to him for supporting their Bill; the liberals for granting them a free vote and the opportunity to throw it out. Rhodes had built up his stocks of goodwill on both sides of the House and lost nothing in the process. The issue of flogging was of no importance to him.

Unsurprisingly, not everyone appreciated the subtlety of Rhodes's political manoeuvres. His support of the bill cost him the friendship of Olive Schreiner, author of *The Story of an African Farm* and one of South Africa's most respected writers. She had once described Rhodes as 'the only great man and man of genius South Africa possesses' but was now refusing to have anything to do with him. Some time later she arrived at a dinner party only to discover that Rhodes was among the guests. There was a violent quarrel, in the course of which Schreiner became so heated that she hit her head on the table.

A year later, a piece of legislation was put before the House that would have a more lasting impact. In August 1892, Hofmeyr introduced the Franchise and Ballot Act. The intention was to continue the process that had been started five years earlier with the Voters' Registration Act (see p. 167). The property requirement would be raised from £25 to £75. There would be an eduction test and an owner's qualification, specifically designed to get poor white farmers onto the electoral rolls.

Five years earlier, Merriman had described the attempt to disenfranchize blacks as 'a miserable sham' and an affront to truth, liberty and justice. Now that he was a serving member of Rhodes's Cabinet, he was willing to support this new measure on condition that a secret ballot clause was inserted. Rhodes grudgingly agreed, but was unhappy with the compromise: 'I like to know how a person votes.'[14]

The effect of this new Bill was to remove a further 3348 non-white voters and add 4506 whites to the electoral rolls in the first year.[14] The property requirement alone halved the number of eligible black voters in Cape Town.[15]

By September 1892, Rhodes felt strong enough to remove the liberals by 'promoting' them out of his Cabinet. He offered to make Rose-Innes a judge and to appoint Merriman to the position of agent-general in London. Both positions were refused, but subsequent events soon played into Rhodes's hands. Sivewright, the Minister of Works and a Bondsman, awarded a scandalous railway contract to 'an ill-favoured friend of his – a drunken and unscrupulous Scot, called James Logan'.[16] Sivewright had not consulted his Cabinet colleagues or invited tenders before giving his friend a monopoly of all railway catering for 18 years.

Merriman and two other ministers threatened to resign unless Sivewright was removed from the Cabinet. Rhodes accepted their resignations, called new elections and was returned with a two-thirds majority. He was now in a position to form a new government free from liberal restraints. Significantly, he added the portfolio of Minister of Native Affairs to his duties as prime minister.

Merriman wrote to his old friend J.B. Currey that it was a relief to be free at last from 'the lobbying, the intrigue and the utterly cynical disregard of anything approaching moral principle in the conduct of public affairs'.[17] With views like that, it may seem surprising that Merriman had remained in Rhodes's Cabinet so long but, as he told his mother at the time, 'the loss of position and means' was a very great sacrifice to bear.[18]

Within weeks of Rhodes's electoral triumph, Jameson's message came down the wire from Fort Victoria – 'We have the excuse for a row over murdered women and children' – to which Rhodes gave his famous reply, 'Read Luke fourteen thirty-one'. As soon as the first term of the new Parliament was over, Rhodes was steaming north on the *German*. Six weeks later he made his triumphant entry into Lobengula's ruined capital and began pegging out the parks and business section of the new township of Bulawayo. In January 1894 the conqueror of Matabeleland returned to Cape Town, determined to solve the 'native question' once and for all.

There is a river in South Africa called the Great Kei river. The land through which it flows used to be called Kaffraria – 'the land of the Kaffirs'. It was home to the Griquas, the Pondos, the Xhosas and the Thembus, and formed a buffer between the British colonies of the Cape and Natal. In time, white farmers encroached into the area and blacks withdrew into shrinking pockets of land which became increasingly overcrowded and overgrazed.

A large tract of Kaffraria north of the Kei river (the Transkei) was formally annexed by the Cape in 1885 and, throughout that decade, Cape magisterial authority was gradually extended over the lands of the Griquas and the Thembus. The Pondos retained their autonomy in a small coastal enclave bordering Natal, but faced frequent complaints from the colonists, including accusations of cattle theft. In 1893 Sir Henry Loch visited the territory in order to discuss these problems with the Pondo chief, Sigcawu, who kept him waiting three days before agreeing to an interview. Nothing was achieved as a result.

Rhodes heard of the High Commissioner's humiliation as soon as he returned from his triumphs in the north. At the earliest opportunity, he set out for Pondoland in a coach drawn by eight cream-coloured horses and escorted by 100 men of the Cape Mounted Rifles. The truculent Sigcawu was summoned and kept waiting for three days, in an obvious tit-for-tat. Rhodes then told the chief to accompany him to a maize field, where the Cape riflemen had set up machine guns. On a signal from Rhodes, the crop was flattened. 'And that is what will happen to you and your tribe,' remarked Rhodes, 'if you give us any further trouble.'[19] He then informed Sigcawu that his country had been annexed by the Cape. The old chief understood the message of the machine guns and offered no objection.

Two months after the annexation of Pondoland and just 10 days after Her Majesty's Government had assigned the whole of Lobengula's territory to his company, Rhodes moved the second reading of the Glen Grey Act in the House. He had described this piece of legislation as 'a native bill for Africa'[20] and his 'favourite child'.[21]

The Glen Grey district, after which this Act was named, was an area of some 800 square miles (2074 square kilometres) south of the Kei river in the former Kaffraria. It was here that Rhodes proposed to start a great project that would eventually provide the colony with an inexhaustible supply of workers who would have no say in the government of the country they were compelled to serve.

The Glen Grey district was to be the first 'native reserve'. 'My idea,' Rhodes explained, 'is that the natives should be kept in these native reserves and not mixed with white men at all.'[22] While whites would not be permitted to acquire land or property in the Glen Grey area, blacks would receive eight-acre (3.24-hectare) allotments which they were forbidden to subdivide or sell. By these means, only eldest sons could inherit;

A Pondo.

younger sons and unmarried daughters would have no means of support. The measure would also prevent African advancement. The successful black farmer could not expand by purchasing neighbouring property, and the man who wished to leave the land would be unable convert his asset into cash.

In addition to these restrictions, every family in the district would be compelled to pay a hut tax and every male (landowners and landless) who did not sell his labour outside the area within a 12-month period would be compelled to pay a labour tax. Rhodes described this last measure as a 'gentle stimulus to these people to make them go on working'.[23] Whatever work they did in the colony, they would have no right to vote there. Instead, they would be permitted to elect 'native councillors', responsible for 'various local questions, to which the natives might devote themselves with good results'.[24]

When Rhodes introduced this Act, the missionaries had been running schools and farms in the Glen Grey area. Rhodes intended to put a stop to these activities. The missionaries, he told the House, 'were turning out Kaffir parsons ... a dangerous class [who] ... would develop into agitators against the government.' In place of the mission schools, Rhodes intended to establish industrial schools 'framed by the Government'.[25]

Anyone familiar with the theory and practice of apartheid in South Africa will recognize that all the essential elements were put in place by Cecil Rhodes 54 years before the Nationalist Government came to power. The notorious Bantu Education Act was always regarded as Dr Verwoerd's creation and was widely condemned as a cynical initiative designed to train blacks to be useful labourers and servants. In fact, it was Cecil Rhodes who pioneered this form of instruction through his 'industrial schools', and it is certainly no coincidence that the first Bantustan created by the apartheid regime was in the Transkei, of which Glen Grey is a part.

Rhodes forced his Act through the House in an unprecedented all-night sitting on 30–31 July 1894. There was no apology, no talk of preserving 'native culture and tradition', no recourse to any of the other excuses used by those who try to make racism 'respectable'. This Bill was about votes and labour, particularly labour. Rhodes came straight to the point:

> When I see the labour troubles that are occurring in the United States, and when I see the troubles that are going to occur with the English people in their own country ... I feel rather glad that the labour question here is connected with the native question ... If the whites maintain their position as the supreme race, the day will come when we shall all be thankful that we have the natives with us in their proper position.[26]

The message was brutally simple. Support this Bill, and you will no longer regard 'the native' as a problem but as an asset, a valuable raw material.

Rhodes told his MPs they were 'sitting in judgement on Africa' and reminded them that their prime minister was not only responsible for 'the natives in the colony' but for 'half a million of natives' on this side of the Zambezi and 'another half-million' on the other side. 'The whole of the North,' he told them, 'will some time or another come under this Bill if passed by the House ... This is a Native Bill for Africa.'[27]

In fact, only two months before Rhodes introduced the Glen Grey Act his Land Commission in Rhodesia had recommended that the defeated Matabele should be herded into two largely waterless and fly-infested reserves[28] to allow the majority of the land to be released to whites. Rhodes's Cape interests and his Rhodesian interests were now in perfect harmony.

Merriman and Rose-Innes fought against the Glen Grey Act and London objected, but it was passed into law. Throughout the 1890s its provisions were extended to other districts of the Transkei, including Pondoland.

In tandem with these territorial changes there was a relentless drive to establish apartheid in the towns. Those non-whites who had long been an integral part of urban life now experienced segregation in schools, sports, prisons, hospitals, theatres and on public transport. In the same session as the Glen Grey Act was passed, Rhodes permitted all the cities and towns of the Cape to impose evening curfews on blacks. Local municipalities were allowed to set up separate locations for Africans and Asians and to demand that they carry passes.[29]

At the same time a vicious propaganda programme was conducted in Rhodes's own newspapers to promote racial segregation. The *Cape Argus* inveighed against 'the wasteful, indifferent, and worst of all, filthy' Cape Coloureds, calling them 'the human scum of this city, the offensive and aggressive half-breeds'. In another edition the editor lamented that there were parts of the city 'where poor white and filthy black still live side by side'.[32]

Rhodes had not created this climate of hate, but he had nurtured it. In so doing he had served his business interests and united the bulk of the colony's white population behind him. He was now at the pinnacle of his power, lionized in the Cape and in London, where bus drivers and cabbies shouted out greetings and 'men every here and there along the route would touch their hats to him' as he passed'.[30]

NINETEEN

JAMESON'S RAID

Jameson never makes a mistake.

CECIL RHODES[1]

Rhodes was 41 years old in 1894. To the world, it seemed that everything he touched was bound to succeed. Yet those who were closest to him were noticing worrying changes. Power was going to his head. At times he could be brutal and overbearing, intolerant of dissent. Increasingly, the people he gathered round him were sycophants and yes-men.

His health was also deteriorating. After cheating death for so many years, Rhodes began to suffer a recurrence of the heart problem that had troubled him in his youth. Periodically, he experienced painful chest spasms and only made matters worse by smoking and drinking to give himself the extra stimulus to stay on top of his heavy workload. As he entered his 40s he was also becoming seriously overweight. He had always appeared older than his years; now that gap seemed wider than ever.

Rhodes could not bear physical pain. When his heart troubled him, he would become tearful[2] and yield to self-pity. Those around him would hear that he did not expect to live beyond 45.[3] 'I have only one thing to complain of,' he said to his architect, Herbert Baker, 'that the Almighty won't give me ten more years to live'.[4] To his friend and banker Lewis Michell he complained that 'the great fault in life is its shortness. Just as one is beginning to know the game, one has to stop.'[5]

This combination of failing health and a growing sense of self-importance gave rise to an obsessive concern that he would not survive long enough to achieve the great work that would bring him lasting recognition – the union of South African States. As the 1890s advanced, Cecil Rhodes became impatient. He began to hurry.

Patience had always been Rhodes's great strength. He owed his success to meticulous planning and a determination to devote whatever time was necessary to persuade, convince and cajole. Nowhere had he shown greater patience than in his dealings with Johannes Paulus Kruger, president of the Transvaal.

In 1894 people were beginning to realize that the wealth of the mines around Johannesburg might soon transform Kruger's backward Boer republic into the economic powerhouse of southern Africa. Rhodes and Rudd had been slow to recognize the potential of the Witwatersrand, leaving the field wide open to men like J.B. Robinson. Alfred Beit, who had provided the loan that launched the 'buccaneer' on his spectacular second career, was soon buying extensively on his own behalf. With his partner, Julius Wernher, 'Little Alfred' formed Wernher, Beit and Eckstein (the Corner House Group), which soon developed into the most powerful force on the Rand. Beit gave Rhodes every opportunity to join his consortium, even offering him half-shares in his own holdings at cost, but Rhodes still had a blind spot when it came to the Rand.

Barney Barnato was another late starter. Like Rhodes, he had devoted his energies to the battle to monopolize the diamond industry, but once amalgamation had been achieved, Barnato began to take notice of the consistently optimistic reports he was receiving from the Rand. Late in 1888 he went to see for himself, and in three incredible months spent £2 million (£99 million by today's values) securing every claim, city property and outlying estate he could lay his hands on. Johannesburg, he told the world, would soon become 'the financial Gibraltar of South Africa'.[6] Very soon Barnato was ahead of Beit, while Rhodes with his Goldfields interests was trailing far behind.

Within months of Barnato's buying spree, there was sudden panic on the Rand. In many ways it was a replay of the Kimberley blue-ground scare 15 years earlier. Rumours circulated that the gold was giving out, but the trouble was purely technical. Near the surface it had been easy to process the gold-bearing banket by amalgamating the crushed ore with mercury, but at greater depths the reef was contaminated with iron sulphides that interfered with the electrolytic extraction process. As a result, most of the gold was escaping in the 'tailings' of sand and slime.

The news set off panic-selling of shares and precipitated the Cape banking crisis that overshadowed Rhodes's first years as Prime Minister. Barnato kept his nerve. 'The gold is there in the earth, beyond a doubt', he kept repeating. 'Money and patience, money and patience, will overcome all difficulties here as they did in Kimberley.'[6]

Barnato was soon proved right. Before the end of 1890 salvation came to the Rand through a team of Glasgow chemists. They discovered that, if the ore was first treated with potassium cyanide, the gold could be recovered. Every mine on the outcrop was soon working at full blast and, as the engineers sank their shafts and boreholes, they discovered that the gold-bearing reef continued to depths of 3000 feet (900 metres) and more. A new age of deep-level mining had dawned.

It was the Kimberley story all over again. The deep levels could only be exploited by those with huge financial resources, and the small, under-capitalized claim-owners were soon digested by the likes of Barnato and Beit.

In 1892 Rhodes and Rudd finally woke up to the potential of the Rand and asked Beit for an interest in his mining properties. Beit agreed and saved Gold Fields from oblivion. A new company, Consolidated Goldfields of South Africa Ltd, was registered. Within three years it showed a profit of £2,540,918.

With the 1890s boom came a second gold rush. From all over the world waves of new immigrants poured into the brash new town of Johannesburg. Like Kimberley in the 1880s, it became a place of extremes. Palatial office buildings, clubs and theatres sprang up in the centre, while here and there the magnificent mansions of the new Rand millionaires appeared in the suburbs. However, the majority of the new immigrants lived in shanties, knocked together out of corrugated iron and flattened biscuit tins. Black miners were confined to compounds, this time without the excuse of IDB.

Flora Shaw, a journalist who would soon play a spectacular role in the Johannesburg drama, visited the town in 1892 and was not impressed. Johannesburg, she wrote, was 'hideous and detestable, luxury without order; sensual enjoyment without art; riches without refinement; display without dignity'.[7]

Thirty miles (48 kilometres) away in Pretoria, the Transvaal capital, president Paul Kruger contemplated the growth of this new Gomorrah with mixed emotions. While he was happy to receive the enormous amounts of extra revenue that were pouring into his state coffers, he was determined that the *Uitlanders* (foreigners) who created this wealth should have no say in the running of his country. On one of his early visits to Johannesburg he was shouted down when he began his address to a mixed audience of Afrikaners and *Uitlanders* with: 'People of the Lord, you old people of the country! ... You foreigners, you newcomers, yes, you thieves and murderers!' When Barnato provided the funds to build Johannesburg's first synagogue, Kruger declared the building open 'in the name of Jesus Christ'.[8]

Kruger was, in fact, the personification of everything backward, reactionary and ignorant in the Afrikaner tradition. He only had three months' schooling in his life. It was his proud boast that he read no book except the Bible, and to the end of his days he believed that the world was flat. He had difficulty writing his own name and, whenever there was a document to sign Sanna, his illiterate wife, would shriek through the house '*Stell, kinders! Papa vell ze nam tieken!*' ('Quiet children! Papa wants to sign his name!'). And then she would watch with breathless pride as Oom Paul's big, awkward fingers traced his signature.[9]

Gigantic, fleshy and grotesquely ugly 'with little, sore pouched eyes and [a] straggly beard that fringed his jaw from ear to ear',[9] Kruger presided over his small white tribe like an Old Testament patriarch. 'Oom Paul' (Uncle Paul) was the affectionate nickname given to him by his burghers (citizens), whom he would receive on the *stoep* of his one-storeyed cottage in Pretoria. Swinging his bulk to and fro in a wooden rocking chair, he would punctuate his sentences 'by spitting in the general direction of a huge brass cuspidor ... Only about once out of five times did he hit his mark.'[9]

Kruger's hold on the Transvaal was not monolithic. The judiciary resisted him and in politics there were young and more liberal Afrikaners, some educated in Europe, who might have guided their republic in a different direction. It is one of the great ironies of history that this backward and venal man was able to prevail in his own country and become an enduring symbol of resistance to British imperialism, largely because of Cecil Rhodes – but this is to anticipate events.

In the early years of his premiership, Rhodes showed commendable restraint, and on one occasion found himself in the extraordinary position of counselling his Afrikaner allies in the Cape Parliament to moderate their attacks on Kruger in the interest of neighbourly relations, but the Bondsmen had good reason to be angry. All attempts to persuade Kruger to join a customs union were flatly rejected, even though the other Boer republic – the Orange Free State – was amenable, and Kruger continued to impose heavy duties on all Cape produce sent to the Transvaal. When Cape Afrikaners came to work in his republic, Kruger treated them in the same high-handed manner he treated the detested English. They were refused government jobs, while Kruger's German and Hollander cronies – as well as the members of his own enormous family – were well represented in the over-paid State bureaucracies.

Kruger also rewarded his friends with manufacturing monopolies over a whole range of items, from bricks to soap. Beit's factious cousin, Edward Lippert, was given sole right to manufacture dynamite for 16 years on condition that he built and equipped a factory. No dynamite factory was ever built by 'the red-bearded German', who continued to import duty-free materials at a low price and sell at a massive profit. It is estimated that the dynamite monopoly alone was equivalent to an extra tax of £600,000 on the gold-mining industry.

The list of grievances went on and on. The *Uitlanders* complained that taxes in Johannesburg were 10 times higher than they were in Pretoria and that nine-tenths of all taxes were paid by them. Yet they had no right to vote or to participate in general or local government and were compelled to sustain schools where all instruction had to be in the Dutch language. They were also liable for military duty.[10]

On the question of the vote, one can have some sympathy for Kruger's position, although there was no excuse for the exclusions from municipal affairs. By the mid-1890s, the *Uitlanders* outnumbered the Transvaal Afrikaners by more than three to one. (The Transvaal Africans outnumbered both groups put together, but that was another matter.) Kruger knew that if he gave the *Uitlanders* the vote he would be handing them his country, but instead of making some small concessions, he introduced uncompromising legislation designed to exclude the *Uitlanders* for all time. The franchise was to be restricted to pre-1876 settlers and their descendants. These people would be entitled to vote at the age of 16.[11]

The majority of the *Uitlanders* were English artisans and miners, who had no intention of taking up permanent residence and were probably not over-concerned with the vote. However, settlers from the Cape Colony and Natal were genuinely aggrieved at their exclusion from citizen rights in the country they had chosen as their home and were helping to develop, and both groups resented the excessive living costs, resulting form Kruger's vindictive trade policies, corruption and mismanagement. In 1892 Charles Leonard, a Cape colonist, formed the National Union, a political reform movement. The petition he presented to Kruger had 13,000 signatures. It was ignored.

Only the mine magnates stayed aloof. They were making millions and saw no reason to rock the boat. Barnato was particularly chummy with Oom Paul, and on one occasion presented him with two stone lions that still guard the entrance to Kruger's cottage in Pretoria, now a national monument. For his part, Rhodes paid no attention to *Uitlander* grievances during his first premiership. Although Kruger was fast becoming the greatest obstacle to his dream of federation, Rhodes was convinced he would eventually win him round. Even if he failed, Kruger was nearly 70. He would not last for ever.

On the first occasion Rhodes met Kruger in his capacity as prime minister of the Cape, they discussed railways. Kruger was interested in obtaining an independent outlet to the sea through Delagoa Bay, which was in Portuguese territory. Rhodes had already tried to buy the bay from the impoverished Portuguese, but national pride had prevented them from selling. He now suggested to Kruger that they should join forces and seize the bay, but Kruger was neither tempted nor amused. The following year the two men did reach an accommodation. Rhodes agreed to raise a loan that would enable Kruger to complete his Johannesburg–Delagoa railway in return for permission to extend the Cape line into Johannesburg.

If he had been sure of his health, who knows how long Rhodes might have continued his slow and patient negotiations with Kruger? As late as January 1894 he gave a speech in Cape Town where he talked of achieving federation 'step by step, taking public opinion with me'. (This was the occasion when he illustrated his theme with the parable of the elderly admiral planting acorns – 'with me rests the conception and the shade and the glory' (see p. 35).) 'Step by step,' Rhodes repeated, 'in accordance with the feeling and sentiment of the people as a whole ... You must never hurry anything.'[12] Before the year was out Rhodes would no longer heed his own advice, but there was more to this sudden change than illness. There was John Hays Hammond.

Hammond was a brilliant American mining engineer, reputed to be able to 'smell a gold mine a thousand miles away'. A native of San Francisco and educated at Yale, Hammond originally made his name in the gold mines of Nevada. He had been brought to South Africa by Barnato, who agreed to pay him $50,000 a year. In no time at all, Hammond transformed Barnato's mining operations. Using American methods, he sank shafts at three times the speed considered possible at the time and reached depths that had never been attained before. With Hammond to guide him, Barnato bought new properties, cut out waste and invested heavily in expertise and machinery.

In 1893, the relationship between these two strong-willed individuals started to fray. Rhodes seized his opportunity and wired Hammond to visit him at Groote Schuur. Yale and Oxford took to each other at once. Sitting together on a wooden bench on the spacious back verandah, they agreed terms over a bottle of excellent Rudesheimer. Rhodes offered Hammond $75,000 a year, 50 per cent more than he was getting from Barnato, and promised him a share in the profits as well as the freedom to buy new properties at his own discretion. The final agreement was scrawled on a scrap of paper: 'Mr Hays Hammond is authorized to make any purchases for going ahead and has full authority provided he informs me and gets no protest. CJR.'[13]

When Barnato heard of Rhodes's offer, he was incensed. The next time the two men had occasion to meet was at the Burlington Hotel, London. It is said that Barnato shouted angrily at Rhodes, 'Suppose you had a first-rate chef and after dining with you I lured him away. You'd think I was a rotter, wouldn't you. And you'd be bloody right!'[14]

Hammond wrought the same transformations at Gold Fields as he had done on the Barnato mines. By now Ernest, Rhodes's only married brother, had replaced Harry Currey as company secretary. Knowing very little about the business, he wisely gave Hammond his head.

Hammond's other great responsibility was to oversee Rhodes's mining interests in Rhodesia. Between September and November 1894, Rhodes and Jameson accompanied Hammond on an extensive survey of the country's mineral resources. All three men knew how much was at stake. 'It was of supreme importance,' Hammond wrote later, 'that my report be favourable – on my findings would hinge the investment or non-investment of enormous sums of British capital in the development of the country.'[15]

Hammond was an honest man and his final assessment was uncompromising. 'I urge the investing public to exercise due discrimination', he wrote.[16] When Rutherfoord Harris read the finished report, he added a gloomy prognosis of his own: 'If we have to depend on Hammond's geological report to raise money for this country, I don't think the outlook is encouraging.'[17]

There *were* mineral resources in Rhodesia – nickel, copper, coal and some gold – but Rhodes's dream of finding a second Witwatersrand in the kingdom of Ophir was shattered by Hammond. Once again, Rhodes and Jameson were in the wrong place. There was no vast, stretching seam of payable ore in either Matabeleland or Mashonaland. The gold fields around Johannesburg were unique. They would make Beit, Wernher, Eckstein, Robinson – even Rhodes and Rudd – incredible fortunes, but unless something was done soon they would also turn Kruger's backward republic into the dominant state in southern Africa. Rhodes's great ambition of creating a federation on his own terms would come to nothing.

Of more immediate concern, though, was the impact that Hammond's report was likely to have on the fortunes of the Chartered Company. At the next AGM in London in January 1895, Rhodes did his best to misrepresent Hammond's conclusions, and in this he was remarkably successful.[18] But the clock was ticking. Interest on loans raised to finance the war against Lobengula would fall due in January 1896.

During the long days and nights they had spent together in the Rhodesian veld, Jameson and Hammond worked hard to persuade Rhodes to think the unthinkable: an invasion of the Transvaal, the overthrow of Kruger and the seizure of Johannesburg's gold wealth by force. The economic arguments were self-evident, but for Hammond there were moral questions as well. Kruger's corrupt and backward regime offended him. Monopolies, backhanders and nepotism offended him. Taxation without representation offended him.

A plan began to take shape. The *Uitlanders* would rise up against Kruger. Leander Starr Jameson, the conqueror of Matabeleland, would ride to their rescue at the head of Rhodes's private army. The tyrant would be overthrown and Rhodes would have the Transvaal. Jameson had done it before and he could do it again. He was gung-ho. 'Anyone', he told Rhodes, 'could take the Transvaal with a dozen revolvers.'[19]

But Rhodes was unsure. This was not his way. He had said so himself, many times. 'I have never met anyone in my life, whom it was not as easy to deal with as to fight.'[20] Kaffir kings were dispensable, but the Boers? 'Never hurry anything ... Step by step ... Give it time ...' But did he have time? 'The great fault in life is its shortness. Just as one is beginning to know the game ...'

After the tour of Rhodesia with Jameson and Hammond, Rhodes decided to call on the Transvaal president on his way south. It was a disastrous meeting. Kruger's rail link from Johannesburg to Delagoa Bay had just been completed, thanks to a £700,000 loan negotiated by Rhodes. Now that he had what he wanted, Kruger announced that his government intended to triple the already extortionate rates charged for taking goods on the last 52-mile (84-kilometre) section of the railway from the Cape border to Johannesburg.[21] His obvious intention was to deflect as much traffic as possible on to his new line to Delagoa Bay. In Rhodes's eyes this was an outrage, an act of monstrous ingratitude. How would he ever be able to deal with such a man? 'If you do not take care,' he warned Kruger, 'you will have the whole of South Africa against you'.[22] It is said that the meeting ended with both men shaking their fists at one another. In all probability, this was the moment when Rhodes made up his mind.

From Pretoria, Rhodes and Jameson travelled to Johannesburg and made contact with Charles Leonard and the other leaders of The National Union. Jameson stayed behind after Rhodes's departure and took further soundings until 'he arrived at the conviction that ... whatever its leaders might do, the mining community of Johannesburg was fixed on a political revolution'.[23]

Ironically, the main elements of the plan Rhodes and Jameson now put together had been suggested to the British Government by Sir Henry Loch 18 months earlier. After visiting the Transvaal in June 1893, the High Commissioner was convinced that the mining community would support the return of the Transvaal to British rule. In Johannesburg he had met Lionel Phillips, chairman of the Chamber of Mines, and discussed the possibility of raising an *Uitlander* force strong enough to hold the town. Evidently satisfied with Phillips's response, Loch returned to Cape Town and ordered Bechuanaland Police to be placed along the Transvaal border. At the same time, he requested the Colonial Office to send 5000 British troops to the Cape and give him authority to invade the Transvaal. Loch's requests were refused.

Rhodes probably knew of the Loch plan and would certainly have disapproved of direct British intervention in South African affairs. In the 18 months since Loch had made that proposal, Rhodes had beaten him in the race to Gubulawayo and scotched his attempts to secure Matabeleland for Britain. Rhodes was equally determined that the Transvaal should be secured by his own force and a settlement imposed on his own terms, something he could not achieve entirely on his own. He needed British collaboration – without British interference.

There were four essential components to the plan that now took shape in Rhodes's mind. First, he had to orchestrate an armed rebellion in Johannesburg. To ensure its success, he would have to smuggle large amounts of additional arms and ammunition into the town. Secondly, he would require a base close to the Transvaal border where Jameson could assemble a private army, ready to come to the rebels' assistance. The Rhodesian border was too far from Johannesburg and, for obvious legal and security reasons, Rhodes could not assemble a force and mount an invasion from Cape territory. The ideal solution was to be found in the vast empty wastes of Bechuanaland. Here Jameson could assemble his troops in relative secrecy within 200 miles (320 kilometres) of Johannesburg. (As will be clear later, Bechuanaland would also offer Rhodes and Jameson a cast-iron alibi should the Transvaalers discover the presence of this force and suspect its purpose.)

Thirdly, Rhodes would have to manage public opinion in Britain and Europe. It had not been difficult to find plausible excuses for the invasion and destruction of an independent black kingdom; justifying an attack on an independent *white* republic would be much trickier. Unlike Lobengula, Kruger had access to the European press and the means to repudiate falsehoods put about by Rhodes and Jameson. He had also established good relations with some of Britain's colonial rivals, particularly Germany, and these countries had representatives in his capital. To win the propaganda battle, Rhodes had to be sure of a definite sequence of events. First, there must be a well-coordinated press campaign to draw international attention to *Uitlander* grievances. When the message had been disseminated, Johannesburg would rise up against the oppressor. Only then would it be safe for Jameson to invade – in response to his countrymen's calls for help. If Jameson went in without that excuse, he would be committing an unprovoked attack on a friendly state and the political consequences could be devastating.

Finally, Rhodes had to impose a peace settlement on his own terms. The Transvaal was in Britain's sphere of influence under terms agreed at the London Convention of 1884. The only person with authority to impose a settlement after Kruger's defeat was the senior British official in South Africa – the High Commissioner of the Cape. Given his ambitions to annex the Transvaal for the crown, Loch was out of the question. Rhodes needed someone he could control. The obvious choice was Sir Hercules Robinson.

Fortunately for Rhodes, one important element in this plan was virtually in place. Two years earlier, the Liberal Government in London had promised that when he was ready to build his railway to Rhodesia, Rhodes would be given a strip of land in Bechuanaland running the entire length of the intended line. He would also receive a subsidy of £20,000 for 10 years. At the same time, it was made clear to him that as soon as conditions were right, the Cape would get the crown colony of Bechuanaland (50,000 square miles (129,600 square kilometres) while the 225,000 square miles (583,200 square kilometres) of Bechuanaland protectorate would go to the Chartered Company (see p. 145).

These might seem curious undertakings from a Liberal government, but Gladstone's successor, Lord Rosebery, was an ardent imperialist. He was also son-in-law of Rhodes's friend and backer, Nathaniel Rothschild, and, like him, a devotee.

On returning to Cape Town after his disastrous meeting with Kruger, Rhodes sent a dispatch to the colonial secretary, Lord Rippon, informing him that the time had come for the Liberal Government to honour its promises. At this point, Loch intervened. Rhodes was denied the protectorate. A grant of 6000 square miles (15,550 square kilometres) for the railway line was accepted in principle, but not confirmed. Clearly, Rhodes would have to do some negotiating on the spot.

In December 1894 Rhodes, Jameson, Willoughby and Harris left for London. It was a particularly successful visit and included Rhodes's famous second audience with the Queen ('I have added two new Provinces to your possessions, Madam' 'since we last met'.) as well as the celebrated AGM of the Chartered Company when he told his shareholders that they 'possessed a very large piece of the world'. On this visit Rhodes was also made a Privy Councillor of the realm. From now on he would have to be addressed as the Rt Hon. Cecil John Rhodes.

Jameson was also given the honours due to the conqueror of the Matabele. The Queen made him a Commander of the Bath and he was guest of honour at a banquet and meeting of the Imperial Institute presided over by the Prince of Wales. Jameson told the assembled dignitaries that Rhodes would carry the British flag 'to the end of Lake Tanganyika' and would create 'a country as large as Europe ... where white men and women can live, where children can be reared in health and vigour'. He went on to describe Rhodesia as a land rich in gold, coal and iron with '100,000 fat, sleek cattle to prove its pastoral value'; a happy combination, as *The Times* reported the following day, 'of Canaan, Ophir, and the Black Country.'[24]

In all this excitement, no mention was made of Hammond's report or of the disquieting fact that the 100,000 fat, sleek cattle were booty, looted from a vanquished people.

The famous pair were as successful in their private dealings as they had been in their public appearances. Rhodes secured a promise from the colonial secretary that Loch would be replaced by Sir Hercules Robinson, who was now 70 years old and suffering from dropsy. For the sake of form, the prime minister insisted that Sir Hercules should resign his directorships – he was then on the boards of De Beers, the Chartered Company and the Standard Bank. Graham Bower, Sir Hercules's long-serving assistant in the Cape, loyally agreed to turn down the offer of a governorship in order to return to his former position. It was felt that the aged and infirm Sir Hercules would need the support of an experienced man.

Rhodes had no difficulty in persuading the directors of the Chartered Company to authorize 'a rather sensational increase'[25] in the size of the Rhodesian police force and the purchase of a huge inventory of arms and ammunition. How Rhodes was able to justify these expenses without confiding in his Board remains a mystery, but since the noble directors would later protest that they had no knowledge of the Rhodes–Jameson conspiracy, we must take them at their word and attribute Rhodes's success to his legendary charm.

Rhodes had decided that *The Times* should be entrusted with the task of orchestrating his press and propaganda campaign in Britain and Europe. The paper had correspondents in all the European capitals, close links with the British Establishment and a reputation for probity. Moberley Bell, the forceful managing director, and George Buckle, the editor, were drawn into the conspiracy, but the principal player would be Flora Shaw, the paper's colonial correspondent. Shaw had once been Stead's assistant on *The Pall Mall Gazette*. She was introduced to Rhodes during his famous visit of 1889 to secure the charter and, since then, had been a devoted admirer.

There was one disappointment during an otherwise triumphant visit. The Colonial Office did not feel the time was right to hand the Bechuanaland protectorate to Rhodes. The promise of land for the railway line was repeated. Jameson would have his base, but Rhodes was greedy for more. With the Transvaal *and* Bechuanaland in his hands, his dream of federation would be almost fulfilled. He would have a continuous block of territory stretching from the Cape to Lake Tanganyika, but the Colonial Office could not be persuaded that this was the right time to hand over the protectorate.

On his return to South Africa, Rhodes began to prepare the ground in Johannesburg. He had decided that his brother Francis (Frank) was the right man to lead the insurrection there. Frank was then a colonel in the British army, but Rhodes had no difficulty getting him seconded from his regiment. The great challenge now was to convince the mine-owners and Charles Leonard's National Union that armed rebellion was the only possible response to Kruger. In spite of Jameson's earlier assurances that 'the mining community of Johannesburg was fixed on a political revolution', Rhodes was more realistic. He knew that the National Union was committed to constitutional change and that the mine-owners had deliberately stayed clear of Transvaal politics.

As a first move, Rhodes invited Beit to Groote Schuur and confided his plan. Little Alfred not only offered to share costs with Rhodes, but agreed that on his return to Johannesburg he would approach Charles Leonard, Lionel Phillips and several mine-owners. Robinson and Barnato were deliberately excluded from the conspiracy. They were too close to Kruger and could not be trusted.

Phillips was not hard to convince, but only one mining company unconnected with Rhodes was won over. This was the Anglo-French, represented in the conspiracy by George Farrar. Leonard was not interested at this stage. He wanted a reformed republic and did not trust Rhodes to deliver it. It was an inauspicious start.

At the end of May, Sir Hercules Robinson and Graham Bower arrived in Cape Town. Three weeks later there was an unexpected development in London. Rosebery's Liberal Government fell and the Conservatives, under Lord Salisbury, were back in power. Joseph Chamberlain's Liberal Unionists had joined Salisbury's coalition government. As a reward, the Birmingham screw-manufacturer had been offered any cabinet post he wanted. He asked to be colonial secretary.

Six years earlier, in his capacity as chairman of the South Africa Committee, Chamberlain had sat shoulder-to-shoulder with the Rev. John Mackenzie and grilled Rhodes about his methods and motives (see pp. 207 and 209). He was then a radical minister in Gladstone's government, an 'Exeter Hall negrophile', an emphatic 'Little Englander'. He was also one of the few members of the South Africa Committee who had resisted Rhodes. When Lord Grey was wavering, he had come to Chamberlain for advice and was told: 'I know only three things about Rhodes and they all put me against him: (i) he has made an enormous fortune very rapidly, (ii) he is an Afrikaner (iii) he gave £10,000 to Parnell.'[26]

By 1895, time and the hunger for office had wrought a miraculous change. Chamberlain was now an arch-imperialist and, in his first speech to the House as colonial secretary, nailed his colours firmly to the mast:

'I believe in the British Empire and I believe in the British race'. In this new incarnation, Chamberlain was a man Rhodes could deal with.

Rutherfoord Harris, the trusted go-between, was sent to London. What transpired at his first meeting with Chamberlain cannot be determined beyond doubt, but Harris believed that he had understood the colonial secretary's meaning correctly when he cabled Rhodes on 13 August:

> Chamberlain will do anything to assist except hand over the administration protectorate, provided he officially does not know of your plan ... He will carry out promises made with reference to protectorate by previous Governments but mentioned one year as about time in which question will be settled as you wish.[27]

Joseph Chamberlain.

This was to be the first of the famous missing telegrams that were withheld from the Commission of Inquiry that followed the Jameson Raid. All the telegrams were sent in code. (A copy of the codebook can be seen on microfilm in the Rhodes House Library, Oxford.)

Two of the missing telegrams were discovered in Rhodes House years later by the biographer C.M. Woodhouse. Three others, including the one above, were quoted from memory by J.L. Garvin, Chamberlain's biographer, friend and apologist. There are perhaps eight others (the exact number differs between researchers) that have not come to light. On Rhodes's instructions all his papers relating to the Jameson Raid were destroyed after his death.

Chamberlain would vehemently deny any prior knowledge of the conspiracy, as would Sir Hercules Robinson, the directors of the Chartered Company and a host of others. In fact, Chamberlain had no alternative. A frank admission of British Government involvement in the Rhodes–Jameson conspiracy would have had disastrous political consequences. A war with Germany, at a time when Britain had no European allies, was not inconceivable. Whole volumes – including outstanding works by Jean van der Poel and Elizabeth Longford – have been written about the Jameson Raid. There is not space here to examine the evidence in the same detail. It is sufficient to say that the case against Chamberlain, Robinson and others is overwhelming, and there is very little reason to doubt that the core of

Harris's message was accurate: 'Chamberlain will ... assist ... provided he does not know of your plan ...'

After a second meeting at the Colonial Office Harris travelled to Birmingham, where he ordered 4000 rifles, three Maxims and several hundred thousand rounds of ammunition on the Chartered Company's account. The arms were then shipped to Cape Town. Harris also held a number of meetings with Flora Shaw of *The Times*, who was given the Chartered Company code and her own code name – Telemones.

While Harris was busy in London, there were two developments in South Africa which, in their different ways, created complications for Rhodes. When Kruger had originally imposed his extortionate charges for the use of the Transvaal section of the Cape Town–Johannesburg line, an excellent scheme was devised by the Cape merchants to avoid payment. Goods were taken off the Cape trains at the Vaal river (the Cape–Transvaal frontier) and transported by ox-waggon for the remaining 52 miles (84 kilometres) to Johannesburg.[28] Kruger was not amused, and on 28 August issued a proclamation that the Vaal drifts (fords) would be closed from 1 October. The Cape government protested that this would be in contravention of the London Convention. The protest was ignored.

Rhodes knew that if Kruger kept his word and acted illegally, the Imperial Government would have a legitimate excuse to intervene and Kruger could be brought down without recourse to secret conspiracies. But where would that leave Rhodes? If the fight against Kruger was above-board and directed from London, could he be sure of achieving a Transvaal settlement on his own terms? It was essential, therefore, that he have his own force ready to participate in any action against Kruger but, at this stage, he still lacked a base. The land for the railway line had been promised again and again, but it had not been delivered.

To complicate matters, three Bechuana chiefs had arrived in London in early September to protest against the transfer of their territory to the Chartered Company. For Rhodes, it was a tiresome rerun of a familiar story, with all the predictable ingredients – visits to the Colonial Office, flurries of excitement in missionary and radical circles. Harris, who was on the spot, realized that Chamberlain could scarcely hand over land while the Bechuanaland deputation was still in London, but was confident that all would be well once the chiefs had gone home; so confident that he decided to spend the rest of September grouse-shooting in Scotland.[29]

But Rhodes was not prepared to hang fire. With the active help of Sir Hercules, he arranged for his old friend Shippard and his brother Frank to negotiate with two minor Bechuana chiefs for the purchase of 40 square miles

(104 square kilometres) of bare, flat veld at a place called Pitsani Potlugo, close to the Transvaal border.[30] Chamberlain warned Sir Hercules that the chiefs who had agreed to the deal were under the paramountcy of the men he was talking to in London and had no right to sell the land. A compromise was reached. The deal would be described as 'provisional'. That was enough for Rhodes. Jameson now had a base and the conspirators swung into action.

Rifles, Maxims and ammunition were smuggled into Johannesburg, concealed in oil drums. A bogus company, the 'Rand Produce and Trading Centre',[31] was registered and a string of supply depots was set up between Pitsani and Johannesburg, disguised as a chain of country stores. The man in charge of this brand-new enterprise was Dr H.A. Wolff, Jameson's former medical partner in Kimberley. Wolff will be remembered for permitting the pregnant Mrs Sarsfield to go to her death and for his misguided attempt to eject Dr Sauer from the Kimberley hospital (see pp. 157–9).

It is astonishing how many actors in the smallpox drama took prominent roles in the later conspiracy against Kruger. Jameson, Wolff and Harris had all been signatories to the notorious pink slips, identifying the prevalent disease in Kimberley as pemphigus. Their implacable opponent, Dr Sauer, became an accomplice on the Rand, and the firm contracted to smuggle arms and ammunition into Johannesburg was none other than Pickering & Co. of Port Elizabeth, a transport company owned by Neville's elder brother Edward.[31]

In the midst of all the excitement, Kruger showed that he was a man of his word. On 1 October he closed the Vaal drifts. Rhodes and Sir Hercules successfully used the crisis to prod Chamberlain into action. In the second week of October the Chartered Company's right to the Pitsani enclave was officially recognized. In the following week Sir Hercules asked the Colonial Office to authorize the transfer of Rhodesian police to Pitsani. Permission was granted the same day. Rhodes now felt confident enough to send Chamberlain an ultimatum. He wanted his rights to Bechuanaland confirmed by 7 November.

While the secret plan was being advanced, Rhodes encouraged Chamberlain to keep up the pressure on Kruger with an open threat of force. Chamberlain obliged. The Transvaal consul in London was summoned to the Colonial Office and warned that unless the drifts dispute was settled to the satisfaction of the Cape government, the British Government would be compelled to intervene. Troop ships sailing to and from India were diverted from the Suez route to the Cape in a deliberate attempt to frighten Kruger. The strategy worked. Kruger suggested a conference to discuss a compromise. Chamberlain consulted Rhodes, who was not interested in compromises. Either the drifts were open or they were not. When his proposal was turned down, Kruger retreated a step further. He was prepared to open the drifts pending a new railway agreement. Again Rhodes refused.

On 2 November Robinson was authorized to send an ultimatum to Kruger, but only after the Cape government undertook, explicitly and in writing, to bear half the cost and provide troops if military action was necessary. Rhodes overcame the reluctance of his Cabinet by assuring them that Kruger would climb down. Sir Hercules convinced Chamberlain, who was becoming as nervous as Rhodes's ministers, that the Cape Parliament would support Rhodes even to the point of war.

To the relief of everyone except Rhodes, Kruger climbed down on 7 November. This was also the date that the other ultimatum fell due. There had been a flurry of telegrams between Cape Town and London as the deadline approached. Chamberlain knew enough to be suspicious of Rhodes. He wanted positive assurance that the rebellion would be under the British flag. Rhodes's final answer was uncompromising: 'I of course would not risk everything as I am doing, excepting for the British flag.'[32]

On 6 and 7 November, Chamberlain held meetings with Harris and the directors of the Chartered Company. He agreed to hand over 100,000 square miles (259,000 square kilometres) of Bechuanaland running along the entire length of the Transvaal boundary from the Cape to Rhodesia. Sir Hercules would be instructed to release the Bechuanaland police and sell their arms and equipment to the Chartered Company.

Rhodes still did not have the whole protectorate, although the portion that had been denied him was mostly desert. The important thing, though, was that he now had sufficient land to build his railway (and a great deal more besides). This meant that if the Transvaalers were to discover his troops ahead of time, their presence could be explained. His men were there to protect the railway-builders from hostile tribesmen. That excuse had no validity when the only land Rhodes owned was the 40 square miles at Pitsani.

By early November, Rhodes could claim another success. He had secured the support of Charles Leonard. It had not been easy. The National Union wanted assurances 'that the Union Jack would not be the symbol of the revolt, that the Transvaal would not be forced into federation, and that the Chartered Company would not profit from the affair'.[33] Rhodes left Leonard with the clear impression that all those conditions had been agreed, but on the question of the flag there was an obvious conflict between Leonard's wishes and Chamberlain's.

In a lifetime of private deal-making, Rhodes had succeeded in being all things to all men. For 25 years this policy had served him well, but his luck could not hold out for ever.

The cable Harris sent to Rhodes on 7 November detailing all the concessions granted by Chamberlain is still missing. According to Garvin, whose account is trusted, it contained an important proviso: 'Secretary of Colonies says you must allow decent interval and delay fireworks for a fortnight.'[32] The meaning was clear. Now that you have the police and the border zone, don't light the fuses in Pitsani and Johannesburg with indecent haste.

The two-week delay gave Rhodes time for one last refinement. Jameson was asked to go to Johannesburg. Rhodes wanted a signed appeal for help from the key conspirators in case their nerve failed and they were tempted to leave Jameson in the lurch. There was to be no date on the document. This would be added by Jameson when the time was right.

The letter was drafted by Leonard and signed by him, Hammond, Frank Rhodes and George Farrar. Leonard began with the usual recital of *Uitlander* grievances and then adopted a more emotional tone:

> What will be the condition of things here in the event of conflict? Thousands of unarmed men, women, and children of our race will be at the mercy of well-armed Boers, while property of enormous value will be in the greatest peril ... It is under these circumstances that we feel constrained to call upon you to come to our aid, should a disturbance arise here. The circumstances are so extreme that we cannot but believe that you and the men under you will not fail to come to the rescue of people who will be so situated ... [At this point in the letter there was a sudden shift from the sublime, which Jameson might have had something to do with.] ... We guarantee any expenses that may reasonably be incurred by you in helping us, and ask you to believe that nothing but the sternest necessity ... [and so on]

Jameson pocketed the letter and hurried back to Cape Town for final meetings with Rhodes and Sir Hercules. Four years later he would tell Viscountess Milner (whose first husband was Lord Salisbury): 'The High Commissioner knew every detail of the arrangements, and as the time approached his train was kept in readiness for him to start at a moment's notice'.[34] That waiting train was supposed to take Sir Hercules to the Transvaal to impose a settlement on Rhodes's terms as soon as Kruger had been brought down.

From Cape Town, Jameson headed for Pitsani. On 9 December, Sir John Willoughby's Rhodesian police reached the enclave. Everything seemed to be going to plan until Jameson received an extraordinary telegram from Frank Rhodes. The conspirators in Johannesburg had decided to postpone the 'polo tournament' (code for rebellion) until after the New Year so that it would not clash with race week. A furious Jameson cabled back: 'Do you consider races of utmost importance compared with immediate risk of discovery daily expected ...? Let J.H. Hammond inform weak partners, More delay, the more danger.'[35]

For the first time in his life, Rhodes was starting to lose control. He gave in to Johannesburg's demand and agreed that the revolution should not take place until after the New Year. The very next day Flora Shaw of *The Times* wired back that delay would be dangerous. If the European powers became aware of the plan and lodged a protest, it might be impossible for the British government to play its part. Bell, her editor, followed up with another telegram: 'Chamberlain sound in case of interference European powers but have special reason to believe wishes you must do it immediately'.[36]

Rhodes now agreed to bring the date of the revolution forward. No sooner had he done so than things started to go badly wrong in Johannesburg. The arms were not getting through and there was a sharp revival of the old distrust of Rhodes. The rebels wanted a reformed republic that would include 'liberal' Boers.[37] They insisted on keeping the *Vierkleur* (the Transvaal flag). Would Rhodes confirm his 'undertaking' to Leonard that the Union Jack would not be the symbol of the revolt?

On 19 December, Captain Francis Younghusband paid a special visit to Groote Schuur to bring the rebels' message to Rhodes. Younghusband was *The Times* correspondent in Johannesburg and *The Times* was Rhodes's principal channel to the Colonial Office. If Rhodes agreed to the rebels' demand, it would immediately reach Chamberlain's ears. If he refused, there was no guarantee of a rising. Rhodes was furious. By choosing Younghusband as their messenger the rebels had put him in an intolerable position. 'Is there no *man* up there?' he shouted. Then, turning to Younghusband, he asked: 'Won't you lead them?' Younghusband politely declined. To avoid any further discussion over the flag, Rhodes simply said 'Then we must stop Jameson'.[38]

As soon as Younghusband left Rhodes was in turmoil. Of course he musn't stop Jameson, but why was everyone trying to pin him down – over a flag? Hadn't he made it clear to Phillips and Leonard that there were much more important issues – practical issues like the customs union and the railway convention where they were all in agreement? 'Other things will all come in time ...' he had said when they tried to press him over the issue of the flag. But they were not satisfied. They pushed him as Chamberlain had pushed him. They wanted to know exactly where he stood. Rhodes was not used to challenges like that. He liked to keep his options open, to give himself plenty of room to manoeuvre. It was madness to make a firm commitment to a flag until he was sure which way things were moving. A rebellion under the Union Jack might invite intolerable interference from London. On the other hand, a rebellion under the *Vierkleur* could usher in an *Uitlander* republic controlled by the likes of J.B. Robinson, Barnato and Lippert.

On reflection, he decided that the second alternative would be far worse. He had enough people of his own in Johannesburg. He could count on a rebellion (of sorts) without consenting to the *Vierkleur*. Harris was sent chasing after Younghusband, who had decided to walk to the station. His message was short and to the point. Rhodes will commit to a rebellion under the Union Jack.

Now was the time to be decisive. Rhodes telegraphed Jameson that the rising would take place the following Saturday at midnight – 28 December. He was not to start before 8.00 p.m. All telegraph communications must be destroyed before the men broke camp. Jameson wired back, asking to go sooner. Rhodes was firm: 'You must not leave before Saturday night; we are feeling confident it [i.e. the rebellion] will take place Saturday night. Since Dr Wolff left [Johannesburg] feeling our subscribers greatly improved.'[39]

Rhodes's confidence was misplaced. The situation in Johannesburg had gone from bad to worse. The arms were still not getting through and word of the planned rebellion had leaked out. Several members of the Johannesburg Stock Exchange reacted by calling a meeting to denounce the 'foolish plans for rebellion' and to assure the government of sympathy 'if the worst comes to the worst'. The Mercantile Association, a body of businessmen, had declared that it would take no part in the revolt.[40]

From Johannesburg, Jameson's brother Sam sent a message to Pitsani: 'Absolutely necessary to postpone flotation [rebellion]'.[41] The 'reformers' were insisting that Jameson should make no move until they had received a pledge from Rhodes that the Imperial authorities would not be involved.

Jameson replied that a pledge was superfluous as the 'reformers' in Johannesburg had already given him written authority to invade. Delay was out of the question. Squads had already gone forward for 'distant wire cutting ... Therefore let J.H. Hammond telegraph instantly all right.'[42] The next message was for Rhodes. If it was too late to stop the wire-cutting parties, Jameson would have to abide by the original plan. He then added ominously: 'They have then two days for flotation. If they do not, we will make our own flotation with help of letter which I will publish.'[43]

Hammond, whom he had counted on as one of the bolder spirits, telegraphed back: 'I absolutely condemn further developments at present.'[44] From Cape Town, Francis Rhodes cabled that it was 'absolutely necessary ... to delay flotation' until Jameson had consulted with two special envoys who were on their way from Johannesburg.[45] Maurice Heany was coming via Kimberley, where a special train had been laid on for him, and a Major Holden was riding to Pitsani across country.

All through Saturday 28 December a stream of confusing messages continued to pour into Pitsani. 'Flotation not popular'; 'We cannot have fiasco'; 'It is alright if you will only wait';[45] and 'When you have seen Captain Heany let us know by wire what he says'. But there was nothing from Rhodes. Jameson would certainly have obeyed an explicit instruction from him. When this was not forthcoming, he sent his own message to Cape Town at 5.00 p.m. 'Unless I hear definitely to the contrary shall leave to-morrow evening ...'[46] The message was addressed to the Chartered Company but, by the time it reached Cape Town, the building had closed for the weekend. For the rest of Saturday night it remained in the Cape Town telegraph office.

On Saturday evening, after two meetings with Leonard, Rhodes was finally persuaded that Johannesburg could not be prodded into a rebellion; but no message was sent to Jameson. Instead, Rhodes sent for Sir Hercules' deputy, Graham Bower, and informed him that the revolution had 'fizzled out like a damp squib'. He described his quarrel with the 'reformers' over the flag, but said that he regarded the issue as 'only a pretext; they had never meant to fight and would now make the best possible terms with Kruger'. Rhodes also complained of the way London had pressured him into accepting the Union Jack. He had been against it, as had Sir Hercules. As Bower was leaving, Rhodes's final words were: 'You better tell the Governor the whole thing has fizzled out; he will be glad.'[47]

At 4.30 a.m. on Sunday 29 December, Maurice Heany arrived at the Mafeking railhead, where a cart was waiting to take him the 20 or so miles to Pitsani. Captain Holden, the other envoy, had reached Jameson's camp late the previous night. Both these men seem to have been unlikely choices for the task of restraining Jameson. Before retiring for the night Holden had already agreed to go with the column. Maurice Heany was the West Point dropout whose drunken indiscretions had forced Rhodes to abandon the plot to assassinate Lobengula. His first action on that crucial morning was to knock up a Mafeking trader and purchase a horse, field boots and a kit bag.

He arrived at Pitsani at approximately 10.00 a.m. and handed Jameson a letter from the 'reformers' in Johannesburg. Jameson's instructions were to stay where he was until further notice. The story goes that Jameson walked up and down for some time and then said 'I'm going'.

'Thought you would' said Heany.

'And what are you going to do?' asked Jameson.

'Going with you' said Heany.

'Thought you would' said Jameson.[48]

Jameson then sent a second telegram to Cape Town: 'Shall leave tonight for the Transvaal ...'

Jameson setting out from Pitsani.

Harris's confidential secretary picked up both of Jameson's messages at about 11.00 a.m. By the time he had taken them to Harris for decoding and travelled with him to Groote Schuur it was already 1.00 p.m. Messages to Mafeking went through the Kimberley telegraph office, which closed at 1.20 p.m. on Sundays. After that there was no link to Jameson.

When Rhodes received Jameson's messages he is reported to have 'paced up and down the room with his hair roughed up, repeating mechanically from time to time, "Now just be cool. Let's think this thing out. Now just be cool".'[49]

Deliberations at Groote Schuur continued until 4.00 p.m, when Harris left for the Cape Town telegraph office with Rhodes's message to Jameson. Supposedly, it contained an explicit instruction: 'On no account must you move, I strongly object to such a course'. As the line to Mafeking had been closed for three hours and the message could not be sent, Rhodes was free to do what he liked with the text before submitting it as evidence in the later inquiry, and there are strong grounds for believing that the version quoted above is bogus.[50]

While the drama was unfolding at Pitsani and Groote Schuur, Sir Hercules Robinson and Graham Bower were quietly composing a telegram that would let the colonial secretary know that the whole plot had been abandoned. Unbeknown to them, Chamberlain had heard from his own source (probably Flora Shaw) on Friday that things were starting to go badly wrong. On Saturday, the British ambassador in Berlin had been summoned to the Foreign Ministry and told that the German government could not 'accept any change in the status quo [in the Transvaal] in the direction sought by Cecil Rhodes'.

By Sunday, Chamberlain had lost his nerve and was making desperate moves to cover himself. Before he received the consoling message from Bower and Sir Hercules, he had drafted his own telegram for the benefit of the High Commissioner in Cape Town (and the record). The opening lines were, to say the least, disingenuous:

> It has been suggested, although I do not think it probable, that an endeavour may be made to force matters at Johannesburg to a head by someone in the service of the Company advancing from the Bechuanaland Protectorate with police. Were this to be done I should have to take action under Articles 22 and 8 of the Charter ...[51]

In other words, Chamberlain wanted it known that if there was any truth in the improbable suggestion that someone in the service of the Company might act illegally, the colonial secretary might consider the cancellation of the Company's charter.

At 5.00 p.m. on Sunday afternoon Jameson summoned his Rhodesians and, for the first time, told them they were going to Johannesburg. They were assured that they would get through without a shot being fired. The fraudulent letter from the Johannesburg conspirators was then read to the men. His biographer, Colvin, states, 'The phrase about women and children stuck in every memory' and the men gave Jameson a hearty cheer. 'As one of them afterwards said, we would all have followed the Doctor to hell.'[52]

At 6.30 p.m., in the gathering coolness of a midsummer evening, the column set out in the order of march.[52]

An hour later the Bechuanaland police were called to parade in their camp in Mafeking and told they would be going to Johannesburg. When one of them asked if he would be fighting for the Queen, the colonel in charge replied 'No ... You are not going to fight for the Queen; but you are going to fight for the supremacy of the British flag.' It seemed to satisfy most of the men.[52]

At about this time, wire-cutting squads on standby in remote parts of the veld cut the telegraph wires from Mafeking to Kimberley and Johannesburg. There is a famous story about the squad that had been sent into the Transvaal to cut the line to Pretoria. Apparently they had been drinking heavily during the long hours of waiting. Although they had careful instructions to remove and conceal a five-mile (eight-kilometre) section of the line, they cut two lengths of fencing wire and solemnly buried those instead. Meanwhile, 170 miles (274 kilometres) away, Dr Wolff was waiting for his instructions to nip around the outskirts of Pretoria and cut all the lines into the town, but the message never got through. Whether the first story is true or not, communications within the Transvaal remained intact throughout the Jameson Raid.

At about 11.00 p.m. that night, one of Rhodes's servants arrived on horseback at Bower's house and delivered a note scrawled on the back of a telegraph form. It was a summons to Groote Schuur. Bower was received in Rhodes's bedroom and told that 'Jameson has taken the bit between his teeth and gone into the Transvaal'.

As soon as he had broken the news, Rhodes gave way to self-pity. He was a ruined man. He would have to resign. He had done his best to stop Jameson .... Bower decided that nothing useful could be done that night. All the telegraph offices were shut and there seemed no purpose in waking the sickly Sir Hercules.[50]

At 5.00 a.m. on Monday Bower sent his gardener to deliver a letter to the High Commissioner: 'There is, I fear, bad news from Jameson. He seems to have disobeyed Rhodes and to have taken the bit between his teeth.'[50]

Taking his authority (and his example) from Chamberlain, Sir Hercules now tried to put as much distance as possible between himself and the main conspirators. A telegram was drafted to Francis Newton, the resident commissioner in Bechuanaland, ordering him to send 'a special messenger on a fast horse' after the raiders with the High Commissioner's repudiation of their action and orders to return.

Newton was one of Rhodes's old Oxford chums and as familiar with the details of the plot as Graham Bower and Sir Hercules himself. (Indeed, Rhodes had briefed Newton personally in early December.[53]) He did not receive his instructions until the line was repaired in the early afternoon, but wasted no time in following the example of his seniors. A messenger was sent off with letters addressed to Jameson and his senior officers, warning them individually that they were breaking the law and should return at once.

After drafting his instructions to Newton, Sir Hercules sent an official letter to Rhodes, once again repudiating Jameson's actions and warning that they would probably cause the cancellation of the charter. Now that his star was in decline, Rhodes would have much to learn about friendship and loyalty. 'When I was happy', he said, 'I thought I knew men, but it was fated that I should know them in misfortune only.'[54]

At almost exactly the same time as Bower's gardener arrived at the High Commissioner's residence, Jameson's Rhodesian force and his Bechuanaland force linked up inside the Transvaal. In total, there were 510 mounted police and 75 African drivers with eight Maxims and three field guns. The stores and ammunition were carried by 30 pack horses and 11 mule-carts.

Incredibly, the Transvaalers had believed the fiction that the force at Pitsani was there to protect railway builders from marauding tribesmen and had focused their attentions on Johannesburg. Jameson's invasion took them completely by surprise, but thanks to drunken wire-cutting parties and missed messages, the lines of communication to Pretoria were still intact and the town was alerted at 8.00 a.m. Kruger received the news in the midst of a session of his Executive Council, who were 'resplendent in tall hats, frock coats and brown boots'.[55] He launched spontaneously into the 68th psalm: 'Let God arise, let His enemies be scattered!'

The conspirators in Johannesburg had no clear confirmation that Jameson had gone in until a message arrived late in the afternoon: 'The contractor has started on the earthworks with seven hundred boys; hopes to reach terminus on Wednesday'.[56]

Some of them were furious at this casual disregard of their wishes and interests. Others believed they should swallow their pride and take advantage of the opportunity to wring major concessions out of Kruger. A third faction wanted to get rid of Kruger altogether.

An emergency directorate was set up with its headquarters in the Consolidated Gold Fields company. It would be known as the Reform Committee, but from the start its members were disunited and its aims were confused. The militants fished the arms and ammunition out of Rhodes's oil drums, recruited volunteers, distributed dashing uniforms and sent a letter of welcome to Jameson. Another faction insisted on immediate negotiations with Kruger.

Late that afternoon, two Boer messengers rode up to Jameson and asked him why he was breaking the law. Jameson replied that he had 'no hostile intentions against the people of the Transvaal' but was there 'in reply to the invitation from the principal residents of the Rand to assist them in their demand for justice.'[57] The column rode on.

It was too early for the Boers to strike. They had no machine guns and their artillery had been tied up in a distant punitive action against African insurgents. For the moment Boer horsemen were content to trail and circle the column at a safe distance, leaving Jameson in no doubt that his every move was being watched.

Rhodes's Cabinet colleagues in Cape Town had not seen their prime minister all morning and knew nothing of the crisis until the lines were restored and two telegrams came in from Mafeking. By then Jameson's Raiders had been in the Transvaal for 12 hours. William Schreiner, Olive's younger brother and Rhodes's attorney general, was asked to go to Groote Schuur to find out what these telegrams meant. When he arrived, he was told that Rhodes was riding somewhere in the grounds. He left a message that he had urgent business, and was summoned later that evening. He provided a vivid description of his interview with Rhodes:

> I went into his study with the telegrams in my hand. The moment I saw him I saw a man I had never seen before. His appearance was utterly dejected and different. Before I could say a word he said: 'Yes, yes, it is true. Old Jameson has upset my apple-cart. It is all true ...' Whatever the reason may have been, when I spoke to him he was broken down ... He could not have acted that part ... I said: 'Why do you not stop him? Although he has ridden in, you can still stop him.' He said: 'Poor old Jameson. Twenty years we have been friends and now he goes in and ruins me. I cannot hinder him. I cannot go in and destroy him.'[58]

Schreiner had asked the crucial question: 'Why do you not stop him?' As prime minister, Rhodes had all the resources of the Colony at his disposal. At the very least he could have sent men to order Jameson back. But he did nothing.

Schreiner had no knowledge of the conspiracy and believed that Rhodes's distress was caused by a friend's betrayal and that the inertia was due to his understandable reluctance to take action against someone who had meant so much to him. This was the impression that Rhodes conveyed to all his visitors during the early days of the crisis. To Schreiner he said 'Twenty years we have been friends, and now he goes in and ruins me', repeating himself again and again when Schreiner urged him to stop the raid. To Bower he had said: 'Jameson has taken the bit between his teeth' and 'I am a ruined man'. When Hofmeyr called the following day, demanding that a proclamation should be issued dismissing Jameson as administrator of

Rhodesia and 'providing that the criminal law ... will be enforced to the utmost against him', Rhodes replied weakly: 'Well you see ... Jameson has been such an old friend; of course I cannot do it'.[59]

All Rhodes's callers were touched by this tragic performance and appear to have shared Schreiner's view that Jameson's 'betrayal' was the cause of Rhodes's grief and inertia. They should have known their man better. The writer Jean van der Poel was much more perceptive when she attributed Rhodes's distress to his anxiety lest Jameson fail, and his inertia to 'his determination to give Jameson every chance to get to Johannesburg'.[60] When one considers Rhodes's treatment of his great friend *after* the raid had failed (see p. 303), it is hard to challenge that view.

Alfred Beit's young nephew, Otto, certainly grasped the truth. He was a house guest at Groote Schuur at the time, and in the middle of the night was woken up by Rhodes and asked to come to his room. For the next four hours Otto listened to his host's ramblings between sleeping and waking. His only memory of the monologue was Rhodes's obsessive concern with Jameson's chances of success.[61]

For the first time in his life Rhodes had placed his destiny in the hands of another man – Dr Jim, the gambler. All that was required of him now was to stay out of his office and mope about in the grounds of Groote Schuur in order that Cape administration should remain paralysed. It was an ignominious role for someone who had always been in complete control.

The last of the main players to hear of Jameson's action was Joseph Chamberlain. By that time, Jameson had been in the Transvaal for 16 hours. The colonial secretary had spent a relaxing day after receiving Sir Hercules' telegram advising him that the whole plan had been abandoned. That evening was the occasion of the annual servants' ball at Highbury, Chamberlain's splendid home on the outskirts of Birmingham. The colonial secretary was just starting to dress for dinner when a Colonial Office messenger arrived with a secret dispatch from Sir Hercules advising him that Jameson had gone in. According to Garvin, his biographer, Chamberlain clenched his fists and said: 'If this succeeds it will ruin me'.[62] It seems that the first loyalty of every player in this drama was to himself.

Chamberlain took the night train to London, and from the early hours of Tuesday morning was firing off telegrams to all and sundry. He sent an official warning to the directors of the British South Africa Company that their charter might be revoked. He told Sir Hercules to 'leave no stone unturned' to stop Jameson and to impress on Rhodes that 'this is filibustering'. He wrote to Lord Salisbury, repeating the bit about 'filibustering' and warning his prime minister that if Jameson was given any assistance by the

British Government, 'it would justify the accusation by Germany and other powers that having first attempted to get up a revolution in a friendly State and having failed, we had assented to an act of aggression ...'[60]

Chamberlain even had the gall to send a solicitous telegram to Kruger offering his services as peacemaker,[60] but the president was in no need of assistance. His government was handling the crisis with great skill. It had been decided to concentrate on the invading force and tread very softly at first with Johannesburg.

Early on Tuesday morning (31 December), Newton's messenger caught up with the column and distributed sealed instructions to Jameson, Willoughby and five other senior officers. Newton's orders were ignored and the column moved on. By now the men were exhausted and hungry. They had had practically no sleep since leaving Pitsani on Sunday evening, and Dr Wolff had shown himself to be as unsatisfactory as a conspirator as he had been as a doctor. His supply depots were woefully understocked, and at one stop the fresh mounts he had been asked to supply were mostly carthorses.

On the same morning an 'unofficial' delegation was sent from Pretoria to meet representatives of the Reform Committee. The Transvaalers were conciliatory and the 'reformers', foolishly interpreting this as a sign of Kruger's weakness, agreed to send their own delegates to Pretoria the following day. Kruger did not receive them personally, but the three senior officials who did took full advantage of *Uitlander* naivety and over-confidence. *The Times* had published the 'women and children' letter that morning in a last-ditch attempt to drum up public support for the raid. The matter was raised at the meeting and the 'reformers' let slip that they had given Jameson written authority to invade six weeks before the date that had appeared on the published letter (28 December). Kruger's officials then asked how they could be sure that the visiting delegates were speaking on behalf of Johannesburg since they had no idea who belonged to their Reform Committee. It was a trap, and the 'reformers' walked straight into it. They immediately sent instructions to Gold Fields headquarters for a complete list of committee members to be sent to Pretoria. That list was the only evidence on which the arrests of all 64 members was made after the raid.

On Wednesday afternoon (1 January 1896) Jameson's raiders had reached Krugersdorp, 20 miles (32 kilometres) from Johannesburg and on the main railway line. According to the original plan, Jameson was supposed to rendezvous here with a Johannesburg force under Frank Rhodes, but the 'reformers' had forbidden Frank to offer any assistance to Jameson while their delegates were negotiating with Kruger's officials. Seeing no evidence of Frank Rhodes's force, Willoughby counselled Jameson to skirt around

Krugersdorp and continue the advance to Johannesburg, but his advice was not taken. With or without the promised reinforcements, Jameson was determined to stick to the original plan.

The enemy had continued to trail them and circle round them. There had been a few light skirmishes, but the Boers had not made a stand. When Jameson's men were in sight of Krugersdorp, the enemy's tactics suddenly changed. The terrain here was broken up by gulleys and boulders that offered protection against bombardment and the indiscriminate sweep of machine guns. Boer riflemen now had a chance against Jameson's Maxims and heavy artillery.

Willoughby brought up his big guns and bombarded the enemy positions. Not one Boer was hit. Deceived by their silence, Willoughby ordered his men to charge. The Boer marksmen were waiting for them. A crashing fire rained down from the front and the flanks. Thirty men were killed or wounded. Willoughby ordered a retreat.

Dusk was gathering and Jameson agreed to abandon the attack on Krugersdorp and attempt an all-night march to Johannesburg, but hardly had they started when they heard heavy firing from the direction of Krugersdorp. It was a Boer celebration of the arrival of their long-delayed artillery. Willoughby made the fatal assumption that Frank Rhodes's men had arrived at last and were engaging the Boers. Leaving his carts and pack animals lightly protected on the road, he ordered his main force to advance to Krugersdorp to assist their imaginary allies. They had not gone far when the distant firing suddenly stopped and, instead of friends, they found a large Boer force facing them and others closing in from the flanks. Frightened of being cut off from his ammunition and supplies, Willoughby ordered his men back to the road. The chance of a swift night march to Johannesburg had been frittered away.

It was now almost dark. Jameson and Willougby decided that the only sensible course was to bivouac for the night. Intermittent rifle fire made sleep virtually impossible and at first light Jameson ordered his men to move out. They had been on the march, with only snatches of rest, for 86 hours and had eaten nothing since the morning of the previous day. The Boers now pursued them, usually at a distance. A running fight continued for about 10 miles (16 kilometres) until Jameson's men discovered that they had been driven into a cul-de-sac. Ahead of them was a large Boer force on top of a low cliff. It was impossible to skirt the cliff and impossible to retreat, as the Boers in the rear were closing in.

Jameson's men were exhausted, surrounded and heavily outnumbered, but they put up a brief fight. The Boers poured down rifle fire. Men and horses were shot down, and when the Boers brought up their artillery there was no hope left. Someone – nobody is sure who – raised the white flag, an apron borrowed from a Hottentot servant woman who had somehow got caught up in the scrap. It is said that when Jameson saw the white apron flying he was so surprised that he fell over and was thought to have been hit.

Many of the raiders were boys in their late teens. According to Cronje, the Boer commandant, some were standing around weeping, and all looked dirty and miserable. Jameson, 'trembling like a reed',[63] surrendered unconditionally. Seventeen of his men had been killed and 55 wounded. The Boers lost four men.

Jameson and his officers were taken to Pretoria in carts, his men on horseback. After being paraded twice around the market square for the benefit of the jeering crowds, they were marched off to the Pretoria jail and forbidden to communicate with anybody.

The German Kaiser sent Kruger a congratulatory telegram and the French government presented him with a ceremonial sword that glorified a heroic Boer strangling the Imperial lion. The old president had united his country behind him and Britain had been humiliated.

The consequences for Rhodes were devastating. He had lost the support of Afrikaners everywhere and his grand design for southern and central Africa was in ruins. It was impossible for him to remain prime minister of the

Jameson's last stand.

Cape, but he had not given up yet. He decided to play the Imperial card, and sent telegram after telegram to his directors in London for communication to Chamberlain. In these, he was more or less ordering the colonial secretary to put the screws on Kruger. 'Tell Mr Chamberlain feeling here tremendous; he can demand anything in English interests.'[64]

Chamberlain now began to dance to Rhodes's tune and his messages to Sir Hercules became increasingly arrogant in tone and hostile to the Transvaal. Bower believed that the colonial secretary was eager to see the crisis develop into a war so that a searching inquiry into the raid could be buried and Chamberlain's part in the conspiracy remain a secret.[64]

Until the very the last days of December, Sir Hercules had kept a train in permanent readiness to take him to the Transvaal where he would impose a settlement on Rhodes's terms; but now he was frightened, exhausted and no longer willing to play the Rhodes–Chamberlain game. When he came to Pretoria on 7 January to meet Kruger, he was prepared to offer virtually any concession to secure peace.

Kruger and his Executive Council had already made up their minds to hand the raiders over to the British Government. They knew that this would be unpopular with most of their followers, who were demanding blood, but wisely calculated that it would not benefit the Transvaal's cause to make

Jameson (centre) and his fellow officers on the boat to England.

martyrs out of Jameson and the others. Let Britain be placed in the difficult position of punishing them.

Sir Hercules thanked Kruger for this decision, but the president's magnanimity did not stretch much further. He demanded that Johannesburg should disarm at once and refused to consider any political concessions. Sir Hercules and the 'reformers' meekly complied. On the day after the *Uitlanders* had agreed to lay down their arms, 64 members of the Reform Committee were arrested and jailed.

Now that Rhodes had lost hope of salvaging anything from the Transvaal crisis, he concentrated on protecting his own position. There was already strong pressure on the British Government to revoke the royal charter. Hofmeyr, who was leading the campaign in the Cape, had in the past received De Beers and Chartered Company shares on preferential terms and Rhodes threatened to expose him. 'The mole' was silenced.[65]

Rhodes now did everything possible to repudiate responsibility for the raid. He wrote to the directors of the Chartered Company in London, complaining that Jameson had started without his knowledge and consent. He tried to persuade Bower, who had accompanied Sir Hercules to Pretoria, to visit Jameson in jail and induce him to take the all blame. So much for loyalty and friendship.

On 16 January Rhodes sailed for England. He had one aim: to protect the charter.

Six days later, Jameson and 13 of his officers followed him. Rhodes made no attempt to contact his old friend during the time he was in London. Indeed, the two men would not see each other again for a year.

On 3 February, Rhodes was met at Plymouth by Maguire and Hawksley (Rhodes's London solicitor). On the journey to London they worked out their strategy to protect the charter. The following day Hawksley met Edward Fairfield, Chamberlain's private secretary, and let him know that Mr Rhodes had a quantity of telegrams in his possession which showed that the colonial secretary not only had full knowledge of the plot but had approved it, encouraged it and supported it.

Fairfield reported the visit to his chief, who asked him to write to Hawksley immediately requesting copies of these telegrams. Hawksley refused in smooth and menacing tones: 'I think perhaps enough has been done, and we may leave matters at this point. Mr C [Chamberlain] knows what I know and can shape his course with this knowledge.'[66]

On 6 February Rhodes met Chamberlain. They were together for nearly two hours. Chamberlain assured Rhodes that he would do his utmost to save the charter. He also felt that it would not be necessary for him to resign as managing director of the Chartered Company. Not a word was said about telegrams. His task accomplished, Rhodes left London for Rhodesia, where he planned to lie low until the storm had blown over.

Jameson and 14 of his fellow officers were committed to trial at the High Court in London. Jameson and Willoughby were sentenced to 15 months, without hard labour, for an unprovoked attack on a friendly state that caused 21 deaths! Rhodes considered these sentences excessive and dismissed the whole episode as 'a tribute to the rectitude of my countrymen who have jumped the whole world'.[67]

At the trial of the 'reformers' in Pretoria, all the accused were advised to plead guilty. This course was bitterly regretted when the four ringleaders – Phillips, Farrar, Hammond and Francis Rhodes – were condemned to death. The sentences were commuted the next day. The other accused were sentenced to two years' imprisonment, a fine of £2000 and banishment for three years after serving their terms.

Barnato, whose nephew Solly was among the accused, dressed himself in deep mourning with a crepe band round his hat and called on Kruger. There were 20,000 whites and 100,000 blacks on his payroll and his companies spent £50,000 a week in the Transvaal. Barnato told Kruger that he would pull out of the country unless all the prisoners were released within two weeks. To show that he meant business, he then placed advertisements in the Johannesburg and Pretoria papers advertising a sale of 'all our landed properties in this state'.

Rhodes and Beit between them spent £200,000 settling fines. All the accused were out of jail by the end of the month and Barnato stayed in the Transvaal.

After the trials there was an unwelcome development. Incriminating documents, not called in evidence when the guilty pleas were lodged, were published in the Transvaal press. The whole series then appeared in a Transvaal Green Book. Their effect was devastating. They revealed Rhodes as the chief plotter, implicated the Chartered Company and *The Times* and, worst of all, hinted at the complicity of the British Government.

When this new information came before the British Parliament Chamberlain realized that it would be very difficult to prevent a full inquiry. He was determined to preserve the charter, but knowing that he would have to give some ground immediately, offered the resignations of Rhodes and Beit as directors of the Chartered Company.

Rhodes received this information in Rhodesia and cabled back to Hawksley: 'Let resignation wait. We fight Matabele tomorrow.' He was already embroiled in his next crisis.

TWENTY

REBELLION

What with Jameson's Raid ... rebellion, famine, rinderpest ...
I feel like Job, all but the boils.

CECIL RHODES[1]

W hen Rhodes celebrated Christmas at Groote Schuur in the year 1895
he was at the peak of his power and prestige, respected and admired
in Britain and by her colonists throughout the Empire. In South Africa, he
had united Englishman and Afrikaner behind him, and there was a real possibility that the coming year would see him well on the way towards the fulfilment of a dream – a vast new country stretching from Cape Point to Lake
Tanganyika, 'a country the size of Europe ... where white men and women
can live, where children can be reared in health and vigour'.[2]

Within three months that great project was in ruins. Rhodes had been
forced to resign the premiership; the Cape Afrikaners had deserted him; his
precious royal charter was under threat; the Bechuanaland protectorate had
been denied to him for ever and the Matabele had taken back their country.
By the end of March 1896, white farms, mines and settlements throughout the province had been abandoned and the entire settler population had
taken refuge in two defensive laagers inside their only towns, Bulawayo
and Gwelo.

Directly and indirectly, Jameson was the cause of all these catastrophes.
Although Rhodes was ultimately responsible for the harsh conditions that
had driven his black subjects to revolt, his fundamental mistake had been to
delegate power and authority to Jameson and to rely on his friend's judgement. Jameson lacked Rhodes's great gifts of insight and perception, his
uncanny ability to get inside other people's heads. He was over-confident,
reckless and needlessly provocative. These were not Rhodes's faults. Even at
his worst, Rhodes could not be accused of gratuitous brutality. If he took
away men's votes or locked them in compounds, it was because it profited
him to do so and he was confident that the advantages outweighed the risks.
It would not have occurred to him to introduce tough racist legislation in the

Cape until he had a sizeable white majority behind him and was sure of the Colony's military and police capabilities.

Jameson's position in Rhodesia was very different. By the end of 1895, the white settler population numbered only 5000.[3] The Matabele regimental system was still intact. Most of their weapons were still in their hands and they were seething with anger. Jameson was so out of touch with these feelings that he cheerfully took the Rhodesian police with him on his raid, leaving only three white members of the force behind to guard the entire country.[4] The complacency within Jameson's immediate circle can be judged from the comments of Weston Jarvis, one of Willoughby's aristocratic chums and a former Tory MP at Westminster. A month before the Matabele rising he wrote to his mother, Lady Jarvis of Middleton Towers:

> There is a rumour of a possible rising among some of the tribes in the Matoppo [sic] Hills but that was of course all moon-shine ... This is a *grand* country, exceeding my most sanguine expectations. It is undoubtedly *very* rich and fertile. The natives are happy, comfortable and prosperous and the future must be magnificent.[5]

The reference to happy, prosperous natives is remarkable testimony to the blindness and arrogance of a coterie of men who had ripped the fabric of an African society apart during their three-year occupation. In that time, the Matabele had lost their king. They had been driven off their land and compelled to sell their labour. They had suffered insults and humiliation at the hands of white officials and black police, recruited from the dregs of their society and poorly controlled by Jameson's officers. Worst of all, their cattle had been appropriated as 'loot', leaving them with only 40,000 animals out of a national herd that had originally numbered 300,000. This had a devastating effect on morale. Besides being a measure of status, cattle were intimately connected with Matabele marriage customs, religious beliefs and their concept of social order. When the king was alive, the herds were often regarded as being held in trust for him or for one of the ancestral spirits. The guardianship of cattle 'lay very near that core of self-respect without which a man or a people can break down into degradation or desperate violence'.[6]

On top of all these tribulations, there were natural disasters during the years of white occupation. Locusts and drought had followed the 'pioneer' invasion and never departed. Next came rinderpest, a fatal cattle plague. The tracks through the country were soon choked with rotting carcases and 'the air itself seemed putrid with the odour of decaying flesh'.[7] Thousands of animals that had escaped the plague were shot by the Company's veterinary officers to prevent its spread. Unsurprisingly,

The Bulawayo laager.

the Matabele regarded this cull as just another example of white malice.

When feelings had reached boiling point, Bulawayo heard that Jameson and virtually his entire force of white Rhodesian police had surrendered to the Boers. The news spread through the country like wildfire. The Matabele unwrapped their spears, axes, rifles and old elephant guns, and on 23 March they struck white farms and mining encampments throughout their country. Within a week, 140 white men, women and children had been killed.

The ferocity of these attacks was indescribable. Whole families were hacked and bludgeoned to death and their bodies horribly mutilated. Those who managed to escape the onslaught fled to the two towns. In Bulawayo there was immediate panic. On the night of 25 March the terrified citizens smashed the windows of the government armoury and 'fought their way up to the source of supply, clambering on to each other's shoulders, grabbing and snatching the coveted weapons ... until the last of the supply had been given out'.[8]

The next day defensive laagers were built in the centres of Bulawayo and Gwelo. Selous, who had returned to Rhodesia to manage one of Willoughby's vast estates, described the Bulawayo laager as 'probably the strongest ever constructed in South Africa'.[9] Two rows of waggons were arranged in a square, chained together and packed with sandbags. Machine guns and field guns were mounted at each corner and the whole fortification was surrounded by three barbed-wire fences and a belt of broken glass 30 yards (27 metres) wide. Bundles of oil-soaked faggots were placed in the surrounding streets, to be lit in the event of a night attack.

After the initial shock had been absorbed, councils of war were set up in

307

both white towns and special patrols were formed. At great personal risk, volunteers went out into the countryside looking for possible survivors. The evidence of Matabele ferocity appalled them, as did survivors' accounts of attacks by trusted servants and labourers. Selous spoke for his fellow whites when he described his reaction at the scene of a family murder:

> The remains had been much pulled about by dogs or jackals, but the long fair hair of the young Dutch girls was still intact, and it is needless to say that these blood-stained tresses awoke the most bitter wrath in the hearts of all who looked upon them, Englishmen and Dutchmen alike vowing a pitiless vengeance against the whole Matabele race.[10]

From now on, the war would be fought with unbelievable ferocity by both sides.

After the initial relief and rescue operations, fighting patrols were sent out into the countryside to take on the Matabele, but the whites were now facing an enemy that was very different from the one that had been so easily defeated three years earlier. Most of the Company's African police had gone over to the Matabele side, taking their weapons with them. Lessons had also been learnt about the white man's tactics, particularly his reliance on the Maxim gun. This time the Matabele did not expose themselves in large numbers but, for the most part, fought as guerillas.

During the early engagements the whites suffered heavy losses for very little purpose. Even if they managed to dislodge the enemy, the Matabele would return to their old positions as soon as the whites had moved on. By mid-April, the battered patrols had withdrawn to the laagers and the countryside was still in Matabele hands.

After his crucial meeting with Chamberlain, Rhodes had returned to Africa by the east-coast route through Suez, thereby avoiding an official inquiry into the Jameson Raid, which he had been asked to attend in Cape Town. He arrived in Beira on 20 March, four days before the start of the rising. Jourdan, Le Sueur and Sir Charles Metcalf, the railway builder, were there to meet him. Grimmer, who had settled in Rhodesia, was expected to join the party later. In his hour of tribulation Rhodes would have his favourite young men at his side.

While struggling through the forests of Mozambique Rhodes contracted malaria and was already in a state of high fever when he reached the town of Umtali, near Rhodesia's eastern border. It was here that the news of the Matabele rising was broken to him. He hurried on to Fort Salisbury and appealed for settler volunteers to join him on the march to Gwelo and Bulawayo. At this stage he had no idea of the scale and seriousness of the rising and believed it could be suppressed without outside help. On 31 March, still suffering from fever, he cabled Bulawayo: 'I'm off to Gwelo with 150 men – 100 mounted. I have news that 140 of Jameson's police will arrive 2 April from England and will rejoin.' Bulawayo telegraphed back: 'Much more serious than you think.'[11]

Fortunately, there were others who were better informed than Rhodes. Bulawayo had been communicating with Chartered Company headquarters in Cape Town; the Company had been communicating with the High Commissioner's office and Sir Hercules had been communicating with London. Chamberlain, prodded by British press reports, was now insisting on sending an Imperial force to relieve Bulawayo and Gwelo.

In the first week of April Jameson's successor, the gentle and idealistic Albert Lord Grey, landed in Cape Town to be greeted with news of the uprising as well as London's response. The telegrams from Bulawayo soon convinced him that the situation in Matabaleland was serious, but the decision to accept Imperial troops was not an easy one. London had insisted that the Chartered Company should bear the full cost of the campaign, which was likely to be enormous. Grey was also aware that Imperial involvement, so assiduously avoided in 1890 and 1893, might lead to a much greater degree of Imperial control. On the other hand, if the Company refused outside help, the Matabele might succeed in taking back their country.

The Gatling gun in the corner of the laager in Bulawayo.

After one sleepless night, Grey informed Sir Hercules Robinson that he was prepared to accept London's offer. Much to his relief, Rhodes established telegraphic contact from the Gwelo laager two days later and approved the decision. By now, Rhodes was better informed.

It was during his time in Gwelo that Rhodes sent his cocky telegram to Chamberlain, 'Let resignation wait ...', but, in reality, the loss of his directorship marked the low point of his career. Rhodes no longer had the Company's power of attorney. Strictly speaking, his status was that of an ordinary civilian in his own country and, of course, he held no military rank. Untroubled by these formalities, Rhodes made himself a full colonel and virtually took charge of military operations in Gwelo. Now that he had brought reinforcements he believed the whites should try to carry the fight back into countryside.

In the early stages of the campaign Rhodes was certain that victory could only be secured by meeting terror with terror, as is clear from Le Sueur's recollection of a conversation between Rhodes and an officer who had just returned from an engagement:

> On Rhodes asking how many [enemy] were killed [the officer] replied, 'Very few, as the natives threw down their arms, went on their knees, and begged for mercy.' 'Well,' said Rhodes, 'you should not spare them. You should kill all you can, as it serves as a lesson to them when they talk things over at their fires at night ...'[12]

According to other eyewitness, Rhodes delighted in returning to the scene of fighting to count Matabele corpses.[13] In a letter to his mother, Jarvis described 'looting corn all morning'[14] with Rhodes. The two of them had been on a patrol that had burned crops and captured women and cattle – a strategy that soon drove the Matabele to despair.

Until his arrival at Gwelo, Rhodes had never taken part in any military action. Those who knew him well – Johnson, Le Sueur, Sauer – considered him something of a physical coward, but now he was throwing himself into the fight in total disregard of his own safety. Sauer, who had returned to Rhodesia after serving time in Pretoria for his part in the Jameson Raid, had this to say about Rhodes's performance during a later stage of the campaign:

> The conspicuous courage Rhodes displayed on this occasion is well known. He had a remarkable dread of any mutilation of his person, and it must have been by the exercise of the highest form of moral courage that he forced himself into positions where he was constantly under fire at close range from rifles and elephant guns loaded with slugs and other projectiles which make ghastly wounds.[15]

The Matabele 'rebellion'.

On another occasion, Rhodes had been rushing ahead with the greater part of his force when the waggons and guns in the rear came under fire at short range. He tore back and sized up the situation at once. The officer in charge only had locally recruited Africans under his command and the attackers were harrying them from the cover of dense shrub. Rhodes shouted at him 'We must clear the bush or these fellows will get our waggons and mules', but the African recruits in the rear were only armed with spears and would not obey the order. 'Will they follow me if I lead the way?' Rhodes asked. Without waiting for a definite answer, he turned his horse round and led the attack. The Africans 'plucked up courage and followed, beating the bush and yelling some sort of war-cry'. The Matabele were soon in full retreat.[16]

Rhodes presented an easy target for enemy bullets. He would ride into battle wearing white flannel trousers and armed only with a riding crop. 'He is very like Napoleon', Weston Jarvis told his mother. 'He quite thinks that he was not intended to be killed by a damned nigger ...'[17]

Or was there more to it than that? Now that his life's work was in ruins was Rhodes deliberately courting death? Did he believe he might still redeem his reputation with one final, glorious act? Few men understood better than Rhodes what a powerful hold the idea of self-sacrifice has over men's imaginations. He had exploited the legend of Allan Wilson's last stand to the full. He knew that 'martyrdom' on the steps of the Khartoum residency had secured General Gordon a permanent place in the pantheon of British heroes and inspired his countrymen to reconquer the Sudan in his name. When he heard of Gordon's death Rhodes had said 'I am sorry I was not with him.'

Whatever his motives, Rhodes was denied death and glory on the battlefields of Matabeleland. On 19 May the tide turned and the settlers secured their first decisive victory. Rhodes's Salisbury column linked up with a Bulawayo patrol and routed a large Matabele force at the Umguza river, not far from the site of Lobengula's kraal. Five days later Major Plumer, an Imperial officer, relieved Bulawayo with a mixed force of irregulars and Imperial soldiers and, in subsequent actions, drove the Matabele back from the environs of the town. The laager was dismantled, a coach load of 'tarts' was brought in from Johannesburg[18] and Bulawayo relaxed.

On 1 June Rhodes tried to enter the town unobtrusively, but word of his arrival soon spread and a public holiday was declared in his honour. In an emotional speech he told his settlers: 'Your list of killed and wounded is severe in the extreme ... Now we shall have to hunt the Matabele in the bush and in the stones and in the kopjes [hills], in a country half the size of Europe.'[19]

Two days later General Sir Frederick Carrington, the senior Imperial officer in southern Africa, arrived with a clutch of brass hats, including Colonel Robert Baden-Powell, who would later make a name for himself as the 'hero' of Mafeking and the founder of the Boy Scout movement.

The citizens of Bulawayo mingled with hussars, war correspondents, monocled 'intelligence' officers and Plumer's contingent of irregulars, who swaggered through town 'in sombreros, revolvers hanging from each hip, wristlets crammed with revolver cartridges'.[19] Baden-Powell, always an exhibitionist, exchanged his officer's cap for a stetson, punched out the crown and created the prototype of the Boy Scout hat.

In the midst of all this gaiety, news reached Bulawayo that the Shona had risen in revolt. Their attacks followed the same pattern that the Matabele had adopted three months earlier, and, indeed, there was close co-ordination between the two peoples. Within the first week of the Shona rising (15–22 June) every isolated family and individual within an 80-mile (130-kilometre) radius of Salisbury had been hacked or bludgeoned to death. The townspeople withdrew into a laager.

The Shona had not lost a king or suffered the same collapse of aristocratic self-esteem as the Matabele, but much of their land had been taken, they had been forced to sell their labour and their cattle too had been seized. Once again the whites had been so out of touch with the feelings of their

African subjects that they were taken by surprise, and this time their reaction was even more bitter. 'A terrible example must be made amongst the murderous insurgents', thundered the *Bulawayo Sketch*. 'The Mashonas have less excuse for such crimes, inasmuch as they are not fighting for their independence; they never possessed it in the past, and have experienced infinitely better times than they ever had before the occupation.'[20]

The whites had long convinced themselves that the Shona regarded them as liberators. It was one of the main planks of Chartered Company propaganda – the stock answer whenever Company methods were criticized. By forming an alliance with the Matabele, the Shona had exposed this argument as a lie and weakened the moral position of the Company still more. It made bad reading in London and bolstered the growing campaign to revoke the charter.

But Rhodes had more than London to worry about. Settler anger, particularly in Mashonaland, was now directed against him. He had taken 150 fighting men out of Salisbury, leaving the town hard-pressed to defend itself. Some of the men on his column had lost the wives and children they had left behind, and there was intense anti-Rhodes feeling among them as they hurried back to defend their base.

With Mashonaland threatened, it was essential to secure an immediate and decisive victory over the Matabele, but by the end of June the war had stagnated. The 'rebels' had virtually abandoned the countryside and gone to ground in two mountain strongholds – the Mambo hills and the Matopos. Carrington decided that the Mambo hills would be his first objective and planned to attack with 1000 men under Plumer's command.

It is said that 'Wilder country than the Mambo Hills can scarcely be imagined; even the Matopos seem tame by comparison'.[21] The Matabele were defending a chaotic mass of pink granite *kopjes* that rose abruptly from the plains. Plumer decided to approach by night and mount a surprise attack at first light on 5 July 1896. It was Rhodes's 43rd birthday, and he rode towards the Matabele stronghold with Johnny Grimmer, Gordon Le Sueur and his brother Frank, recently released from Pretoria jail. Sticking close to the party was De Vere Stent, war correspondent for *The Times*.

As dawn was breaking, Plumer ordered his cavalry to charge. 'One man drew out ahead', wrote Stent. 'In spite of warnings and expostulations, I spurred [on] to see. It was Rhodes himself, riding unarmed, switch in hand, leading the hunt.'[22] By the curious mistake of a staff officer, Rhodes was almost cut off by the rebels. Le Sueur recalled: 'Rhodes was nearly hit, a bullet striking the ground under his horse. "Do you know," he said afterwards, "it was a very near thing. I might have been hit in the stomach, which would have been very unpleasant, and I should have been very angry."' A report in the *Cape Times* noted that 'he also added "I was in a horrible funk. But I stayed at the front because I was far more afraid of being thought afraid.""[23]

Plumer won the day and dislodged the Matabele from the hills. His men rounded up '10,000 head of cattle as loot, and a large number of men, women and children as prisoners'[22].

At sundown the bodies of the 18 whites killed in battle were wrapped in the skins of newly flayed oxen. The 'still bleeding' shrouds were then fastened with thorns. According to Stent, the experience 'cut Rhodes to the heart'. It was a pivotal moment in his life, vividly described by *The Times* correspondent:

> As the procession passed through to the burial place, one of the bodies, carelessly fastened in its skin shroud, fell to the ground. Rhodes and Plumer were walking together behind it. I caught sight of the shocked and pained expression upon Rhodes's face. This rough and hurried burial of the men who had given their lives for Rhodesia brought home to him, as nothing else could have done, the meaning of war – the cruel bloodiness of war ...
>
> We walked back to camp. Rhodes sat over a fire, his shoulders again hunched up. He was not restless. He was thinking, gazing into the coals ... It was then that there came to him the idea of meeting the Matibili [sic] themselves, learning what they fought for, and trying to bring Peace.[22]

There were other reasons – hard, financial reasons – why Rhodes's thoughts now turned to peace, but this is not to deny him his moment of grace. After the battle of the Mambo hills he forgot the impatience, cruelty and arrogance that the years had laid on him and recovered his finest quality – a readiness to recognize the other man's point of view and come to terms with it. For the first time since his days as a cotton farmer he also understood that 'the other man' might equally well be black. In his new incarnation, he told his friend and biographer Louis Michell: 'You cannot have real prosperity in South Africa until you have first established complete confidence between the two races, and henceforth I shall make that part of my work, but all must help, all must help'.[24] For once in his life, Rhodes did not mean English and Afrikaner when he spoke of 'the two races', but black and white.

The transformation was immediately apparent. On the morning after the Mambo hills battle, Stent was shocked to discover boy prisoners, 14 or 15 years old, with their wrists bound so tightly that they bled. He complained to the officer in charge, who threatened him with arrest. Someone went off to warn Rhodes that Stent was planning to 'work off a scandal' and suggested that all his telegrams should be censored. Rhodes came to the spot at once and ordered the officer to untie the boys. As Stent related: '"You must not be cruel," said he, "cruelty does no good." He then ordered the boys to be well treated, and to be sent home with messages that the white man wanted peace.'[22]

This was not an empty gesture, calculated to earn good copy. Talk of peace was dangerous. The settlers were thirsting for Matabele blood and would not be satisfied until they had avenged dead friends and loved ones. The soldiers would not be satisfied until they had achieved total victory. Rhodes knew that the camp would be in a 'rage' when news of this incident spread, and he was right. But he had set his heart on peace and nothing would stop him now.

Carrington was not prepared to discuss the matter. After their defeat in the Mambo hills, the Matabele had withdrawn to their last stronghold, the Matopos, and the old general could smell victory. He decided to 'let the troops blood themselves a little'[25] before moving them on to crush the Shona.

Unfortunately, Carrington had underestimated the task ahead of him. The Matopos are a mass of steep granite hills and gigantic boulders, chaotically heaped together. They cover an area of some 35 miles by 50 miles (56 by 80 kilometres) and are riddled with caves and surrounded by dense bush. 'A ghastly country for fighting,' the irrepressible Jarvis told his mother, '... and these niggers are so nippy.'[26]

The Matabele had 10,000 men guarding the hills, their women and children sheltering in the steep, narrow valleys where their cattle could graze. This was no longer a rebellion to drive the white men out of the country but a struggle for national survival.

Carrington launched attack after attack. In three days of fighting he suffered 100 casualties without making the slightest impression on the rebels. He now concocted a plan to starve them into submission. He would encircle the Matopos with a string of forts and ask for an additional 10,000 men. His transport officers were told to draw up cost estimates. Their final figure ran into millions. Rhodes was appalled – the additional burden would break the Chartered Company. Peace was imperative.

Rhodes established his own 'Sugar Bush Camp' on the edge of the Matopos and two miles from Carrington's encampment, where it would be 'much easier to carry on our nefarious experiments in peace-making'.[27] For most of the time he had Sauer, Metcalf, Grimmer, Jourdan, Le Sueur, De Vere Stent and Frank with him. Johann Colenbrander, Rhodes's former ambassador at the court of Lobengula, now owned a large farm on the outskirts of Bulawayo and was a regular visitor to the camp. However, the key figure in the peace-making 'conspiracy' was Johnny Grootboom, a Thembu from the Cape who had originally come to Matabeleland as the Rev. Helm's waggon-driver. He was a fluent Ndebele speaker and renowned for his bravery.

This little clique made several attempts to contact the 'rebels' but were unsuccessful until one of their daily rides brought them close to a village, where there appeared to be no sign of life apart from a few chickens. Rhodes and the others had started to help themselves when, according to Sauer, 'an old native lady emerged from a hut and attacked Rhodes in voluble Zulu, calling him a stealer of hens and other uncomplimentary names'.[27]

Rhodes, who spoke Zulu moderately well, discovered that his accuser was Nyamabezana, one of the last surviving wives of Mzilikazi, father of Lobengula and founder of the Matabele nation. He appreciated the significance at once, but while he was trying to deal with the old lady, 60 Matabele 'rebels' were seen running down the main mountain to attack. Mzilikazi's widow was immediately bundled into a 'skin' and, 'notwithstanding her furious indignation',[28] taken back to Sugar Bush Camp. For the next 48 hours she refused to speak to her captors, 'contenting herself with spitting whenever she saw any of us'.[27] With great patience, Rhodes and Colenbrander finally overcame her resistance and persuaded her to go into the Matopos accompanied by two released prisoners. She was to bring a message to the leaders of the rebellion. Rhodes wanted peace. If they were prepared to discuss terms they should display a white cloth on a prominent tree on one of the peaks of the Matopos. If they were determined to continue the fight, they should hang a red flag.

After four anxious days the white cloth was raised. It was the opportunity that Rhodes had been waiting for. In gratitude, he would always keep a photograph of Nyamabezana in his bedroom at Groote Schuur, where it still hangs today. It was the only photograph of a woman ever to be displayed in Groote Schuur during his lifetime.

Rhodes persuaded Johnny Grootboom and two other African scouts to contact the rebels. Each of these brave men was offered a reward of £25, one of them confessing later that he had bolstered his courage with brandy before leaving for the hills.

On 21 August the three scouts were back at Sugar Bush Camp. The Matabele *indunas* were prepared to discuss peace, but they were suspicious of Rhodes and had stipulated that he should bring no more than three whites with him and that no member of his party should be armed. The *indunas* had also specified the meeting place, which was well inside the Matopos. Rhodes agreed to all their conditions.

To accompany him Rhodes chose Colenbrander and Grootboom for their fluency in Ndebele, Stent for the publicity and Sauer for companion-ship. 'He told me', Sauer wrote afterwards, 'that he wanted me to be with him because I had sufficient funk mixed in with my courage to make him feel safe.'[27]

Colenbrander did not rise to the occasion immediately. He believed he had 'no business risking [his] life at the request of Mr. Rhodes for the benefit of the Chartered Company',[29] but was eventually persuaded with an offer of 1000 guineas, which his lawyers tried to increased tenfold after the event.

Before the party could move off word got to Carrington, who immedi-ately rode over to Sugar Bush Camp. He made it clear that he was opposed to any peace deals until the Matabele had been defeated 'and brought to sub-mission' and that he resented the fact that Rhodes had gone this far without consulting him.

Rhodes led the irate general to one side. When they were out of earshot of the others the two men began pacing up and down, 'carrying on an ani-mated conversation'. Sauer was fascinated as he watched them from a dis-tance. 'I noticed that the General gradually became less and less vehement while Rhodes grew more and more impressive.'[27] After a quarter of an hour Rhodes bounced back to the camp and told the others to prepare to start. Before they moved off Mrs Colenbrander, 'the only woman allowed in the camp', insisted on distributing revolvers. Sauer stuffed one into each pocket of his riding breeches, but Rhodes refused the offer. He would be the only member of the party to go into the hills unarmed, carrying nothing more lethal than his riding crop.

The party entered the hills through a narrow canyon with a towering bluff on one side and a deep wooded valley on the other. They were all ner-vous and said little until Rhodes suddenly turned to Sauer and asked, 'What are our chances?' Tactlessly, Sauer reminded him of the fate of the Boer leader, Piet Retief, who had gone on a similar peace mission to the kraal of the Zulu king, Dingaan. Retief and his party had entered the royal enclosure unarmed, as custom demanded. After signing a treaty with the Boers, Din-gaan gave the signal and Retief and all his followers – 100 men – were mur-dered. According to Sauer, Rhodes's only response to this cautionary tale was 'I shall take my chance'.

After three miles, the path led to an open space surrounded by granite hills. At its centre were some tree stumps and the remnants of a big ant heap. It was the appointed place. As they waited, the surrounding hills began to fill with Matabele. Colenbrander said quietly to Sauer in Afrikaans: 'Don't let Rhodes dismount.' Rhodes overheard and immediately jumped off his horse, ordering the others to do the same: 'Dismount. It will give them confidence.

They are nervous too.' Flinging the reins over his horse's head, Rhodes led the way to the ant heap, where he sat down and waited.

> A second or so later... the folds of a great stretch of white calico showed dead white against the evergreen shrubs that fringed the granite *kopjes* ... At the same time a number of dark forms could be seen gathering around it. Slowly a little procession formed, headed by the flag, and came towards us. The wonderful smile broke out on Rhodes' face as he said, 'Yes, yes, there they are. This is one of those moments in life that makes it worth living. Here they come!'

> The tableau was as unique as it was impressive. The four white men, seated upon the remains of the ant-heap, dominated the foreground. Rhodes – the central figure. To his left, Colenbrander, interpreting and advising. To his right, Sauer and myself, spectators, silent. Below us the demilune of natives, in the centre of which sat the high chiefs – the commoners squatted on their haunches ... 'Is it peace?' asked Rhodes. 'It is peace, my father,' answered Somabhulana, 'but we would speak with you.' The *indaba* had begun.[30]

Somabhulana, whom Stent described as 'one of the finest native orators in Africa', was the rebel leader and spokesman. Forty other *indunas* and officers were also present, among them Babayane, who still wore a gold bracelet given to him by Queen Victoria. A large crowd of servant and mat-bearers attended the dignitaries.

At Rhodes's invitation, Somabhulana rose to speak and told the saga of the Matabele people, whom he called 'the children of the stars'. He described how Mzilikaze had fled from Shaka's wrath along a path of blood to a new home in the north. He told of the coming of white men, greedy for gold, and of their guns that 'spat bullets as the heavens spat hail', of the deaths of the king's envoys on the Tati river, of the theft of Lobengula's gold by the two troopers, of the death of their king and the confiscation of their cattle. The atmosphere warmed. 'You came, you conquered. The strongest take the land. We accepted your rule. We lived under you. But not as dogs! Is it not better to be wiped out than to live as dogs?' An angry murmur. A restless stirring in the crowd. 'The moment,' wrote Stent, 'was inflammable. The least indiscretion might precipitate a massacre.'[30]

Rhodes, speaking through Colenbrander, calmly urged Somabhulana to continue, asking: 'By whom and how were [you] treated as dogs?'

This gave Somabhulana his opening. He told of the tyrannies of the native commissioner and the abuses of power by the police. Babayane and the other *indunas* now entered the discussion, describing how their cattle and land had been seized and how they had been treated with contempt when they came to pay their respects to the Bulawayo magistrate.

Rhodes listened for two and a half hours. Then suddenly, he turned to Colenbrander and said, 'Ask them why they killed my women and children?' At first, Colenbrander refused to translate, believing that the question would lead to trouble. Rhodes was angry and insisted. Somabhulana replied, 'Because you did it first', and he then told the story of four women, shot by cattle collectors. The incident had never been reported to anyone in authority but Colenbrander confirmed that all the details were true.

Rhodes was genuinely moved. While insisting that he had come to discuss peace and not grievances, he offered significant concessions. He promised to disband the Native Police, strongly implied that he would reform the administration and gave his pledge that he would remain in the country to oversee all the changes. He also guaranteed the security of the *indunas* who were at the gathering on condition that they had not ordered any specific murders. None would be punished for a general order to kill whites.

'Tell them that the past is done with ...', he said. The sun was setting. Somabhulana rose. 'Is it peace?' asked Rhodes. Somabhulana lifted a stick and placed it on the ground before him. 'Here is my rifle; I lay it down at your feet.' Others followed. 'Here is my assegai ... Here is my rifle.' They were tokens of surrender, but the *indunas* still needed time to consult other leaders of the nation who had not attended this gathering.

Rhodes and his party rode home elated. 'I have been sitting with the rebel chiefs in the hills for about four hours,' Rhodes wrote to Grey, 'and the war is over as far as this part is concerned.' Stent and Sauer rode on to Bulawayo that night with an escort of troopers. Stent telegraphed his copy to London and Cape Town and both men instructed their agents 'to buy Chartereds'.[31]

Rhodes moved his camp into the Matopos and stayed there for eight more weeks until he had made peace with the Matabele. Three other *indabas* followed and every day Rhodes received delegates in his camp. He showed patience and courage in all his dealings, not only with the Matabele, but with soldiers and settlers alike. His task was never easy. At the second *indaba* he was met, not by a handful of chiefs, but by 2000 truculent young warriors in battle array. Colenbrander, suspecting treachery, shouted to his companions to remain on their horses. Again, Rhodes ignored him, and walked straight towards the hostile crowd, ordering them to lay down their arms. 'The young men muttered and looked sullen, and then at last one dropped his assegai, then another followed, and another, until the whole regiment stood unarmed.'[32] Rhodes then beckoned them to sit down with him and dealt 'dispassionately and without prejudice with their quarrels'.[33]

The third and final *indaba* was a very grand affair, attended by Lord Grey and an escort of lancers, but it was Rhodes the *indunas* wanted to hear. Again and again they expressed their overriding wish that he should stay among them and protect them, but he would not remain, he told them, unless the last warrior came out of the hills and laid down his arms. The threat was effective.

While the negotiations were in progress, news reached Rhodes that some of Plumer's soldiers had looted Mzilikazi's tomb, a cave deep in the Matopos. Rhodes called for horses and Matabele guides and set off at once.

When his party reached the spot, Rhodes stared into the cave and was deeply moved. 'The corpse of Mziligazi [sic] was sitting upright in a stone chair, looking out from the cave in which his body had been embalmed, over a wonderful stretch of the country he had conquered.'[34] Rhodes stared at the eyeless skull under its headdress of blue jay feathers and whispered 'What a poet that man was'. The grave was restored under his personal supervision and ten oxen were specially selected and sacrificed to appease the spirit of the dead king.

Some days later Rhodes discovered the granite dome of Malindidzuma – Matabele for 'the dwelling place of the spirits' – with its circular crown of boulders. He was riding with Sauer and suggested that they both dismount.

> We tied our horses to a tree, and after a long but gradual ascent reached the summit. On arrival there we were rewarded with a magnificent view over the rugged masses of the Matopos, with the deep twisting valleys and gigantic boulders heaped up in profusion wherever we looked. Rhodes was profoundly moved by the impressive panorama before us, and said: 'This is the World's View.'[35]

Later, he took Le Sueur to the same place and told him: 'I admire the imagination of Umzilagazi [Mzilikazi]. There he lies, a conqueror alone, watching over the land that he had won. When I die, I mean to be buried here ...'[36]

Rhodes's romantic identification with the Matabele was complete. The founder and the present father of their nation would be permanently linked in death.

Rhodes's handling of the crisis in Matabeleland revealed his great gifts of imagination and perception, as well as his extraordinary qualities as a leader. One would like to say that he had been transformed by these experiences, but his later actions do not bear this out. This single episode in his life stands apart, perhaps because it was one of the few occasions when his own interests coincided with the best interests of others. The peace that saved the Matabele from destruction also saved Rhodes from financial catastrophe.

This is not to denigrate the meetings in the hills. They were as important to Rhodes as they were to the Matabele. They touched him deeply, but they did not change him. His promise to stay with the Matabele was never honoured. How could it be? His interests demanded that he should be elsewhere. He would return briefly to the farm near the Matopos that he bought from Hans Sauer. He would hold a ceremonial *indaba* or a great birthday feast and then he would leave. Certainly, the administration softened, but that had more to do with Lord Grey than with Cecil Rhodes.

Above all, the lesson he had learnt in Matabeleland was never applied in Mashonaland, where the military requirements were different. There were no natural fortifications, no demands for a string of forts or 10,000 extra troops. In Mashonaland the villages could be blown apart with field guns and Maxims. The caves where the women and children ran for shelter were easy to reach and could be cleared in no time by tossing in sticks of dynamite. For those reason there was no call for an *indaba* in Mashonaland – only for bullets, high explosives and the rope.

The Shona struggle continued for another year, but by then Rhodes had moved on. He had other battles to fight, other interests to defend; and the methods he used were the familiar methods, unredeemed by his experiences in the hills.

TWENTY ONE

NEMESIS

You can conquer anything. You can conquer, if you will allow me to say it,
even Raids; but Time you can never interfere with.

CECIL RHODES[1]

A few days before Rhodes's party abducted Nyamabezana and set the Matabele peace process in motion, an important visitor arrived at Sugar Bush Camp. He was George Wyndham, a Conservative MP and one of Rhodes's many admirers at Westminster. The mission that had brought him to Rhodesia was a delicate one. Ever since the Transvaal Government had published incriminating documents – which the raiders and reformers had failed to destroy – a full parliamentary inquiry at Westminster had been unavoidable (see page 404). It had been put off until early the following year, but Chamberlain needed an immediate assurance from Rhodes that he would not show the same contempt for the Mother of Parliaments as he had done for the Cape Assembly when the inquiry into the Jameson Raid was held there. He also wanted Rhodes to be in London from the start of the inquiry to restrain Hawksley, who was showing, 'a disconcerting desire to reveal all'.[2] The documents that Rhodes's solicitor had in his possession were far more dangerous than anything the Transvaal Government had been able to produce, and Chamberlain needed to be sure they would remain under cover. In return for these services, Wyndham was able to guarantee that the charter would be safe.

Rhodes was delighted to accept Chamberlain's terms. As long as the charter was safe, all would be well. His spirits rose even further when the peace negotiations were concluded, and within a month of the final *indaba* with the Matabele he felt confident enough to press the Colonial Office to honour its long-standing promise to transfer the Bechuanaland protectorate to the company. It seems as if he was blissfully unaware of the fall-out from the Jameson Raid and the implications of such a move on the eve of an inquiry.

By November, the withdrawal of Imperial forces was already under way.

Many of Jameson's police were back in the country, and there was sufficient manpower to pursue the campaign against the Shona to its bloody conclusion. At the beginning of December, Rhodes decided it was time for him to leave. Carrington and Baden-Powell agreed to accompany him and his party.[3]

The road from Bulawayo to Salisbury and Umtali was now secure and Rhodes was determined to leave the country by this route. Throughout his time in the Matopos, he had been pestered with telegrams from Salisbury[4] that left him in no doubt that the Mashonaland whites blamed him personally for allowing them to face the first Shona onslaught without the protection of the police and their best fighting men. If he went to Salisbury he knew he would be walking into a hornet's nest, but he was back on form and relished the challenge.

As soon as the party reached the town, Philip Jourdan was told to invite the settlers to send a deputation to meet Rhodes. While on this errand, Jourdan heard enough to convince him that feelings against Rhodes were very strong and that a stormy meeting could be expected.

The next day, Rhodes received the settler deputation, sitting at the head of a long table. 'With the full light on his face and his commanding forehead, he looked every inch a Colossus and a giant amongst pygmies,' noted Jourdan.[4] Each delegate was asked to state his grievances and Rhodes took laborious notes without saying a word. In his silent presence, the fiery agitators of the previous day soon lost their nerve. When they had all finished, Rhodes dealt with their complaints, point by point. The delegates listened 'in awe of his personality,' Jourdan observed. They left quite pleased with themselves, although they got practically nothing.'[4] Rhodes had put out another fire.

Lord Grey had agreed to accompany the party as far as the border. Somewhere between Salisbury and Umtali, he received a telegram with the momentous news that Groote Schuur had been burnt down, along with most of its contents. Rhodes's famous response is repeated in every biography and obituary. This is Stead's version, which was the first to appear in print and is certainly the most colourful:

> Knowing how intensely Mr. Rhodes was attached to his home, Lord Grey shrank from breaking the news to him until they were alone. He feared that Mr. Rhodes might lose his self-control. They rode out together that morning, and not until they were far out in the country did Lord Grey think of telling the evil tidings which arrived that morning ... 'Well, Mr. Rhodes, I am very sorry, but I am afraid I must give you a rather ugly shock.'

Mr. Rhodes reined up his horse, and turning to his companion he exclaimed, his face livid, white and drawn in an agony of dread – 'Good heavens! Out with it man! What has happened?'

'Well,' said Lord Grey, 'I am sorry to tell you that Groote Schuur was burnt down last night.'

The tense look of anguish disappeared from Rhodes's face. He heaved a great sigh, and exclaimed with inexpressible relief – 'Oh, thank God, thank God! I thought you were going to tell me that Dr. Jim was dead ... We can always rebuild the house, but if Dr. Jim had died I should never have got over it.'[5]

If this story is true, the timing of Rhodes's remark is extraordinary. When he received the news that Groote Schuur had burnt down, Jameson was hovering between life and death following a serious bout of fever and an operation for gallstones[6]. Rhodes had not seen him or communicated with him for a year. His first reaction, when he heard the Raid had failed, was to ask Bower to pressure Jameson into taking full responsibility. (As it transpired, this was unnecessary. Jameson remained loyal without pressure.) Rhodes then told the world that Jameson had invaded the Transvaal against his orders and allowed him to go to trial, knowing that the deal to withhold the telegrams would throw the full responsibility for the Raid on to his friend, greatly prejudicing his defence.

Against this background, what can one say about the remark to Lord Grey? Did it suggest remorse? Was this the real Rhodes finally speaking out after a year consumed by the rebellion and the fight to save the Charter? Or was the story of Lord Grey just another fable put about by Rhodes and his admirers in order to convince his many critics of his qualities of loyalty and compassion? Frankly, when one's only sources are Rhodes and his friends, it is impossible to establish the truth.

By the end of December 1896, Rhodes's party had left Rhodesia and was steaming down the Pungwe river towards the port of Beira. From there Rhodes took a coastal steamer to Port Elizabeth, where he received a welcome that exceeded all expectations.

It was soon clear to dispassionate observers that Rhodes had reinvented himself in the wake of the Jameson Raid. To meet the changing circumstances, he had simply rearranged the pieces on the board. His Afrikaner alliance and a lifetime's work in politics had been dumped. He was now the arch-imperialist, proudly wrapped in a Union Jack. It was this image that his propagandists worked hard to establish during Rhodes's final years and which has been perpetuated in simplistic histories. It should be said that the brand of Imperialism Rhodes now embraced was not one that would have appealed to Southey, Mackenzie or the early governors of the Cape. It was raw English nationalism, and it had its own special label, 'jingoism' (taken from the chorus of a music-hall song).

Rhodes had long despised the jingoists in Cape politics, but the Jameson Raid had given him an opportunity to pose as their champion, and after his triumphant tour of the colony he was convinced that he was on to a winning streak.

In Port Elizabeth, 40 old Rhodesians unhitched the horses from his carriage and drew him through the streets to the Town Hall, where he was due to make a speech.[7] 'I am going home,' he told the crowd, 'to face the unctuous rectitude of my countrymen.' He had struck the right pugnacious note and they loved it, but his friends were nervous when the speech was reported in the press the next day. Couldn't he say he was misquoted? Anxious rectitude ...? Upright rectitude ...? 'No. Unctuous rectitude. And I meant it.'[8]

At every station between Port Elizabeth and Cape Town the crowds came out to meet him. At Cape Town he had, according to Jourdan, 'the reception of his life. Thousands were gathered in the market square'· Formal speeches were made in his honour, and the crowd followed him all the way to Groote Schuur, shouting and clutching at him. The grounds were 'overrun by people in their excitement'. Rhodes stood amongst the blackened ruins of his home and made another speech, which was wildly cheered. Days later he sailed for England, 'to face the music'.[9]

Rhodes was apprehensive of the reception he would receive in London, but he need not have worried. 'As he said afterwards, "When I arrived in London, and saw the busmen and cabbies and working men touch their hats to me in a friendly way, I knew I was alright and that the man in the street had forgiven me".'[9]

It was more than forgiveness. During his months in the veld, Rhodes had been out of touch with the popular mood in England, which was not very different from the mood in the Cape. The nation's pride had been hurt by a Boer triumph over Englishmen, by the Kaiser's congratulatory telegram, by that damned French sword and other insults. A press campaign, spearheaded by *The Times*, had strengthened the feelings of resentment and xenophobia and exalted Rhodes in the popular imagination. He had not been in London long before it was clear that, by and large, the nation had taken him to its heart. Knowing how sensitive politicians are to the popular mood, he began to feel much more confident about the forthcoming inquiry.

Ten members of Parliament had been selected to serve on the House of Commons select committee into the Jameson Raid. Among the five

Conservatives who would be 'cross-examining' Rhodes were Chamberlain and his messenger boy, George Wyndham. Rhodes would have very little to fear from that quarter. The lone Irish member was hardly likely to embarrass the party's generous benefactor. That left the five Liberal members. Any of them who were aware of Rhodes's earlier dealings with Lords Rosebery and Rippon would be unlikely to delve deeply.

Rhodes made six appearances before the committee between 16 February and 5 March 1897. Two of the Liberals, Henry Labouchere and William Harcourt, cross-examined him tolerably well, but the Tory chairman, William Jackson, always made sure that Rhodes was never pressed too hard. Once, when Labouchère was a little too insistent, Rhodes asked if the session could be adjourned for the rest of the day to give him time to think of his reply. Permission was granted at once, even though it was only 2.50 p.m.

As Rhodes became increasingly confident that Chamberlain had the whole charade under control, he began to relax and enjoy himself, 'once a day, to save the time of the committee, eating a plate of sandwiches and sipping a tumbler of stout as he gave evidence'.[10] No-one had suggested digging into Colonial Office files for crucial telegrams, and when Rhodes was asked to produce cables that had passed between the Chartered Company's London and Cape Town offices, he flatly refused. The matter was dropped. Rhodes also declined to answer a number of questions on the grounds that his answers might implicate others, such as Sir Hercules Robinson, who had been deliberately kept away from the proceedings. Again, no-one complained.

Rhodes kept to the agreed script throughout. He had supported the revolution in Johannesburg. He was privy to the plan to send a force into the Transvaal, but Jameson went ahead without his authority. Chamberlain, Sir Hercules, and the noble directors of the Chartered Company had no prior knowledge of the conspiracy and were innocent of any involvement.

Rhodes made no attempt to contact Jameson during his first days in London. He finally agreed to visit the nursing home where Jameson had a private room, 'at the urgent insistence of Jameson's servant, who maintained that the doctor was dying':

> The servant opened the door, and the two men whose names had been bandied together for a year across the very world, came face to face at last. There was a silence, but before he closed the door, the servant heard Rhodes say gruffly, 'Both of us have had a rough time, but you have had a rougher time than I'.[11]

According to Jameson's biographer, Ian Colvin, Rhodes poured 'his own blood into Jameson's veins with talk of telegraphs and Tanganyika, and work to be done and accounts to be squared'.[11] This does not seem to have been a great exaggeration. Within days of Rhodes's visit, Jameson was out of the nursing home and sharing rooms in Piccadilly with Sir John Willoughby. On 26 March he was fit enough to appear before the committee and loyally kept to the script. He had indeed gone in against Rhodes's wishes. Chamberlain, Sir Hercules Robinson and the noble directors of the Chartered Company were innocent, and so forth.

Beit, Harris, Hawksley, Flora Shaw, Bower, Willoughby and a host of others were called to the proceedings, which dragged on until July. The final conclusions were predictable. Rhodes was castigated for planning the raid, but there was no suggestion that any action would be taken against him (for an unprovoked attack against a friendly power) and he was allowed to remain a privy councillor. Chamberlain, Sir Hercules and the noble directors were declared blameless. The royal charter was secure.

There was one unpleasant ramification. Some highly placed individual had evidently decided that it would be stretching credibility too far to suggest that no-one in the Colonial Office had any knowledge of this conspiracy, and it was decided to create scapegoats in the junior ranks. The first choice was Chamberlain's late secretary, Edward Fairfield. A year earlier he had been given the unpleasant task of dealing with Hawksley, Rhodes's blackmailing solicitor (see page 303), but had subsequently died. He was an ideal person on whom to dump blame. The other decisions were not quite as painless. Graham Bower, who had loyally turned down a governorship to support Sir Hercules, and Rhodes's old Oxford friend, Francis Newton, were both found guilty of complicity.

Not everyone was delighted with the committee's final report. Lord Rosebery declared that he had never seen a document 'at once so shameful and absurd',[12] and Arnold Morley, a fellow Liberal, described the entire charade as 'The Lying in State at Westminster'.[13] In Cape Town, Merriman was wracked with pity for 'poor Bower and poor Newton',[14] who were clearly shielding others but were nonetheless being shunted off to inferior posts with their chances of promotion destroyed.

Rhodes left London long before the proceedings had ground to an end. After a grand tour of Europe with Grimmer and Bobby Coryndon, he returned to Cape Town on 20 April 1897. There was a 'tremendous reception' for him at the docks where Jourdan and Le Sueur were waiting. He looked 'bright and well ... really in excellent health',[9] and delivered a triumphant speech to the crowd: 'My public life is only beginning. It is not over. It cannot be over'.[15]

Le Sueur takes up the story:

[Rhodes] then drove out to the ruins of Groote Schuur, where the new house was rising phoenix-like from the ashes. He paid one or two flying visits to Kimberley, and then determined to throw himself into northern expansion and development. 'I have always loved the north,' he said - 'my north. They can't take that away. The can't change the name. Did you ever hear of a country's name being changed?'[16]

It was certainly unusual in 1897.

There was an extraordinary incident during Rhodes's northward journey. Late one night, the sumptuous De Beers train stopped at Vryburg in the northern Cape where Le Sueur collected the telegrams that were being held at the station. One of them contained distressing news and Le Sueur decided not to disturb Rhodes, who was already asleep. When he was presented with the telegram the following morning, Rhodes flew into a rage and demanded to know why he had not been woken immediately. According to Le Sueur, Rhodes shouted at him, 'I suppose you thought this would affect me and I should not sleep. Why, do you imagine that I should be in the least affected if you were to fall under the wheels of this train now?'[17]

The telegram brought the news that Barney Barnato was dead. He had been on his way to England to join the celebrations to mark Queen Victoria's golden jubilee. Shortly after his ship called at Madeira, Barnato leapt from his deckchair, cried out 'They're after me', rushed to the nearby railings, climbed up and jumped over.[18] One of the ship's officers immediately dived overboard. He caught sight of Barnato but the rough sea kept them apart. By the time the lifeboat reached him, Barnato was floating face downwards. All attempts to revive him failed.

In describing the incident, Le Sueur was less concerned with the circumstances of Barnato's death than with Rhodes's reaction. 'He tried to give the impression of being without feeling, but nothing is more absurd. He was crammed with sentiment to his finger-tips, but adopted a brutal manner and a rough exterior to cover up the weakness of sentiment.'[17]

One can certainly believe that Rhodes was badly shaken by the news of Barnato's death. The Rhodes–Barnato relationship went back a long way. Barnato was also the first of this group to die. (He was 44 in 1897, the same age as Rhodes.) At a time when Rhodes was so preoccupied with thoughts of his own mortality, that telegram must have had a profound effect.

The full circumstances of Barnato's suicide have never been revealed. Many people believed that Barnato had achieved his early success in Kimberley by dealing in stolen diamonds (see p. 123) and that his past had finally caught up with him. Le Sueur alleged that Barnato's criminal associates had driven him to a frenzy with blackmail letters, 'rudely embroidered with skull and cross-bones and coffins etc.'.[19] There is no surviving evidence of this. What is certain, though, is that Barnato was seriously deranged during the last months of his life. Although his doctors and his family begged him to rest, he continued to drive himself hard and live on his nerves.

At the time of Barney's death, Rhodes could certainly take comfort in his own remarkable recovery. He had saved his Rhodesian base from rebellion and his company from threats to the charter. He still had large reserves of private power through De Beers and Consolidate Goldfields, and although he was no longer Premier of the Cape, the tide of popularity was turning in his favour. When he told the Cape Town crowds that his public life was 'only beginning', he was not being totally unrealistic.

There was another important new development soon after Rhodes's return to South Africa. Sir Hercules Robinson, who had been deliberately kept in office so that he would not have to appear before the inquiry, was finally allowed to retire in May 1897 and rewarded with a peerage. His successor, who had been waiting all the while in the wings, was Sir Alfred Milner, another of Rhodes's famous Oxford contemporaries. After a brilliant university career – Milner was described as the 'finest flower' of his generation at Balliol – he had made a name for himself as an efficient financial administrator and the author of *England in Egypt*. Milner described imperialism as 'a great movement of the human spirit with all the depth and comprehensiveness of a religious faith'. Again, this was not the Southey/Mackenzie brand of Imperialism with its idealistic notion that Britain was merely the temporary guardian of Africa's future. The British, as Milner made clear in *England in Egypt*, were there to stay.

Merriman sensed Milner's fanaticism from the start, describing him in a letter to Harry's father, J.B. Currey, as, 'a strong Rhodes and anti-Transvaal man'.[20] At their first formal meeting, Milner revealed his intention to force reforms on Kruger, and Merriman soon gained the impression that the British Government was now determined to continue the fight that Rhodes had begun. This time, though, there would be no need for secret conspiracies. It would be open confrontation. Merriman was so alarmed at Milner's attitude that he warned him he was in danger of creating 'another Ireland in South Africa'.[20] Milner dismissed Merriman as a crank.

As far as Rhodes was concerned, the Cape administration was now in capable hands and he could concentrate on 'his' north. The railway line was extended from Mafeking towards Bulawayo at the rate of a mile a day, and a second line was put down connecting Delagoa Bay and Umtali. Dr Jameson, now back in Africa and raring to go, was asked to supervise the construction of Rhodes' great African telegraph line, which would eventually link Cape Town to Cairo. Bobby Coryndon, one of the original 'angels' on the 'pioneer column (see page 217) was dispatched to administer Rhodes's territory north of the Zambezi. Although white settlement there had scarcely begun – there was just a handful of missionaries and traders – Rhodes was confident that once the railway had crossed the Zambezi, the territory would come into its own. Harry Pickstone, a horticulturalist, was brought out from California to plant 150,000 fruit trees in Rhodes's two Rhodesian estates – at Inyanga in the eastern highlands and near the Matopos.

At the height of all this activity, Rhodes was again struck down with malaria. This time his heart was badly affected. Jameson, who was in Beira at the time, rushed up to Inyanga and 'brought the sick man back to some degree of health'.[21] Not long afterwards, Rhodes told a friend, 'I never lie down on my bed at night without wondering whether I shall wake in this world or the next'. It was the beginning of the end.[22]

In the last week of October 1897, the railway reached Bulawayo. The formal celebrations were held back until 4 November, the fourth anniversary of Jameson's victory march through the smouldering ruins of Lobengula's capital. Nowhere in the British Empire had there been such a rapid transformation.

Rhodes was too ill to attend the ceremonies. Sir Alfred Milner declared the new line open in the presence of a huge gathering of distinguished guests from all parts of the world and described the occasion as, 'a performance of *Hamlet*, without the Prince'.[22]

In December 1897, Rhodes returned to Cape Town. Although he knew his heart had been affected by his recent illness, he was determined not to let go. Before the year was out, he had plunged back into Cape politics after an absence of two years. With the active encouragement of Edmund Garrett, editor of the *Cape Times*, Rhodes took over the leadership of the Progressive Party and set in motion an extraordinary game of political musical chairs. The Progressives had started out as a loose affiliation of liberals, that had grouped round Merriman and Rose-Innes after their resignation from Rhodes's Cabinet. Their original purpose had been to resist racist legislation, but once Rhodes had taken over the leadership the 'jingos' rallied to the Progressive banner and the liberals formed an alliance with the Bond. The issue that now divided the colony was the Transvaal. Would the people of the Cape back Rhodes and Milner in their determination to compel Kruger to accede to all *Uitlander* demands, even to the point of declaring war?

In readiness for the next election, Rhodes and Beit poured money into

Progressive Party coffers. Rhodes's agents purchased farms secretly in Afrikaner strongholds and settled men on them 'about whose politics there could be no question'.[23] Ministers of the Dutch Reformed Church warned their congregations not to sell to the men from De Beers, but the prices on offer were irresistible.

Rhodes's most cynical move was his all-out attempt to capture the non-white votes. The man who laid the foundations of apartheid and had once campaigned for 'equal rights for all white men', replaced one word and came up with a new slogan 'equal rights for all civilized men.' When asked what he meant by a civilized man, Rhodes's answer came back, straight off the cuff: 'Well ... He is a man, whether White or Black, who has sufficient education to write his own name, who has some property, or works ... In fact, is not a loafer.'

The resignation of that hardy perennial, Gordon Sprigg, in June 1898 precipitated the long-awaited elections. Cape politics, which had often been a confusion of shifting alliances, break-ups and regroupings, now came as close as it had ever been to a straight two-party contest. The Progressives faced a Bond-liberal alliance calling itself the South Africa Party and led by Rhodes's former attorney general, William Schreiner.

It was to be the most corrupt, libellous and aggressive election campaign in Cape history. In his desperate effort to secure the premiership, Rhodes was prepared to use any weapon that money could buy. Hired thugs broke up political meetings and an election agent, well-versed in the campaign stratagems of Lord Salisbury's Conservative Party, was specially imported from England.[24]

Rhodes used his virtual monopoly of the English-speaking press to mount a vicious campaign against his opponents, whom he described as 'a little gang terrorizing the country'.[24] Merriman, his life-long friend, was castigated as a fraud and a turncoat. Schreiner's lukewarm support for the Vaal drifts ultimatum (see page 287) was used as a stick to beat him with. The leader of the South Africa Party was branded as a hypocrite and also accused of misusing election funds (a particularly vicious falsehood)[25] After his 17-year courtship of the Bond, Rhodes now portrayed his former allies as a bunch of traitors, fighting the elections with 'Transvaal gold'[25] and conspiring to hand the Cape to Kruger. Behind this scurrilous campaign stood Sir Alfred Milner, supporting Rhodes 'more or less openly'.[24]

In the murk of lies and abuse, it was easy to lose sight of what this election was about. South Africa Party supporters feared that Rhodes, Milner and Chamberlain were hell-bent on pushing South Africa into a war and they were determined to prevent them. No-one expressed the central issue more cogently than Merriman when he sent this personal appeal to a member of Milner's staff, some time after the elections: 'War to you would be an incident of what you call 'Empire'; to us it would mean absolute ruin, financially and socially, undertaken at the bidding of a subsidized press in order that those who are bursting with riches may grow richer.'[26]

Rhodes lost the election by one seat, although he secured the majority of the votes. He appealed to Milner to invalidate the results, but this was impossible. Schreiner took office as Prime Minister with Merriman as his treasurer. Their victory probably delayed the outbreak of the eventual war by a few months, but it could not prevent it. Exhausted by the contest, Rhodes withdrew to 'his' north. It would be left to Chamberlain and Milner to keep up the pressure on Kruger.

A new chapter had begun. It was a time for grandiose schemes and dreams. Rhodes was now determined to fulfil his great ambition of extending the railway line northwards until he had linked Cape Town to Cairo. 'We shall not relax our efforts,' he said, 'until by our civilization and the efforts of our people we reach the shores of the Mediterranean.'

In 1899, Rhodes met Leopold II of the Belgians and the German Kaiser to discuss the laying of the telegraph line and the railway through their African territories. He took an instant disliking to Leopold – 'He haggles like an old Jew' – but hit if off with the Kaiser, 'who met him in the most friendly and broad-minded spirit'.[27] The two of them even managed to joke about the infamous telegram to Kruger. Although an agreement was reached over the telegraph, the Kaiser and his advisors were much more cautious about the railway. The written agreement they eventually offered Rhodes was useless to him.[28]

It was also the year when Rhodes drafted his sixth and final will. It began with the famous instructions for his final resting place:

> I admire the grandeur and loneliness of the Matoppos [sic] in Rhodesia and therefore I desire to be buried in the Matoppos on the hill I used to visit and which I called the 'View of the World' in a square to be cut in the rock on the top of the hill covered with a plain brass plate with these words thereon - "'Here lie the remains of Cecil John Rhodes.'"[29]

A monument was to be erected nearby to Allan Wilson and his Shangani patrol, but no-one else would be laid to rest on Rhodes's granite hill without the approval of the Government of Rhodesia or the Federal Government of the future 'States of South Africa'.[30] Fittingly, Jameson was allowed a place at Rhodes's side after his death in 1917.

Among his many other bequests, Rhodes left his English properties to his brothers and sisters, and his Rhodesian estates in trust 'for the instruction of the people of Rhodesia'. The sum of £100,000 was bequeathed to Oriel, his old Oxford college, and Groote Schuur was left as a residence for future South African Prime Ministers.

The most significant section of the will was Rhodes's provision of a scholarship fund to instill into young minds the advantage 'of the retention of the unity of the Empire'[31] and the 'union of the English-speaking peoples throughout the world'.[32] Twenty scholarships a year would be awarded to students from the British Colonies, the United States and Germany, to enable them to study at Oxford for three years. It was said that the idea to add the Germans came to Rhodes after his visit to the Kaiser.

The Rhodes scholars were to be chosen not merely for their 'literary and scholastic attainments' but for 'success in manly outdoor sports', and qualities of leadership, as well as 'kindliness, unselfishness, manhood, devotion to duty'.

It is clear from the language of the will that women were not considered for these scholarships. The student had to be judged by *his* attainments, *his* qualities, *his* character, and so on. There was a provision that 'no student shall be qualified or disqualified ... on account of his race or religious opinions',[33] but that was to ensure that French Canadians and Afrikaners would not be excluded. Rhodes never envisaged African scholars. Later trustees quietly and wisely ignored his intentions, and there have been many distinguished Rhodes scholars who were neither white nor male.

The idea behind the scholarships harks back to 'A Confession of Faith' and a 23-year-old's dream of establishing a secret society with members 'in every part of the British Empire ... placed in our universities and schools ...' (see page 113).

As Rhodes approached his end, his concern for an immortal place in history was taking him back to his youthful obsession: 'What is life worth with no object, no aim?'[34]

Rhodes knew that men and women are not remembered for their great wealth or their entrepreneurial flair, but for their vision. He began to rummage through the ideological baggage he had carried with him in his youth. He rediscovered his early imperialist and racial 'dreams', and his public utterances became increasingly mystical and pompous. 'I find that up the mountain one gets thoughts, what you might term religious thoughts, because they are thoughts for the betterment of humanity ... '[35] In his final two years he also posed continuously for portraits and statues.

His public loved it. Rhodes was now the great English hero, worshipped 'at home' and throughout the empire. On 21 June, Oxford awarded him with an honourary doctorate. As his boat docked at Cape Town on his return, the police band played 'Behold the Conquering Hero Comes'. The streets were decked with flags and banners proclaiming, 'Welcome Home Empire Maker' and 'Go ahead, Rhodes, Claremont Backs You'.[36]

Sadly for Rhodes, he would be brought down from these great heights by someone who was neither a business rival, a political opponent, nor a victim of his laws, military campaigns or company take-overs. After a lifetime spent squaring opponents and covering himself from every angle, Rhodes was finally ambushed by someone outside any of his spheres of influence – and a woman!

Princess Catherine Radziwill (née Ekaterina Adamevna Rzewuska) was the only daughter of a Polish nobleman living in exile in southern Russia. At the age of 15 she had married Prince Wilhelm Radziwill, fellow Polish exile living in Berlin. She hated the Prussian capital and eventually wrote a vicious exposé of aristocratic and court life with the innocuous title, *Berlin Society*. The book was considered a gross insult, not only to those she had attacked personally, but to the pride of the nation. Catherine had written under a pseudonym, but she was eventually unmasked. She and her husband left Berlin in disgrace, but were welcomed by London and Parisian society. Catherine also remained a particular favourite of the Russian Czar, Alexander III. In 1895, Catherine and her prince separated and she settled in London, where she continued to move in the highest social circles. She was 39 years old at the time but still beautiful and vivacious, with talents to match her looks. She spoke four languages fluently and was a gifted writer and raconteur. Stead admired and trusted her. She knew Labouchère and other radical politicians and, on several occasions, was invited to stay at Hatfield House, the country residence of Lord Salisbury, the Prime Minister.

In February 1896, Catherine was introduced to Rhodes at a dinner party given by Moberley Bell, the managing director of *The Times*. The Jameson Raid had ended in disaster a month earlier and Rhodes was in London to remind Chamberlain that he had certain telegrams in his possession and wished to retain his charter.

Rhodes had apparently forgotten Catherine when she wrote to him some time later, asking for advice on investments.[37] She became a persistent correspondent, claiming in one letter that she was 'blessed or cursed with the gift of second sight' and had had a premonition that within six months there would be an attempt on Rhodes's life. To protect him, she had enclosed a gold talisman. Rhodes lost it almost at once.[38]

After receiving his Oxford doctorate, Rhodes changed his bookings for the return voyage to South Africa at least four times. Jourdan was surprised to hear from an official of the shipping company that Catherine Radziwill had been making repeated visits to their offices to inquire about Rhodes's travel arrangements. Apparently, she had cancelled and rebooked a passage for herself every time Rhodes had changed his plans.[39]

According to Jourdan, there was mock surprise when Catherine walked into the first-class dining room on their first evening at sea and discovered she was on the same boat as Rhodes. She immediately contrived to get a permanent place at his table, and thereafter used all her skills to win his affection. 'In a soft, trembling, hesitating voice full of pathos and sadness',[39] she complained of the cruelties she had suffered at the hands of her husband, whom, she announced, she was now divorcing. On one occasion, she even managed to faint skilfully into Rhodes's arms. He was less impressed with these antics than with Catherine's obvious talents. She seemed to have a remarkable grasp of South African affairs and was certainly well connected. By the time Rhodes stepped ashore to the strains of 'Behold the Conquering Hero', Princess Radziwill had a standing invitation to his home.

Cape society was in awe of this Russian princess and she was an instant success, establishing friendships with Hofmeyr, Milner and other South African notables. She tried to encourage Rhodes to fight to regain the Premiership, but it was not long before their relationship soured. Her visits to Groote Schuur were too persistent, as was her determination to discuss politics. He began to suspect her motives and invented outside appointments whenever she arrived at the house. He then discovered to his horror that she was telling some people that they were having an affair and others that they were engaged, but before this personal drama reached crisis point, larger events had taken over their lives.

Rhodes had returned to Cape Town in an atmosphere of mounting tension. Two months earlier, Kruger and Milner had faced each other over a conference table in Bloemfontein, the capital of Orange Free State. Milner had opened the session with a demand that the *Uitlanders* in the Transvaal should qualify for the vote after five years. Kruger wanted to know what he could expect in return for such a far-reaching reform, and brought up the matter of reparations for the Jameson Raid. Milner curtly dismissed what he called a 'Kaffir bargain'.

The tone had already been set. As the discussions continued, Kruger offered significant concessions but Milner was not interested in negotiation. At the conclusion of the conference, Kruger told Milner, 'It is our country you want'.[40]

From now on, British policy was to turn the screw tighter and tighter, to demand more and more. Moderate Afrikaners everywhere rallied round

Kruger, while Englishmen like Merriman were ashamed and angry. At the beginning of August, he wrote: 'Milner and Chamberlain in two years by their rampant Imperialism and their neurotic desire for notoriety have put the clock back for twenty-five years ... It is difficult as an Englishman to see one's country playing the part of a bully.'[41]

In the following month, the British Cabinet agreed to raise the number of regular British troops in South Africa to 22,000. Chamberlain then issued an ultimatum, rejecting the Transvaal's claim to be a sovereign State. A whole set of new demands was imposed on Kruger, and the five-year franchise requirement was repeated. In effect, the Transvaal Boers were being asked to surrender their country. Schreiner sent Chamberlain an official minute on behalf of the Cape Government, 'unanimously begging Her Majesty's Government to pause before plunging into war'.[42]

Rhodes, in the meantime, was playing a intricate game. In the midst of the crisis his newspaper, the *Cape Argus* , proclaimed: 'War, with all its horrors, is the only solution to the problem of the Englishman in the Transvaal'.[43]

The very next day, Rhodes told his supporters:

> There is not the slightest chance of war. The notion of the Transvaal being able to trouble Great Britain seriously is too ridiculous ... If you were to tell me that the native chief in Samoa was going to cause trouble to the Imperial Government, then I would discuss the proposition that the Transvaal was a danger to the British Empire.[44]

In his unpublished memoirs, Harry Currey put a very sinister interpretation on Rhodes's antics:

> It has often been asked how it was that England embarked on that fatal step, the Boer War – and the answer has always been, 'We trusted the Man on the Spot.' In this case it was Cecil Rhodes. ... Percy Ross Frames, formerly chairman of the De Beers Consolidated Mines, told me that he once asked Rhodes in Bulawayo how, knowing the Boers as he did, he could ever have expressed such an opinion. Rhodes' reply was cynicism itself for he said, 'Do you think there would have been a war if I had at any time expressed a different opinion?'[45]

Harry Currey had come a long way, both politically and personally, since he had been thrown out of Groote Schuur. In 1899, he was editor of a pro-Merriman newspaper and on the point of being elected to the Cape Parliament in a by-election. He cannot be described as impartial, but he was always honest.

Kruger knew that war was inevitable and took the only course open to him. He presented his own ultimatum to the British before they had a chance to build up their forces. On 8 October he asked the British Government to agree to a number of conditions within 48 hours. They included a commitment to peaceful arbitration and assurances that all British forces would be withdrawn from the Transvaal border and that troops already on the high seas would not be landed at South African ports.

'They've done it,' exclaimed Chamberlain jubilantly, for he knew that the *casus belli* was the insuperable difficulty. Lord Lansdowne, the minister of war, congratulated the colonial secretary. And Lord Salisbury declared that 'a defiance so audacious ... liberated us from the necessity of explaining ... why we are at war.'[46]

The British rejected Kruger's ultimatum, and it was war; in many ways, Rhodes's war. Merriman divided the blame. He identified two aggressors, 'stockjobbing capitalism' and 'imperial militarism',[46] but Jan Smuts believed that the primary responsibility was with Rhodes. He wrote:

> The Jameson Raid was the real declaration of war in the Great Anglo-Boer conflict ... And that is so in spite of the four years truce that followed ... [the] aggressors consolidated their alliance ... the defenders on the other hand silently and grimly prepared for the inevitable.[47]

Boer commandos.

Colonial Kekewich

On the night of 11 October, Rhodes excused himself from dinner at Groote Schuur and left for the station with Jourdan. The two of them travelled on the very last train to reach Kimberley before the town was surrounded by the Boers.

'As for Jameson, he made a bee-line for the point at which the fighting was to be.'[48] That was the town of Ladysmith in Natal, which remained under siege for the next four-and-a-half months. Much to Jameson's disappointment, the British Army did not require his military talents.

The citizens of Kimberley had heard a rumour that the Transvaal Boers had one great ambition – to catch Cecil Rhodes and parade him through the streets of Pretoria in a lion's cage. They were convinced that his presence among them would focus enemy attention on the town and they did their best to stop him leaving Cape Town. The message from the harassed mayor read, 'Under all circumstances would ask you kindly postpone coming'. Rhodes, of course, paid no attention. He was not going to be told when he could come and go to his diamond capital.

As soon as he arrived, he took over the Sanatorium, a luxurious semi-private hotel built and run by De Beers, which 'compared favourably with the best hotels in London'.[49] He would have a complete staff to run the place throughout the siege.

Once installed, Rhodes decided to see what the military were up to. The commander of the British Army garrison in Kimberley was Lieutenant-Colonel Robert Kekewich, a pleasant, plump, bald, unassuming man in his mid-40s, who had fought in minor colonial wars without attracting a great deal of notice. He had been in Kimberley since August, preparing its defence. The town's perimeter was now well-fortified with sandbags and an observation tower atop the De Beers main headgear commanded a view across an infinity of bare, flat veld.

In the early days of the siege, Rhodes and Kekewich got on well. Rhodes proposed that he should raise and equip a cavalry troop that could be sent out to harry the Boers and prevent them from establishing trenches near the town. In the De Beers stores were eight machine guns, over 400 rifles and some 700,000 rounds of ammunition which Messrs Pickering & Co had failed to deliver to their intended destination four years earlier. Rhodes was happy to put these at Kekewich's disposal.

In the first major battles of the Boer War the British suffered a series of devastating setbacks. On 22 October, the town of Dundee in Natal was abandoned to the Boers, who found 40 days' military supplies for 5000 men. By 31 October, Ladysmith, the main British supply base in the colony, was under siege. Just as Jameson had done four years earlier, the British had made the great mistake of underestimating their enemy.

The Boers cut all lines of communication into Kimberley, but nothing much else happened until the first week of November, when a party of Boer horsemen approached the fortified perimeter of the town, bearing a white flag and a letter, addressed to 'The Senior British Officer'. It was an ultimatum from Commandant-General Wessels, the Boer commander, for Kimberley to surrender or, alternatively, for 'all women and children to leave Kimberley, so that they may be placed out of danger'. Safe passage was also offered to 'all Afrikander families who wish to leave Kimberley'.[50]

Surrender was out of the question and the evacuation of women and children impractical. Kekewich composed a polite reply to Wessels and, out

The Sanatorium Hotel (Kimberley), sandbagged against shellfire.

of courtesy, sent one of his officers to the Sanatorium Hotel with the Wessels letter and his proposed reply. Rhodes insisted that the Boer ultimatum should be reworded and then published in the *Diamond Fields Advertiser*. No mention would be made of the offer of safe passage to '*all* women and children', only to the *Boer* women and children. In Rhodes's view, such obvious discrimination on the part of the enemy would anger the people of Kimberley and stiffen their resolve. Kekewich meekily complied. It was the start of his troubles.[50]

The Boers now began to shell the town in a desultory fashion. After the initial panic, the population soon took the bombardment in their stride. During the first seven days, 'the amount of damage done both to life and property was so small that it would hardly be believed'.[51] There were two deaths in that time – an African woman, whose head was blown off as she walked past the Kimberley Club, and an Afrikaans woman who died of shock when a shell burst near her house.[51]

On the second day of the shelling, Kekewich had another unpleasant experience of Rhodes. Following his normal routine, he had climbed to the top of the observation tower at first light, when he was astonished to see a 'living mass' of men approaching the town. He gave orders for the field guns to open up at point-blank range. As the light improved, Kekewich suddenly realized that he had been shelling unarmed African mine-workers. Rhodes had been emptying his compounds without bothering to inform the military authorities. The Boer shelling had put a stop to mining operations, and Cecil Rhodes saw no reason why he should continue to feed an unproductive 'hoard of savages'.[52]

At midnight on 9 November an NCO arrived at Kekewich's quarters with an African runner who had got through Boer lines. He brought a message from the commander-in-chief, Sir Redvers Buller: 'Civilians in Kimberley representing situation there as serious. Have heard nothing from you. Send appreciation of the situation immediately'.[53]

Kekewich was astounded. He had been sending out regular reports of his own by runner since mid-October. The situation in Kimberley was certainly not serious, but it was now obvious to Kekewich that Rhodes had been sending alarmist messages behind his back. Kekewich decided to say and do nothing.

Rhodes was fast losing his judgement and his self-control. Only a week after he had cabled the news of the impending fall of Kimberley, he was insisting that Kekewich should release 800 of the men under his command to assist Baden-Powell, who was besieged in Mafeking, 220 miles to the north. Kekewich patiently explained the realities. The men were needed in Kimberley. If they went north, they would be cut off by much larger Boer forces, which would be armed with artillery. Rhodes refused to listen. He was abusive and lost his temper. 'You are afraid of a mere handful of farmers. You call yourselves soldiers of an Empire-making nation. I do believe you will take fright at a pair of broomsticks. Give it up. Give it up.'[54]

The tantrums continued. A few days later, Rhodes was complaining to Kekewich that Kimberley now needed *more* troops to defend itself, and offered to send instructions to Cape Town for a force of 2000 volunteers to be raised at his own expense. Kekewich tried to make Rhodes understand that experienced officers would have to be taken off other duties to train this force and that it would all take a great deal of time. Again, Rhodes flew into a rage.

On 23 November, the long-awaited message came. A relief column under General Methuen was on is way. Patient, courteous, long-suffering Colonel Kekewich would soon have Cecil Rhodes off his hands.

Kimberley waited and waited ... but the column never arrived. At the Magersfontein hills, 60 miles southwest of Kimberley, the British Army had suffered another terrible setback. Methuen would not be coming to Kimberley's relief. The town prepared for a long siege.

Rhodes was now determined to prove to Kekewich that he was king of this town. Against military orders, he sent women and children down the mine shafts for shelter. It was a pointless exercise, but it showed that the people of Kimberley followed Rhodes's lead. He had a four-inch gun built in the De Beers workshops by his enthusiastic chief engineer, George Labram. Christened 'Long Cecil', it was capable of firing 28-pound shells. All Kekewich had in his armoury was a few 7-pounders – 'pop-guns' Rhodes called them – and they were no match for the Boer artillery. But as soon as Long Cecil went into action, the tables were turned. The very first shell flew 5 miles and landed 'right in the midst of the Boer camp'.[55]

Five days later, the Boers replied with 'Long Tom', a 90-pounder they had just brought up from Natal. It achieved more for them in three days than all their other guns had done in four months. By an extraordinary twist of fate, one of Long Tom's early victims was George Labram. He was shaving in his hotel bedroom when a shell passed through four walls and killed him instantly.[55]

Long Tom went into action on 23 January 1900. The siege was now in its 14th week and Rhodes had had enough. He was ready to surrender to the Boers – or rather, to blackmail the British high command with the threat that he was ready to surrender to the Boers.

By this time the counter-invasion had begun. Lord Roberts's great army was rolling up from the south to take Bloemfontein, capital of the Boer republic of the Orange Free State. Africa had never seen anything like 'the Imperial steam-roller':

British fatalities at Spion Kop.

... A whole army corps in motion across the sand, under the canopies of dust and amid the yells of African drivers, the wheep of the long whips and the squeeling [sic] of the mules ... It was the sheer scale of this army that took one's breath away. Roberts and Kitchener had five divisions - about forty thousand men, with one hundred guns, including a whole division of cavalry commanded by Lieutenant-General John French.[56]

Suddenly, this behemoth was stopped in its tracks by a message from Colonel Kekewich in Kimberley. Cecil Rhodes was demanding that the course of the war should be changed. Unless the army made the relief of Kimberley its first priority, Cecil Rhodes would surrender the town and the mines to the Boers.

It would not require the whole army to relieve Kimberley, but it would certainly mean sending the cavalry division dashing up, while the infantry brigades engaged the attention of the Boers with a massive artillery barrage. Because supply problems had not yet been resolved, it would mean half-rations for the cavalry while they were on the move. It would mean horses, as yet unacclimatized, dropping dead with heat, hunger and exhaustion.

But if that was what Cecil Rhodes demanded ...

On 15 February 1900, General French's cavalry rode into Kimberley. The 124-day siege was over. So heavy was the toll in dead and exhausted horses that the cavalry division was virtually destroyed as a fighting force.

Rhodes made a speech to his Kimberley shareholders immediately the siege was lifted. It was one of his most astounding public statements:

When we look back at the troubles we have gone through, and especially all that has been suffered by the women and the children, we have this satisfaction – that we have done our best to preserve that which is the best commercial asset in the world – the protection of Her Majesty's flag.[57]

This speech was delivered in the middle of a war that would claim at least 70,000 lives.

Some time later, Rhodes complained to his friend Stead that he had been unjustly 'abused' for making this speech. He was quite hurt about it, and his defence is as revealing as the speech itself:

People talked as if I were making a political speech, or speaking as a politician. I was not. I was addressing a meeting of the De Beers shareholders, half of whom were Frenchmen ... French feeling is very strong against England, and the French shareholders ... had lost an enormous sum of money from the cessation of industry during the war ... I finished up with a declaration that I had been sending their money in defending ... the greatest commercial asset in the world ... I was addressing not the world at large ... I had my eye on the French shareholders.[57]

All things to all men.

It is strange how that phrase 'the women and the children' reverberates through the darker episodes of Rhodes's life. 'We have an excuse for a row over murdered women and children' was the excited message Jameson sent to Rhodes when he saw his opportunity to destroy the Matabele nation, and it was the phrase about 'women and children' that stuck in every memory when the bogus letter from the Johannesburg conspirators was read out on the eve of the Raid.

After the siege of Kimberley had been lifted the Boer War dragged on for another two years and four months. In the final stages, the Boers fought as guerillas. Their spirit was only broken when their women and children were taken off the farms and placed in the world's first concentration camps.

Rhodes would not live to see the end of the wear, nor would he find his own peace. His crises continued to overlap. No soooner had the fire been put out in one place than another was raging somewhere else.

There is one important postscript to the story of the Kimberley siege. No sooner had the relief column entered the town than Rhodes was scheming to destroy Kekewich's career. When that decent man returned to his headquarters in Cape Town, he found somebody else sitting at his desk. He had been relieved of his command because he had been 'overbearing and tyrannical towards Rhodes'.[58]

During Rhodes's four-and-a-half months in Kimberley, Princess Radziwill had launched herself on a one-woman crusade to restore the political status quo that had existed in the colony during Rhodes's first Premiership, when Merriman and the 'liberals' were united with Bondsmen under his leadership. She even had a name for her new political creation. It would be called the 'Anglo-African party'.

Catherine had meetings with Merriman, Hofmeyr and other prominent politicians. She briefed journalists, including Leo Amery, the *Times* correspondent in Cape Town. Whether she was after power or a reconciliation with Rhodes or was genuinely concerned to see peace and harmony restored, she was pursuing an absurd course at the height of the war, when passions were so inflamed.

Rhodes was horrified when he returned to Cape Town and heard what she was up to. It was not the plan itself that he found so offensive, but the fact that she was claiming to be acting under his instructions. To make matters worse, she started pestering him in his home again, and behaving as though their previous rupture had never occured. More than once he lost his temper with her and (on her own admission), shouted at her to leave him alone, but her tenacity was remarkable.

In the middle of March 1900, Rhodes left for England. Catherine followed him, but before she landed Rhodes had already turned round and was heading back to Cape Town.

In London, Catherine lost no opportunity to publicize her association with Rhodes and 'their' plans for South Africa's future. She even spread the old story of their engagement. By July, she was back in Cape Town. Rhodes was now in Rhodesia, under orders from his London heart specialist to take a long rest. Undaunted, Catherine continued her campaign to restore him to the Premiership.

When Rhodes finally returned to Cape Town at the end of October 1900, he organised Groote Schuur on siege lines. It is said that a look-out was posted to warn him of Catherine's approach and that there was always a horse saddled and waiting in the stables so that he could make a rapid escape.[59] But she kept on coming, sometimes sitting down to meals while Rhodes was hiding in the grounds. She continued to pursue her political campaign and in January 1901 took the extraordinary step of launching her own newspaper, *Greater Britain*, to promote the cause.

From this point, the intrigue (and Catherine's motivation) becomes almost impenetrable, although she herself provided an important clue. According to her own testimony, she managed on one occasion to corner Rhodes in his study, where they had a 'violent quarrel ... He wanted me to return certain documents which I possessed ... I utterly refused'.[60]

In an unpublished account, she expanded further:

> I had some [papers] very compromising for certain persons and especially a few of them which, after having been stolen [from] their own proprietors fell into my hands ... We had, Rhodes and I, a tragic scene about it. He insisted upon my giving him all what I possessed in the matter of letters and papers, I refused vehemently. 'Very well,' said he. 'Whatever happens, I will have those papers.'[60]

In the days when she had been a welcome visitor at Groote Schuur, Catherine was often seen wandering into Rhodes's private office. Historians believe that she stole compromising documents – perhaps the 'missing' telegrams – and had been blackmailing Rhodes for some time. This is certainly the only theory that would account for the extraordinary measures Rhodes was prepared to take to avoid her, when the obvious remedy was to forbid her entry to Groote Schuur. It would also explain why Milner eventually became so concerned that he ordered the chief of his CID to search Catherine's house; a measure – as she had great pleasure in telling the intruder – that was a complete waste of time, since all her important documents were in a sealed envelope at the German consulate.

If the theory is correct, we have the extraordinary situation of someone prepared to go to any lengths in her determination to be king-maker – even if it meant blackmailing the reluctant king.

Greater Britain was not a success and Catherine was soon in serious financial difficulties. Her blackmail – if blackmail it was – now took a new direction. She started forging Rhodes's signature on promissory notes, to a value that eventually totalled £29,000.[61]

Rhodes took no direct action. Instead, a mysterious Mr Louw appeared on the scene. Acting through an intermediary, he offered Catherine sufficient cash to redeem the first forged note she had issued, and on the very day it was due. In return, Mr Louw was prepared to accept a fresh promissory note from Catherine. She obliged with another forgery, which was due for payment in eight weeks' time (23 September). When that day arrived Catherine made no attempt to redeem the note, and Mr Louw took an action against Princess Catherine Radziwill *and* Cecil John Rhodes in the High Court. This was curious as Mr Louw was a loyal and long-standing friend of Cecil Rhodes, and one of the few Bondsmen in the Cape Parliament who had stuck by him after the Jameson Raid.[62]

On the day of the hearing, neither defendant appeared in court. Rhodes was in England and the court was advised that he was too ill to travel and had denied all knowledge of the document he was alleged to have signed. Mr Louw's counsel had no objection to postponement of the case against Rhodes, but as no explanation had been given for Catherine's absence and she was not represented in the court, he asked for a judgment in her case. A provisional sentence was passed and on 20 November she was arrested and charged with 24 counts of fraud and forgery. A week later, funds miraculously arrived from England and she was released on bail.

The involvement of Mr Louw in the case against Catherine *and* Rhodes is fascinating. None of the newspaper accounts written at the time of the trial mentions any connection between Rhodes and Louw. Indeed it was not until 1969 that the historian Brian Roberts was able to establish a link. May I offer a theory that fits all the facts of the case. I emphasize that this is only a theory, but one based on some knowledge of Rhodes's methods.

Rhodes could not take legal action against the Princess for fear that she might publish compromising documents. Instead, he instructed Louw to acquire a forged promissory note from the Princess, which would give him sufficient grounds to go to law. Very few people (and certainly not Catherine) knew of the Rhodes–Louw connection, and to obscure the fact still further Louw issued a claim against Rhodes as well as Catherine. At the trial Louw accepted Rhodes's requests for a postponement of his case *and never followed it through*, but demanded that immediate action should be taken against Catherine, thereby setting in motion her arrest and subsequent trial. She remained completely unaware that Rhodes had any part in the scheme and did not activate the blackmail.

Weeks of complicated manoeuvring and intrigue followed Catherine's release on bail. There were offers from the Rhodes camp to redeem all Catherine's outstanding notes if she 'consented to give up the papers that were wanted'.[63] There were approaches from Rhodes's political opponents, who appeared to be willing to handle her defence. The date of Catherine's trial was eventually set for 6 February 1902.

When Rhodes was informed of this in early January he insisted on returning to Cape Town. His friends were alarmed at the state of his health and pleaded with him not to go, but Rhodes would not be deterred. He was under no obligation to be present at the trial, and one can only assume that he was determined to bring all the weight of his personal prestige against Catherine. If he could prove decisively in court that she was a forger, any documents she might produce would be suspect. It was a fatal miscalculation.

Rhodes was returning to one of the hottest Cape summers anyone could remember. On the voyage his condition worsened. He could not breathe in his cabin and a bed was made up for him on the chart-room table. All the portholes were kept open and he caught a cold. In a storm, he was thrown off the table and badly injured. Every effort had been made to keep his arrival a secret. Rhodes's party (which included Jameson) was taken off the ship by a tug and landed in a quiet sector of the dock. Le Sueur, who was there to meet him, was shocked at Rhodes's appearance: 'His face was bloated ... livid with a purple tinge'.[64]

Rhodes was so ill that the trial was eventually transferred to Groote Schuur. Catherine then pleaded illness herself and a postponement was granted until 10 March, but by then it was too late for Rhodes. He was already confined to his little seaside cottage, with an oxygen cylinder at his bedside and silver tubes to drain off the fluid from his legs.

The princess, still on bail, continued to haunt him, pacing up and down the road outside the cottage.

Shortly before 6.00 pm on Wednesday 2 March 1902, 'to the accompaniment of the thunder of the surf breaking on the beach in front of his little bedroom, the greatest of modern Englishmen ... passed away'.[65] He was 48 years old.

Dr Jameson made the announcement to the waiting crowd. When asked for the great man's last words, he replied: 'So little done. So much to do.'

There is a traditional ending to a Rhodes biography. Usually it takes the form of a lengthy assessment of his life and career, with page after equivocal page on the theme: 'Cecil Rhodes, the enigma; Rhodes, the man of contradictions'. I hope readers feel they have progressed beyond that point and have a clearer understanding of who Rhodes was and the forces that drove him. I hope too that they will leave this story feeling that the days of Rhodes and the empire are less remote than they had previously imagined; that there are political, business and moral issues that still resonate today.

'Was Rhodes a great man?' asked his obituary writer in the *Cape Argus*. Before answering in a loud affirmative, he wrote about 'much fierce controversy as to whether Rhodes was a great man or merely a big man'. I would prefer to side-step the moral distinction implied and describe Rhodes as a giant, who towered above his contemporaries. Very few historical figures have had the ability to reach out to others, whatever their race, sex or background, and inspire them with a great sense of purpose. The tragedy for southern Africa (and perhaps the rest of the world) was that Rhodes squandered his great gift.

He also squandered a great opportunity. He had arrived in southern Africa at that defining moment when a source of unimaginable wealth had been discovered in a backward country, largely inhabited by black, white and brown farmers. No-one in those early days of the diamond diggings had any particular expertise. The diggers (including Rhodes) learnt as they went along, and claim owners from one particular group were neither more or less qualified than anybody else to make the adjustment from a pastoral to an industrial way of life. Indeed, this was probably the only time in history when people from so many races and backgrounds had a chance to cross that threshold together.

Rhodes, at the age of 21, sided with men like Richard Southey, who believed that everyone was entitled to the same opportunity. Seven years later, he had thrown in his lot with those who were determined to see that this would not happen.

The timing of Rhodes's arrival in Africa was important in another respect. An industrial and technological revolution in Europe and the United States had given him unique advantages at the precise moment he was able to profit from them. When he first arrived in Africa in 1870, the voyage from Tilbury to Durban took nearly three months by sailing barque. Overland journeys in Africa were at the pace of the ox or the horse. It took eight months to receive a reply to a letter from England.

In the next decade, when Rhodes was ready to expand his interests, southern Africa had been transformed. The telegraph offered instantaneous communication. Cape Town and Kimberley were linked by rail and the journey time to London had shrunk to 19 days. The opportunities for men like Rhodes were unlimited. They could be in touch with the world and the world' financial markets. They had means to mine to depths of 3000 feet (914 metres) and more. They had dynamite. They had electricity. They had the Maxim machine gun, and Africa was powerless to resist them. With 200 inexperienced youngsters, a man could take a country considerably larger than the British Isles.

Conquest and the acquisition of wealth were not the greatest challenge, though. When Rhodes was at the height of his power, men and women of vision were already sounding warnings of a terrible future for their country unless power and wealth were shared; unless black and white, Afrikaner and Englishman were made to feel part of the same nation. Nobody was pretending that this would be easy, but if there were one man capable of achieving that unity it was Cecil Rhodes. The English, of course, were his natural supporters, but he had proved again and again that he could lead and inspire Africans, Afrikaners, Coloureds and any other group he wanted to draw to himself. Instead, he used his great gifts to pursue ends that were pragmatic and in the end a disaster for southern Africa.

Can we blame Rhodes entirely? In an early moment of cynicism he had said that every man has his price. Perhaps the most shocking lesson we take from his life is that his experiences invariably proved him right. On Rhodes's return from that triumphant visit to England with Harry Currey, Merriman wrote: 'Personally just now [Rhodes] is very charming … but he trusts no one really and thinks everyone can be bought … except Jameson and Harry'. That was the reverse side of Rhodes's success and glory, and Merriman could sense the underlying pain. How hard it must have been to retain any sense of idealism when everyone Rhodes dealt with showed themselves to be corruptible. Perhaps if there had been one bishop or prime minister, newspaper editor or Cabinet colleague or field marshal with the moral strength to resist Rhodes his life might taken a different course. Perhaps we might not be looking back now with the same sense of tragedy and waste.

The miracle is that after decades of conflict, repression and lost opportunities another 'giant' has appeared, capable of inspiring all the peoples of South Africa. This time, though, his experiences have made him neither a cynic nor a pragmatist, but a moral force. South Africa has been given a second chance.

EPILOGUE

The Boer War continued for two months after Rhodes's death. Twenty-two thousand soldiers from Britain and the Empire died in the conflict, many from disease. It is estimated – though it cannot be confirmed – that 7000 Boers were killed in action, while 28,000 of their women and children died in British concentration camps.

No accurate figure has ever been given for black casualties. In Mafeking alone, nearly 2000 of the African garrison under the command of Baden-Powell were shot by the Boers or left to die of starvation by the British.

In the first elections to be held after the Boer defeat, Dr. Jameson led Rhodes's Progressive Party to victory in the Cape, and was appointed prime minister of the colony. He was subsequently knighted by King George V and made president of the Chartered Company and chairman of De Beers. He died in 1917.

In 1910, Rhodes's dream was partially realized. Cape Colony, Natal and the Boer republics of the Orange Free State and the Transvaal were welded into a single nation. The Union of South Africa was born.

John Merriman, who succeeded Jameson as prime minister of the Cape and was considered the only candidate for the premiership of the new South African nation, acceptable to black South Africans as well as the Boers, was passed over by H.J. Gladstone, the British High Commissioner.

Harry Currey resigned from parliament in disgust and never resumed his political career. He was financially secure, thanks to compensation he had been awarded for unfair dismissal by Cecil Rhodes. He died in 1945, aged 83.

Alfred Beit survived Rhodes by only four years. He never married and much of his vast fortune was left to charity.

Johnny Grimmer, who had accompanied Rhodes's coffin as far as Bulawayo, was taken ill with malarial fever and could not attend the ceremonies in the Matopos. Two months later he contracted blackwater fever and died.

Gordon Le Sueur, Philip Jourdan and Bobby Coryndon all married and had families. Jourdan lived until 1962. His youngest daughter Susan is still active and has given me valuable assistance with this book.

On 28 April 1902 Princess Radziwill was sentenced to two years in

The Colossus of Africa.

prison. She served 16 months. After an erratic career as a journalist, she died in St Clare's Hospital, West 51st Street, New York on 12 May 1941. She was 84 years old. No papers relating to the Jameson Raid were found after her death. All papers that had been in Rhodes's possession were destroyed by his executors in 1902, according to his instructions.

In 1923, Southern Rhodesia (Mashonaland, Matabeleland and Manicaland) passed directly from Chartered Company rule to settler self-government without ever experiencing a period of direct Colonial Office control.

In 1964, all the land that Rhodes had acquired north of the Zambesi (Northern Rhodesia) became the independent African State of Zambia. The British South Africa (Chartered) Company had continued to control all the mineral rights of the country.

Sixteen years later, after a long and bitter struggle, the people of Mashonaland and Matabeleland won their independence. The nation of Zimbabwe was born and Rhodes's name was removed from the map of Africa.

In South Africa, the struggle continued for another 12 years. In 1994, Nelson Mandela became the first democratically elected president of a non-racial South Africa. He was also the first head of State not to reside in Groote Schuur, the home that Rhodes had created for himself at the foot of Table Mountain.

BIBLIOGRAPHY

BBC Books would like to thank the following for granting permission to reproduce quotes for this book. While every effort has been made to trace copyright holders, we would like to apologise should there have been any errors or omissions.
Books are referred to in Notes by author and page number only for brevity.
The complete bibliography is given below.

Angove: *In the Early Days* by John Angove (Kimberley and Johannesburg, 1910)

Ashe: *Besieged by the Boers* by E. Oliver Ashe (Hutchinson, London, 1900)

Baker: *Cecil Rhodes by His Architect* by Herbert Baker (Book of Libraries Press, New York, 1938)

Beet: *The Grand Old Days of the Diamond Fields* by George Beet (Cape Town, 1931)

Bell: *Flora Shaw – Lady Lugard DBE* by E. Moberly Bell (Constable, London, 1947)

Bickford-Smith: *Ethnic Pride and Racial Prejudice in Victorian Cape Town* by Vivian Bickford-Smith (Cambridge University Press, 1995)

Blue Book: *Further Correspondence Respecting the Affairs of Bechuanaland* (HMSO, London, 1890)

Boyle: *To the Cape for Diamonds: A story of Digging Experiences in South Africa* by Frederick Boyle (Chapman & Hall, London, 1873)

Bryant: *Olden Times in Zululand and Natal* by A.T. Bryant (Longmans, Green & Co., 1929)

Buss: *The Lure of the Stone* by W. M. and Vincent Buss (Howard Timmins, Cape Town, 1976)

Chapman: *A Voyage from Southampton to Cape Town and Illustrations of the Diamond Fields* by Charles Chapman (London, 1876)

Chesterton: *Miscellany of Men* by Gilbert K. Chesterton (New York, 1912) for 'The Sultan'. This was first published in the *Daily News* (London), 11 June 1910, under the title, 'Orientalism in the Empire'

Churchill: *Men, Mines and Animals in South Africa* by Randolph Churchill (London 1892)

Cohen: *Reminiscences of Kimberley* by Louis Cohen (Bennett & Co., London, 1911)

Colvin: *The Life of Jameson* by Ian Colvin (Edward Arnold & Co., London, 1922), 2 volumes

Colquhoun: *Dan to Beersheba* by Archibald Colquhoun (Heinemann, London, 1908)

Cook: *Edmund Garrett* by C.T. Cook (London, 1909)

Crewe: *Lord Rosebery* by the Marquis of Crewe (New York, 1931)

Currey: *John Blades Currey, 1850–1900: Fifty Years in the Cape Colony* (Johannesburg, 1986)

Currey, Ronald: *Rhodes: A Biographical Footnote* by Ronald Currey (Carmelite Press, Cape Town, 1964)

Decle: *Three Years in Savage Africa* by Lionel Decle (Methuen, 1898)

de Kiewiet: *The Imperial Factor in South Africa* by C.W. de Kiewiet (Cambridge University Press, 1976)

De Waal: *With Rhodes in Mashonaland* by D.C. De Waal (J.C. Juta, Cape Town & London, 1896)

Dixie: *In the Land of Misfortune* by Florence Dixie (Bentley, London, 1882)

Doughty: *Early Diamond Days* by Oswald Doughty (London 1963)

Fisher: *The Transvaal and the Boers* by W. Garret Fisher (London, 1896)

Fitzpatrick (SAM): *South African Memories* by J. Percy Fitzpatrick (Cassell & Co., London, 1932)

Fitzpatrick (TFW): *The Transvaal From Within* by J. Percy Fitzpatrick (Heinemann, London, 1900)

Flint: *Cecil Rhodes* by John Flint (Hutchinson, London, 1974)

Foley: *Autumn Foliage* by Cyril P. Foley (Methuen & Co., London, 1935)

Fort (Jameson): *Dr Jameson* by G. Seymour Fort (Hurst & Blackett, London, 1908)

Fort (Beit): *Alfred Beit: A Study of the Man and His Work* by G. Seymour Fort (Ivor Nicholson & Watson, London, 1932)

Fuller: *The Right Honourable Cecil Rhodes – A Monograph and a Reminiscence* by T. E. Fuller (Longmans, Green & Co., London, 1910)

Galbraith: *Crown and Charter: The Early Years of the British South Africa Company* by John S. Galbraith (California, 1971)

Gale: *One Man's Vision* by W. D. Gale (Hutchinson & Co., London, 1935)

Gardner: *The Lion's Cage* by Brian R. Gardner (Arthur Barker, London, 1969)

Garrett & Edwards: *The Story of an African Crisis* by E. Garrett and E. J. Edwards (London, 1897)

Garvin: *The Life of Joseph Chamberlain* by J. L. Garvin (Macmillan & Co., London, 1937), 3 volumes

Gibbs: *A Flag for the Matabele* by Peter Gibbs (Fred Muller, London, 1955)

Giliomee: *The Shaping of South African Society* by Herman Giliomee (Wesleyan University Press, Middletown, Connecticut, 1988)

Gross: *Rhodes of Africa* by Felix Gross (Cassell & Co., London, 1956)

Jackson: *The Great Barnato* by Stanley Jackson (Heinemann, London, 1970)

Hammond: *The Autobiography of John Hays Hammond* (New York, 1935)

Harris: *The Chartered Millions* by John H. Harris (Swarthmore

Press, London, 1920)

Hiller: *The Concession Journey of Charles Dunnel Rudd, 1888* edited by Constance E. Phipp & V. W. Hiller (Chatto & Windus, London, 1949)

Hyam: *Empire and Sexuality* by Robert Hyam (Manchester University Press, Manchester & New York, 1990)

Imperialist: *Cecil Rhodes – A Biography and Appreciation* by Imperialist with Personal Reminiscences by Dr Jameson (Chapman & Hall, London, 1897)

Johnson: *Great Days* by Frank Johnson (G. Bell & Sons Ltd, London, 1940)

Jourdan: *Cecil Rhodes – His Private Life By His Private Secretary* by Phillip Jourdan (John Lane, London, 1911)

Keppel-Jones: *Rhodes and Rhodesia* by Arthur Keppel-Jones (McGill-Queen's University Press, Kingston & Montreal, 1983)

Knight-Bruce: *Memoirs of Mashonaland* by G.W.T. Knight-Bruce (Edward Arnold, 1895)

Knox Little: *Sketches and Studies in South Africa* by W. J. Knox Little (London, 1900)

Le Sueur: *Cecil Rhodes – The Man and His Work* by Gordon Le Sueur (John Murray, London, 1913).

Lewsen ('Selections'): *Selections from the Correspondence of J. X. Merriman* edited by Phyllis Lewsen (Van Riebeck Society, Cape Town, 1960)

Lewsen (JXM): *John X. Merriman* by Phyllis Lewsen (Yale University Press, Newhaven and London, 1982)

Lockhart and Woodhouse: *Rhodes* by Lockhart and Woodhouse (Hodder & Stoughton, London, 1963)

Longford: *Jameson's Raid* by Elizabeth Longford (Weidenfeld & Nicolson, London, 1982)

MacKay Wilson: *Behind the Scenes in the Transvaal* by David Mackay Wilson (London 1901)

McDonald ('A Heritage'): *Rhodes: A Heritage* by J. G. McDonald (Chatto & Windus, London, 1943)

McDonald ('A Life'): *Rhodes: A Life* by J. G. McDonald (P. Allen & Co., London, 1927)

McNish: *Graves and Guineas* by J. T. McNish (C. Struik, Cape Town, 1969)

Mason: *The Birth of a Dilemma* by Philip Mason (Oxford University Press, London, 1958)

Mathers: *Zambesia, England's Eldorado* by E. P. Mathers (Knog, Snell & Railton, London, 1891)

Michell: *The Life of the Rt. Hon. Cecil John Rhodes* by Sir Lewis Michell (Edward Arnold, London, 1910), 2 volumes

Millin: *Rhodes* by Sarah Gertrude Millin (Chatto & Windus, 1933)

Moffat: *John Smith Moffat by his Son Robert U Moffat* (John Murray, London, 1921)

Moorhouse: *The Missionaries* by Geoffrey Moorhouse (Readers Union, Newton Abbot, 1975)

Murray: *South African Reminiscences* by S. A. Murray (Cape Town, 1894)

Nutting: *The Scramble for Africa* by Anthony Nutting (Constable, London, 1970)

O'Meara: *Kekewich in Kimberley* by Lt. Col. W. A. J. O'Meara (Medici Society, London, 1926))

Pakenham: *The Boer War* by Thomas Pakenham (Weidenfeld & Nicolson, London, 1979)

Payton: *The Diamond Diggings of South Africa* by Sir Charles A. Payton (London, 1872)

Plomer: *Cecil Rhodes* by William Plomer (Peter Davies, London, 1933)

Preller: *Lobengula* by G. S. Preller (Afrikaanse Pers-Boekhandel, Johannesburg, 1963)

Ranger: *Revolt in Southern Rhodesia* by T. O. Ranger (Heinemann, London, 1967)

Ransford: *Bulawayo: Historic Battleground of Rhodesia* by Oliver Ransford (A. A. Balkema, Cape Town, 1968)

Reade: *The Martyrdom of Man* by Wynwood Reade (London, Edinburgh, 1872)

Ripp and Hiller: *Gold and Gospels in Mashonaland* edited by Constance E. Ripp and V. W. Hiller (London, 1949)

Roberts (CRP): *Cecil Rhodes and the Princess* by Brian Roberts (Hamish Hamilton, London, 1872)

Roberts (KTC): *Kimberley: Turbulent City* by Brian Roberts (David Philip, South Africa, 1976)

Roberts (TDM): *The Diamond Magnates* by Brian Roberts (Hamish Hamilton, London, 1969)

Rose-Innes: *The Autobiography of James Rose-Innes* (Oxford University Press, 1949)

Rotberg: *The Founder – Cecil Rhodes and the Pursuit of Power* by Robert I. Rotberg (Oxford University Press Inc., New York, 1988)

Rouillard: *Matabele Thompson, An Autobiography* edited by Nancy Rouillard (Faber & Faber, London, 1936)

Rorke: *Melina Rourke, Told By Herself* (George G. Harrap & Co., London, 1939)

Samkange (OTFMC): *On Trial for My Country* by Stanlake Samkange (Heinemann, London, 1966)

Samkange (OR): *The Origins of Rhodesia* by Stanlake Samkange (Heinemann Educational, London, 1968)

Sauer: *Ex Africa* by Hans Sauer (Geoffrey Bles, London, 1937)

Schreiner: *Trooper Peter Halket of Mashonaland* by Olive Schreiner (T. Fisher Unwin, London, 1895)

Scully: *Reminiscences of a South African Pioneer* by W. C. Scully (London, 1913)

Selous: *Sunshine and Storm in Rhodesia* by F. C. Selous (Rowland Ward, London, 1896)

Shee: *The Ill Health and Mortal Sickness of Cecil John Rhodes* by J. G. Shee (April, 1965)

Stead: *The Last Will and Testament of Cecil John Rhodes* edited by W. T. Stead (Review of Reviews Office, London, 1902)

Stent: *A Personal Record of Some Incidents in the Life of C. J. Rhodes* by De Vere Stent (Maskew Miller, Cape Town, 1925)

Strage: *Cape to Cairo* by Mark Strage (Harmondsworth, Cape Town, 1973)

Symonds: *A Problem in Modern Ethics* by John Addington Symonds (London 1891)

Tidrick: *Empire and the English Character* by Kathryn Tidrick (Tauris & Co., London, 1992)

Turrell (CLKDF): *Capital and Labour on the Kimberley Diamond Fields* by Rob Turrell (Cambridge University Press, 1987)

Trollope: *South Africa* by Anthony Trollope (Chapman & Hall, London, 1878)

van de Poel: *The Jameson Raid* by Jean van de Poel (Oxford University Press, Cape Town, London, New York, 1950)

van de Sandt de Villiers: *The Life of Jan Hendrik Hofmeyr* by Van de Sandt de Villiers (Druckpers, Cape Town, 1913)

Vindex, pseud. (Rev. F. Verschoyles): *Cecil Rhodes: His Political Life and Speeches* (Chapman & Hall, London, 1900)

Walker: W. P. Schreiner: *A South African* by Eric A. Walker (Oxford University Press, London, 1937)

Wheatcroft: *The Randlords* by Geoffrey Wheatcroft (Weidenfeld & Nicolson, London, 1985)

Williams, Basil: *Cecil Rhodes* by Basil Williams (Constable & Co. Ltd, London, 1921)

Williams, F. Gardner: *The Diamond Fields of South Africa* by F. Gardner Williams (Macmillan & Co., New York, 1902)

Williams, Ralph: *How I Became a Governer* by Ralph Williams (London, 1922)

Wilson: *With the Flag to Pretoria* by H. W. Wilson (London 1900)

Newspapers, Manuscripts, Journals and Periodicals

BS: *Bulawayo Sketch*
CA: *Cape Argus*
CFC: *A Chronicle of the Funeral Ceremonies* (Cape Town, 1905)
CH: *Cape Hansard*
COF: Rhodes's 'Confession of Faith' (1877)
CT: *Cape Times*
CTWE: *Cape Times Weekly Edition*
DF: *The Diamond Field*
DFA: *Diamond Fields Advertiser*
DI: *Daily Independent*
DN: *Diamond News*
Elliot: 'Gold From the Quartz' by W. A. Elliot (Ms, London, 1910)
EPH: *Eastern Province Herald*
FR: *Fortnightly Review*
JSAS: *Journal of Southern African Studies*, vol. 7 (see 'The Black Flag Revolt on the Kimberley Diamond Fields' by Rob

Turrell, April 1981; 'Rhodes, Rhodesia and the Rand' by I. R. Phimister, Oct. 1974)
JICS: *Journal of Imperial and Commonwealth History*, vol. 10 (see 'Rhodes, De Beers and Monopoly' by Rob Turrell, May 1982)
KI: *Kimberley Independent*
MHLC: 'Memoirs of Harry Latham Currey' (unpublished ms written by Harry Currey and kindly loaned to the author by his granddaughter, Phillida Brook Simons)
Ms. Afr: Rhodes House Library
NG: *National Geographic Magazine* (for 'Africa Since 1888, With Special Reference to South Africa and Abyssinia' by Hon. Gardiner G. Hubbard, May 1896; 'British South Africa and the Transvaal' by F. F. Hilder, March 1900)
NY: *New Yorker*
Phillips: 'My Journey and Experiences in Mashonaland' by Francis Gamaliel Phillips (Ms, Rhodes House)
RH: *Rhodesian Herald*
Turrell (CFF): 'Class Formation on the Fields' by Rob Turrell
Turrell (ISS): 'IBD, Searching and Strikes' by Rob Turrell

NOTES

Introduction
(1) CA 27.3.1902
(2) Stead, pp. 93–98
(3) COF
(4) TC 1.8.1971
(5) Ch. 15 pp. 214–215
(6) CA 27.3.1902
(7) Vindex, pp. 159–163
(8) Bickford-Smith, p. 6
(9) Vindex, p. 371
(10) Bickford-Smith, pp. 138–164
(11) See later refs to Rev. John
Mackenzie, Olive Schreiner
and John X. Merriman
(12) See Ch. 2, p. 33
(13) Stead, p. 55
(14) See Ch. 15, p. 210
(15) Vindex, p. 440
(16) See Ch.17, p. 259
(17) See Ch. 4, pp. 60 & 63
(18) This figure includes the territories Rhodes gave to British
protection (today's Malawi
and Botswana), the territory
he acquired for Cape Colony
(the former Crown Colony of
Bechuanaland) and the
countries he acquired on
behalf of his Chartered
Company (today's Zambia and
Zimbabwe)
(19) Basil Williams, p. 327
(20) See Ch. 21, pp. 332–333

Chapter One
(1) CFC, pp. 7–9 and CT,
14.03.1902
(2) Le Sueur, p. 305 and
pp. 311–320, also Millin, p. 1.
(3) Gross, p. 259
(4) Knox-Little, pp. 21–24
(5) CT, 2.4.1902
(6) Baker, p. 22
(7) See Ch. 16, pp. 217–220
(8) Lord Salisbury's alleged advice
to Rhodes in August 1889.
See Samkange, p. 142 and
Gross, p. 173
(9) Millin, p. 1
(10) Le Sueur, pp. 311–320
(11) Michell, vol. 2, pp. 310–312
(12) CA. 27.3.1902
(13) Jourdan, pp. 267–271
(14) MHLC (MS) pp. 104–105

(15) Millin, p. 351 and Roberts,
CRP p. 357
(16) Rotbert, p. 675
(17) From Le Sueur's two
accounts, CA 31.3.1902 and
Le Sueur, pp. 326–327
(18) CA, 29.3.1902
(19) CA, 28.9.1902
(20) CTWE, 16.4.1902
(21) RH, 29.3.1902
(22) CTWE, 9.4.1902
(23) CFC, pp. 7–9
(24) The full text of the sermon is
given in CFC, pp.27–31 and
CTWE, 9.4.1902
(25) See Ch. 6, p. 81 and Ch. 10,
p.145
(26) Le Sueur, pp. 328–330
(27) Millin, p. 353
(28) Based on CTWE, 9.4.1902
and Millin, p.352. (Millin,
however, makes the mistake of
adding the armoured train
after Mafeking, where there
were no hostilities. The *Cape
Times* report was correct.)
(29) Based on Millin, p. 352;
CTWE, 16.4.1902; CFC, pp.
53–57; Le Sueur pp. 331–333;
Jourdan pp. 276–281
(30) McDonald ('A Heritage')
pp. 96–97
(31) An anonymous poem,
published in CTWE,
9.4.1902
(32) Fuller, p. 269
(33) NG, 5.1895, p. 151
(34) Rhodes ('A Heritage') p. 38
(35) COF
(36) Rhodes ('A Heritage') p. 14
(37) Schreiner (Halket) pp. 135,
136, 155
(38) Basil Williams, p. 328
(39) Chesterton, p. 293
(40) The quotations from
Spengler and Hitler are given
in McDonald ('A Heritage').
He identifies the Hitler
quotation as one published in
the German press on
4.11.1941.
(41) Flint, p. 233
(42) COF
(43) See Ch. 19

Chapter Two
(1) Le Sueur p. 1
(2) Gross, p. 3
(3) Rotberg, p. 25
(4) CA, 27.3.1902
(5) Rhodes's speech at a Cape
Banquet (Jan 1894), quoted in
Imperialist, p. 345 and
repeated in many subsequent
biographies
(6) Ch. 15, pp. 206–211
(7) Millin, p. 3
(8) Michell, vol. 1, p. 18
(9) Lockhard & Woodhouse,
p. 39
(10) Letter to *The Times* by Henry
Wilson (April 1902), quoted
in Michell, vol. 1, pp. 19–20
(11) 'Mrs Newman Says', 15, in
Mss. Afr.s.641 (Rhodes
House)
(12) Rotberg, p. 28
(13) 'Fragments' 9: 'Mrs Gervis'
Reminiscences' 4, Mss. AFr.
641 (Rhodes House)
(14) Michell, vol. 1, pp. 12–17
(15) 'Fragments' 9: 'Harrington's
Ideas', pp. 8–9, Mss. Afr. s.
641 (Rhodes House) and
'Fragments', 11: 'Mrs. Purkis
Says', p. 18, Mss. Afr.s.641
(Rhodes House)
(16) McDonald ('A Life') p. 4
(17) See Ch. 4, pp. 55 and Ch 7
p. 91
(18) Baker, p. 13
(19) See Ch. 4, pp. 58–59
(20) Yerburgh, interview with
Basil Williams, 26.6.1914,
Mss.Afr.s.134 (Box 1,
Notebook 1) – Rhodes House
(21) Michell, vol. 1, pp. 18–20
(22) 'Fragments' 11; 'Mrs Purkis
Says,' 18 (Rhodes House)
(23) Le Sueur, pp. 2–5
(24) Roberts (CRP) p. 6
(25) C.J.R. to Sophy Peacock,
17.7.68
(26) Mss. Afr. Morris/t/l/f/10
(Rhodes House) & Lockhart
& Woodhouse p. 43
(27) Shee, April 1965 & Wheatcroft p. 42, etc.
(28) Rotberg, pp. 33–35

(29) C.J.R. to Francis Rhodes, 19.8.1875
(30) Stead, p. 68
(31) C.J.R. to his mother, 11.9.1870
(32) Mss. Afr. t.II.f.47 and Lockhart & Woodhouse p.63

Chapter Three
(1) Giliomee, pp. 3–65, particularly the essay 'The Khoi-San' in 1828 by Richard Elphick and V.C. Malherbe
(2) See Trollope, vol. 1, pp. 20–21
(3) NG, 1900, p. 88
(4) Wheatcroft, p. 18
(5) Cape Colony Census for 1806
(6) Trollope, vol. 1, p. 30 & Wheatcroft, p. 18
(7) Trollope, vol. I, p. 35
(8) Garret Fisher, p. 15
(9) Public Records Office (War Office) 1/343, 57
(10) Trollope, vol. 1, p. 242
(11) Mackay Wilson, pp. 194–195
(12) Unattributed quotation from Wheatcroft, p. 24
(13) Trollope, vol. 1, p. 68
(14) Attributed to Louisa Rhodes (See Ch. 2, p. 39)
(15) The Atherstone quotation appears in Buss and is unattributed. There are almost as many versions of the story of the discovery of the 'Eureka' diamond as there are written accounts; all invariably unsourced. In some versions, the diamond was originally found by the Jacob's 15-year-old son, Erasmus; in other accounts another (unnamed) child is credited. Usually, the Jacobs family is described as tenants of van Niekerk and his stepfather, but in some versions they are neighbours and in others the relationship is reversed, the Jacobs being described as the owners and van Niekerk the tenant. In Wheatcroft there's a further twist: we learn that van Niekerk was trying to sell his portion of 'de Kalk' to the Jacobs family when he discovered the stone. However, the basis facts, common to all accounts, are that a diamond was discovered by a member of the Jacobs family on the banks of the Orange River. It was given to Schalk van Niekerk, who passed on to O'Reilley who, in his turn,

took it to Lorenzo Boyes, who then forwarded it to Dr Atherstone, who was able to confirm that the stone was a diamond.
(16) At least the word 'gregory' was still current in the 1930s: see Millin, p. 11
(17) Wheatcroft, p. 26

Chapter Four
(1) Michell, vol.1, p. 28
(2) C.J.R. to his mother, 11.9.1870
(3) C.J.R. to his sisters, 17.11.1870
(4) C.J.R. to his mother, 17.3.1871
(5) C.J.R. to his mother, 2. 1871
(6) See Michell, vol.1, p. 24 and Lockhart and Woodhouse, p. 46
(7) See footnote to p. 48
(8) C.J.R. to his mother, 19.9.1870
(9) Michell, vol.1, pp. 27–31
(10) As quoted by the Archbishop of Cape Town in his funeral address. CFC, pp. 27–31, and CTWE, 9.4.1902
(11) C.J.R. to his mother, 17.6.1871
(12) C.J.R to his mother, 18.10.1870
(13) C.J.R to Louisa Rhodes, 1872
(14) C.J.R. to his mother, 16.12.1870
(15) C.J.R to hi mother, 11.4.1871
(16) C.J. R to his mother, 17.1.1871
(17) C.J.R. to his mother, 16.7.1871
(18) C.J.R to his mother, 11.4.1871
(19) Roberts (CRP) p. 11
(20) Buss, p. 24
(21) The details of Rhodes's journey to the diggings are not taken from the letters, but are provided (unsourced) in most biographies.

Chapter Five
(1) Roberts (TDM), pp. 3–4
(2) C.J.R. to Sophy Peacock, 26.2.1880
(3) Beet, pp. 19–21
(4) Doughty, p. 101
(5) Cohen, pp. 17–18
(6) C.J.R. to his mother, 1872
(7) Boyle, p. 110
(8) Doughty, p. 51
(9) Payton, p. 189

(10) Doughty, p. 66
(11) Payton, p. 205
(12) Trollope, vol. 2, p. 177
(13) Doughty, p. 88
(14) C.J.R. to his mother, 1877 and Doughty, p. 85
(15) Chapman, pp. 122–123
(16) JSAS, p. 209
(17) Payton, p. 190
(18) Doughty, p. 42
(19) Cohen, p. 60
(20) Doughty, p. 42
(21) Throughout the text, all conversions to present-day values are as provided by the Bank of England.
(22) Michell, vol. 1, p. 42
(23) Doughty, p. 90
(24) Ibid, p. 169
(25) Payton, p. 147
(26) Doughty, pp. 171–172
(27) Cohen, p. 75
(28) Doughty, p. 164
(29) Doughty, p. 77
(30) Roberts (KTC) p. 83
(31) Doughty, p. 74
(32) Roberts (KTC) p. 108
(33) Cohen, p. 24
(34) Lockhart and Woodhouse, p. 57
(35) Payton, p. 150
(36) Basil Williams, p. 31
(37) Scully, pp. 128–132
(38) Cohen, p. 46
(39) Millin, pp. 20–21
(40) Lockhart and Woodhouse, p. 58
(41) Flint, p. 20
(42) JICS, p. 313
(43) Millin, p. 126
(44) Lockhart and Woodhouse, p. 59
(45) Basil Williams, p. 32

Chapter Six
(1) Lockhart and Woodhouse, p. 59
(2) Le Sueur, pp. 7–8
(3) Flint, p. 17
(4) C.J.R. to Frank Rhodes, 19.8.1875
(5) From Stead's first impression of Rhodes, published in November 1899 (pp. 84–85)
(6) Colvin, vol.1, p. 48
(7) Doughty, p. 82
(8) Trollope, vol. 2, pp. 177–178
(9) Turrell (CFF) p. 125
(10) Ibid, p. 147
(11) Wheatcroft, p. 38
(12) Payton, p. 195
(13) Roberts (KTC) pp. 26–32
(14) Cohen, p. 216
(15) Murray, p. 201
(16) Roberts (TDM) p. 44

(17) JSAS, p. 233
(18) Roberts (KTC) p. 122
(19) McNish, pp. 273–274
(20) Gross, p. 50
(21) C.J.R. to C.D. Rudd, 1.6.1876
(22) Basil Williams, p. 42

Chapter Seven
(1) Stead, p. 68
(2) Michell, vol. 1, pp. 50–53
(3) See Ch 6, p. 81
(4) C.J.R. to Sophy Peacock, 26.2.1880
(5) C.J.R. to John X. Merriman, 16.5.1880
(6) Michell, vol.1, pp. 50–53
(7) Millin, p. 27
(8) Ibid, p. 31
(9) See the quotation and the head of this chapter, also Ch 2, pp. 43–44
(10) C.J.R. to Rev. Francis Rhodes. (Two letters undated, but probably Dec 1873 and Jan 1874.)
(11) From the author's interview with H.L.F. Curry, 23.11.1995
(12) With minor variations, the story of Devenish's pump and the Boer transport driver appears in most of the better biographies, e.g. Michell, vol. 1, pp. 64–66; Lockhart and Woodhouse, pp. 72–73; Roberts (TDM) p. 57, etc. However, in all these accounts, it is assumed that the pump was acquired so that Rhodes could fulfil his second contract (i.e. with De Beers Mining Board). In JICS, p. 316 Rob Turrell, an expert on the early history of the diamond mines, provides a convincing argument for the time sequence I have followed.
(13) Fort ('Jameson') p. 72
(14) Michell, vol. 1, p. 45
(15) Rouillard, pp. 198–199
(16) See Le Sueur p. 8, Michell, vol. 1, p. 66
(17) Lewsen ('Selections'), vol. 1, p. 9
(18) DF, 28.11.1874
(19) Cohen, pp. 216–222
(20) Roberts (KTC) p. 135
(21) JSAS, pp. 194–195
(22) Roberts (TDM) pp. 45–49
(23) C.J.R. to Frank Rhodes, 19.8.1875
(24) de Kiewiet, p. 55
(25) Roberts (KTC) p. 139

(26) Turrell (ISS) p. 246
(27) Lockhart and Woodhouse, p. 72
(28) DN, 6.1. 1876
(29) DN, 8.1. 1876
(30) See Roberts (TDM), pp. 53–56, for a complete account of the bribery charges and Robert's own conclusions
(31) JICS, p. 317
(32) C.J.R. to either E.W. Tarry or William Alderson, undated, probably Oct 1876

Chapter Eight
(1) C.J.R. to C.D Rudd (May 1876)
(2) C.J.R. to C.D. Rudd (undated)
(3) Michell, vol. 1, p. 78
(4) Rotberg, p. 90
(5) Lockhart and Woodhouse, p. 64
(6) Michell, p. 81
(7) Moorhouse, p. 28
(8) Ibid, p. 21
(9) Ibid, p. 27
(10) Ibid, p. 23
(11) Ibid, p. 31
(12) Nutting, p. 220
(13) Bickford-Smith, p. 64
(14) Wheatcroft, p. 17
(15) Bickford-Smith, pp. 78 & 85
(16) From correspondence between Dr Richard Dawkins and the author
(17) Quotations are from Reade
(18) Bickford-Smith, p. 79
(19) NG, May 1896, p. 163
(20) Bickford-Smith, p. 80
(21) See CT 8.1.1890 and the *Lantern* 29.6.1889
(22) Fuller, p. 247
(23) Baker, pp. 10–11
(24) All quotations from Ruskin's Inaugural Address at Oxford University
(25) C.J.R. to Frank Rhodes, 19.8.1875
(26) Flint, pp. 26 & 27
(27) Millin, p. 131
(28) COF
(29) Stead, pp. 88–98

Chapter Nine
(1) Ronald Currey, p. 21
(2) Michell, vol. 1, pp. 61 & 62
(3) JICS, p. 320
(4) Boyle, pp. 376–377
(5) Roberts (TDM) p. 126
(6) JICS, p. 319 Rhodes, De Beers and Monopoly
(7) Jackson, pp. 5–9
(8) Cohen, p. 51
(9) Roberts (TDM) pp. 29–30

(10) Cohen, p. 61
(11) Ibid, pp. 81 & 82
(12) Jackson, p. 27
(13) Ibid, p. 37
(14) Cohen, pp. 92–94
(15) Gross, pp. 69–70
(16) KI, 10.3.1881
(17) Millin, p. 45
(18) JICS, p. 326
(19) From articles and press reports quoted in Michell vol. 1, pp. 91–96
(20) CT, 28.4.1881
(21) From an article in CA, April 1881, also partially reproduced in Rhodes's obituary in CA 27.3.1902
(22) Lockhart and Woodhouse, p. 83
(23) COF
(24) Michell, vol. 1, p. 94
(25) Bickford–Smith, p. 41
(26) Lewsen (JXM), p. 98
(27) See Rhodes's obituary in CA, 27.3.1902
(28) See Basil Williams, p. 63 and Lewsen (JXM) p. 90
(29) See Vindex, p. 34
(30) KI, 27.7.1881
(31) Rotberg, p. 140
(32) C.J.R. to Thomas Scanlen, 3.9.1883
(33) Michell, p. 135
(34) This story is repeated in many biographies, although not all versions include the phrase 'for the benefit of mankind'. This is the version given by Rhodes's secretary, Harry Currey, who would have heard the story many times from Rhodes (MHLC, p. 23).
(35) Roberts (KTC) pp. 197–198
(36) Cohen, pp. 142–144
(37) Turrell (ISS), p. 249
(38) Wheatcroft, p. 96
(39) Rouillard, pp. 81–89 and F. Gardner Williams, pp. 411–420
(40) Rorke, p. 62

Chapter Ten
(1) COF
(2) See Ch 6, p. 80 and ref 2 to that chapter
(3) McDonald ('A Heritage') p. 38
(4) JICS, p. 326
(5) Michell, vol. 1, p. 145
(6) Vindex, p. 34
(7) Michell, vol. 1, pp. 154–156
(8) Stead, pp. 142–143
(9) Vindex, pp. 62–69
(10) Johnson, p. 5

(11) Lockhart and Woodhouse, p. 99
(12) Basil Williams, p. 4
(13) This story is repeated in virtually all the biographies – e.g. Millin, p. 67
(14) This quote is repeated in many biographies – e.g. Millin, p. 66
(15) Lewsen, p. 124
(16) Johnson, pp. 4–6
(17) MHLC, p. 28
(18) Millin, p. 70
(19) MHLC, p. 33
(20) Ralph Williams, p. 119
(21) A quote attributed to Kruger in most biographies, e.g. Lockhart and Woodhouse, p. 102
(22) From Vindex, pp. 120–127
(23) Flint, p. 73
(24) Rotberg, p. 177

Chapter Eleven
(1) Quotation attributed to Rhodes in Gross, p. 261
(2) Colvin, vol. 1, p. 59
(3) Wheatcroft, p. 100
(4) C.J.R. to John X Merriman, April 1883
(5) Turrell (CFF) pp. 162–164
(6) Colquhoun, p. 257
(7) Pickering letter quoted in Roberts (KTC), p. 193
(8) Rotberg, p. 194
(9) Jackson, p. 54
(10) Bower to Basil Williams, 5.11.1918, Mss. Afr.s. 134
(11) Basil Williams, p. 53
(12) Ms. Afr.t.l. (6)
(13) Francis S. Dormer, interview with Basil Williams, 14.7.1919, Mss. Afr. s. 134
(14) EPH, 18.10.1886
(15) Colvin, vol. 1, p. 79
(16) Millin, p. 53
(17) Rotberg, p. 147
(18) Colvin, vol. 1, p. 79
(19) Roberts (CRP) p. 61
(20) Colvin, vol. 1, p. 13
(21) Fort ('Jameson') p. 7
(22) Rorke, pp. 50–51
(23) Colvin, vol. 1, p. 14
(24) Ibid, p. 27
(25) Lockhart and Woodhouse, p. 76
(26) Colvin, vol. 1, p. 80
(27) Sauer, p. 74
(28) Turrell (Iss) p. 258
(29) Sauer, p. 74
(30) Angove, p. 158
(31) Colvin, vol 1, p. 30
(32) Sauer, p. 37
(33) Ibid, pp. 38–39

(34) Ibid, p. 42
(35) Ibid, p. 67
(36) Ibid, p. 72
(37) Ibid, p. 73
(38) Ibid, p. 76
(39) Ibid, p. 79
(40) Ibid, p. 81
(41) Ibid, p. 84
(42) Ibid, p. 85
(43) Ibid, p. 86
(44) Ibid, p. 87
(45) Ibid, p. 88
(46) Turrell (ISS) pp. 254 & 258, Colvin, p. 33
(47) Colvin, vol. 1, p. 32
(48) Turrell (ISS) p. 259
(49) UCT, Judge Papers, 8, 46, Medical Commission 1883
(50) Reminiscences of Mrs Tiny Hickman, Ms Afr. T 11. (Rhodes House)

Chapter Twelve
(1) Sauer, p. 119
(2) Ibid, p. 107
(3) Ibid, p. 109
(4) Ibid, p. 112
(5) Ibid, p. 113
(6) Ibid, p. 129
(7) EPH, 18.10.1886
(8) Sauer, p. 70
(9) DFA, 18.10.1886
(10) According to Gross, p. 129
(11) According to Colvin, vol. 1, p. 81
(12) Fitzpatrick, pp. 87–89
(13) Plomer, p. 42
(14) MHLC, p. 35
(15) Sauer, p. 137
(16) MHLC, p. 37
(17) Sauer, p. 43
(18) Lewsen (JXM) pp. 132–133
(19) Vindex, pp. 150–165
(20) CH, 1887, pp. 99–201, 296
(21) John. X. Merriman to Agnes Merriman, 16.1. 1886 in Lewsen ('Selections') p. 205

Chapter Thirteen
(1) Fort ('Beit') p. 50
(2) Ibid, p. 69
(3) Ibid, p. 104
(4) Lockhart and Woodhouse, p. 111
(5) Fort ('Beit') p. 69
(6) Ibid, p. 86
(7) Michell, vol. 1, p. 62
(8) Roberts (TDM) p. 159
(9) Fort ('Beit') p. 111
(10) Ibid, p. 70
(11) Ibid, p. 71
(12) Ibid, p. 88
(13) Ibid, pp. 89 & 58
(14) Ibid, pp. 72–73
(15) See Roberts (TDM) p. 164

(16) Fort ('Beit') p. 76
(17) Lockhart and Woodhouse, p. 75
(18) The phrase used by Kenneth Griffith in his documentary, *A Touch of Churchill, a Touch of Hitler*
(19) See Rhodes's speech on 'The Great Diamond Mines Amalgamation', Vindex, p. 754
(20) JICS, p. 329
(21) Fort ('Beit'), p. 107
(22) See Vindex, pp. 748 et seq. and Colvin, vol. 1, p. 63
(23) Basil Williams, p. 99
(24) DFA, 22.9.1987
(25) Vindex, p. 752
(26) Ibid, p. 754
(27) Jackson, pp. 77–78
(28) C.J.F. to Philipson-Stow, 22.10.1887
(29) JICS, p. 332
(30) Quoted from the original De Beers Trust Deed
(31) This quotation, with minor variations in the wording, is repeated (unsourced) in many biographies
(32) Vindex, p. 774
(33) Ibid, p. 760
(34) Ibid, p. 779
(35) Rotberg, p. 210
(36) John X. Merriman to J.B. Currey, 6.9.1886
(37) Flint, p. 92
(38) CLKDF, p. 92
(39) DI, 5.6.1888

Chapter Fourteen
(1) C.J.R. to Lord Rothschild, 29.10.1888
(2) There are a number of different translations: 'He that drives like the wind'; 'Driven by the wind'; 'The scatterer'; 'The over-turner of a shield'.
(3) Ransford gives an alternative translation, 'The place of he who has been maltreated', a reference to Lobengula's tribulations during the inter-regnum of 1868–1870.
(4) Ranger, p. 35
(5) Ibid, p. 28
(6) Elliot (Ms) p. 81
(7) Blue Book, p. 123
(8) Bryant, p. 426
(9) Knight-Bruce, pp. 56 & 70
(10) Johnson, p. 36
(11) Lockharts Woodhouse, p. 135
(12) Cook, p. 254
(13) Sidney Shippard to Hercules

Robinson, 18.10.1888, Colonial Office: Africa (South) no. 369

(14) See Samkange (OTFMC), Millin, p. 100 and Colvin, p. 99

(15) 'Sixty wives' was Rudd's estimate; 'two hundred wives in all' was Thompson's

(16) Gibbs, p. 15

(17) Mathers, p. 190

(18) Ransford, p. 44

(19) According to Johnson, p. 77, Dr Knight-Bruce found two Matable converts in Kimberley, but it was not clear to him whether this was the result of missionary work in Matabeleland or in Kimberley.

(20) Johnson, p. 77

(21) Keppel-Jones, p. 55

(22) Johnson, p. 11

(23) Ibid, p. 19

(24) Ibid, p. 41

(25) Mason, p. 119

(26) See Ch 13, p. 179

(27) C.J.R. to Shippard, 14.8.1888

(28) Mason, p. 120

(29) Moffat, p. 212

(30) Ibid, p. 217

(31) Ibid, p. 221

(32) Quoted in Millin, p. 101

(33) For a full account of the murder of Grobler and the subsequent inquiries see Keppel-Jones, pp. 60–63

(34) NG, May 1896, p. 159

(35) Rotberg, p. 252

(36) Mss Afr. s 73, p. 23 (Rhodes House)

(37) Cook, p. 254

(38) Rouillard, p. 95

(39) Galbraith, p. 62

(40) Cook, p. 256

(41) Rouillard, p. 102

(42) Rudd's diary entry from 25.8.1888 in Hiller

(43) Rouillard, p. 126

(44) Colonial Office, 879/30/372, nos. 1, 2

(45) Ransford, p. 48

(46) Cook, p. 255

(47) Rudd's diary entry from 21.9.1888 in Hiller

(48) Helm, 11.10.1888 (Ms papers LO 6/1/5)

(49) Thompson's papers, diary, 24.11. 1888

(50) Rouillard, p. 124

(51) Ibid, p. 127

(52) Colonial Office, Africa (South), no. 369; Encl. to no. 64

(53) Colonial Office, Africa (South), no. 369

(54) Ibid

(55) Keppel-Jones, p. 72

(56) Shippard to Francis Newton, 29.11.1888, quoted in Galbraith, pp. 68–69

(57) Rouillard, p. 128

(58) Ibid, p. 129

(59) Ibid, p. 130–131

(60) Rudd's diary entry for 31.10.1888, reprinted as Appendix D in Rouillard

(61) Helm, 29.3.1889 (LMS papers LO/6/1/5)

(62) Colonial Office 879/30/369, no. 89, encl., p. 210

(63) Rouillard, pp. 129–131

(64) Colonial Office Africa (South) no. 358, p. 88) 1144/81

(65) Quoted in Millin, p. 108

(66) Knight Bruce's speech of 8.10.1888, quoted in Ripp and Hiller, p. 138

(67) C.J.R. to F.D. Rudd, 26.12.1888 (Ms. 16.097, Cory Library)

(68) CT, 26.11.1888; also CA (weekly ed), 28.11.1888

(69) Keppel-Jones, p. 85

(70) Rouillard, p. 140

(71) Samkange (OR) p. 89

(72) Keppel-Jones, p. 84

(73) Rorke, p. 142

(74) (Rhodes House) 17, p. 11 and Samkange (OR), p. 95

(75) Keppel-Jones, p. 105

(76) See Selous's article in FR, May 1889

(77) Cook, pp. 256–257

(78) Colvin, pp. 78–90

(79) Rudd to Thompson and Maguire, 4.2.1889, Ms. Afr. S 73, p. 122

Chapter Fifteen

(1) Stead, p. 190

(2) See particularly Strage, pp. 65–66

(3) Ibid and Samkange (OR) p. 127

(4) *The Times*, 6.3.1889

(5) Samkange (OR) p. 126

(6) Colonial Office 5918–163

(7) Le Sueur, p. 124

(8) Colonial Office 879/31/380, p. 4

(9) Samkange (OR) pp. 132–133

(10) Nutting, p. 182 and Samkange (OR) p. 132

(11) Stead, p. 82

(12) Flint, p. 103

(13) Rouillard, p. 174

(14) Ibid, pp. 178–179

(15) Ibid, pp. 181–182

(16) Ibid, p. 155

(17) Ibid, p. 184

(18) Colvin, vol. 1, p. 131

(19) Ibid, p. 117

(20) Rouillard, pp. 185–186

(21) Johnson's account of the plot to assassinate Lobengula was removed from his biography *Great Days*. Unfortunately for the censors, he had already described the incident in an interview which was published in the *Cape Times* on 12. 9.1930, from which all the details of the plot are taken.

(22) Johnson, p. 109

(23) Ibid, p. 107

(24) Ibid, p. 113

(25) Fort ('Jameson'), pp. 94–95

(26) For an account of the incident on the Shasi river, see particularly Johnson, p. 136 and Gibbs, p. 60

(27) Johnson, pp. 136–137

(28) Ibid, p. 152

(29) C.J.R. to Lord Rothschild, 29.10.1888

(30) C.J.R. to Sidney Shippard, 14.8.1888

(31) Jourdan, p. 44

Chapter Sixteen

(1) Jourdan, p. 165

(2) Rose-Innes, p. 47

(3) Herbert Baker, as quoted by Jourdan, pp. 188–189

(4) Baker p. 22

(5) Le Sueur, p. 253

(6) Knox-Little, pp. 21–24

(7) Except where otherwise indicated, all quotations in pp. 291–298 are taken from two accounts – Ronald Currey, pp. 12–23 and MHLC (MS), p. 55 et seq. Ronald Currey based his account on this manuscript and discussions with his father.

(8) McDonald ('A Heritage') p. 26

(9) John X. Merriman to John Blades Currey, 22.4.1891

(10) Johnson, pp. 104–105

(11) Jourdan, pp. 21–25

(12) Hyam, p. 68

(13) Cohen, pp. 269–270

(14) Hyam, p. 210

(15) Le Sueur, p. 52

(16) From the author's interview with Harry Currey's

granddaughter, Phillida
Brook Simons
(17) Hyam, p. 39
(18) Foley, p. 46
(19) Roberts (CRP) p. 105
(20) Le Sueur, p. 195
(21) Jourdan, p. 25
(22) Le Sueur, pp. 200–201
(23) Jourdan, p. 162

Chapter Seventeen
(1) Colvin, vol. 1, p. 48
(2) Johnson, pp. 94–95
(3) The account of the attack on
the Portuguese at Macequece
and the subsequent encounter
with the Bishop of Mashonaland and Major Sapte is based
on several accounts, including
the Bishop's own – see
Knight-Bruce, pp. 88–89,
Johnson, p. 174, Gibbs,
p. 102, and Colvin, vol. 1,
pp. 203–205.
(4) Le Sueur, p. 164
(5) For a complete account of the
conditions see Gale,
pp. 107–113: also Colvin,
vol. 1, pp. 209–210 and
Phillips (Ms)
(6) De Waal, p. 67
(7) Colvin, p. 172
(8) Johnson, p. 103
(9) Galbraith, p. 278
(10) Gale, p. 125
(11) Different numbers are given
in the various accounts. I have
accepted the figures given by
Jameson's biographer, Colvin.
(12) Colvin, vol. 1, p. 220
(13) William H. Milton to his
wife, 18.9.1896, quoted in
Galbraith, p. 280
(14) Strage, p. 79
(15) Based on several accounts,
e.g. the incident at Chiconga,
described in Gale, p. 145 and
the many other incidents
described in Ranger,
Ch 4
(16) Lendy's report, 24.3.1892;
Hole to Acting Secretary,
Cape Town, 21.3.1892, Cape
Town Office of the British
South Africa Company
1/15/7
(17) The account of Rhodes's
first journey to Mashonaland
is taken from De Waal,
pp. 124–258, Johnson,
pp. 205–208 and Colvin,
vol. 1, pp. 211–218
(18) Colvin, vol. 1, p. 213
(19) For a full account see
Churchill, pp. 198–207,

De Waal, pp. 234–245 and
Strage, pp. 77–79
(20) De Waal, p. 277
(21) Se Ch 14, pp. 188 & 195
(22) Mason, p. 164
(23) Ibid, p. 165
(24) Colvin, vol. 1, pp. 251–252
(25) Jameson to Harris,
17.7.1893, Ms. Afr.s. 228,
C. 3B
(26) The description of the
indaba at Fort Victoria is
taken from Sauer,
pp. 220–221 and Colvin,
vol. 1, pp. 254–255
(27) Keppel-Jones, p. 243
(28) Jameson to Harris,
19.7.1893, Ms. Afr.s.228,
C.3B
(29) Imperialist, pp. 399–401
(30) Strage, p. 88
(31) Ranger or Keppel-Jones
(32) Mason, p. 170
(33) Sauer, pp. 226–228
(34) Preller, p. 218
(35) Colvin, vol. 1, p. 268
(36) Samkange (OR) p. 258
(37) Knight-Bruce, p. 237
(38) For an account of this
incident , see Tidrick,
p p. 79–80; Keppel-Jones,
p. 260 and Colvin,vol. 1,
p. 269
(39) Lockhart and Woodhouse,
p. 259
(40) Keppel-Jones, p. 369
(41) This allegation was made in
the journal *Truth* by the
Radical British MP, Henry
Labouchere. The Zimbab-
wean historian, Professor
Stanlake Samkange, later
discovered supporting
evidence, including the
unpublished memoirs of
H.A.J. de Roos, a Boer
volunteer in Jameson's force,
see Samkange (OR) p. 260.
(42) Ransford, p. 58
(43) Colvin, vol. 1, p. 283
(44) Ransford, p. 60
(45) Knight-Bruce, p. 234
(46) Millin, p. 196
(47) In Matable oral tradition,
there are slight variations on
the words Lobengula actually
used, but the meaning is
always the same. See Harris,
p. 117 and Keppel-Jones,
p. 279.
(48) Mason, p. 181
(49) Keppel-Jones, p. 283
(50) McDonald ('A Life') p. 162
(51) Vindex, pp. 328–335
(52) Ranger, pp. 99–100

(53) Vindex, p. 418
(54) Keppel-Jones, p. 286
(55) Moffat, p. 346
(56) Nutting, pp. 275–276
(57) Strage, p. 91

Chapter Eighteen
(1) Lewsen, p. 186
(2) CA, 27.3.1902
(3) Basil Williams, p. 214
(4) Fuller, pp. 152–153
(5) See the Archbishop of Cape
Town's fineral oration,
quoted in full in CFC,
pp. 27–31 and CTWE,
9.4.1902
(6) A famous Rhodes maxim,
quoted in many biographies,
e.g. McDonald ('A Heritage'),
p. 22
(7) Quotations attributed to
Barney Barnato in Jackson,
p. 83 and Gross, p. 122
(8) Lewsen (JXM) p. 143
(9) Flint, p. 160
(10) Le Sueur, p. 29
(11) Basil Williams, p. 214
(12) Stead, pp. 144–145
(13) John X. Merriman to Agnes
Merriman, 18.3.1891
(14) Flint, p. 164
(15) Bickford-Smith, p. 145
(16) Colvin, vol. 1, p. 236
(17) John X. Merriman to J.B.
Currey, 9.5.1893
(18) John X. Merriman to Julia
Merriman, 17.5.1893
(19) Basil Williams, p. 209
(20) Vindex, p. 390
(21) Basil Williams, p. 213
(22) Vindex, p. 386
(23) Ibid, p. 381
(24) Ibid, p. 381
(25) Ibid, p. 383
(26) Ibid, p. 371–372
(27) Ibid, p. 372 & p. 390
(28) Mason, pp. 185–186
(29) See particularly Bickford-
Smith, pp. 139–151
(30) Le Sueur, p. 29

Chapter Nineteen
(1) Fuller, p. 75
(2) Le Sueur, p. 34
(3) Basil Williams, p. 251
(4) Baker, p. 122
(5) Michell, vol. 2, p. 48
(6) Jackson, p. 105
(7) Bell, p. 108
(8) Millin, p. 251
(9) Rorke, p. 91
(10) NG, May 1896
(11) John Fisher, p. 274
(12) Imperialist, p. 345
(13) Hammond, p. 252

(14) Jackson, p. 157
(15) Hammond, p. 257
(16) Ibid pp. 277–278
(17) JSAS 10, 1974 vol. 1 no. 1 p. 75
(18) Vindex, pp. 417–442
(19) Longford, p. 45
(20) See page 263 and accompanying footnote
(21) Colvin, vol. 2, p. 27
(22) Lockhart and Woodhouse, p. 194
(23) Colvin, vol. 2, p. 15
(24) Ibid, pp. 18–19
(25) van der Poel, p. 24
(26) Basil Williams, p. 136
(27) van der Poel, p. 30
(28) Colvin, vol. 2, p. 41
(29) van der Poel, p. 32
(30) Ibid, p. 33
(31) Ibid, pp. 58–59
(32) Colvin, vol. 2, p. 44
(33) Flint, p. 186
(34) van der Poel, p. 63
(35) Colvin, vol. 2, p. 41
(36) van der Poel, p. 67
(37) Ibid, pp. 75–76
(38) Colvin, vol. 2, p. 116
(39) van der Poel, p. 77
(40) Ibid, p. 80
(41) Longford, p. 73
(42) van der Poel, p. 78
(43) Colvin, vol. 2, p. 50
(44) Longford, p. 74
(45) van der Poel, p. 84
(46) Colvin, vol. 2, p. 52
(47) van der Poel, p. 85
(48) Colvin, vol. 2, p. 53
(49) CT, 2.4.1902
(50) van der Poel, pp. 91–93
(51) Ibid, p. 82
(52) Colvin, pp. 61–62
(53) van der Poel, p. 94, Colvin, pp. 66–67
(54) Millin, p. 169
(55) Longford, p. 56
(56) Fitzpatrick (TFW) p. 138
(57) Colvin, p. 56, van der Poel, p. 109
(58) Walker, p. 71
(59) Hofmeyr, p. 499
(60) van der Poel, pp. 97–98
(61) Colvin, pp. 132–133
(62) Garvin, vol. 3, p. 89
(63) Garrett and Edwards, p. 113
(64) van der Poel, p. 145
(65) Lewsen (JXM), p. 179
(66) Garvin, vol. 3, p. 109
(67) Michell, vol. 2, p. 177

Chapter Twenty
(1) Millin, p. 317
(2) See p. 310
(3) Le Sueur, p. 117
(4) Sauer, p. 289

(5) W.A. Jarvis to Lady Jarvis, 24 & 29.2.1896, JA 4/1/1 (Zimbabwe archives)
(6) Mason, p. 186
(7) Rorke, p. 174
(8) Keppel-Jones, p. 445
(9) Selous, p. 90
(10) Ibid, p. 102
(11) Michell, vol. 2, p. 153
(12) Le Sueur, p. 159
(13) Flint, p. 205
(14) W.A. Jarvis to Lady Jarvis, 17.6.1896, JA 4/1/1 (Zimbabwe Archives)
(15) Sauer, p. 305
(16) Rotberg, p. 560
(17) W.A. Jarvis to Lady Jarvis, 19.8.1896, JA 4/1/1 (Zimbabwe Archives)
(18) Ransford, p. 105
(19) Millin, p. 305
(20) BS, 11.7.1896
(21) Ransford, p. 112
(22) De Vere Stent, pp. 12–26
(23) Le Sueur, p. 119 and CT, 2.4.1902
(24) Michell, vol. 2, p. 168
(25) Ranger, p. 235
(26) W.A Jarvis to Lady Jarvis, July 1896, Ja 4/1/1/(Zimbawe Archives) (22)
(27) Sauer, pp. 312–322
(28) Lady Grey to her children, GR 1/1/1/ (Zimbabwe Archives)
(29) Ranger, p. 241
(30) The entire account of the first indaba is based on Sauer, pp. 312–322 and De Vere Stent, pp. 46–67
(31) C.J.R. to Lord Grey, 21.8.1896, AM/1/2/1 (Zimbabwe Archives)
(32) Gibbs, p. 186
(33) DFA, Special Memorial Number (Kimberley, 1902)
(34) Mc Donald ('A Heritage') p. 97
(35) Sauer, p. 324
(36) Le Sueur, p. 121

Chapter Twenty–One
(1) Vindex, p. 639
(2) Flint, p. 207
(3) Keppel-Jones, p. 510
(4) Jourdan, pp. 47–48
(5) Stead, pp. 178–180
(6) Colvin, vol. 2, p. 157
(7) Millin, p. 317
(8) Le Sueur, p. 130
(9) Jourdan, p. 52–53
(10) Colvin, vol. 2, p.162
(11) Ibid, pp. 159–160
(12) Marquis of Crew, p. 441
(13) Longford, pp. 298–299

(14) Lewsen (JXM) p. 184
(15) Millin, p. 328
(16) Le Sueur, p. 131
(17) Ibid, p. 19
(18) Nellie Mackintosh's testimony, quoted in Roberts (TDM) p. 234
(19) Le Sueur, p. 66
(20) Lewsen (JXM), pp. 191–192
(21) Colvin, vol. 2, p. 176
(22) CT, 2.4.1902
(23) Le Sueur, p. 68
(24) Nutting, p. 381
(25) Lewsen (JXM), pp. 198–199
(26) John X. Merriman to Sir David Tennant, 7.6.1899
(27) Jourdan, p. 70
(28) Colvin, vol. 2, p. 185
(29) Stead, pp. 3–4
(30) Ibid, p. 5
(31) Ibid, p. 23
(32) Ibid, p. 27
(33) Ibid, p. 39
(34) C.J.R. to Frank Rhodes, 19.8.1875
(35) Stead, p. 86
(36) CT, 19.7.1899 & 26.7.1899
(37) Jourdan, p. 83
(38) Le Sueur, p. 65
(39) Jourdan, pp. 86–89
(40) Nutting, p. 402
(41) John X. Merriman to Goldwin Smith, 9.8.1899
(42) Nutting, p. 420
(43) CA, 17.7.1899
(44) CT, 2. 4.1902
(45) MHLC, p. 94
(46) Lewsen (JXM), pp. 216–217
(47) Pakenham, p. 10
(48) Colvin, vol. 2, p. 189
(49) Jourdan, p. 116
(50) See Wilson, vol. 2, p. 373, Gardner, p. 52, O'Meara, p. 53
(51) Ashe, pp. 38–39
(52) O'Meara, pp. 55–56
(53) Ibid, p. 58
(54) Ibid, pp. 64–66
(55) Jourdan, pp. 121–122
(56) Pakenham, pp. 311–312
(57) Stead, pp. 174–175
(58) O'Meara, pp. 133–137
(59) Roberts (CRP), p. 237
(60) Ibid, p. 246
(61) Millin, p. 343
(62) Roberts (CRP) p. 309
(63) Ibid, p. 293
(64) Le Sueur, p. 305
(65) See Ch 1, p. 5 and accompanying footnote

INDEX

Picture credits

BBC Books would like to thank the following for providing photographs, and for permission to reproduce copyright material. While every effort has been made to trace and acknowledge all copyright holders, we would like to apologize should there have been any errors or ommisions.

Author's collection 70–1; Rhodes House Library/Bodleian Library Photo 22, 38 left, 56, 90, 103, 111, 142, 175, 262, 265, 339; Hulton-Getty 19, 46, 110, 119, 144, 170, 285, 301, 302, 342; Mansell Collection 47, 49, 50, 105, 165; McGregor Museum, Kimberley 69, 73, 75, 83, 85, 88, 97, 125, 133, 149, 150, 151, 176, 337, 338; Museum Africa, Johannesburg 61, 146; National Archives, Zimbabwe 29, 57, 185, 191, 197, 205, 206, 216, 233, 237, 241, 244, 252, 257, 258, 293, 307, 309, 311; Popperfoto 62; Punch 350; Rhodes Museum, Bishop's Stortford 34, 38 right, 41, 214; University of Cape Town Library 2.